# Let Haiti LIVE
## Unjust U.S. Policies Towards Its Oldest Neighbor

**Melinda Miles and Eugenia Charles**
**Editors**

# Let Haiti LIVE
## Unjust U.S. Policies Towards Its Oldest Neighbor

**Editors**          **Melinda Miles and**
**Eugenia Charles**

For information, please contact:
Educa Vision Inc.,
7550 NW 47th Avenue,
Coconut Creek, FL 33073

Telephone: 954 725-0701.
E-mail: educa@aol.com.
Web: www.educavision.com

**ISBN**: 1-58432-188-1

# DEDICATION

*This book is dedicated to our girls ---*

## Mikaelle Dantiana Mathurin

**and**

## Simbi Gisele Duplan

*--- two daughters of Haiti.*

# Table of Contents

# Let Haiti LIVE!
## *A Note from the Editors*

## HAPPY BIRTHDAY TO HAITI!

Happy Bicentennial to Haiti and her children all over the world, and congratulations for being the first country to practice the concept of human rights by abolishing slavery – by making every human who sets foot on Haiti's soil a FREE person. January 1, 1804 to January 1, 2004 marks 200 years of Haiti's story and the struggle of her people to build a democratic nation. Bòn Fèt Ayiti!

In March 2002, publisher Féquière Vilsaint of EducaVision approached us about making a book based on our Haiti Solidarity Week First Annual Conference. The conference came at an important time for Haiti – during the darkness of a humanitarian crisis, a protracted political standoff and an international embargo on humanitarian aid. On the eve of the bicentennial, the Haitian people's historic victory over slavery, Haitians were suffering from the effects of two hundred years of unjust U.S. policies.

We took Féquière up on his idea, and decided to take it a step further and ask experts on Haiti to contribute essays to make this book. We gathered analysis from our friends and colleagues and we teamed up to make this project a success. Nevertheless, it was a challenge to organize the book and present the text to you. We decided to let the words of the Haitian people guide you through the book. Each chapter opens with a Haitian proverb and deals with a different aspect of U.S. policy, both foreign and domestic. The final two chapters give us some insight into Haiti's future by detailing the U.S.-Haiti solidarity movement and the Haitian Diaspora in the United States. It is only the efforts of these two communities, united, that will change U.S. policy towards Haiti.

We are honored to bring you the story of Haiti. The Haitian people are striving to build democracy for the next 200 years. We hope as you read this book, you will feel the spirit of the Haitian people and their struggle, and that you will be inspired - as we are, each and every day.

Please join us in our efforts to Let Haiti LIVE! Visit the website of the Let Haiti LIVE: U.S. Coalition for a Just U.S. Policy at www.lethaitilive.org and become a member of the campaign today.

January 1, 2004
Melinda Miles and Eugenia Charles
*The staff of Haiti Reborn, a program of the Quixote Center*

# Foreword:
# Time to Say Thank You to Haiti

*Reverend Jesse L. Jackson, Sr.*
*July, 2003*

Earlier this month, we celebrated July 4th and the spirit of American independence – the commitment to the ideals of, in Thomas Jefferson's immortal words, "life, liberty, and the pursuit of happiness."

Only 10 days later, we commemorated Bastille Day on July 14th, the day the common people of France freed the prisoners from the dread Bastille prison, in the name of "liberty, equality, and fraternity."

These are worthy days to celebrate, and worthy revolutions to remember. The American Revolution and the French Revolution forever changed the world, and the way we look at freedom.

There is another revolutionary anniversary coming up, however, one just as deserving of celebration and commemoration – in 2004, it will be 200 years since the successful Haitian revolution, the first revolt in human history to outlaw slavery.

Think about that – a group of enslaved Africans, led by their great General, Toussaint L'Ouverture, threw off their own shackles and fought back against the French, the greatest army in the world at that time. And they won. They overthrew the colonizers, forced Napoleon to give up his hopes of an empire in the Western hemisphere, and ended slavery on the island.

African Americans should know this history, and we should celebrate it. Enslaved Africans rose up and overthrew the mighty armies of Napoleon, sending them home in defeat, and putting an end to slavery. A milestone in human history. A turning point in African and American history. 1804 – a date that all who love freedom should hold dear.

Indeed, the day of the revolt of former slaves in Haiti is a day that everyone in the United States should hold dear. Why? Because it changed the size, the shape, the history of this nation as well.

First, it increased the pressure against slavery in the South, and greatly worried Southern slaveowners, concerned that the inspiring Haitian model might be emulated in this country as well.

Second, the interesting historical fact is that the revolt in Haiti helped pave the way for the Louisiana Purchase, a massive land purchase which doubled the size of the mainland United States. Faced with a serious revolt in Haiti, and planning for an attempted conquest of Europe, Napoleon came to the conclusion that there was no hope for re-establishing a major French Empire in the Western hemisphere. Instead, he decided to sell French territory in the New World, and surprised Jefferson's land negotiators in Paris, who were trying to buy New Orleans, with an offer to take all of the Louisiana territory off France's hands.

For $15 million, President Jefferson was able to buy more than 800,000 square miles of the Great Plains and Rocky Mountains, stretching all the way from New Orleans up to Montana. The territory he purchased now makes up most of Louisiana, Arkansas, Missouri, Iowa, Minnesota, both Dakotas, Nebraska, Oklahoma, most of Kansas, and parts of Montana, Wyoming and Colorado east of the Rocky Mountains.

The ironies abound in this story. African slaves defeated Napoleon, a decade before Waterloo. The rejected stones of the American Revolution, the enslaved Africans who were counted by our Constitution as only three-fifths human, led the revolt in Haiti which accomplished what our Founding Fathers could not. And a French retrenchment led to a land deal which time has proven to be one of President Jefferson's greatest accomplishments in office.

Think of that – the American slave owner Jefferson, already a walking contradiction given his eloquent writings on freedom, owes his greatest accomplishment as President to the rebellion of enslaved Africans in a French colony, two centuries ago.

The people of one-fourth of our states owe their homes and status to the bravery and commitment of an unsung group of Haitians. And one of the great Generals who made it possible for our nation to grow to the West, without slaughtering a single Native American, was Toussaint L'Ouverture.

We are not taught this history in our schools – so we must teach each other. The weight of the debt that the United States of America owes to enslaved Africans rising up in Haiti will never be lifted unless we do the heavy lifting. The talking heads of today's corporate mass media do not worry too much about either the history of Haiti, or the problems of modern-day Haiti – so we must do what we can to educate ourselves, and to educate our children.

And we will certainly never be taught about the uglier history that comes after the Haitian revolution – the invasions; the occupations; the support for the repressive and corrupt Duvalier family; the disparate treatment given to Haitian refugees when they risk their lives on leaky rafts to land on our shores, compared to Cuban refugees; the failure to stand up for democracy when Aristide won by a landslide.

We know that it was only when African Americans in the United States stood up and fought back, in the U.S. Congress, in the press, and in the streets, that the democratic rights of Haitian voters were recognized, and Aristide was restored to his rightfully earned position as President. We must teach our children.

Today, Haiti still lives with the scars of centuries of colonization, occupation, and repression. Today, the people of Haiti still suffer from the withholding of $500 million in humanitarian aid, the payment of which the Quixote Center's "Let Haiti LIVE Campaign" has been pressing for. Today, the politics of Haiti still suffer from the legacy of the Duvaliers and the secret police.

We can do better. U.S./Haiti relations do not have to be based on suspicion and fear and threats. We could help Haiti, with debt relief, humanitarian aid, and building bridges between Haitians and African Americans.

And we could start today. It is far past time for America to say "thank you" to Haiti. Thank you for leading the way to abolish slavery. Thank you for a revolution that valued enslaved Africans as people. Thank you, Haiti, for making it possible to purchase so much of our current nation—the rich farms of Iowa, the wheat fields of Kansas, the Big Sky country of Montana, Colorado's Rockies, and so much more.

Again, think of the irony. Our Presidential race always begins in Iowa, a state made available to our nation because of the bravery of thousands of enslaved Africans, who rose up against Napoleon's troops two centuries ago. Two seemingly disconnected places, Iowa and Haiti, bound together by history, by the courage of our freedom-minded forebears.

Then again, that is what Dr. Martin Luther King, Jr. taught us. In his great speech, "Remaining Awake Through a Great Revolution," he reminded us that everything really is tied to everything else:

"We are tied together in the single garment of destiny, caught in an inescapable network of mutuality. And whatever affects one directly affects all indirectly. For some strange reason I can never be what I ought to be until you are what you ought to be. And you can never be what you ought to be until I am what I ought to be. This is the way God's universe is made; this is the way it is structured."

So the next time the U.S. press talks about the Presidential candidates campaigning in Iowa, think for a moment about the Louisiana Purchase. Then think about Toussaint L'Ouverture, and his victorious slave rebellion against Napoleon. Then think about how far we still have to go until the descendants of enslaved Africans in both this nation and in Haiti are finally treated as fully human, fully free, fully equal.

Go out and educate yourself about Haiti and history. Read this book. Help the Haiti Reborn program of the Quixote Center. Continue the struggle for peace and justice on both sides of the U.S./Haiti divide.

And take a quick minute to say "Thank you, Haiti." The people of Haiti have earned it.

Keep hope alive.

# INTRODUCTION

## Kite m Viv
### *Edwidge Danticat*

A few years ago, in April 1989, my cousin Marie died of a heart attack in the Bel-Air neighborhood where I grew up. She was thirty-six years old. Marie's death would eventually be the subject of a *New York Newsday* article written by staff correspondent Ron Howell, a man who would later become an acquaintance.

> "The marching band stepped solemnly down Rue de L'Enterrement, tapping drums and blowing horns all the way to the cemetery at the end of the long street. Thursday was burial day for 36-year-old Marie Micheline Danticat Marol," begins Ron's article. He would continue, explaining that my cousin Marie – a nurse's aid who had both taught me to read and made me her first child's godmother when I was five – was "apparently one of the casualties of the confrontation earlier this month between rival units within the Haitian army. The woman, doctors said, died of a heart attack. Her father, Joseph N. Danticat... put it this way: "She heard the fighting and the cannons and saw soldiers running up and down and fighting outside the house. And she was frightened to death."

At twenty, Marie's death was the biggest tragedy of my adult life. It was the first time I had lost a loved one so close to my age. And it made me bitter and angry. I was angry at the neighborhood where she'd spent her whole life, at the soldiers who fought outside her house. I was angry at my uncle who'd never wanted to move and had encouraged her to stay, "among the people" to help with the small school and clinic they ran together. Marie's life, it seemed, had been unnecessarily squandered by a country that desperately needed her. And she was not the only one. Later, I would lose, among others, one cousin to an ocean crossing to Miami and another to AIDS. Like many other families, mine would be robbed of my kin's love, humor and brilliance, but would also wonder what could have been, had they been allowed to live. Could Marie have saved lives? Could my cousin Laris, who'd succumbed to AIDS, have finished the Law degree he'd started and become a staunch defender of his people? Could my cousin Joël who'd perished at sea have become a great artist, just as he'd dreamed since he was a little boy? Only had they lived would we have known.

For as long as Haiti as existed, people like my cousins Marie, Laris and Joel and millions of others who came before and after them, have been demanding, either with their voices or their actions, to be allowed to live. The Taïnos who warmly greeted a murderous Columbus when he set foot on their land in 1492 wanted to live. The slaves who suffered the most egregious treatment under French colonial rule wanted to live. Their desire was so strong that on August 1791 many gathered in the woods of Bois Caiman and swore to live freely or die. And even as many died, others did live to see their land become a free nation in 1804. Though marginalized by the rest of the world, the new citizens of this budding republic wanted desperately to live. So much so that they made a Faustian deal with France that would rob them of much needed funds to have their independence recognized. The Cacos, my paternal grandfather among them, who rebelled when the United States occupied Haiti from 1915 to 1934, wanted to live. But many of them were slaughtered, among them Charlemagne Péralte whose corpse was nailed to a door by American Marines and left on display for days as an example to others who would dare dream of complete sovereignty for their land. The men and women who took to the streets and put an end to the twenty nine year Duvalier dictatorship wanted to live and those who voted in the democratic elections of December 1990 wanted to live with renewed hope. On the two hundred anniversary of Haitian independence, those who are protesting both in support and against the current administration want to live, even though they may not agree on the path they must follow to do it together.

*Memwa se paswa,* says the proverb. Memory is a sieve. We all can filter through it what we will. But as we commemorate the bicentennial of our yet greatest accomplishment as a people, the collective memory of our ancestors' triumphs and strife should bring us closer together rather than further apart. Because of my own family's *memwa,* my faith tends to lie more with the people of Haiti than with any one person or institution, people like my living cousins who are battling to remain in their own country and somehow contribute to its future. *Zwazo ki gra pa chante* says another proverb. *Fat birds don't sing.* For Haiti to live freely, peacefully, democratically, we must listen to the singing from all sides. The egg-eater must feel the pain of the mother hen or at least acknowledge its sacrifice. The rocks in the water and the rocks in the sun must at last realize that they're both from the same river. I hope that everyone who cares about Haiti and Haitians will be energized and encouraged by the testimonies and analyses in this book. And hopefully we can all harvest a few more solutions that might bring us closer to the full realization of a now two hundred-year-old dream.

# CHAPTER ONE

*Wòch nan dlo pa konnen doulè
wòch nan soley.*

The rocks in the water do not know the
suffering of the rocks in the sun.

# The Trials of Haiti
*Tracy Kidder*

In the winter of 2003, when war loomed in Iraq and every rock was suspected of concealing a terrorist, one might have imagined that the last thing on the minds of American diplomats would be a little impoverished country like Haiti, a mere third of an island, which lacks even an army. But the United States has a foreign policy everywhere, and, as a rule, the weaker and poorer the nation, the more powerful the policy is.

Most Americans if they visited Haiti would, I imagine, come away with new definitions of poverty. What you notice most of all are absences of the most basic things. Water, for instance. In a recent survey of the potable water supplies in 147 nations, Haiti ranked 147th. It's estimated that only 40 percent of Haiti's roughly eight million people have access to clean water.

In the capital, Port-au-Prince, the morning after rain, you see working men take up manhole covers and lean in beneath the pavement, dipping buckets into the city's brimming drainage channels. They use the water to wash cars for pay, and occasionally, when the day gets hot, you'll see one of them invert a bucket over his head. This is very dangerous, because any contact with sewer water invites skin diseases and a mere thimbleful swallowed can cause bacillary dysentery.

All over Haiti, you see boys and girls carrying water, balancing plastic buckets on their heads as they trek long distances up and down the hillsides of Port-au-Prince or climb steep footpaths in the countryside. Many of the water-carriers are orphans, known as *restavek* – children who work as indentured servants for poor families. Contaminated water is one of the causes of Haiti's extemely high rate of maternal mortality, the main reason there are so many orphans available for carrying water. "Sanitation service systems are almost nonexistent," reads one development report. Many Haitians drink from rivers or polluted wells or stagnant reservoirs, adding citron, key lime juice, in the belief that this will make the water safe. The results are epidemic levels of diseases such as typhoid, and a great deal of acute and chronic diarrhea, which tends to flourish among children under five, especially ones who are malnourished. Hunger is rampant. "Haitians today are estimated to be the fourth most undernourished people on earth, after Eritrea, Ethiopa, and Somalia," the World Bank reported in 2002. The cures for many waterborne ailments are simple. But in Haiti, it's estimated (almost certainly overestimated) that only 60 percent have access even to rudimentary healthcare. In the countryside, the vast majority have to travel at least an hour, over paths and main roads that resemble dry riverbeds, to reach health centers, which not only charge fees that most can't afford to pay but also lack the most basic provisions.

Last winter, I visited the centerpiece of Haiti's public health system, the University Hospital in Port-au-Prince. It was founded in 1918, during the time when American Marines occupied and essentially ran the country. It's a large complex of concrete buildings in the center of the city, and it seemed to be open when I arrived. My Haitian guide and I strolled over toward the pediatric wing. It seemed unnaturally quiet. No babies crying. Inside, the reason was obvious. There were no doctors or nurses or patients in sight, only a young male custodian, who explained that the doctors had recently ended a strike but that the nurses had now launched one of their own. Strikes at the hospital are frequent; this one had to do with current political strife.

"Where did the sick children go?" I asked my Haitian guide.

"They went home." She made a face. "To die."

We walked past rows of empty metal cribs, and then, turning a corner, down at the end of a long row of old metal beds with bare, stained mattresses, we saw a lone patient. A girl lying on her side, very thin in the arms and legs, with a swollen belly. Her mother, standing beside the bed, explained that the girl had been sick for a long time. The doctors said she had typhoid. When the strike began, the mother and daughter had simply stayed, because the mother didn't know what else to do. But a doctor did stop in now and then, and had left behind some pills.

At the hospital, the morgue, at least, was functioning. I looked into the one reserved for victims of diseases, mostly diseases that could have been prevented or cured. The door was made of corroded metal, like the door to a meat locker. The room inside was filled with trays on racks, stacked horizontally, several bodies per tray, the majority children, the little girls still in their dresses, bows in their hair.

Diarrhea alone kills sixty-eight Haitian children out of every 1,000 before the age of 5. "Did many of the people in the morgue die because of dirty water?", I asked the medical director.

"Oh, of course!" he said. He also told me, "Sometimes we have to put more bodies together than we're supposed to, because there isn't room."

Haiti is in dreadful shape. No one disputes the fact. So it seems odd that over the past few years foreign aid to the country has actually declined. Haiti still receives assistance, from the United States, the European Union, Canada, Japan and various United Nations organizations, but the total amount has been reduced by about two-thirds since 1995. The United States has cut its donations by more than half since 1999. The World Bank, meanwhile, has shut down its lending to the country, for the time being at least, and has closed its Haiti office, leaving behind only an administrator and driver.

Then there is the case of the Inter-American Development Bank. The IDB isn't as well known as some of the other IFIs (the international financial institutions, or "Iffies" in aidspeak) but ranks as a major player in Latin America and the Caribbean. It has long been one of the most important lenders to Haiti. In the late 1990s it made comprehensive plans for a passel of new low-interest loans to address some of the country's most pressing needs--$148 million in all for improving roads, education and the public health system, and for increasing the supplies of potable water. But in the spring of 2001, when the loans were about to be disbursed, the U.S. representative on the IDB board of executive directors wrote the bank's president asking that the process be halted. This was unusual. No member nation is supposed to be able to stop the disbursement of loans that are already approved. Nevertheless, the IDB complied. The Haitian government also lost access to loans it could have received from the IDB over the next several years, worth another $470 million.

The State Department seemed reluctant to discuss this matter. I was granted an interview with a senior department official only on condition that I not use his name. He told me it wasn't just the United States that had wanted to block the IDB loans; it was "a concerted effort" of the Organization of American States. The legal justification for blocking the loans, he said, originated at an OAS meeting called the Quebec City Summit, which produced something called the Declaration of Quebec City. But that document is dated April 22, 2001, and the letter from the IDB's U.S. executive director asking that the loans not be disbursed is dated April 6, 2001. So it would seem that the effort became concerted after it was made. The reason for blocking the loans, according to the official, was "to bring pressure to bear on the Aristide government, to address what the OAS itself and other members of the international community saw as serious flaws in the 2000 electoral process."

The official was referring to elections held in May 2000, in which Jean-Bertrand Aristide's Lavalas political party won large majorities in both houses of the Haitian Parliament. Each candidate had to win a clear majority to avoid a runoff, but the election procedures made it impossible to determine whether some had won majorities or merely pluralities. This was the case with eight Senate seats, in seven of which Lavalas candidates had received the most votes. But the Provisional Electoral Council eschewed runoffs, and declared those eight the winners. Opposition parties claimed the elections had been stolen, and many foreign diplomats made a fuss. Soon, many were calling the entire election "fraudulent." This seemed rather harsh, given the fact that to a great extent, foreigners had financed, managed and monitored the proceedings, and in the immediate aftermath many observers had declared a victory for Haiti's fledgling democracy. Sixty-five percent of Haiti's eligible voters had turned out, many walking miles along mountain paths and waiting for hours in the hot sun to vote. Moreover, those eight contested Senate seats didn't affect the balance of legislative power. Even if they'd lost them all, Lavalas would still have had control of Parliament.

The election didn't seem like a sufficient reason for cutting aid to Haiti. To me the State Department's explanation seemed like obvious diplomatic obfuscation, what diplomats called "irregularities in vote-counting" serving as the pretext for reducing the amount of money that went to Haiti's government.

Back in 1990, after centuries of slavery and dictatorship, Haitians finally got the chance to vote in free and fair elections. They chose Aristide, a Catholic priest from a poor parish of Port-au-Prince, as their president by an overwhelming margin—he received 67 percent of the vote in a field of thirteen candidates. Aristide's liberation theology--a doctrine whose central tenet is "to provide a preferential option for the poor"--won him a devout following among Haiti's poor but few friends in the first Bush Administration. After just seven months Aristide was deposed by a military junta, which ruled the country with great violence and cruelty for three years. Finally, in 1994, the Clinton Administration sent troops, which restored Aristide and his government. In the remaining year and a half of his term, Aristide made some small progress in rooting out the endemic corruption that various juntas and dictatorships had left behind. With the help of the United States, he also disbanded the Haitian Army, which the U.S. Marines had reconstituted during the American occupation of Haiti in the early part of the century--an army, it was often said, that never knew an enemy besides the Haitian people.

An array of foreign governments and Iffies pledged their help in rebuilding Haiti, but many of the donors insisted that in return for their aid Aristide institute "structural economic adjustment"—the privatization of state-owned enterprises, for example. According to one diplomat who spent a great deal of time conferring with him, Aristide was "privately ambivalent and publicly ambiguous" about the Iffies' recipes for Haiti. Too ambiguous to suit some of his former admirers on the left, for whom neoliberal economic reform is anathema, but also too ambiguous to win over any of his numerous detractors on the right.

In 1996, Aristide, barred from seeking a consecutive term by the Haitian Constitution, endorsed as his replacement an old friend, Renè Prèval, and for the first time in Haitian history, a democratically elected head of state turned over power to another. Aristide ran for president again in November 2000. Citing the unresolved flaws in the May legislative elections, the United States declined to assist or monitor the presidential elections, which the political opposition in Haiti also boycotted. Aristide won easily, though--and legitimately, in the eyes of most of the world. But by then he had acquired many detractors, a large and varied cast, mostly situated outside Haiti.

To the American right, liberation theology had long seemed like an especially dangerous doctrine, combining Marxist analysis with a call to connect the struggles of Christ to those of the poor. And Aristide's preaching and criticisms of the United States, combined with his great popularity among the Haitian poor, made him a natural target for right-wing politicians, such as Jesse Helms, who had denounced Aristide, even retailing slanders against him. Some of Aristide's early detractors are still in the American government. One of Helms's chief aides on the Senate Foreign Relations Committee, Roger Noriega, was until recently the permanent U.S. representative to the OAS. In that capacity, he issued a number of statements criticizing Aristide and his government. Recently he was nominated as the Bush Administration's chief of policy on Latin America.

Today, Aristide's critics argue variously that he is guilty of fomenting corruption and violence, or of condoning them, or, at the very least, of being too irresolute to put a stop to them. And it may be that, as one former diplomat told me, Aristide returned to power in 1994 with a "never again" attitude, resolving that if his enemies had guns and thugs, he would not be without them either. When I interviewed Aristide, he allowed that the issue of controlling his supporters was "a preoccupation," and added that he couldn't control agents provocateurs who committed crimes in the name of Lavalas. (A common sort of charge in Haiti. Opposition leaders have claimed, for instance, that Lavalas staged the notorious armed attack on the presidential palace on December 17, 2001, in order to have a pretext to attack them.) Aristide also told me, "I will do more to try to provide security and push the judicial system to render justice and not to delay and delay."

I wasn't sure he'd get very far in those efforts. Haiti now has about 3,500 poorly trained and ill-equipped police, including many amenable to payoffs and bribes, and some involved in drug trafficking. The United States has withdrawn all its support for the police and judicial system and, with the OAS, has been demanding that Aristide improve security and the administration of justice. A State Department official told me that the United States was trying to give "recognized political parties as much training as possible so they can compete nationally." In fact, Washington has long tried to create a counterforce to Aristide's vast popular support — most preposterously back in the mid-1990s, when the American soldiers temporarily occupying the country were told by their commanders that a right-wing terrorist organization called FRAPH was the "loyal opposition" to Aristide. More recently, public documents show, the United States helped to create the main political opposition, the Democratic Convergence, and has aided it in developing platforms and strategies. In theory, this could be a laudable program; democracy benefits from real competition. But it is sinister if, as Aristide's supporters say, part of Washington's strategy is to make room for an opposition by crippling Aristide's government--by blocking IDB loans, for example.

Over the past few years, the United States and the OAS have placed increasingly onerous conditions on the Aristide government, which have included satisfying the demands of the political opposition. Foreign diplomats insisted that the senators in the contested seats resign; all did so several months after Aristide's re-election as president. Aristide has continually called for new elections, but the opposition has demanded that Aristide resign before they will cooperate. A State Department official in Haiti told me that the United States won't countenance such intransigence but also said that no support for new elections in Haiti will be forthcoming until Aristide improves "security," among other things. But it may be, as Aristide's supporters believe, that no support will be forthcoming until Washington thinks elections will yield the result it wants.

There is no telling, of course, how new elections would turn out, but it is possible to guess. The United States has commissioned opinion polls in Haiti. These have not been released publicly, but I managed to obtain one, dated March 2002. The most striking thing about the data is that on many significant issues between 40 and 46 percent of those surveyed either refused to answer or said they had no opinion. Among those who responded, the poll reveals a rise in national cynicism. And the poll does show significant declines in Aristide's ratings from a poll conducted a year before, but those are declines from a very high level. About 60 percent of those who responded in 2002 named him as the leader they trusted most, and no more than 4 percent named anyone else. About 40 percent of respondents also named Lavalas as the political party they sympathized with, while only about 8 percent named the Convergence.

One foreign journalist recently wrote, "Among the disaffected former supporters [of Aristide] are virtually all of Haiti's leading intellectuals and artists, the persons who had best articulated the humane values that should be at the basis of any new Haitian society." But should Haiti's leading artists and intellectuals, however well articulated and humane their values, be the ones to define a new Haitian society? Perhaps 80 percent of Haitians live in poverty, about 70 percent in poverty so desperate that they've never had a chance to go to school, let alone become intellectuals. These are the people most often invoked in discussions about Haiti's suffering, but they are also the people least often consulted on the question of what should be done. The main exception has been elections. The Haitian poor demanded the right to vote. They ran grave risks to get it--in the aborted elections of 1987, for instance, when thugs employed by the junta in power gunned down would-be voters at polling places. And when they've finally had their chance, the impoverished majority has, time and again, turned out in large numbers and expressed their hopes by electing Aristide.

The saga of the blocked IDB loans has continued. In September 2002, the OAS seemed to relent a little, and resolved that the Iffies should resume normal relations with the Haitian government. But this had no immediate practical effect. The World Bank had no plans to make new loans. And the IDB couldn't disburse the loans for clean water and health, and roads and education, because arrears had accumulated since 2000. Haiti now owed the bank millions more in debts on previous loans, ones taken out, ironically enough, by Aristide's predecessors--by "Baby Doc" Duvalier and by various military juntas that had tried to kill Aristide several times back in the late 1980s. Haiti didn't qualify for the international program of debt relief because Haiti didn't owe enough. It did, however, owe more than it could pay. So if the loans were going to be released, some foreign government or institution would have to make a bridge loan to Haiti. One senior State Department official told me that the United States was in favor of a bridge loan, but only if Aristide's government met various conditions. Clearly, the IDB loans were still being used to exert pressure on Aristide.

This past summer the Haitian government decided to pay the arrears itself, a total of $32 million, a sum that represented more than 90 percent of the country's foreign reserves. In effect, the government has all but bankrupted itself for the sake of those loans with the hope of more to come.

Last winter I made a call to the World Bank, to the person then serving as its Caribbean country director, Orsalia Kalantzopoulos. I knew that the World Bank had run into the same problems as the IDB, and that loans were being held up by about $25 million in arrears. But I wondered why it had pulled out of the country. It seemed like a strange thing to do, given that its mission statement reads, "Our dream is a world free of poverty."

Kalantzopoulos told me, "The problem was that most of the projects, with very few exceptions, did not meet their objectives. In addition, the projects had a lot of execution problems. There was not proper procurement and sometimes money was not going to the projects described." She added, " The bottom line is, if there is not the political will to use the money properly, does it really make sense to mortgage the next generation?"

Of course, the status quo doesn't promise future generations much of a future in Haiti. And the Iffies are already making the current generation of Haitians pay for the sins of the past.

Today, the United States is passing almost all of its direct aid to Haiti through USAID, which then funnels the money to various NGOs. But according to Gerard Johnson, until recently the IDB's representative there, this tactic is only a palliative, not a cure. "In the sense of development, NGOs cannot replace the government. They can satisfy short-term humanitarian problems, they're very important as a partner to government, but I don't think you can avoid the government and do lasting development." The only real solution in the long run, Johnson felt, was to strengthen the institutions within Haiti, and one way to do that was through IDB loans. Haiti, he explained, has an informal economy, untaxed and untaxable, that probably accounts for about 85 percent of the country's employment. Incompetence and corruption are problems, but the bigger problem is that the government can't raise enough in taxes to do much more than pay its employees salaries. Low-interest IDB loans could provide the capital for making real improvements.

There are a few examples of successes even in Haiti. One of Johnson's favorites was a recent Canadian project that had brought reliable electricity to the city of Jacmel. One of the most harmful legacies of the American occupation early in the twentieth century and of the Duvaliers' long rule has been the centralization of everything. The Jacmel project was so far fairly successful, Johnson thought, because the Aristide government had ceded control, including that of revenues, to the local government. "This is exactly the model that we would like to replicate with the water loan," Johnson told me. "Support good governance, support local government, and that's definitely linked to democracy. The people are to stand in relation to the state to the point where they're willing to trust enough to pay their water rates, which sounds like something automatic in Washington, DC, but in Haiti when you pay your water rate, you may or may not get water."

Of course, some opponents of neoliberal economic reform believe that poor countries should have no truck with the Iffies, because the conditions that are invariably attached to their aid usually end up doing further harm to the poor. I raised this objection with Dr. Paul Farmer. He is a professor of medicine and medical anthropology at Harvard and the medical director of a remarkably effective and expanding public health system in a desperately impoverished region of rural Haiti. He has also published a number of articles critical of the Iffies and neoliberal economic reforms. He told me, "Anti-neoliberal people say Haiti would be better off without the IMF and the World Bank and the IDB, but there's no topsoil left in a lot of the country, there are no jobs, people are dying of AIDS and coughing their lungs out with TB, and the poor don't have enough to eat. These are problems in the here and now. Something has to be done. Haiti is flat broke, and I don't see what else the government can do but turn to the Iffies. It's the job of the true friends of Haiti to protect it from the hypocrisies of the Iffies."

I have spent portions of the past three years in Haiti, mostly in the country's famished, deforested central plateau. During that time I've met a number of people who describe themselves as peasants, among them a man in his 30s, named Ti Jean Gabriel. When I spoke with him last winter in Haiti, he said he wished he could talk with President Bush and tell him about the problems in the country. He could tell his own story, how when he was 8 he had so few clothes that he used to work naked in his father's field. "I feel like if I could get to the right person, so I could explain the situation..."

I told him that some people thought giving more aid to Haiti now would be a mistake. What was his response to that?

He leaned toward me. "I will answer your question with a question," he said. "You have seen Haiti. Do you think Haiti needs more aid?"

* * *

Reprinted with permission from the October 27, 2003 issue of *The Nation*. For subscription information, call 1-800-333-8536. Portions of each week's *The Nation* magazine can be accessed at http://www.thenation.com.

# Liberation Medicine and U.S. Policy toward Haiti

*Adam Taylor and Paul Farmer, M.D., Ph.D.*

## Introduction

The world's failure to globalize health as a human right stands as a stark indictment to today's era of economic globalization. All too often the health of people living in poverty serves as collateral damage in the pursuit of economic growth and advancing commercial interests at all costs. The stakes of globalization have never been higher than around the crisis of HIV/AIDS due to the lethal relationship between AIDS, inequality, and poverty. The nation of Haiti serves as a microcosm of this trend and as a clear reminder that U.S. policy gone awry has devastating outcomes in the realm of health and human rights.

The culpability of the United States in the suffering of the Haitian poor is too often ignored and understated. Despite previous U.S. policy that propped up the brutal and corrupt governments of past Haitian leaders, such as Baby Doc and Papa Doc, U.S. policy continues to be unjust and biased against the will of the Haitian people. U.S. programs that alleviate suffering in the poorest nations often begin from a paradigm of either charity or humanitarianism. While these goals represent noble sentiments, they belie and at worst come at the expense of demands for justice based upon the long history of U.S. intervention into the affairs of the Haitian people. One recent and seemingly confounding double standard stands in the way of halting the spread of HIV/AIDS and promoting health. On the one hand the U.S. government designated Haiti as a recipient for Bush's new AIDS initiative and yet with the other hand has been blocking access to loans approved by the Inter-American Development Bank for water, health, and education programs. The duplicitous nature of this policy is costing lives at a moment in which the Bush Administration is using HIV/AIDS as evidence of a more compassionate face of its foreign policy.

This chapter explores how contradictions in current U.S. policy toward Haiti exacerbate an already grave health crisis and how the groundbreaking HIV/AIDS programs at the *Clinique Bon Sauveur* provide a replicable model for implementing rights-based HIV/AIDS programs across the poorest parts of the Caribbean and sub-Saharan Africa.

# Health Conditions in Haiti Today

Simply put, health conditions in Haiti are among the worst in the world. All of Haiti's public health indices are bad. Life expectancy, for example, is the lowest in our hemisphere. As elsewhere in the world, infant mortality rates fell fairly slowly but steadily over the course of the past few decades, but in Haiti some of these trends have reversed and infant mortality now stands at 80.3 per 1,000 live births.[1] This is unacceptable, since the majority of infant deaths are readily preventable. Juvenile mortality rates, similarly, are the worst in the region, in large part because of malnutrition, low vaccination rates, and other by-blows of poverty. Maternal mortality rates are appalling. Even the low-end estimates (523 per 100,000 live births)[2] are the worst in the hemisphere, and one community-based survey conducted in the 1980s pegged the figure at 1,400 per 100,000 live births.[3] For a sense of scale, those same figures in the United States, Costa Rica, and Grenada are 7.1, 19.1, and 1.0 per 100,000 live births, respectively.[4,5,6]

What about infectious diseases? Polio, announced eradicated from the Western hemisphere in 1994,[7] resurfaced on the island in 2000.[8] This unexpected resurgence occurred because of a sharp decline in vaccination rates under military rule. Haiti's self-appointed leaders had scant interest, it would seem, in public health. National vaccination rates for measles and polio reached their lowest point ever, with one PAHO survey suggesting that, in 1993, only 30% of Haitian children had been fully vaccinated for measles, polio, mumps, and rubella.[9] It was only a matter of time— in this case, a few months to a few years— before these diseases came back. The measles epidemics came quickly, as was documented in central Haiti.[10] But even polio, deemed vanquished forever, could and did return. The strain of polio that spread was actually derived from a vaccine, we should point out. This strain was fully capable of causing paralysis and death and able to spread only because so few children had been vaccinated during the early nineties.[11]

You know already that AIDS is a serious problem in Haiti, perhaps the only country in this hemisphere in which HIV stands as the number-one cause of all adult deaths.[12] The Haitian epidemic has been described as "generalized," since it affects women as much as or more than men; it is not confined to any clearly bounded groups; and it has spread from urban areas to the farthest reaches of rural Haiti, such as the villages in which Partners In Health works. What's worse, HIV not only kills 30,000 Haitians each year and orphans 200,000 more,[13] it has also aggravated an already severe tuberculosis epidemic. In one careful survey conducted in an urban slum in Port-au-Prince, fully 15% of all adults were found to be infected with HIV.[14] Stunningly, the rate of active and thus potentially infectious tuberculosis among these HIV-positive slum dwellers was 5,770 per 100,000 population. Again, for a sense of scale, the number of Americans with active TB is pegged at 5.6 per 100,000 population.[15] For Jamaica, Haiti's neighbor, the number is 5 per 100,000 population;[16] for Cuba, rates of active TB are only slightly higher than those registered in Jamaica.[17]

As for food and water, again the story is grim. According to the World Bank, Haiti is the third hungriest country in the world,[18] the only hungry country located close to our shores. The water story is even worse: a group in the U.K., the Centre for Ecology and Hydrology, recently developed a "water poverty index" and carefully surveyed 147 of the world's countries for supply and quality. Haiti was ranked in 147th place.[19]

# U.S. Policies: Healthy and Unhealthy

Social conditions in Haiti are deteriorating, mostly because resources and medical personnel are scarce, and because there is a growing burden of disease. There are many reasons for worsening conditions, but it is important to assess the connection between unnecessary suffering, increased mortality, and an aid embargo which has greatly diminished the ability of the public-health system to respond to the needs of the Haitian people.

The United States is the richest country in the world and produces a third of the world's GDP. By virtue of its location, historical development, and power, it stands to reason that U.S. policies towards that country have an overwhelming influence. But has the influence of our policies been a good one? Here, of course, is where the dispute comes in. An examination of history reveals that a concerted effort has long been under way to upset the Haitian people's efforts to build an egalitarian society. It began in 1791, when the only independent country in the hemisphere, our own, weighed in on the side of the slave owners. And so it has gone on for years, as Haiti grew poorer and the U.S. grew richer.

If ever there were a little known tale that involved epic struggle, injustice (specifically, the abuse by the powerful of the poor), and more epic struggle, it would be Haiti's. Distorted versions of that story make it into the popular consciousness, with images of tinpot dictators and voodoo and brute poverty dominating. But that's not the real story. The real story, the one that bears the most resemblance to history, is even uglier. To understand Haiti today - "the poorest country in the western world" – one has to understand five centuries of history.

Haiti is the story of a small group of people in struggle with powerful forces and people far from the western part of the island on which Haiti now sits. The history of Haiti is the story of European expansionism, the rise of plantation slavery, slave revolts and war, exploitation by colonial powers, the ascendancy of the United States, and – in recent years – the domination of the Caribbean by the United States. Through twists of fate and history, citizens of rich countries like the U.S. and affluent Europe have had undue influence in Haiti and in other impoverished nations. Haiti became "the poorest country in the Western world" the hard way, by being subjected to this history, which invariably involved Europe and, later, the United States.

During each of these periods of time, some Haitians fought against domination and slavery. Usually they lost; usually they had few allies. But the struggle was never snuffed out. Haiti's is a story that is both local and global, and comprehensive understandings of these connections are critical if we are to help Haiti to advance its centuries-old struggle for independence and equity. For those self-determinationists who suggest that "Haiti and Haitians are going to have to solve their own problems," we say that if Haitians had created these problems on their own, then they might reasonably be expected to resolve them on their own. But as we shall see, the tragedy that is now Haiti has been a transnational project for hundreds of years.

We will not dwell on what some non-Haitians would call "ancient history" (that is, anything that occurred prior to the 21st century), but can't resist noting that while the Haitians willingly sent troops to aid us in the Battle of Savannah, in 1779,[20] our own response to their appeal for assistance in their war of independence was to support the slave owners. And when, against all odds, the Haitians defeated the French on the battlefield – which led, according to John Adams and to many others, to the Louisiana Purchase – we continued to behave ungraciously. From 1804 until 1862, when Lincoln changed our policy, we simply refused to recognize the existence of "the Black Republic."[21] Worse, we later pressured other countries in the hemisphere not to recognize Haiti's sovereignty.[22]

Our policies did not improve much during the late 19th century, and in the early 20th century we invaded and occupied Haiti militarily.[23] Evidence shows that our past policies towards Haiti were remarkable for their consistently antidemocratic tilt. Modern U.S. historians agree on this, as do the Haitians.

# Successes

Many good things are happening in Haiti, though, and surely the most important of these is the transition, however painful, from dictatorships to democracy. There are medical victories, as well—and most of them are the result of genuine public-private partnerships, such as the one between Partners In Health/Zanmi Lasante and the Haitian public sector, to combat AIDS.

For too many years AIDS has been considered impossible to prevent or treat in the poorest parts of the world. But in Haiti, non-governmental organizations (NGOs) working closely with the Ministry of Health have spent a decade developing culturally appropriate prevention tools, providing voluntary counseling and testing, and working to improve care for people living with HIV. These efforts are among the reasons why the predicted "explosion" of HIV did not occur in Haiti. That is, the situation is grim and AIDS is, as noted, the leading killer of young Haitian adults. But seroprevalence studies suggest that the Haitian epidemic is slowing down. Again, Haiti formed a public-private partnership, one of the strongest in the world, in order to pull together a successful proposal to the Global Fund for AIDS, Tuberculosis, and Malaria.[24] The National AIDS Commission is chaired by the First Lady, Mildred Aristide, who has made AIDS and the rights of poor children her primary concerns as a public figure. As we write, Haiti is probably the country in the poor world with the most promising integrated AIDS prevention and care project already up and running.

# The Cange Syndrome

To an AIDS activist, traveling to the *Clinique Bon Sauveur* in Cange is akin to a pilgrimage to the mecca of modern medicine benefiting the world's poorest peoples. Located in the Central Plateau of Haiti, the hospital, operated cooperatively by the Boston-based medical NGO Partners in Health (PIH) and its NGO partner *Zamni Lasante* (ZL), represents a symbol of what is possible even in the most remote, unfavorable public health conditions. Practically impassable roads lead from Port-au-Prince to Cange. The hospital overlooks an impoverished squatter community that was displaced by the construction of a hydroelectric dam project. PIH's approach applies tenets in liberation theology by providing health care to the poor, regardless of their ability to pay, thus lending a preferential option in health care to the poor.

Partners in Health has been carrying out AIDS prevention programs for over 15 years in Cange. PIH was the first to introduce voluntary counseling and testing into central Haiti, and the first to develop culturally appropriate prevention tools. In 1995, Zamni Lasante introduced the provision of AZT in rural Haiti to block mother-to-child transmission of HIV. Subsequently, the proportion of women accepting free Voluntary Counseling and Testing during pregnancy increased from between 15%-20% to greater than 90% of all women[25]. PIH recognized that the social death that precedes a physical death from AIDS represented a powerful factor in driving HIV/AIDS underground and preventing public education and testing from reaching those most at risk.

In 1998 PIH/ZL launched the HIV Equity Initiative to complement its prevention efforts by offering highly active antiretroviral (ARV) therapy free of charge to patients with advanced HIV disease judged to be in imminent danger of death[26]. The program utilized the directly observed therapy model that has been so successful in administering complex treatment regimens for multidrug-resistant tuberculosis. Community health workers called *accompagnateurs* visit patients daily and supervise their pill-taking, while at the same time providing social support[27] for patients receiving medicines. Referred to as angels by their patients, these accompagnateurs come from the local community; in addition to medications, they supply limited nutritional supplements[28] and often provide assistance with children's school fees. The antiretroviral program follows 3,000 HIV positive patients, 10-12% of whom are on AIDS therapy, even though 25% are in need of life-prolonging medicines. The Zamni Lasante experience suggests that improving clinical services can dramatically improve the quality of prevention efforts and reduce AIDS-related stigma[29]. The majority of patients have shown striking health improvements, characterized by weight gain and abatement of AIDS-related symptoms. Many patients have returned to work and family life after extreme debilitation[30]. The success and publicity around the treatment program in Haiti has led to what human rights lawyer Nicole Lee terms "the Cange syndrome." This contagious syndrome provides credence to the reality that treatment is indispensable to effective prevention and can be effectively administered in even the most resource poor setting.

# Contradiction and U.S. Policy

While the Clinique Bon Sauveur represents a life-saving dam that stops a flood of premature death and unnecessary suffering in the Central Plateau, the hospital cannot alter the harsh realities of underdevelopment and social injustice that envelop the nation of Haiti. In 2002, Zamni Lasante had capacity to receive 35,000 visits per year but saw almost 200,000 ambulatory patients, a three-fold increase from the previous year[31]. This flood of high child and maternal mortality sweeps across the rest of Haiti unabated. NGOs across Haiti provide localized barriers to obstruct this flood; however, only the government of Haiti is in position to address the poverty that lies at the source of this tragedy. In a practical sense, the Ministry of Health is the only institution with the reach to replicate local, concentrated successes throughout Haiti. Yet, current U.S. policy toward Haiti would preclude funding to the Ministry of Health. Aid to Haiti has been reduced by about two-thirds since 1995 with the U.S. cutting its donation by more than half since 1999, none of which goes through the Haitian government[32].

Realizing health as a human right in Haiti will require engagement by the U.S. government with the government of Haiti. Five years from now, Haiti could be the success story of the Caribbean in a similar way that Uganda provides hope for the rest of sub-Saharan Africa[33]. However with scaled up treatment programs across the island, Haiti could avoid the same degree of painful loss and death that coincided with Uganda's remarkable reduction in HIV prevalence. The crucial ingredient of political will that contributed to the success of Uganda is also evident in Haiti. For example, Madame Aristide chairs the National AIDS Council of Haiti. Even in the midst of sanctions, the government of Haiti has increased its expenditures in health from 1.2% of GDP in 1990 to 2.4% in 2000[34]. In the case of Haiti, it is confounding that in a nation with an incredibly high quotient of political will, the whims of the United States seem to undermine this commitment at every turn.

The impact of the U.S. government's withholding $146 million in loans from the Inter-American Development Bank goes far beyond this sum. The European Union and other multilateral organizations have followed suit and not released funding to the Haitian government in recent years. These sanctions have dramatically reduced publicly available funds for Haiti, which in turn has led to the deterioration in Haiti's public health infrastructure[35]. U.S. development programs will not have their intended impact as long as they isolate the Haitian government. Through the context of health and HIV/AIDS, the U.S. government has an opportunity to engage the government of Haiti around a program that constitutes a clear priority for both the U.S. and the Haitian people.

# The Fight We Are Fighting

Only three years ago, during the 2000 International AIDS conference in Durban, South Africa, the debate between prevention and treatment came to a head with experts from the World Bank alleging that anti-retroviral (ARV) treatment is not cost-effective. Denial around HIV/AIDS was not simply a condition that plagued the President of South Africa, Thabo Mbeki, during the conference. A more subtle and sophisticated form of denial has characterized the response by governments and the public health establishment in its response to the crisis of HIV/AIDS. Both have argued against the feasibility of treatment programs, contending that AIDS treatment is too difficult and expensive for poor settings or that investments in treatment would divert resources from other less costly health programs and fuel drug resistance. By the 2002 International AIDS conference in Barcelona, the AIDS world at least tacitly embraced the notion that treatment and prevention programs were mutually reinforcing.

AIDS brings new urgency to the need to establish the right to the highest attainable standard of physical and mental health as stated in Article 25 of the Universal Declaration of Human Rights and Article 12 of the International Covenant on Economic, Social, and Cultural Rights. The human rights approach taken by Partners in Health in Haiti provides a crucial model in the fight against AIDS. This approach can be replicated across the country of Haiti and serve as a best practice in other countries. People living with HIV are not treated simply as patients that require diagnosis and treatment, but as people whose life chances have become circumscribed by disease and whose right to basic services has been callously abridged. For example, visitors walking the grounds of the hospital find it striking to see children from the outlying community attending classes in a community school built within the compound. Equally astounding is the opportunity for members of the community from the squatter settlement to find employment within the constructs of the hospital.

PIH recognizes that turning back the advance of HIV/AIDS is inextricably linked to combating abject poverty, empowering women, and improving overall public health. The widely accepted prevention approach known as "ABC" standing for abstinence, being faithful, and using condoms leaves out an important E for economic and social empowerment. The work carried on in Cange provides evidence that the integration of women's empowerment, antipoverty, and vulnerability reduction programs significantly strengthens AIDS prevention and treatment programs.

# HIV/AIDS and the Imperative for U.S. Reengagement

The miracle at Cange should not, however, be romanticized. It is clear that significant private funding and extraordinary leadership have played key roles in the program's success. However, these factors can be replicated in other parts of Haiti and other parts of the world. Resignation and denial represent the greatest obstacles to fighting AIDS, not simply among the most marginalized but also among those charged and trained to promote the health of societies and communities. Even though the number of patients on treatment in Haiti pales in comparison with the overall need, the evidence from Cange has given treatment activists new ammunition beyond a moral and human argument that AIDS need not equal a death sentence.

Haiti provides an immediate opportunity to show the merits of a treatment and human rights-based approach within the new Bush initiative. Evidence in Cange disproves popular arguments that complex and sophisticated care is impossible in resource-poor settings. Yet this assumption still seems to be at the heart of the glacial pace of the United States in appropriating the adequate resources required to build health infrastructures in Africa and the Caribbean. Too often the racism of low expectations infects our U.S. foreign policy to the point that we no longer question why infrastructure remains so weak in impoverished countries, nor do we promote levels of foreign assistance that would enable poor countries to truly invest in that infrastructure. To make matters even worse, the World Bank and IMF-imposed structural adjustment programs often force countries to balance their already tight budgets on the backs of those that can least afford it through cuts in health care and social services

The implementation of Bush's Emergency Plan for AIDS Relief has been characterized by an incremental approach and deferred promises. After Bush's State of the Union announcement that the U.S. would provide $15 billion over five years to fight AIDS in Africa and the Caribbean, only a vague fact sheet has been released outlining their approach[36]. The Bush Administration's procrastination in designing and implementing the Emergency AIDS Plan could cost millions of lives. The goal to provide treatment to 2 million people in Africa and the Caribbean within five years will be increasingly difficult to reach the more valuable time is lost[37]. AIDS advocates as well as leading Democrats and Republicans in the Senate and the House authorized $3 billion to spent in fiscal year 2004 for global AIDS with $1 billion going to the already up and running Global Fund to Fight HIV/AIDS, Tuberculosis, and Malaria. Yet Dr. Joe O'Neill, Director of the Office of National AIDS Policy, stated that "Congress should not appropriate more than $2 billion because even though treatment is central to the AIDS initiative, treating AIDS patients is very complex and requires the United States to build much more infrastructure, including training health care workers"[38].

The Bush Administration is playing politics with people's lives in asserting that money must be ramped up slowly to fund the AIDS initiative because of lack in health infrastructure, then denying the very funding that would help to build that infrastructure. The U.S. has engaged in a dangerous and irrational game of cart and horse in which the inability of countries to absorb large amounts of funding serves as a convenient smokescreen to delay U.S. commitment. According to a UNAIDS report, "lack of capacity to absorb increased resources allocated to HIV/AIDS, while posing challenges, is no reason to delay the boosting of responses in countries expressing commitment to an expanded response"[39].

Fortunately, Haiti received a $66.7 million grant from the Global Fund in 2002 to provide resources to scale up a number of effective treatment and prevention programs. By the end of the year 2003, money from the grant will be used to provide antiretroviral therapy to more than 1,200 people living with HIV through the Partners in Health directly observed therapy approach. The program will couple strategies for behavioral change communication with social marketing of over 15 million condoms throughout the country and a massive expansion of prevention services targeting youth, reaching more than 400,000 by the year's end[40]. These are the types of programs that the Bush plan could support right now. It is seemingly contradictory that Haiti was the first country to meet the Global Fund's strict monitoring and accountability requirements for the dispersal of funds, yet if the new Bush AIDS initiative follows current U.S. policy, the Government of Haiti will be denied access to bilateral funding.

# Why Haiti, Why Now?

Through the lens of Haiti, the AIDS movement and public health community have the opportunity to embrace a broader development and human rights agenda to fully halt the onslaught of HIV/AIDS. Haiti is already serving as a demonstration site to develop best practices around AIDS treatment programs in resource-poor settings and implement strategies that link HIV/AIDS to poverty and marginalization. Throughout the over 20-year history of HIV/AIDS, one can trace a series of defining chapters. During the first chapter, the world coped with pervasive stigma, shame, and silence that surrounded the virus. AIDS activists demanded increased funding for research and for their civil rights. The second chapter challenged the notion that life is expendable and that AIDS should represent a death sentence for the poor and a manageable disease for the privileged.

The final chapter must call for the full realization of political, social and economic rights in order to guarantee access to treatment and eliminate the vulnerabilities that fuel the spread of AIDS. Many parts of the world are in different stages of this continuum. While the world at large seems to be turning the corner in chapter two by embracing the need for treatment programs, it has yet to embrace a human rights and comprehensive development-based response to AIDS.

# Epilogue: Moving Forward

As the poorest nation in the Western Hemisphere, Haiti's health crisis mirrors many of the most AIDS-afflicted countries in sub-Saharan Africa. Based on this reality and the long-standing interference of the U.S in Haitian politics, there are at least two crucial lessons that must be learned from Haiti. First, the community-based programs of Partners in Health and Zamni Lasante highlight the need to situate the fight against AIDS into a broader development and human rights framework. Secondly, Haiti demonstrates that the fight against AIDS is profoundly influenced by U.S. policies, whether due to direct sanctions or economic prescriptions imposed by international financial institutions. While we might hope to depoliticize this fight, the U.S. government's disregard for Haiti's sovereignty and undermining of Haitian democracy cripples efforts to address health and development issues.

Until recently, the world lacked concrete examples that demonstrate treatment programs are both cost-effective and feasible even in settings with very little health infrastructure. Médecins Sans Frontières (MSF) has also led successful treatment projects begun in 2001 in Cambodia, Cameroon, Guatemala, Honduras, Kenya, Malawi, South Africa, Thailand, Uganda, and Ukraine, enrolling nearly 2,200 patients by 2002[41]. The pioneering work around Highly Active Antiretroviral Therapy by PIH and MSF has catalyzed a paradigm shift in both public policy and public health circles that supports the notion that poor people not only deserve access to care but that care itself can be provided even in the face of weak health infrastructure and limited resources. "The Cange syndrome" is grounded in a moral and medical imperative to include ARV treatment as an indispensable part of a comprehensive AIDS program. The approach is also based in the belief that a human rights approach to medicine will empower poor people to make better health decisions.

The Chinese symbol for crisis has two roots, one meaning opportunity and one meaning danger. The world already associates AIDS with the danger to human life, though this danger is often underestimated and miscalculated. Yet we have been slower to understand AIDS as an opportunity to achieve real development and human rights victories for the world's most impoverished nations. The fight against AIDS is not simply a fight to get information, services, and medicine into the hands of those at risk or living with HIV. At an even deeper level, the fight against AIDS is about empowering those in our midst that are marginalized and vulnerable. The fight is about changing the very fabric of international relations and promoting a broader development and human rights agenda that can rectify the social conditions that contribute to the spread of the virus.

The visibility and momentum surrounding the AIDS crisis should not come at the expense of other infectious diseases, of course. The AIDS movement will be characterized as shortsighted and myopic if we don't use the AIDS crisis as a vehicle for building real health infrastructures or for accelerating anti-poverty initiatives. Zamni Lasante and Partners in Health's work in Haiti is more accurately described as practicing liberation medicine. Through the context of addressing inequalities in health, poor people's lives are being restored, transformed, and empowered. Haiti provides an immediate opportunity to scale up to the national and global level a commitment to promoting health as a human right not just in rhetoric, but also in practice.

---

[1] Infant mortality in Haiti has actually risen since 1996, when it was 73.8 per 1,000 live births; PAHO attributes this rise to increasing poverty, the deterioration of the health system, and HIV. See Pan American Health Organization. Country Profiles: Haiti. 2003. Available at: http://www.paho.org/English/DD/AIS/be_v24n1-haiti.htm.

[2] Pan American Health Organization. Country Profiles: Haiti. 2003. Available at: http://www.paho.org/English/DD/AIS/be_v24n1-haiti.htm. These numbers are likely to be even higher if one measures maternal mortality at the community level.

[3] The only community-based survey done in Haiti, conducted in 1985 around the town of Jacmel in southern Haiti, found that maternal mortality was 1,400 per 100,000 live births. See Jean-Louis R. Diagnostic de l'état de santé en Haïti. *Forum Libre I (Médecine, Santé et Démocratie en Haïti)* 1989: 11-20. During that same period, "official" statistics reported much lower rates for Haiti, ranging from a maternal mortality rate of 230 for the years 1980-1987 and a maternal mortality rate of 340 for 1980-1985 to a higher estimate in the years that followed, 1987-1992, of 600 maternal deaths per 100,000 live births. See United Nations Development Programme. *Human Development Report, 1990.* New York: Oxford University Press for UNDP, 1990; and World Bank. *Social Indicators of Development.* Baltimore: Johns Hopkins University Press, 1994; respectively.

For additional maternal mortality data from that period, see World Health Organization. Maternal Mortality: Helping Women Off the Road to Death. *WHO Chronicle* 1985; 40: 175-183.

[4] Pan American Health Organization. Country Health Profile: United States. 2001. Available at: http://www.paho.org/English/SHA/prflUSA.htm.

[5] Pan American Health Organization. Country Health Profile: Costa Rica. 2001. Available at: http://www.paho.org/English/SHA/prflCOR.htm.

[6] United Nations Development Programme. Human Development Indicators 2003: Grenada. Available at: http://www.undp.org/hdr2003/indicator/cty_f_GRD.html.

[7] Centers for Disease Control and Prevention. International notes certification of poliomyelitis eradication— the Americas, 1994. *Morbidity and Mortality Weekly Report* 1994; 43(39): 720-722.

[8] Centers for Disease Control and Prevention. Outbreak of poliomyelitis— Dominican Republic and Haiti, 2000. *Morbidity and Mortality Weekly Report* 2000; 49(48): 1094-1103.

[9] Pan American Health Organization and World Health Organization. *Haiti— L'Aide d'Urgence en Santé.* Port-au-Prince: Pan American Health Organization, 1993.

[10] Farmer PE. Haiti's Lost Years: Lessons for the Americas. *Current Issues in Public Health* 1996; 2(3): 143-151.

[11] Kew O, Morris-Glasgow V, Landaverde M, et al. Outbreak of poliomyelitis in Hispaniola associated with circulating type 1 vaccine-derived poliovirus. *Science* 2002; 296 (5566): 269-70.

[12] Pan American Health Organization. "Haiti." In: *Health in the Americas 2002: Vol. II.* Washington, D.C.: Pan American Health Organization, 2002: 336-349.

[13] Joint United Nations Programme on HIV/AIDS. Epidemiological Fact Sheets on HIV/AIDS and Sexually Transmitted Infections: Haiti. 2002. Available at: http://www.unaids.org/hivaidsinfo/statistics/fact_sheets/pdfs/Haiti_en.pdf.

[14] Desormeaux J, Johnson MP, Coberly JS, et al. Widespread HIV counseling and testing linked to a community-based tuberculosis control program in a high-risk population. *Bulletin of the Pan American Health Organization* 1996; 30(1): 1-8.

For a more comprehensive overview of Haiti's burden of treatable and preventable infectious diseases, see Farmer P. *Infections and Inequalities: The Modern Plagues.* Berkeley, CA: University of California Press, 1999.

[15] Centers for Disease Control and Prevention. Reported in *Tuberculosis in the United States, 2001.* Atlanta, GA: U.S. Department of Health and Human Services; 2002. Available at: http://www.cdc.gov/nchstp/tb/surv/surv2001/content/T1.htm.

[16] United Nations Development Programme. Human Development Indicators 2003: Jamaica. Available at: http://hdr.undp.org/reports/global/2002/en/indicator/indicator.cfm?File=cty_f_JAM.html.

[17] In 1999, the rate of active tuberculosis in Cuba was 11 per 100,000 population. See United Nations Development Programme. Human Development Indicators 2003: Cuba. Available at: http://hdr.undp.org/reports/global/2002/en/indicator/indicator.cfm?File=cty_f_CUB.html.

[18] United Nations Food and Agriculture Organization. *The State of Food Insecurity in the World.* United Nations Food and Agriculture Organization: Rome, 2000. Available at: http://www.fao.org/FOCUS/E/SOFI00/img/sofirep-e.pdf.

[19] Sullivan CA, Meigh JR, and Fediw TS. *Derivation and Testing of the Water Poverty Index Phase I.* Centre for Ecology and Hydrology: Wallingford, 2002. Available at: http://www.ciaonet.org/wps/suc01/suc01.pdf.

[20] Madeline Diaz, in the U.S. Consulate's Haiti newsletter, describes the event this way: "... Haitian soldiers fought and died on a Georgia battlefield to help the United States gain its independence from England. About 1,500 volunteers from their country, then a French colony, joined forces with the Americans to fight the British in the 1779 Siege of Savannah." See Diaz MB. Haitians seeking recognition of war effort in U.S. *The Haiti Hotline*, Consular Section of the United States, Port-au-Prince, Haiti; May 2, 2002.

[21] Lawless R. *Haiti's Bad Press.* Rochester, VT: Schenkman Books, 1992.

[22] In 1825, the United States blocked Haiti's invitation to the famous Western Hemisphere Panama Conference. See Lawless R. *Haiti's Bad Press.* Rochester, VT: Schenkman Books, 1992.

[23] Heinl R and Heinl N. *Written in Blood.* Boston: Houghton Mifflin Co., 1978.

[24] For information on Haiti's proposal to the Global Fund, see http://www.globalfundatm.org/proposals/round1/fsheets/haiti.html.

[25] Farmer, Paul. Including ARV's in Resource-poor settings. http://www.pih.org/library/essays/IntroducingARVs/plenarytalk.pdf

[26] Irwin, Millin, and Fallows. Global AIDS: Myths and Facts. Cambridge, South End Press, 2003; 83.

[27] Farmer, Paul. Including ARV's in Resource-poor settings. http://www.pih.org/library/essays/IntroducingARVs/plenarytalk.pdf

[28] Irwin, Millin, and Fallows. Global AIDS: Myths and Facts. Cambridge. South End Press, 2003; 84.

[29] Farmer, Paul. Introducing ARVs in Resource-poor Settings: Expected and Unexpected Challenges and Consequences. http://www.pih.org/library/essays/IntroducingARVs/plenarytalk.pdf

[30] Irwin, Millin, and Fallows. Global AIDS: Myths and Facts. Cambridge. South End Press, 2003; 84.

[31] Farmer, Smith, and Nevil. Unjust embargo of aid for Haiti. *The Lancet.* Vol 361. February 1, 2003; 422.

[32] Farmer. Testimony of Dr. Paul Farmer before the Committee on Foreign Relations. United State Senate. Washington, DC. July, 2003.

[33] President Museveni assumed prominent leadership in the fight against AIDS in 1986, declaring the AIDS struggle a national priority. Due in large degree to political leadership, HIV/AIDS infection rates decreased dramatically in Uganda between 1986 and 2000.

[34] Human Development Report 2003. UNDP. New York, 2003; 297.

[35] Farmer, Smith, and Nevil. Unjust embargo of aid for Haiti. *The Lancet.* Vol 361. February 1, 2003; 422.

[36] According to the Fact Sheet "Implementation of the President's Emergency Plan for AIDS Relief will be based on a network model: being employed in countries such as Uganda...The model will employ uniform prevention, care, and treatment protocols and prepared medication packs for ease of drug administration".

[37] Fact Sheet: The President's Emergency Plan for AIDS Relief. http://www.whitehouse.gov/news/releases/2003/01

[38] Congressional Record S9956 (daily ed., July 17, 2003)
[39] UNAIDS. Report on the global HIV/AIDS epidemic 2002. Geneva, 2002.
[40] Global Fund Money to Scale Up AIDS Treatment and Prevention Efforts in Haiti. December, 2002.
http://www.globalfundatm.org/journalists/press%20releases/pr_021202.html
[41] Irwin, Millin, and Fallows. Global AIDS: Myths and Facts. Cambridge. South End Press. 2003; 86.

# An Open Letter to Activists
*Congresswoman Barbara Lee*

Thanks to all of you who have fought for Haiti. Your advocacy for our neighbor country has worked to overcome the reality that aid for Haiti has been the victim of politics, its humanitarian and medical crises overlooked, and its people ignored.

My colleagues and I have sought to educate our Congressional colleagues. The Congressional Black Caucus' Haiti Task Force has been especially strong in advocating for Haiti: Representatives Conyers, Christian-Christensen, Waters, Meek, and I have mounted both a congressional and a public campaign on issues related to Haitian asylum seekers and immigrants; trade, economic, and infrastructure development; and debt relief. We have pushed for investments to develop Haiti's infrastructure, roads, and water resources, which would ease the country's health crisis. We have sought to ensure that money long overdue from the international financial community be delivered, including the $146 million in loans approved by the Inter-American Development Bank.

Our efforts have succeeded because you have been so adamant in your lobbying efforts. It is you who do the hard and difficult work of carrying the message of Haiti throughout the halls of Capitol Hill and the corners of the country. We have pushed the Bush Administration to provide money for Haiti, including the loan money, and we have been able to generate a new direction for U.S. policy through Ambassador Terrence Todman and the Organization of American States.

We have made enormous progress in helping Haiti, but we cannot stop here. We must also address political reforms and overall U.S. policy. Haiti is at a crossroads, and we must now be equally bold in supporting the next step: democratic, free and fair elections. We must also renew our commitment to bring about peace, stability, and sustainable development to all of the Caribbean.

Commit to alleviating the suffering of the Haitian people. This is a moral imperative that we cannot and should not ignore.
Let Haiti LIVE. Kenbe fèm.

Lapè avek ou,

Barbara Lee
Member of Congress

# When Major Powers Stage a Coup
*Randall Robinson*

A bloodless coup, led by the world's richest and most powerful nations, is taking place in Haiti.

For two years now, the world's wealthiest nations and the Bretton Woods institutions they control have maintained a crushing international financial embargo on eight million Haitians. They have done this "to protest an electoral dispute stemming from Haiti's May 2000 national elections." At issue was the formula used to calculate the votes for seven senate seats - out of some 7,500 filled nationwide at that time. The seven senators have long since resigned, yet the sweeping financial embargo their election triggered remains in place.

In the original dispute over the vote count, anti-government figures inside Haiti, with powerful connections abroad but no political support at home, saw a priceless opportunity. If, instead of having to create the screaming victims and ricocheting bullets of the 1991 coup, the international community would, this time, simply block every penny of international capital to the Government of Haiti, then that government could, effectively, and without the negative headlines, be again overthrown. A government with no access to capital soon becomes no government at all. And so, for more than a year now, Haiti has been hog-tied and thrust face into the dirt by a financial embargo initiated and maintained by the wealthiest nations on earth.

There may not be the bullet-ridden bodies along Haiti's streets that we saw after the coup of 1991. But there are bodies. They are the bodies of Haiti's nameless, faceless poor who, no longer able to bend, break. They buckle under the weight of an embargo that, incredibly, denies their elected government already-approved loans for safe drinking water, literacy programs, and the health care that they need. They die out of earshot, out of sight, and unremarked by "those who matter" beyond their shores.

Professor Paul Farmer of Harvard Medical School established a health clinic in Haiti's Central Plateau some 20 years ago and travels there regularly. Day after day, he and his staff do battle against the ravages of the embargo. He has been writing and speaking extensively in an attempt to alert the outside world to the impact of the world's powerful on Haiti. "They are doing severe harm to millions of

Haitian men, women, and children.... If the American people could observe first hand the ravages of this embargo, they would strongly condemn it," he says.

Profoundly concerned by the human costs of the embargo, the fourteen English-speaking democracies of the Caribbean dispatched a high-level delegation to Haiti in January of 2002. In their view, the widespread human suffering the embargo has wrought has gone unaddressed, and unremarked, for far too long. These democracies, the oldest and most stable in the hemisphere south of the United States, have stepped forward to serve as a bridge between those imposing the embargo and those suffering under it. They note that the Government of Haiti has made significant concessions in an attempt to end this crisis, key among them being the long ago resignation of the seven senators whose election triggered the embargo. At the same time Caricom (Caribbean Community) is working in earnest with Haiti's unelected opposition figures in an attempt to encourage them to work with their government to end the stalemate.

According to Julian Hunte, Minister of External Affairs in the Government of St. Lucia and Head of Caricom's Special Haiti Mission for the entire international community, "the social, economic, and political interests of eight million Haitians must now become paramount." Indeed, Dame Eugenia Charles, former Prime Minister of Dominica and rock solid partner of Ronald Reagan in the 1983 US/Caricom invasion of Grenada, lamented after participating in an official fact-finding mission to Haiti in July 2001, "No one is listening to the Haitian people. No one is asking what the Haitian people want!"

Caricom is trying to alert the Organization of American States, and indeed the entire international community, to a number of stark realities. In this special period in world relations, it is morally untenable and politically unwise for the wealthiest nations on earth to maintain a financial stranglehold on eight million men, women, and children in Haiti. Haiti has no nuclear weapons. It has attacked neither American property nor American citizens. Indeed, it is trying its very best, even with its limited material resources, to be a responsible nation and to support U.S. priorities in the region. As an active participant in the U.S. led regional war on drugs, for example, even with its inexperienced police and coast guard, Haiti was able to double the size of its cocaine seizures last year over the year before.

Throughout the Caribbean, there is a keen sense that the duly elected Government of Haiti must now be allowed to govern. The financial embargo robs the Haitian people of their government, and therefore of their democracy. There is also, throughout the Caribbean, respect for the right of Haiti's opposition figures to continue criticizing their government while awaiting their turn at the polls, for this is the essence of democracy.

Caribbean democracies are urging that the loans successfully negotiated by the Government of Haiti on behalf of the Haitian people be released without delay. It is only when this is done, Caricom feels, that the benefits of Haiti's hard-won democracy will, at last, be made manifest to the very special people of that very special land.

This piece is reprinted, in its entirety, from www.BlackCommentator.com with permission of the author.

# CHAPTER TWO

*Lè yo vle touye yon chen, yo di'l fou.*

When they want to kill a dog, they say it's crazy.

# Haiti:
# Lies My Media Told Me
*Kim Ives*

It was sometime in the summer of 1986 or 1987. I was riding in a car with three other journalists, two from the Associated Press (AP) and one from the Washington Post. We were weaving our way through burning barricades and angry crowds on eerily car-less streets to the far end of the Port-au-Prince's Carrefour district to make an assessment of the general strike which had been called that day.

Finally we decided to get out and talk to some people. I went up to the largest nearby group. The people were watching us with the mix of curiosity, reserve and excitement often seen when a carload of journalists alights in a tense situation.

The people in the crowd were passionate but articulate in denouncing the military dictatorship and in laying out their reasons for supporting the strike. I went back to my colleagues and invited them to come over to hear what the people had to say. Being the only Creole speaker in our group, I told them I would translate for them.

"No," the junior AP reporter responded, "we're going to talk to that guy."

Standing almost alone on a stretch of sidewalk on the other side of the street was an elderly man in a suit and glasses. We went over to him. Speaking in careful French, he told us that the strike was the work of "trouble makers" who were causing disorder and whipping up the people. He said that no good would come from it and that the soldiers who periodically chased the crowds were just trying to keep order.

We then drove back to the Holiday Inn. The AP and Washington Post journalists never spoke to the larger group.

This example illustrates how the mainstream press covers Haiti, or anyplace else, for that matter. While proclaiming its "objectivity," the corporate media spins, shades and shapes its stories by choosing what to cover and with whom to talk. This lies at the core of how news from Haiti is twisted today.

Do a Google internet search engine news search for the word "Haiti," as most people who want to know something about the country are apt to do. You will likely get a slew of hits on the same handful of AP or Reuters stories reproduced in several of Google's touted "4,500 news sources." These are generally U.S. urban dailies, which all subscribe to these two wire services and also reproduce articles from the Washington Post and the New York Times, the two flagships of the U.S. establishment.

Usually, the stories carry almost identical omissions, distortions, and even, sometimes, lies. If the story happens to be broadcast by one of the large U.S. television or radio networks, it too will have the same spin.

The misinformation (and disinformation) bandied about by the corporate press is drawn from and echoed by the conservative Haitian press to create a powerful synergy which is being used today to condition minds and provoke events in Haiti.

# U.S. Media Concentration

The uniformity and pervasiveness of the mainstream media's message results from its growing concentration. A tiny handful of companies now own and control most of the news U.S. Americans see, hear, and read.

The largest media conglomerate is AOL Time Warner, whose assets include CNN, the WB Television Network, HBO, Cinemax, and the magazines Time, Life, and Fortune. The next largest media giant is Viacom, which owns the CBS Television Network, United Paramount Network (UPN), MTV Networks, Black Entertainment Television, Paramount Home Entertainment and the Simon & Schuster publishing group. According to the Center for Digital Democracy, the company has a global reach of about 166 countries and territories.

The weapon-manufacturing multinational General Electric owns NBC and its thirteen affiliates, as well as CNBC, MSNBC, Paxson Communications, Bravo, and the second largest U.S. Spanish-language television network Telemundo. The Walt Disney Company owns ABC, the Disney Channel, ten televison stations, and five daily newspapers.

Four behemoths – Comcast, AOL Time Warner, Charter Communications, and Cox Enterprises – feed two-thirds of the U.S. cable television audience. Australian media mogul Rupert Murdoch's News Corporation controls the Fox Network and rabidly pro-war Fox News, the No. 1 rated cable news channel in the U.S.

Similar concentration exists in the print media. Gannett, Knight Ridder, the Hearst Corporation, Dow Jones & Co., Advance Publications, Lee Enterprises, the MediaNews Group, and the Liberty Group own the majority of U.S. urban and regional newspapers. The New York Times owns 18 other newspapers, including the Boston Globe and the International Herald Tribune (as well as eight TV stations nationwide), while the Washington Post owns Newsweek magazine, the Gazette Newspaper chain, and six TV stations.

Meanwhile, radio station ownership is dominated by Clear Channel Communications, with some 1200 stations, as well as Cumulus Media, Citadel Communications, and Viacom.[1]

This thumbnail sketch of U.S. media concentration in the third quarter of 2003 gives an inkling of how a simple dispatch from the AP or Reuters can be so easily inserted into the consciousness of so many unwitting U.S. Americans. Few of them realize that most of the news and images they consume comes from a pair of wire/photo agencies, which in turn generally rely on "official sources" in U.S. government and business for their orientation and news-framing.

# Right-Wing Media Dominance in Haiti

In Haiti, there is not the same concentration of ownership, but the vast majority of the 60-odd radio stations and news departments are controlled by Haiti's small right-wing bourgeoisie. Thus most of what Haitians hear on the airwaves, the country's major news medium, is an opposition point of view.

The preeminent conservative station is Herby Widmaier's Radio Métropole. Widmaier is from a prototypical bourgeois family, which founded the station in 1970. Most of its programming is in French. It articulates the vision of Haiti's traditional *comprador bourgeoisie*.

Now rivaling Métropole as a reactionary voice is Léopold Berlanger's Radio Vision 2000, which represents the bourgeois sector most linked to U.S. investments, particularly in the assembly industries. The lineage of this station deserves special attention.

Vision 2000 was founded by members of the putschist bourgeoisie during the 1991-1994 coup against President Jean-Bertrand Aristide and financed by the U.S. State Department's Agency for International Development (USAID). Apart from Radio Nationale, it is the only station which completely covers mountainous Haiti, thanks to its sophisticated and expensive satellite technology.[2]

Berlanger has long been favored by Washingon. Once a subaltern of U.S.-backed economist and perennial presidential candidate Marc Bazin, Berlanger became infamous as the head of the Haiti International Institute for Research and Development (IHRED) in 1986. This organization was spawned by the National Endowment for Democracy (NED), the quasi-official foundation for promoting Washington's agenda in the Third World in a more "legal" and overt fashion than its cousin agency, the CIA. IHRED's launching was "enthusiastically endorsed by the U.S. Embassy," according to a NED report from that time, with the mission of "helping independent democratic institutions to take root and flourish in the country."

An Aristide arch-enemy, Berlanger has also positioned himself as a Haitian election "observer" over the years, most recently as the "coordinator general" of the National Council of Electoral Observation (CNOE) in 2000.

Other opposition-aligned stations include Radio Kiskeya, Radio Caraïbes and Radio Signal FM.

There are a few stations that are considered fair or pro-Lavalas. Jean-Lucien Borges' Radio Ginen, which reports in-depth on news around the country, is wildly popular and generally considered "objective" by most Haitians. Radio Solidarité is considered pro-Lavalas. The Lavalas Family party (FL) also controls Tele Ti Moun, Radio Ti Moun, and, now TeleMax, a small television station. Despite frequent guests from the opposition, Haitian National Television (TNH) naturally favors a government viewpoint, but is offset by the powerful and arch-conservative Tele-Haiti.

Given this skewed balance of forces among media, tiny opposition organizations like the Organization of Struggling People (OPL), with very few adherents in Haiti, have air time equal to or greater than an organization like the FL, whose ranks number in the tens of thousands. The relevance of these tiny opposition groups is sustained only by the attention lavished on their every utterance by the U.S. corporate and Haitian anti-government press.

It is ironic that the picture many U.S. Americans are given is that the Haitian press is muzzled and repressed by a dictatorship. Quite to the contrary, the airwaves are dominated by the opposition, which voices its opinions and charges against Aristide with no regard to etiquette or professional ethics. The most outlandish rumors are reported as fact.

In contrast, on July 25, President Hipolito Méjia of the Dominican Republic had two journalists from Radio Montecristi arrested for taking an on-air poll of whether listeners would vote for him or the devil for president. Satan won by a margin of 14 to 2. Neither Guyler Delva's Association of Haitian Journalists, the National Association of Haitian Media, or the Paris-based Reporters Without Borders registered any protest, as they regularly do when there are murky reports of unidentified individuals making vague threats against radio journalists. They also are quick to condemn perceived press freedom violations in Haiti's other neighbor, Cuba.

The Haitian people are perfectly aware of the political shading of every press outlet, regardless of how often it pronounces itself neutral. Any casual conversation with a person in Cité Soleil or Bel Air reveals that. The people generally have the stations pegged. This is why there have often been demonstrations in front of some of the conservative stations, which the people, with justification, see as important agents in the destablilization campaign against the Haitian government.

# The Foundation Myths

The myths and misconceptions about Haiti planted in the minds of U.S. Americans go back decades. Confusion about the current situation in the country also has deep roots. To get a clear picture of what's happening in Haiti today, we must first unravel four underlying distortions about Haiti which lace most AP and Reuters reports, and their downstream feeders, in recent years.

**Myth #1:** President René Préval (1996-2001) was Aristide's "hand-picked successor" in 1996.

**Reality:** Préval was "hand-picked" by the OPL in 1995 in opposition to the call by most Haitians for Aristide to serve out the three years that he spent in exile from his five year term during the 1991-1994 coup d'état, a perfectly legitimate interpretation of Haiti's 1987 Constitution. But that wasn't Washington's interpretation, since Aristide was proving to be mercurial and uncooperative in privatizations and other neoliberal reforms. The tension burst forth on Nov. 11, 1995 when Aristide verbally pilloried U.S. Ambassador William Swing and U.N.

Haiti Chief Lakhdar Brahimi at the National Cathedral during a funeral for one of the president's slain partisans.[3] "The game of hypocrisy is over" Aristide exclaimed with a fire reminiscent of his sermons when a priest at St. Jean Bosco in the early 1980s. "We don't have two, or three heads of state, we have one."

Peeved and alarmed, Washington, whose troops still occupied the country, turned to the OPL to push Aristide out. Having no viable presidential candidates of their own, the OPL selected Préval, who had been Aristide's prime minister in 1991. The move galled Aristide, who didn't announce his support for Préval until the day before his Dec. 17, 1995 election.

Préval turned out to be his own man and gradually struck a course of growing independence from his OPL sponsors, starting with his refusal to name OPL Secretary General Gérard Pierre-Charles as Prime Minister, forcing a compromise on a lower level OPL cadre, Rosny Smarth.

**Myth #2:** President René Préval was Aristide's "surrogate" while in power, carrying out Aristide's orders.

**Reality:** The relationship between Préval and Aristide was often prickly. Their approaches and power bases are different. Préval was more linked to the "enlightened" bourgeoisie, as epitomized by his mentor radio journalist Jean Dominique. Aristide's base, on the other hand, is in Haiti's growing urban lumpen-proletariat.

Préval did take account of Aristide's positions. He walked a line between the OPL, which controlled the Parliament, and Aristide, who formed his own party, the Fanmi Lavalas (FL), in Nov. 1996. Préval was never a member of the FL, nor was his Prime Minister Jacques Alexis, nor were most of the ministers.

Préval had to make a choice, however, in January 1999 when the terms of most OPL parliamentarians ran out due to the political gridlock they had imposed. Préval refused to unconstitutionally decree an extension of their terms, as they demanded. This brings us to the next distortion.

**Myth #3:** President Préval "dissolved the Parliament" in January 1999.

**Reality:** Haiti's 46th Legislature simply expired. Parliamentarians had even signed statements before taking office affirming that their terms would end on January 11, 1999. The OPL-dominated legislature blocked all of Préval's efforts to install a Prime Minister and hold elections for new lawmakers. Haitians generally applaud the way Préval ran the government and held elections after the obstructionist parliament self-destructed.

**Myth #4:** There were "flawed elections" in May 2000, which render the Haitian government "contested."

**Reality:** The May 21, 2000 elections were marked by peace, discipline, and a massive participation of more than 60%, despite the difficulties many Haitians had in obtaining a voting card. Hundreds of election observers expressed their satisfaction with the voting as "acceptable," in the words of Orlando Marville, who headed the 200 observers of the Organization of American States (OAS). Rep. John Conyers (D-MI), who led a U.S. Congressional delegation, was "totally pleased and happy" with how the vote was conducted. Oscar Tarranco, the representative of the United Nations Development Project (UNDP), called voter participation "impressive." The International Coalition of Independent Observers (ICIO) reported that "voters were able to participate without fear" at over 100 voting stations which they visited. The Mission of Francophone States also gave its seal of approval. Even Léopold Berlanger of the CNOE admitted that "we cannot say there was a situation of massive fraud," as some losing candidates charged.

The OAS's dubious objection about the May 2000 elections didn't come until ten days later. It was that eight of the 19 Senate races should have gone to a second round. (Seven of those eight senators voluntarily stepped down in early 2001, one of the FL's early concessions.)

In fact, the OAS had no business meddling in Haiti's vote calculation method. "It is the same method used in '90, '95, and '97," said CEP member Carlo Dupiton said at the time. "Haiti is an independent and sovereign nation, and the electoral institution doesn't receive orders from anybody."

Under Haiti's Electoral Law, the CEP, half of whose members were selected by the opposition, is the final arbiter of Haitian elections, just as the U.S. Supreme Court was when it appointed George W. Bush as president after the U.S. elections in 2000. The OAS made no attempt to cast doubt on Bush's presidency.

Furthermore, the opposition and Washington have inflated the quibble over how eight run-offs were calculated into questioning the validity of the entire polling for some 7,200 posts from about 30,000 candidates. The U.S. and France even encouraged then, President Préval to unconstitutionally overrule the CEP's verdict, which he refused to do.

# THE MISCONCEPTIONS: Blaming the Victim

Following the May 2000 elections, Aristide was elected president for a second time in November 2000, and took office in February 2001. The opposition, which had formed itself into a 15-party front called the Democratic Convergence, briefly established a "parallel government," and has consistently called for Aristide's removal by extra-constitutional means. The Convergence and complementary "civil society" organizations like the "Group of 184" have received some $120 million in backing from Washington.

During this time, the U.S. mainstream press by and large followed the lead of the U.S. State Department and the Haitian opposition. Journalists and their editors frame their stories to reinforce the message that Aristide is the aggressor and the U.S.-coached opposition the victim, when the opposite is true. An analysis of a few mainstream articles on key events since 2001 illustrates the technique.

## Dec. 17, 2001: The attempted assassination of Aristide

On this date, some 30 heavily-armed uniformed commandos attacked and seized the National Palace for several hours with the help of 50-millimeter machine guns bolted onto pick-up trucks. Aristide did not stay at the Palace that particular Sunday night, as had been his custom, and thus escaped harm. Two policemen and one assailant, a former Haitian soldier, were killed in the attack. The gunmen escaped from the Palace grounds and fled back towards the Dominican border, shooting up the gate at Aristide's Tabarre residence and wounding and killing several people along the way.

Understandably, the attack created panic in the population and the government. Large crowds of people, believing another coup d'état was underway, ransacked the homes and offices of Convergence politicians who had been calling for Aristide's removal. Some government officials went into the streets to try to calm the mobs. There is no evidence that any high-level government official encouraged or sanctioned the reprisals.

One can only imagine Washington's fierce reaction if such a commando attack had been launched against the White House or an ally, like, say, Israel. The attack, after all, was the moral equivalent of the Sept. 11, 2001 terrorist attacks on the World Trade Center and the Pentagon. But Washington and the U.S. mainstream press favored the Convergence's charge that the coup attempt was "theater" and then condemned the people's perfectly predictable reaction.

"Police hunted for the leaders of an assault on Haiti's National Palace and some opposition leaders charged the failed coup was really staged by the government as a pretext to crush dissent," wrote the AP's Michelle Faul in the lead to her Dec. 19, 2001 article on the event. Faul goes on to feature the analysis of Convergence leader Evans Paul who gave the piece's principal quote: "The so-called coup d'etat was a masquerade."

Faul also cites unnamed "Aristide loyalists" to assert that "demonstrations [...] in response to the violence at the National Palace weren't spontaneous" but pre-arranged. She closes the piece by putting the coup attempt and the people's response on equal footing by quoting State Department spokesman Richard Boucher who "condemned the raid on the palace and the mob violence that followed." Boucher called for "dialogue and reconciliation," a far cry from Bush's tone after the Sep. 11 attacks.

In the week and months that followed, Washington, the OAS, and corporate press would focus increasingly on the people's retaliation and decreasingly on the attack itself.

## November - December 2002: Convergence/Macoute alliance vs. the People's Response

On November 17, some 8,000 demonstrators led by Convergence politicians and former Haitian soldiers marched in the northern city of Cap Haïtien to call for the ouster of President Aristide and the formation of a provisional government to hold new elections. The march was the culmination of a week-end opposition rally which was heavily promoted by powerful conservative radio stations like Radio Métropole in Port-au-Prince and Radio Maxima in Cap Haïtien.

The two-day event drew complete coverage from Haiti's capital-based press corps as well as a CNN television crew. The network reported the march to be 70,000 to 80,000, surpassing the euphoric estimates of 50,000 by media-sponsor Radio Métropole.

Counter-demonstrations of similar proportions were organized by the government immediately after the opposition march, but these were barely mentioned or were ignored by the local press and U.S. mainstream press. Similarly, the corporate press said not one word when the leftist National Popular Party (PPN) organized a march of some 4000 of its militants in Port-au-Prince on May 1, 2002 and some 3000 in Cap Haïtien on October 17.

Since the opposition had never had such a turnout before, it figured a groundswell was occurring and planned to duplicate the action in Port-au-Prince on December 3. A groundswell was indeed happening, but not the one they thought.

It is true that many Haitians, out of frustration with hunger and uncertainty, joined in the Nov. 17 march. But when they saw the march's leader was Himmler Rébu, a former officer in Duvalier's counter-insurgency force called the Leopards, a backlash began. Haitians did not, and still do not, want the return of a neo-Duvalierist dictatorship. On November 25, 2002, some 30,000 demonstrators rallied in front of the National Palace to express their opposition to the Convergence's call for Aristide's ouster. Reuters obliquely reported that "thousands of people," and later in the same piece, "hundreds of marchers" demonstrated to support Aristide.

The AP was even more inaccurate. In a piece entitled "Haiti Crowds Call for President's Ouster," correspondent Michael Norton wrote: "In the capital, more than 2,000 Aristide supporters marched through the streets. Some demonstrated outside the National Palace and, on the way, stoned an African studies center where anti-government students were meeting."

In reality, it was less than twenty students behind a locked gate at the State University who taunted and threw stones at the throngs marching by. Furthermore, the "Aristide supporters" were about 15 times "more than 2,000."

Meanwhile the AP photo service chose to run photos of the much-smaller anti-government demonstrations and none showing the massive pro-government rally.

Dueling, impromptu demonstrations continued around Haiti throughout much of the week, with the opposition demonstrations highlighted in mainstream coverage. But when Convergence politicians began rallying on Dec. 3, they were faced with an angry multitude of counter-demonstrators, much as a Ku Klux Klan rally might be greeted in Harlem. Sixteen people were hurt in scattered skirmishes between the two groups of demonstrators.

A Dec. 4 anti-government general strike by the bourgeoisie fizzled, and on Dec. 16 tens of thousands of government supporters again rallied in front of the Palace. By then, the wind had gone out of the opposition's sails. Its leaders and other "civil society" big-shots flew to Santo Domingo that weekend and met with the NED's International Republican Institute (IRI) coaches to plan their next move.

## March 20, 2003: Visit from the OAS and Student Demonstrations

On this date, the Associated Press reported the visit of a high-level OAS "mission to help resolve Haiti's political stalemate." In fact, there was, and is, no "stalemate," at least not between forces within Haiti. Aristide is hugely popular while the opposition is not. Only Washington's meddling, largely through the OAS, has caused blockage. The very international body that helped create and helps maintain the "stalemate" is presented as wanting to resolve it.

But the AP argued that "Haiti has been in crisis since flawed 2000 legislative elections swept by Aristide's Lavalas Family party." As mentioned above, almost all election observers and Haiti's electoral council, the polling's final arbiter, found the 2000 elections exemplary in participation, order, and lack of violence. The "flaw" raised by an OAS official, which was a minor calculation dispute, has been blown up into what the PPN calls a "false crisis."

The AP goes on to blame ensuing violent political clashes on one side – Aristide's partisans. Therefore, it is not surprising when the report claims that "as the delegation met with officials, police fired tear gas and used nightsticks to disperse about 300 anti-government demonstrators near the National Palace." In reality, anti-government protestors numbered less than 200 and insisted, over police objections, on changing their march itinerary to the National Palace where hundreds of pro-government protesters were rallying. Predictably, a melee ensued, which the police broke up. The AP closed their account with a quote from the opposition's main leader Gérard Pierre-Charles: "The government is more repressive than ever."

## March & July 2003: Anti-Government Guerrilla Attacks

On Mar. 17, the Miami Herald ran a story that sought to cast doubt on the provenance, or even the existence, of Duvalierist guerillas which have carried out deadly strikes throughout Haiti since July 28, 2001, primarily on the Central Plateau. After perfunctorily citing Police spokesman Jean Dady Siméon that "they are former soldiers and they are part of the opposition" and "want to overthrow President Jean-Bertrand Aristide," the Herald also turned to Gérard Pierre-Charles. "We consider this whole thing a fake," he says.

The story quotes U.S. filmmaker David Murdock, who was held at gunpoint by the guerillas on Dec. 19. Murdock corroborated police accounts saying the guerrillas boasted that they were former soldiers and lectured him "on how they would overthrow Aristide." But in the next paragraph, the Herald says the "origin" of the band is "unclear because of difficulties confirming police versions of events."

The Herald summarizes the many indisputable killings of the guerillas – "a judge, a police officer and five civilians" – with the qualifier "according to Siméon." It cites Siméon's account of a police raid in which two guerillas were killed, weapons and vehicles recovered, and six men arrested, but notes "he did not supply their names... Journalists have not seen the men allegedly arrested, the weapons recovered or the bodies of the victims." The message: this all may be bunk.[4]

In fact, this insinuation is bunk. The six captured men whom "journalists have not seen" were presented in a cover photo of the Feb. 12 edition of *Haïti Progrès* – over a month before the Herald piece – along with their names. The police presented them, along with the "unseen" captured weapons, at a very public Feb. 10 press conference.

The Herald piece closes by giving the last word about a Dec. 17, 2001 assault on the National Palace[5] to the OAS, which claimed it was not an "attempted coup d'état" as the government says, but a piece of theater because "there was police complicity." All evidence indicates, however, that it was carried out by the same Duvalierist guerrillas.

Ironically, David Murdock, in a letter to the U.S. Embassy about his encounter with the guerrillas wrote: "It struck me that the sole press notice I read regarding reports of ex-military activity in central Haiti, a Miami Herald article from December 21, 2002 entitled, Haitian Government Says Ex-soldiers Mount Insurgency was largley devoted to airing the views of those who doubted that such incidents were occurring."

The guerillas, known as the San Manman (Motherless) Army struck again on July 25, 2003. They ambushed a car of officials from the Interior Ministry, killing four men and burning their bodies. A fifth man was wounded, but escaped.

The AP entitled its story about the attack "Haiti Gang Kills Four Government Officials." Michelle Karshan, the Haitian government's press liaison, wrote an open letter to the AP saying "the use of the word 'gang' in the title of the article... serves to minimize the gravity of the situation and misleads your readership regarding the true nature of the attack." Karshan noted that the killings came in "the same locality where, for nine months, a pattern of sustained terror and continuous attacks have been waged by armed men who use Pernal, in the border region of the Central Plateau, as their base. The countless incidents include the murder of twenty people, including a judge and police, abduction of doctors and a foreign journalist, attacks on police stations, arson of the main hydroelectric plant, and more. The use of the word 'gang' leads readers to believe that this planned ambush of government officials was a random, isolated act committed by ordinary criminals. In the body of the article, the author further dilutes the situation by stating that the government alleges the attackers are the armed wing of the opposition when the terrorists themselves have previously identified themselves to the press as former military men bent on violently overthrowing Haiti's government."

These examples, of which there are many more, illustrate how the U.S. mainstream press presents the news in a way that distorts reality and furthers the U.S. government's agenda. One notices several threads of distortion: the opposition always dismisses attacks against the government as staged; U.S. government officials are always presented as aloof and paternalistically trying to calm down two fighting children – the warring parties – which don't understand the workings of democracy; and the Haitian government is always cracking down on demonstrators who were peaceful, orderly and disciplined.

# One Case Study

Every so often, there is a feature story on Haiti by one of the wire services or big dailies which tends to reinforce the message that "Haitians are just not fit to govern themselves." One such paternalistic story was a May 20, 2003 Reuters piece by Jim Loney entitled "U.S. nation-building in Haiti founders amid turmoil."

"As the United States launches its nation-building project in Iraq, analysts say Haiti holds few lessons in success," Loney writes. "The poorest country in the Western hemisphere," another constant refrain in the corporate press, "is stumbling toward its 200th anniversary of independence next year as troubled as ever, mired in political turmoil, burdened by poverty and unable to solve its own problems." No hint that Haiti's "turmoil" and "problems" are being stoked by Washington.

Loney then cites Ken Boodhoo, a professor of international relations at Florida International University, parroting an often-heard riff from clueless academics and bureaucrats: "Haiti is the perfect example of the failed state."

The Reuters piece goes on to trace Aristide's rise to power, the coup against him, and his return to Haiti on the shoulders of U.S. troops.

When U.S. troops left, Loney writes "Haiti was, to a large extent, on its own, analysts said, leaving a country with no history and little understanding of democracy to figure it out on its own."

Loney cites President Bill Clinton's Haiti envoy Lawrence Pezzullo making a frank admission about the U.S. designs in occupying Haiti in 1994: "If you're going to be an imperialist, at least have a sense of how you're going to run the thing," Pezzullo said. But then he complained that the U.S. "abandoned Haiti far too soon."

Loney includes the aforementioned refrains that "officials improperly calculated the results of several Senate seats to favour Aristide's party," and that "Haiti has been mired in a political stalemate since."

"The United States needed to stay here for 20 years," said Richard Desorme, "a Haitian who said he is unemployed and homeless", writes Loney, using the corporate media's technique of culling a quote from a "man in the street" to get across their editorial intent. "Then maybe there is hope for Haiti," Desorme and the piece concludes.

# The Role of the Press

As Prof. Robert McChesney has noted "journalism can never be an entirely neutral enterprise." The U.S. corporate press tries to sustain the myth of its "objectivity" and gravitates naturally to taking its orientation from U.S. Embassy briefings, State Department reports, and bourgeois spokespeople. As veteran journalist Ben Bagdikian said: "Journalists become oblivious to the compromises with authority they constantly make."

Many young journalists have arrived in Haiti, eager to prove their mettle as the new correspondent for one of the wire agencies or perhaps a big daily. But very quickly, like the AP apprentice I rode with in a car in 1986, they learn that if you rock the boat and tell the truth, you will soon have no more "official sources," and possibly no more job.

Destabilization of progressive and populist governments – Aristide in Haiti, Hugo Chavez in Venezuela, the Sandanistas in Nicaragua, Michael Manley in Jamaica, Maurice Bishop in Grenada, Allende in Chile – has been refined into a science by Washington, and many in the present Bush administration helped perfect its techniques in the 1980s. Some of the tools in their bag of tricks include "Contra" guerilla forces, "civil society" fronts, "broad opposition" coalitions, infiltration of agents into the upper ranks of the police or military, fanning of urban gang warfare, and, most importantly, effective, subservient, trained, and dedicated agents in the media, who can influence public opinion, color events, demoralize the masses, embolden the reaction, deny and fabricate truth, and generally do the lion's share of "winning hearts and minds," as the Pentagon terms it. Haiti today provides a petri dish in which we can see the mechanics of such media manipulation.

What is to be done? Whether in the U.S. or Haiti, look to the alternative press. The Pacifica Radio Network, *Haïti Progrès,* Truthout.com, *In These Times, Workers World,* Commondreams.com, *Le Monde Diplomatique,* and *The Catholic Worker* are just a few examples of alternative sources of news and analysis. Listen to them. Read them. Use them. Support them.

And above all, don't despair. The Haitian people, although in majority illiterate, are connoisseurs of news and analysis. They don't swallow disinformation easily. *Twou manti pa fon:* the hole created by a lie is not deep, says a Creole proverb. North Americans must subject the news they ingest from an ever-concentrating circle of media conglomerates to the same skepticism and critique that Haitians apply to their media. Write a letter to the editor when you see a distorted presentation. Call into radio talk shows when it's appropriate. Challenge untruth wherever it raises its ugly head.

**Postscript:** Since this piece was written in August 2003, the media campaign vilifying President Aristide and his government has intensified. At this writing, in early December 2003, the mainstream press continues to portray Aristide as repressive.

Amiot "Kiben" Métayer was assassinated under mysterious circumstances on September 21. Mainstream media reports have favored opposition speculation and blamed the government, even though Métayer was a government supporter and the man he was last seen with a government foe.

A handful of armed men created turmoil in Gonaïves following the killing. The corporate press resurrected the popular organizations it had previously taxed as "thugs" and cast them now as a popular uprising. But even this distortion was flawed.

The Haitian government presented evidence that the protesting "Raboteau residents" were in fact outside armed infiltrated agitators who had been active in previous months on Haiti's Central Plateau. This was never reported.

Demonstrations were also selectively reported. On Sept. 30, the anniversary of the coup, the AP reported on a demonstration of less than 100 people in St. Marc in solidarity with demonstrators in Gonaïves. A march of over 10,000 organized by the PPN in Port-au-Prince, denouncing the opposition and critically supporting the government was never mentioned.

On Nov. 14 in Port-au-Prince, thousands of pro-government demonstrators surrounded and had minor skirmishes with anti-government demonstrators organized by the Group of 184 (G184). The G184 leaders called off their demonstration and accused the government of disrupting their march. The mainstream press, along with the U.S. embassy, favored the opposition's charge, even though the police worked aggressively to separate the demonstrators.

Many tens of thousands rallied in Cap Haitian four days later to hear Aristide on the bicentennial of the Haitian revolution's final Battle of Vertières. The mainstream press downplayed this massive outpouring, never mentioning its huge size and emphasizing more the boycott of the ceremony by the U.S. and France.

Such are the highlights of the continuing media campaign against Haiti. This fall, the Haiti Action Committee in California put out a very useful pamphlet, *Hidden from the Headlines: The U.S. War Against Haiti*, which helps to counter the lies, omissions, and distortions.

---

[1] Outline of corporate ownership concentration distilled from the website of the Columbia Journalism Review "Who owns what" www.cjr.org/tools/owners.
[2] Author's interviews.
[3] *Haïti Progrès*, Vol. 13, No. 34, November 15, 1995.
[4] *Miami Herald,* March 17, 2003.
[5] *Haïti Progrès,* Vol. 19, No. 40, December 19, 2001.

# "To the Editor -- A Little Story of Censorship"
*by Tom F. Driver*

The *New York Times* is not, we might say, overly inclined to do the right thing by Haiti. Of this I had long been aware as a daily reader of "All the News...", etc., but it was dramatized for me one day in December, 2000, when the *Times* rang my phone after receiving from me a letter to the editor. They wanted to know.....

But I'm ahead of myself. The story needs some background.

Flawed as it is, *The New York Times* is essential to American journalism. On the very day I began to write this article, two of its top editors resigned because the paper published stories by two staff writers that were later found to have been less than true -- one had fictionalized some of his "news"; the other had used another person's research for a story filed under his own name. These events bring to the fore the ambivalence with which many regard America's "newspaper of record." Although without it, the American public would be far less well informed than it is, the *Times* is often not reliable. This is not mainly because on rare occasions reporters such as Jayson Blair or Rick Bragg will cook the news for self-serving reasons but because of the *Times'* closeness to the corridors of power.

To get from the *Times* ALL the news that's fit to print, you have to read the paper very closely and over a long period of time. I'm particularly fond of a confession of kowtowing to government officials that the *Times* made 44 years after the fact in an obituary of one its ace reporters, Sydney Gruson, who it had once assigned to cover news from Guatemala.[1] In 1954 the CIA was preparing to orchestrate a coup against Guatemala's President Arbenz. Judging Gruson to be too "liberal" to cover the news "objectively," the then Director of Central Intelligence, Allen Dulles, asked the *Times'* publisher, Arthur Hays Sulzberger, to keep Gruson away from Guatemala, which he did. A clear case, long hidden, of letting the Government decide what's fit to print.

Because the *Times*, known as a flag-bearer of liberal journalism, is also a bastion of establishment thinking, it is hard for the paper to entertain a view of Haiti that comes anywhere near approximating the perspective seen from the streets of Port-au-Prince or the hills of Fondwa. Haiti has the misfortune of being both below and outside the point of view of most North Americans -- "below" because of its extreme poverty and consequent lack of influence on the international stage; "outside" because of race and culture. African in origin, dark-skinned, self-liberated from slavery, independent-minded and proud of it, Haitians speak two languages alien to most of the hemisphere: French, in a region dominated by either Spanish or English, and Kreyol, which is falsely assumed by many non-Haitians (and a few of Haiti's own elite) to be no genuine language at all. Most Haitians, while nominally Roman Catholic, practice Vodou, a name which, when spelled as Voodoo, has become synonymous with superstition and danger.

Although *The New York Times* does not disseminate the worst of the anti-Haitian stereotypes prevalent in North America, it tends to echo Washington's prevailing idea that Haiti is a hopeless case, incapable of democratic governance, and a fit subject for paternalistic treatment. Readers of the *Times* are not likely to be reminded how great a role the U.S. has played in the impoverishment of Haiti, in supporting (as well as bringing to power) some of the most corrupt and brutal of its dictators, and in subversion of its efforts to democratize itself. In recent years, the *Times*, like the U. S. Government, has been deeply suspicious of Jean-Bertrand Aristide, the first of Haiti's presidents ever to have been chosen by the people in a free and fair election, who won in a landslide vote in December of 1990, was the object of a U.S.-aided *coup d'état* nine months later, was restored to office in 1994 by the U.S. army on terms dictated by the U.S. Government, left office in 1996 in because the U.S. insisted that his years in exile had to be counted as part of the five-year term that Haiti's constitution allowed him, and (once he became elligible to run again) displeased the U.S. by being re-elected in yet another landslide vote (in November of 2000). During this history, elements of the U.S. Government have at one time or another worked to prevent his election, to depose him, to control him, and to delegitimize him.

Throughout this history of negativity, which is not unlike what the U.S. Government has shown to other democratic and social reform movements in Latin America, the *Times*, has kept its distance from Aristide, tending to present him in unfavorable light. But there have been occasional exceptions, and one of these became the occasion for the story I have to tell.

\*\*\*

On November 30, 2000, a few days after Haiti's presidential election, the *Times*' Op-Ed page carried an article by Tracy Kidder called "Give Aristide a Chance." I was surprised to see such a sensible piece in the *Times*. However, I remembered that in the previous July Kidder had published a long article in *The New Yorker* magazine about Paul Farmer, the Harvard-based physician whose concern for Haiti's social ills as well as its medical ones is legendary. Most likely, that article induced the *Times* to let Kidder have his say about Aristide.

Kidder's message was that "the United States, which has done a great deal in the past to harm Haiti, should now do all it can to help Haiti's duly elected government." (Three years later these words ring with bitter irony.) In order to lend point to this conclusion, Kidder reminded his readers that Aristide had enemies in Washington. After noting that the U.S. Government had scorned Haiti's recent elections, refusing even to send observers, thereby repudiating the legitimacy of Aristide's presidency before it began, Kidder observed that "America's foreign-policy bureaucracy has long disliked Mr. Aristide...."

Upon reading the article, I thought I saw an opportunity. If you want to get a letter to the editor published in the *Times*, find something positive to say about what they have already printed. Since I liked Kidder's offering, I could praise it and then go on to fill in some things I felt the *Times'* readers should know. So I went to my computer, where I wrote and then sent the following email:

November 30, 2000

I have been following events in Haiti for 20 years. Thanks to your editors and Tracy Kidder ("Give Aristide a Chance," Op-Ed page, Nov. 30) Haiti's former President and now President-elect Aristide has at last been given a fair shake in a major American news medium. Alas, vilification of Aristide holds sway in most of our media.

Kidder correctly observes that "American's foreign-policiy bureaucracy has long disliked Mr. Aristide." More than that, some parts of our government gave aid and support to his enemies during the crucial years 1991-94 when he was driven into exile.

Although Kidder does not say why Aristide has been disliked in Washington, the reason is that Aristide aims to bring Haiti's poor, who are the vast majority of its people, into a fair participation in the political and economic life of the nation. This runs counter to the United States' habit of supporting those governments and strong men in the Americas who try to maintain 'stability' by opposing efforts to bring about long-overdue social change. Such change is nowhere more needed than in Haiti, and Aristide is the only major figure there who holds out any promise of its happening. It would be in the best interests of the United States and its people to encourage him in the process.

Tom F. Driver
The Paul J. Tillich Professor of Theology and Culture Emeritus
Union Theological Seminary in New York

My letter did not appear the next day. I then realized I had neglected to include my phone number. The *Times* requires one in order to verify the origin of the letters it receives. Much to my surprise, later in the day someone from the *Times* did call, presumably having looked me up in the phone book. They wouldn't have done that, I figured, if they had not found the letter to be of interest. Sure enough, the caller said they liked my letter but had a problem with one sentence.

"Which one?"

> "The one that reads: '... some parts of our government gave aid and support to his [Aristide's] enemies during the crucial years 1991-94 when he was driven into exile.'"

"What's wrong with it?"

"We need to know if you have anything to back that statement up."

I was surprised that people at the *Times* would question that point, since it seemed well known. The military junta that ruled Haiti by terror druing the period of the *coup* got help from their friends in Washington. That was one reason why Aristide had had to wait three long years before being restored to office. Why was the *Times* balking at this?

The caller repeated the question: could I find backup for the statement? "Yes," I replied, "I am sure there is something in my files."

"Please fax it to us right away."

So I dropped what I was doing and started digging in my files, which were in fact a large cardboard box containing innumerable clippings and articles deposited in something approaching chronological order but without any kind of indexing. It took about half an hour to find two items that I thought would be sufficient: an article published by the Institute for Policy Studies in Washington, DC, and "Haiti Under the Gun," a special report by Allan Nairn published in *The Nation* magazine in 1996.[2] Nairn's article begins as follows:

> In the face of rising outrage in Haiti that paramilitaries are still armed and at large, the U.S. government has again denied collaborating with the perpetrators, including FRAPH, the hit squad whose leader, Emmanuel Constant, worked for the C.I.A. (see Nairn, "Our Man in FRAPH," October 24, 1994). But evidence just discovered indicates that, starting in mid-1993,

FRAPH was launched on its reign of terror with secret shipments of U.S. arms, and that still-active FRAPH members have been used recently in U.S. occupation operations, sprung from jail with Washington's help, freshly recruited by the C.I.A. and, as a matter of high-level U.S. policy, allowed to keep their arms.

This information comes from interviews in Haiti and the United States with military, paramilitary, and intelligence officials, including Green Beret commanders, and also from internal documents from the U.S. and Haitian armies. Pieces of the story also come from Constant himself... who has said that he started the group that became FRAPH at the urging of the Defense Intelligence Agency (D.I.A.) -- an acount confirmed last year by a U.S. official who worked with him...."

I faxed the caller from the *Times:*

Herewith are two documents in support of the sentence you questioned. Given time, one could track down even more documentation. For example, I seem to remember that the *N.Y. Times* itself ran stories in the fall of 1993 that contained reference or allusions to covert U.S. support for Haiti's army, which had carried out the *coup d'état* against Aristide and was then ruling the country by terror and opposing all moves to return him to Haiti. But these stories would have to be researched.

Within minutes my phone rang. When I heard the now familiar voice from the *Times*, I thought something must have gone wrong with the faxing, for surely they had not had time to read the two articles. The caller declared: "We cannot accept these documents as backup."

"What do you mean?"

"They are from two left-wing sources."

"I beg your pardon?"

"That's what I said. I've checked with the people here, and they say we cannot accept what is said in these leftist publications."

You would think I had sent them something disreputable. Dumbfounded, I tried to think what to say.

"The *Nation* article," I began as soon as I could find words, "is by Allan Nairn. You must know that he is one of the best investigative journalists in the United States."

Silence greeted this statement, so I went on: "He has reported on the Haiti situation for several years. He risked his life reporting a massacre he witnessed in East Timor. He has just finished testifying about East Timor before a Congressional investigating committee in Washington."

"I'm sorry," she said. "The people here say we can't use this. *The Nation* is a leftist magazine."

With my blood pressure rising, I tried to stay cool. You can't win arguments if you get hot. Especially not on the telephone. I tried another tack.

"Did you see what I said in my fax about stories in the *Times* itself back in 1993 that would probably confirm that sentence in my letter?"

She answered: "We don't have time to look for those. It's Friday afternoon, and we have to leave soon. If this is all you've got, we won't print that sentence."

"And if I take it out?"

"We'll print the rest of the letter."

What to do? Let them kill the whole letter, or agree to delete the contested sentence? There were other things in the letter I did want read. So I caved. Out came the sentence about aid and comfort going to Aristide's enemies from parts of the U.S. government while he was in exile. That was something they deemed not fit to print. And after all, it's their printing press.

\*\*\*

Although the incident is a very small blip in the history of *The New York Times*, it is significant in two ways.

First, it shows the narrow range of opinion and interpretation that is admissible in the *Times* and other major news media in America. The *Times* has a reputation for liberal journalism, and it is frequently attacked by right-wing commentators for its liberalism, but the fact is that it seldom strays far from the views that are dominant in Washington. If it has no columnist the likes of Rush Limbaugh, neither does it have a Noam Chomsky. If the editors of the letters page on that Friday afternoon, December 1, 2000, did look at the Allan Nairn article I sent them they would have read that "the U.S. government has again denied collaborating with the perpetrators" of Haiti's *coup*. If the government denies something, who are Allan Nairn and *The Nation* to say otherwise, whatever investigations they have made? The *Times* must not stray far from the center of the road. And the center of the road is wherever Washington says it is. Since the *Times* is America's flagship newspaper, it sets the tone for the rest of the major media. Or did until recently. Today, in 2003, one could argue that CNN and Fox News are worse than the *Times*. Which means that the case for Haiti's best interests is getting harder and harder to represent in the so-called "news."

Second, the story indicates that the editorial views of the *Times* do not necessarily reflect, indeed may contradict, the news reported in its own pages. I think the worst thing about the *Times'* censoring of my letter was their refusal to look in their own indices of past issues to follow up my suggestion that they could confirm my statement from some of their own stories published in 1993. They said they had no time to do that, but surely it would not have taken long, and they did not run my letter until December 6 -- five days after we talked.

Eventually I located the following materials from back issues of the *Times*:

Saturday, October 23, 1993, p. 1: "Administration is Fighting Itself on Haiti Policy", by Steven A. Holmes.

The article reports an attempt by the C.I.A. to destroy the character of President Aristide, "portraying him as a mentally unstable man," or, in the quoted words of an Administration official, a "murderer" and a "psychopath." It tells of classified briefings to this effect given to Senators and members of the House of Representatives that week by a C.I.A. analyst named Brian Latell, who in 1992, the article reports, had "produced a report praising Lieut. Gen. Raul Cedras, Haiti's current military dictator, as 'one of the most promising group of Haitian leaders to emerge since the Duvalier family dictatorship was deposed in 1996.'" Cedras, of course, had led the 1991 the coup against Aristide. The Congressional briefings described in the article were arranged by Senator Jesse Helms to support leglislation that he and Senator Robert Dole introduced to restrict "the Administartion's ability to dispatch American troops to Haiti." The article concludes by saying that "Lawrence Pezullo, the Admninistration's special envoy to Haiti, told colleagues that he found the briefing to House members 'distasteful.'" Although the article does not say so, Senator Helms allied himself with Gen. Cedras throughout the latter's three-year reign of terror in Haiti.

**Monday, November 1, 1993, p. 1:** "Key Haiti Leaders said to have been in the C.I.A.'s Pay," by Tim Weiner.

In his lead sentence, Mr. Weiner wrote: "Key members of the military regime controlling Haiti and blocking the return of its elected President, Jean-Bertrand Aristide were paid by the Central Intelligence Agency for information from the mid-1990's at least until the 1991 coup that forced Mr. Aristide from power, according to American officials."

With the phrase, "at least until the 1991 coup," Mr. Weiner implied that the payments may have continued during the coup. He reinforced the point later: "It was not clear when the payments ended...." The article quotes former Congressman Michael D. Barnes, who had become a spokesman for Aristide: "Given what the C.I.A. has done in the past two weeks, namely the attempted character assassination of Jean-Bertrand Aristide, it wouldn't be surprising to learn that the C.I.A. had been working with his political enemies in Haiti for many years."

**Sunday, November 14, 1993, p. 1:** "C.I.A. Formed Haitian Unit Later Tied to Narcotics Trade," by Tim Weiner.

The article recounts the C.I.A.'s role in establishing a Haitian counter-narcotics unit known as S.I.N. (*Service Nationale d'Intelligence*) made up entirely of officers from the Haitian army. The article implies that the agency was ineffective in narcotics work, that some of its leaders were themselves involved in drug trafficking, and that its main effects may have been to undermine support for Aristide.

The Haitian intelligence service provided little information on drug trafficking and some of its members themselves became enmeshed in the drug trade, American officials said. A United States official who worked at the American Embassy in Haiti in 1991 and 1992 said he took a dim view of S.I.N.

> "It was a military organization that distributed drugs in Haiti," said the official, who spoke on condition of anonymity. "It never produced drug intelligence. The agency gave them money under counternarcotics and they used their training to do other things in the political arena."

Like the earlier article by Tim Weiner, this one strongly hints that the C.I.A.'s payments to Haitian army officers (in this case those involved in S.I.N.) did not end with Aristide's overthrow in 1991 although the American agency claimed that they did:

> A 1992 Drug Enforcement Administration document described S.I.N. in the present tense, as "a covert counternarcotics intelligence unit which often works in unison with the C.I.A. at post."

The article also highlights the role of the C.I.A. analyst Brian Latell (mentioned in an earlier article) in persuading members of Congress to look favorably upon Haitian army officers who had ousted Aristide and were his sworn enemies:

> The agency's leading analyst of Latin American affairs, Brian Latell, traveled to Port-au-Prince in July 1992 and recorded his trip in a three-page note that he later shared with members of Congressional intelligence committees. He met with General Cedras, who he said impressed him as "a conscientious military leader who genuinely wishes to minimize his role in politics."

> That impression, Father Aristide's supporters say, contributed to the faith placed in General Cedras by United States policy makers, a faith broken when the general abrogated the Governor Island accord.

> Mr. Latell also reported that he "saw no evidence of oppressive rule" in Haiti... "I do not wish to minimize the role the military plays in intimidating, and occasionally terrorizing real and suspected opponents," the analyst said, but "there is no systematic or frequent lethal violence aimed at civilians."

> That conflicts with a State Department report for the same year, which said, "Haitians suffered frequent human rights abuses throughout 1992, including extrajudicial killings by security forces, disappearances, beatings and other mistreatment of detainees and prisoners, arbitrary arrests and detention, and executive interference with the judicial process."

**Monday, December 13, 1993, Op-Ed page:** "Signals to Haiti," by Anthony Lewis (then a regular columnist for the *Times*).

> "... If a reasonably well-informed Haitian civilian must be confused about the policy of the Clinton Administration, imagine the effect on the military thugs in Port-au-Prince. The mixed signals from Washington encourage them to think there is no real committment to dislodge them: encourage them to continue their defiance.

> "... the history of U.S. relations with Haiti, as with many Latin-American countries, has featured close links between the U.S. military and theirs....

> "Young Haitian officers have often attended U.S. military training schools. In fact, at least 10 are known to have taken training courses here after the 1991 coup, although the Pentagon said it had sent them all home....

> "In sum, there is a long record of closeness between U.S. military and intelligence agencies and Haitians who have turned out to be the country's tyrants and plunderers."

**Sunday, April 10, 1994, Op-Ed page:** "Abandoning Democracy," by Bob Herbert (a regular columnist):

After recounting the reasons for Aristide's popular support in Haiti before and during the period of the coup, which was still going on, Mr. Herbert wrote:

> "The interests of the vast majority of Haitians, on the one hand, and the alliance of the United States Government and American businesses on the other, are different. And so the Clinton Administration -- in its actions, if not its words -- has abandoned Father Aristide and his followers and sided with the murderous enemies of democracy in Haiti."

***

One wonders what had happened at *The New York Times* between 1993, when it was willing to run both news stories and Op-Ed columns claiming that parts of the U.S. Government were siding with Aristide's enemies and the autumn of 2000 when its letters page was not willing to print one sentence to the same effect. I can think of three possible reasons, all of which might be true: 1) the shift of public opinion, at least as expressed in the media, toward the right, which has been happening in America since the 1970s at an ever accelerating rate; 2) the appointment of Howell Raines (later discredited) as the *Times'* executive editor; 3) the turbulent presidential election process in November-December of 2000, which, by the time I wrote my letter, had brought George W. Bush almost to the White House.

With the latter development has come an increased reluctance in our major media to cast doubt upon the motives of any branches of the Government that so-called "conservatives," who are really reactionaries, favor. Although our citizenry are greatly disturbed by the increasing militarism of American foreign policy, the major media seem reluctant to say so, or to give voice to those concerns.

Today (2003) Haiti has largely disappeared from the news. There are days when I think this is a blessing, for if Haiti were to return to the front pages readers would undoubtedly be subject to a flood of disinformation.

---

[1] Excerpts from the obituary of Sydney Gruson, 81, written by Eric Pace, published in *The New York Times*, March 8, 1998:

He ... was transferred in 1951 to Mexico City.

From that base, he did much reporting about Guatemala. In 1954, there were widespread rumors that a coup was going to be mounted against the leftist Guatemalan Government of Col. Jacobo Arbenz Guzman.

At the time, Allen Dulles, the director of the United States Central Intelligence Agency, told his Princeton classmate, Gen. Julius Ochs Adler, The Times's general manager, that he did not believe that Mr. Gruson, who the agency thought had "liberal" leanings, could report objectively on that forthcoming revolution. He asked that The Times keep Mr. Gruson away from the story.

Later that year, Colonel Arbenz was indeed overthrown, and it subsequently became known that the C.I.A. had played a central part in bringing on the revolution that led to his downfall. In 1977, The Times reported that the C.I.A.'s files contained some evidence that it had feared that Mr. Gruson's reporting, while based in Mexico City, was edging toward a premature discovery of the agency's role in Guatemala.

Mr. Gruson said in an interview in 1977 that he had learned later that Arthur Ochs Sulzberger's father, Arthur Hays Sulzberger, who was The Times's publisher in 1954, had complied with the C.I.A.'s request by arranging to keep him in Mexico City and away from Guatemala.

Mr. Gruson said the elder Mr. Sulzberger had brought this about by claiming to have received a tip that the fighting might spill across the Guatemalan border into Mexico. A newly declassified C.I.A. history of the Guatemala coup gave confirmation last year that Mr. Gruson was spied on by the C.I.A. before being kept out of Guatemala by The Times.

[2] "Haiti Under the Gun: How U.S.-Backed Paramilitaries Rule Through Fear," by Allan Nairn, *The Nation*, 262.2 (January 8/15, 1996):11-15.

# CHAPTER THREE

*Bay kou, bliye. Pote mak, sonje.*

The one who gives the blow forgets.
The one who gets hurt remembers.

# *Lave Men, Siye Atè:* Taking Human Rights Seriously
### *Brian Concannon, Jr.*

The United States has historically advanced civil and political human rights in Haiti, by pushing dictators out the door, financially supporting law enforcement and encouraging respect for human rights norms.[1] At the same time, we have undermined human rights by supporting the very same dictatorships, blocking urgently needed development assistance to democratic governments, and inducing politicians to represent our interests over those of Haitian voters. Such flexibility may serve short-term, shifting U.S. interests well, but its long term consequence is what Haitians call *lave men, siye atè*: wash your hands, dry them in the dirt. The harmful policies not only cancel out the positive contributions, they leave poor Haitians more vulnerable to human rights violations than they would be without U.S. interventions. Over the long term, the policies decrease stability in Haiti, frustrate the development of sustainable institutions that support human rights, and undermine the effectiveness of both past and future positive measures.

This essay will explore areas of inconsistency in U.S. human rights policy towards Haiti, and discuss the impact of those failures on the current situation. It will show how the failure to take human rights seriously as an end in itself, rather than as a tool for other policy objectives, has stunted Haiti's democratic development, led to expensive U.S. intervention, and generated adverse consequences for the U.S.' credibility in Haiti.

## I. U.S. Human Rights Policies Towards Haiti's Dictatorships

Four Haitian dictatorships in the 1980's and 1990's illustrate how U.S. policies undermine respect for human rights. The U.S. forcefully condemned human rights abuses under the reigns of Jean-Claude Duvalier (1971-1986), the *Conseil National du Gouvernement* ("CNG", 1986-1988), Prosper Avril (1988-1990) and the *de facto* military *junta* (1991-1994). We imposed some types of economic sanctions against all four, and were instrumental in forcing all from office. But the U.S. also provided support, including military support, to each of them, and helped downplay their atrocities. After they lost their grip on power, we helped three of the four to escape the legal consequences of their actions, and provided them support and safe havens.

## A. Jean-Claude Duvalier

Jean-Claude Duvalier's reign, although not as bloody as his father's, did imprison or kill hundreds of opponents, outlawed both political organization and a free press, and set new standards for corruption. The U.S. helped rid Haiti of Duvalier, through behind-the-scenes maneuvers, public withdrawals of support, and, finally, by sending a plane to pick him up.[2] U.S. officials also criticized the regime's human rights record, and threatened to cut off economic support if human rights did not improve. But U.S. military and economic support was the hated dictatorship's foundation, and was never completely withdrawn no matter how many opponents were killed or imprisoned, no matter how many newspapers were shut down.

By 1980, the Duvalier regime's continued use of political prisons,[3] attacks against journalists (including closing one newspaper down and forcing forty journalists out of the country in that year alone) and widespread, persistent corruption led the international donors to condition aid on progress on both fiscal reforms and human rights.[4] However the reality never matched the rhetoric: at a year-end meeting with foreign donors, an official of the (outgoing) Carter administration broached the issue of human rights abuses. Duvalier's Planning Minister felt able to interrupt, declare the human rights references "not acceptable," and command the official to "pass to the technical part of your speech." The Minster knew what he was doing: the donors made no more references to human rights, and increased Haiti's foreign aid by 20%.[5]

Five years later, increased repression, including outlawing political parties and jailing journalists, generated international pressure for reforms in Haiti. The U.S., in particular, urged Duvalier to rescind the ban on political parties. In response, the Duvalier-controlled Parliament duly passed a law that permitted parties to exist in June 1985. Yet this "progress" required the parties' bylaws to recognize Duvalier as President-for-Life and gave the Ministry of the Interior broad discretion to suspend party operation without giving any reason.[6] At the same time, Parliament voted to amend the Constitution to expand Duvalier's powers, including the right to designate his successor.

The U.S., despite its earlier human rights rhetoric, failed to criticize this entrenchment of dictatorial powers. On his Independence Day speech of July 4, 1985, U.S. Ambassador Clayton McManaway called the political parties law "an encouraging step forward." An anonymous State Department official told *Newsweek* "with all of its flaws, the Haitian government is doing what it can" while the official State Department report boasted that "the press in Haiti has known a growing freedom of expression in recent months."[7] With this seal of approval,

Duvalier submitted the constitutional changes to a referendum on July 22, which passed, according to "official" statistics, with 90% of registered voters participating, and 99.98% of them voting "yes." The State Department then certified Haiti's human rights "progress," and the aid flow to the official hereditary dictatorship continued.[8]

In the months after the Ambassador's July 4 speech, a wave of anti-government protests swept across Haiti, precisely because the Haitian people saw no "encouraging step forward." The popular movement had all but ousted the dictatorship by February 1986, when the U.S. joined in. Secretary of State George Schultz announced that Haiti should have "a government put there by a democratic process."[9] On February 7, the U.S. sent an Air Force plane that whisked Duvalier and several supporters to France.

## B. The CNG

For the next five years, Haitians struggled to achieve "a government put there by a democratic process." Control of the government alternated between brief democratic openings and longer military dictatorships. The dictatorships were often described as "Duvalierism Without Duvalier," because many of the same repressive policies were carried out by many of the people who had served the Duvalier dictatorship. The first of these, the *Conseil National de Gouvernement* or CNG, ruled with various compositions, from Duvalier's departure until 1988. Although civilians, some with democratic credentials, were usually part of the *Conseil*, the military never intended to relinquish effective power to civilians.

The army's intention to rule became apparent in 1987, the year a new constitution was ratified and Haiti's first democratic elections were scheduled. The CNG permitted the adoption of a progressive constitution, but balked at actually implementing its provisions. In July, landowners in the northern town of Jean-Rabel massacred over three hundred peasants, with complete impunity and with the tacit support of military authorities.[10] In August, a gunman attacked a church service near St. Marc, and a mob intercepted the fleeing priests and nuns down the road, a few dozen yards from a military checkpoint.[11] Throughout the year, soldiers gunned down dozens of demonstrators and pro-democracy activists. Labor unions were dissolved. When the Provisional Electoral Council (CEP) charged with running the elections showed too much independence, it was temporarily stripped of its powers. CEP members and facilities were regularly attacked.

These attacks against civilians and electoral officials did not stop the generous U.S. military aid to the dictatorship. As election day, November 29, approached, many pro-democracy activists, noting the CNG's obvious unwillingness to share power, argued that the elections should be cancelled or postponed. In response, the U.S. Embassy declared "… we are confident that the CNG will guarantee the safety of the voters and the honesty of the election." [12]

This confidence was lethally misplaced. On election day, paramilitaries backed by regular soldiers attacked polling stations and election offices throughout the country, mowing down voters by the dozens. At least 34 were killed, hundreds were injured, and the CNG, in hiding, cancelled the elections. The international protests against the violence did not throw the dictatorship, or the most ambitious candidates, off stride. New elections were set for January 17, and although any candidate with democratic convictions refused to participate in the charade, the CNG was able to find three to run. Leslie Manigat topped the official results, and was installed as President on February 7, 1988.

U.S. support for the CNG and its allies in the election process was not limited to exhortations. At the beginning of 1987, the CIA began a covert operations program to encourage a high turnout, support specific candidates and undermine the influence of election critics, including Jean Bertrand Aristide, then a parish priest.[13] The program was terminated by the Senate Select Committee on Intelligence after a staff visit to Haiti revealed it. The reason for the Senate action, according to one Committee staffer, was that "there are some of us who believe in the neutrality of elections."[14]

## C. Prosper Avril

Former General Prosper Avril may be the most enduring subject of U.S. *lave men, swiye atè* policy. A U.S.-trained career soldier, Avril was a key member of the notorious Presidential Guard, under both Francois and Jean-Claude Duvalier, where he was reported to be involved in human rights violations and financial and political impropriety.[15] Avril was a member of the first CNG in 1986,[16] and with the help of the Presidential Guard, he seized power for himself in September 1988.

A U.S. District Court found that Avril's regime engaged in "a systematic pattern of egregious human rights abuses." It found him personally responsible for enough "torture, and cruel, inhuman or degrading treatment" to award six of his victims $41 million in compensation. [17] His victims included opposition politicians, union leaders, scholars, even a doctor trying to practice community rural medicine. Avril's repression was not subtle: three torture victims were paraded on national television with faces grotesquely swollen, limbs bruised and clothing covered with blood. He also suspended thirty-seven articles of the Constitution,[18] and declared a state of siege.

The U.S. criticized Avril's human rights abuses, and backed the rhetoric up by withholding large amounts of aid.[19] It helped push the dictator out of power in March, 1990, and transported him, like Duvalier, out of the country on an Air Force jet. But once democracy had been established in Haiti, the U.S. resuscitated Avril and promoted him as counterweight to the *Lavalas* political movement. The U.S. supported Avril's political party, arranged a private reconciliation with many of his former victims, and has opposed efforts to bring him to justice in Haiti.

The U.S. started protecting Avril shortly after the 1994 restitution of Haiti's elected authorities. In November, Secretary of State Warren Christopher relayed to the U.S. Ambassador intelligence reports that the "Red Star Organization," under Mr. Avril's leadership, was "planning [a] harassment and assassination campaign directed at the Lavalas Party and Aristide supporters. The campaign is scheduled to commence in early December 1995" (just before the Presidential elections). This information was not shared with the Haitian government.[20]

That same month an assassination attempt was made against prominent Lavalas legislators, and in December the Haitian police team investigating the case sought to arrest Mr. Avril at his home. A U.S. Embassy official admitted that he visited Avril the day before the arrest, and immediately after the Haitian police arrived at Avril's house, U.S. soldiers arrived. They tried to dissuade the Haitian police from making the arrest, and it was only after Haiti's President intervened personally on the police radio that the police were able to enter Avril's house. Although Avril had been spotted on a balcony when the police arrived outside his gate, by the time they entered the premises he had fled to the neighboring residence of the Colombian Ambassador. Police searching Avril's house found several military uniforms, illegal police radios and weapons.[21]

Avril escaped to Israel, but later returned to Haiti, where his international support and feared military capacity deterred further arrest attempts. He founded the CREDDO political party, which has never fielded candidates for elections, but was invited by the U.S. International Republican Institute (IRI) to participate in developing an opposition to Lavalas. IRI brokered a rapprochement between Avril and two of his torture victims, Serge Gilles of PANPRA and Evans Paul of the KID party, as part of the creation of the Haitian Conference of Political Parties (CHPP).[22] Mr. Avril admitted his "moral responsibility," and all three signed the CHPP's Declaration of Principles.[23] No financial settlement was disclosed, but both Serge and Paul subsequently dropped their substantial civil complaints against Avril.

In May 2001, after U.S. soldiers had left the country and while Avril was at a book signing away from his home and guns, the Haitian police finally seized the opportunity to execute Avril's arrest warrant. The successful arrest was greeted with applause by the vast majority of Haitians and by human rights and justice groups in Haiti, the U.S., and Europe. Amnesty International in England asserted that the arrest "could mark a step forward by the Haitian justice system in its struggle against impunity," and that "[t]he gravity of the human rights violations committed during General Avril's period in power, from his 1988 *coup d'état* to his departure in March 1990, cannot be ignored." France's Committee to Prosecute Duvalier concluded that "the General must be tried." California's Global Exchange added that Avril's arrest "sends a loud message that Haitians have not forgotten the crimes of the past and are ready to take action against criminals like Avril."[24]

Avril's allies in the U.S. and the Haitian opposition rallied to his defense. The IRI's George Fauriol called the torture arrest evidence of "the arbitrary nature of the police and uses of arrest warrants."[25] Serge Gilles and Evans Paul, despite their criminal and civil complaints in Haiti against Mr. Avril, despite a multi-million dollar verdict each had won from the U.S. District Court, and despite voluminous affidavits detailing their extreme torture and disabling injuries, publicly called for his release.[26] Official Embassy statements periodically call for Mr. Avril's release, or categorize him as a political prisoner.

Such open support for a notorious dictator and torturer raised questions among Haitians and non-Haitians concerned about human rights in Haiti. Avril's victims, especially the victims of the 1990 Piatre massacre, persistently demonstrate against any efforts to pry Avril away from the justice system. The Paris-based Committee to Prosecute Duvalier warned that "to forget the violence of General Avril, as Evans Paul proposes, is the best way to prepare the return of the ex-dictator, or of other future military dictators."[27] An op-ed by a prominent Haitian American leader and an American intellectual called Avril "the latest cause célèbre for an opposition whose quest increasingly appears to have no other goal than ascension to power through means other than elections." [28]

Mr. Avril's consistent resorting to undemocratic behavior in four different decades disqualifies him as a viable political candidate. The vast majority of Haitian voters, seconded by human rights groups throughout the world, agree that Mr. Avril should be prosecuted, not elected. Association with Mr. Avril, by U.S.-based political initiatives and by Haitian politicians, serves only to soil the image of the associates and eliminate their credibility with Haitian voters.

## D. The *De Facto* Dictatorship

Prosper Avril's ouster in March 1990 led to Haiti's first ever democratic Presidential elections the following December. The interlude was however, brief, as another military junta, known as the "*de facto* regime," overthrew the elected officials on September 30, 1991. The ensuing three years were among the bloodiest periods in modern Haitian history, with an estimated 5,000 killed, and hundreds of thousands tortured, imprisoned, or forced into internal or external exile.[29]

The U.S. condemned the *de facto* dictatorship quickly and forcefully. It continued to denounce human rights violations throughout the regime, and participated in UN and OAS sanctions. It financially supported MICIVIH, the UN/OAS human rights observation mission to Haiti. American troops led the UN-sponsored multinational force that chased the *de facto* regime from power in September of 1994. But alongside these positive efforts, the U.S. also provided moral, financial and other support to the *de facto* regime and its paramilitary allies. This support certainly prolonged the dictatorship's duration, and most likely allowed it to increase its terror.

The most striking example of U.S. inconsistency on human rights was the support for FRAPH, the Revolutionary Front for the Advancement and Progress of Haiti (at one time the "Armed Revolutionary Front of the Haitian People"), and its founder, Emmanuel Constant. FRAPH was the principal paramilitary ally of the *de facto* dictatorship. Secretary of State Warren Christopher described it as "a paramilitary organization whose members were responsible for numerous human rights violations in Haiti in 1993 and 1994." [30] A less restrained U.S. Embassy cable called FRAPH a group of "gun carrying crazies," eager to "use violence against all who oppose it." Numerous monitors, including MICIVIH, the Organization of American States, Amnesty International, and Human Rights Watch documented FRAPH's multitude of atrocities.[31]

FRAPH targeted Americans as well as Haitians. In October 1993, a FRAPH mob turned back the USS *Harlan County*, carrying American soldiers sent to help implement the Governor's Island Accords, a U.S.-sponsored attempt to negotiate the *de facto* regime's departure. FRAPH members, some armed, assembled at Haiti's principal port, brandishing their arms and shouting "Kill whites, Kill whites" in English.[32] The *Harlan County* turned back, and the dictatorship endured another year. A year later, after President Clinton ordered U.S. troops to lead the multinational force into Haiti, Constant declared: "Each FRAPH man must put down one American soldier."[33] When American troops stormed the FRAPH headquarters, Constant threatened foreign journalists with: "Everybody who is reporting the situation bad.... by the grace of God, they will end up in the ground." After the troops arrested some FRAPH leaders, Constant threatened to break out weapons and begin an all-out war against the foreigners.[34]

Despite his public animosity towards the U.S., Constant was in fact a paid CIA operative who regularly met with U.S. officials, some of whom encouraged his activities.[35] Constant admits that U.S. intelligence operatives encouraged him to delay the return of the Constitutional authorities, and that he in turn kept them informed of his activities, including his plans to demonstrate against the *Harlan County*.

U.S. support for FRAPH become public after the U.S. troops arrived. American soldiers were told by their officers that FRAPH was a legitimate political party, and needed to be protected.[36] The U.S. even set up a press conference for Constant, in front of the National Palace, ringed by U.S. troops, to announce his entry into politics. Shocked and enraged Haitians rushed the barricades, shouting "assassin" and "murderer." The soldiers were forced to cut the press conference short and whisk Constant to safety.[37]

The U.S. has also protected Constant from the Haitian justice system. When an investigating judge invited him in for questioning, Constant fled to the U.S. Under pressure from Haitian officials, the U.S. Immigration and Naturalization Service ("INS") commenced deportation proceedings. The State Department publicly intervened in support of the move. Warren Christopher wrote a letter to the Court explaining that due to his terrorist activities in Haiti, Constant's "presence and activities in the United States have potentially serious adverse foreign policy consequences..." The Judge agreed, and added that "allowing [Constant] to remain in the United States fosters the impression that the United States endorses FRAPH and its actions."[38]

The Judge ordered Constant deported in September 1995. Three months later, while his case was pending appeal and he was in a detention facility, Constant went on CBS' *60 Minutes* television program, admitted his relationship with U.S. intelligence officials, and hinted that he could divulge more.[39] Officials quickly offered Constant a deal: he could remain in the U.S., a free man, as long as he checked in regularly and did not talk about what he did in Haiti. A 30-year INS veteran who supervised Constant in detention "cannot understand why [Constant] is not rotting in a U.S. jail.... He was just treated differently than any other murderer or terrorist."[40]

In December 2000, a Haitian court convicted Constant of murder *in absentia* for FRAPH's role in the 1994 *Raboteau Massacre*, a military/paramilitary attack on a pro-democracy neighborhood. Despite repeated calls by human rights advocates and victims,[41] the 1995 deportation order has not been executed. Constant has not, however, given up his political ambitions. In early 2001 he promised "I'm either going to be President of Haiti or I'm going to be killed."[42]

Assistance to the de facto repression was not limited to paramilitary organizations. The U.S. had originally organized the Haitian army during the 1915-1934 U.S. Marine occupation of Haiti, and had maintained close ties ever since, regardless of the army's human rights record. Emmanuel Constant reports that the U.S. military attaché in Haiti was in military headquarters the night of the coup. A Canadian advisor to the dictatorship reports the same in the following days.[43] The *de facto* regime's top military leaders had all received training in the U.S., and the U.S. continued to train Haitian army personnel after the 1991 coup, at least into 1993.[44] Many of the coup leaders had been on the CIA payroll for years.[45] One CIA analyst, in a widely-circulated report in 1992, praised the *junta*'s leader, General Raoul Cedras, as one of "the most promising group of Haitian leaders to emerge since the Duvalier family dictatorship was overthrown in 1986." Other CIA reports fabricated accusations that President Aristide suffered from mental illness.[46]

The U.S. has also worked to protect the *de facto* military leadership from justice. In 1993, U.S. negotiators pressured Haiti's elected, but exiled, authorities to grant a broad amnesty for the dictatorship's crimes as part of the 1993 Governor's Island Accords.[47] That amnesty, like the peace accords, never went into effect, but the U.S. pushed for a new amnesty with the arrival of the Multinational Force in 1994. This time the Haitian authorities granted a very narrow amnesty, covering only the *coup d'état* of September 1991 itself, not the consequent murders, torture and other crimes.[48]

The U.S. made the exiles of many *de facto* leaders possible. The two top generals, Raoul Cedras and Philippe Biamby, were flown to refuge in Panama, aboard U.S. planes. The American Embassy even rented three of Cedras' luxurious villas for expatriate housing. Most of the remaining members of the high command were allowed to settle in the U.S.[49] After pressure from Congress and human rights groups, the INS did deport two members of the High Command convicted in the *Raboteau* case in January of 2002.[50]

The U.S. has downplayed the *de facto* regime's atrocities. When human rights advocates (including the UN/OAS mission) and victims denounced the introduction of rape as a political weapon, the U.S. denied it. An embassy cable leaked to the press concluded that "[t]he Haitian left, including President Aristide and his supporters in Washington and here, consistently manipulate or even fabricate human rights abuses as a propaganda tool.... A case in point is the sudden epidemic of rapes reported... by pro-Aristide human rights activists...." The rapes were suspicious because "rape has never been considered as a serious crime [in Haiti]." [51] In order to justify a policy of repatriating Haitian refugees intercepted at sea, the U.S. denied reports by human rights organizations of persecution of returned refugees. One CIA analyst declared "that there is no systematic or frequent lethal violence aimed at civilians," and called the head of the military junta, Raoul Cedras, "a conscientious military leader."[52]

## II. U.S. Human Rights Policies Towards Haiti's Democracy

The U.S. has made substantial contributions to Haiti's democracy since the restoration of the Constitutional authorities in 1994. The return itself was made possible by the 20,000 U.S. troops spearheading the UN-sponsored force. U.S. soldiers remained in the country for the next four years, helping to maintain stability and providing the elected officials breathing space to begin developing democratic institutions. The U.S. invested heavily in training, for the civilian Police Nationale d'Haiti (PNH) that replaced the army, and for judicial officials.

Yet even this assistance fell into the *lave men, swiye atè* trap. The most egregious example is U.S. intelligence agency recruiting of agents during U.S.-sponsored police training programs. PNH officers report that this recruiting began as soon as the first class of trainees arrived at the training center set up at Ft. Leonard Wood in Missouri. It continued under the U.S. Department of Justice's ICITAP training program in Haiti.[53] When ICITAP's own director attempted to stop the practice, she was forced out of her position. Although other employees objected as well (one former ICITAP contractor called the spying program wrong, and "not good for those cadets, not good for Haiti, and not good for the program. We were to make civilian police out of them, not spies"), the intelligence recruitment continued.[54]

U.S. policy was also inconsistent regarding disarmament of former soldiers and paramilitaries. Disarmament was a central part of the multinational force's UN mandate, and U.S. soldiers engaged in some disarmament activities, including destroying the army's heavy weapons and running "buy-back" programs for handguns and other weapons. Yet top officials repeatedly refused to authorize operations to confiscate large caches of weapons, even though soldiers on the ground believed they had the intelligence and capacity to make safe, successful seizures.[55]

The failure to pursue aggressive disarmament had the effect of strengthening the military and paramilitary elements that the U.S. had supported under the dictatorships, and that had most effectively resisted democracy. It also created an instant common crime problem, as the weapons' owners, unemployed by the military and paramilitary demobilization, made their own democratic transition to economically motivated robbery and murder.[56]

Perhaps the most damaging legacy of the intelligence infiltration during police training and the failure to disarm is their examples to Haiti's current police officers. Many, in the international community, notably the OAS and the U.S., have criticized the PNH as not sufficiently independent from elected officials. They claim that politicians exercise control over the police, and influence it to accomplish objectives beyond the scope of police work,[57] undermining the rule of law. These complaints ring hollow in the ears of officers whose very training, by the people now championing the rule of law, included recruitment for politically motivated treason, a betrayal of the officers' loyalty to their country, and a violation of the law. Officers deciding whether to risk their lives in operations to seize weapons from people that may have them outgunned understandably pause when they remember that the world's best trained and equipped military refused to take up that task.[58]

In contrast to the often gentle treatment of the dictatorships' human rights violations, the U.S. has been quick to criticize and punish Haiti's democratic governments. Many of the U.S. government's critiques of human rights under democracy have been justified, and the threat of economic sanctions can be an effective tool in promoting human rights. However, the way that the U.S. has brandished and implemented sanctions and human rights critiques over the last nine years implies that those actions, like the refusal to punish the dictators, were motivated more by political calculation than by an interest in human rights. As a result, U.S. policy has promoted cynicism more effectively than it has human rights.

Democratic Haiti certainly has its share of human rights violations, but they are neither quantitatively nor qualitatively comparable to those of the dictatorship. The prisons are overcrowded, and prisoners' procedural rights are not always respected. But there is nothing like the horrors of Fort Dimanche, the political prison that Duvalier opponents rarely left alive. There are too many killings, some by police officers, but none of the systematic massacres organized under the Duvalier, CNG, Avril, and *de facto* dictatorships. In that sense, Haiti has undergone a democratic transition: the human rights violations of a dictatorship peasant massacres and other large-scale killings, political prisons, and official censorship of the media, the courts and political dissent have been left behind, but have been replaced by the human rights violations of democracy non-systematic police brutality, judicial corruption and inefficiency, and difficulty protecting citizens from acts of other citizens. Although there have been some notable successes – the army's demobilization is probably Haiti's most significant human rights advance since emancipation – Haiti has struggled in this area. It has struggled about as much as one could expect of a new democracy with no tradition of democratic policing or justice and little money to invest in them.

Haitian authorities could do better, and the U.S. should play a role in encouraging them to do so. This encouragement, to be effective, must be consistent and clearly motivated by human rights principles, not short-term, transparently political objectives. Such misuse of the term "human rights" breeds cynicism among both the targets of the discourse, and the largest constituency for human rights in Haiti, the poor majority.

The best example of hijacked human rights discourse, and the damage it can do, is the prosecution of the April 2000 murder of Jean Dominique and his bodyguard Jean-Claude Louissant. Dominique was Haiti's most prominent journalist ever, by far, and one of its most eloquent pro-democracy activists. His strength as a journalist and activist was that he made an option for the poor: he innovated Creole language radio broadcasts, so the vast majority of Haitians who did not speak French could understand the news. He persisted in covering issues that peasants cared about – land reform, agricultural policy, rural development – and in making their voices heard. Dominique insisted on a democracy that was not merely formal, with elections, but one where the majority of Haitians who were poor actually decided its destiny. He was courageous and unrelenting in criticizing those he believed responsible for the poor's suffering: the country's elite (from where he himself came), the foreign imperial powers, and the military that served both. Although he considered himself part of the *Lavalas* movement, Dominique gave government officials no quarter when he felt criticism was due. He relentlessly called for justice for the victims of the preceding dictatorships, and a more honest and representative government. No one has felt the loss of Jean Dominique more than Haiti's rural and urban poor.

The investigation of the killing has been controversial, and in many ways unsuccessful. No one has been charged with ordering or planning the crime. Two suspects were killed in police custody. The main investigating judge publicly feuded with police officials and the executive branch until he finally left the country. Elected officials have interfered with the investigation.

But the Dominique case has also had some successes. First is its mere endurance: after four years of controversy, sometimes involving high-ranking public officials, it is still moving. The case has elicited unprecedented time and resources from the government, and it has advanced through several procedural steps that have stymied other prominent cases. Dozens of witnesses have been interviewed, and four suspects are in custody.

The Dominique case's successes are, in large part, due to public pressure on the Haitian government and justice system. This pressure raises its priority among the Haitian government's many urgent concerns, allowing it a larger share of scarce funding and management attention. Officials trying to pursue the case use it as a lever to remove resistance to their work. The fact that so many people care about the case ensures that it cannot be put aside and forgotten.

Pressure from the U.S. and other members of the international community can be an important part of the mobilization. Unfortunately, this pressure has been exerted in a patently political manner, and has demobilized the most powerful and motivated pressure group, Haiti's poor. The U.S. opposed most of Jean Dominique's justice efforts while he was alive, so the sudden adoption of his cause by them seemed suspicious. From the beginning, U.S. pressure on the investigation was focussed narrowly on the possibility that an elected official may have been involved.[59] The U.S. also allied closely with the economic elite and the traditional political class, many of whom had served in dictatorships that had forced Jean into exile.

In the first days after Dominique's assassination, no one called for justice louder than Haiti's poor. A march from his radio station down to the National Palace was coordinated by middle-class organizations, but the majority of marchers were from grassroots groups. At Dominique's funeral in the national stadium, busloads of peasants joined throngs streaming on foot from Port-au-Prince's poor neighborhoods. Everywhere on the streets, on the radio, and in grassroots meetings, Haiti's poor called out for justice.

These calls were soon joined by calls from other, better-financed voices: opposition politicians and business leaders, and the U.S. government. These voices had not joined Dominique's when he called for land reform, less foreign interference in Haitian politics, prosecution of the *de facto* leadership, or the arrest of Prosper Avril. Their calls for justice focused less on Dominique and his work, and more on the prospect that people associated with the government were involved. Soon, these voices dominated the mobilization in the Haitian and international press.[60]

The dominance of voices that had not previously supported Jean Dominique's causes resulted in a demobilization among those who had cried out for justice most early and loudly. Afraid that Dominique's death and the justice movement were being usurped to undermine other gains that Haiti's popular movement and Jean Dominique had fought so hard to attain, many grassroots activists decreased their activities. For example, at a screening of a movie about Dominique's life, billed as an event in the mobilization, a large percentage of the attendees were foreigners working in Port-au-Prince, and most of the rest were middle-class Haitians. The grassroots groups that had brought huge numbers of demonstrators to the streets were almost completely absent.

Poor Haitians still feel Jean Dominique's loss as much as ever. When things happen that should not - a human rights case mired in the courts, international interference in Haitian affairs, public corruption, provocations and violence by anti-government groups Haitians will often sigh and say "if only Jean were still here...." Grassroots leaders still participate in some aspects of the fight for justice for Jean Dominique, and include the Dominique case in their litany of complaints against the system. But their efforts are limited, because poor Haitians believe that too much of the mobilization has been taken over by people whose primary agenda is not justice, but the undermining of the very democracy that they, and Jean, fought so hard to obtain.[61]

Another recent example of the politicization of a legitimate human rights issue is the disparate treatment of Jean Pierre, a.k.a. "Jean Tatoune," and Amio Metayer, a.k.a. "Cubain" after both escaped from prison in August 2002. Although Tatoune had been actually convicted and sentenced for murder, and Metayer had no serious allegations against him before the Haitian courts, the U.S. and its allies in Haiti continuously chastised the Haitian government for not arresting Metayer,[62] but rarely if ever mentioned Tatoune.

Metayer and Tatoune grew up in adjacent (and feuding) poor neighborhoods of Gonaives. Both first made names for themselves in the fight against the Duvalier dictatorship, although Tatoune became a local FRAPH leader during the *de facto* regime. Both were in prison in early August, 2002: Tatoune serving a life sentence for murder for his role in the 1994 Raboteau massacre, Metayer officially in pre-trial detention on arson charges. Most observers felt the real reason for Metayer's detention was accusations by the MOCHRENA political party and the OAS that he had been involved in a December 2001 attack on the MOCHRENA headquarters, in which a guard was killed. There were no official complaints against Metayer for the December attacks with the Gonaives police or courts, and no eyewitnesses identified him publicly. The OAS case consisted of a single sentence.[63]

Both Metayer and Tatoune escaped from prison during a jailbreak organized by Metayer's supporters on August 2, 2002. Although both initially called for the the forcible overthrow of the government, only Tatoune continued to do so after the first few weeks. Yet the escaped convicted murderer and paramilitary member calling for forced regime change was not the one who attracted the attention of the U.S. Instead, the U.S. called only for the arrest of Metayer, who was still innocent until proven guilty, and the proof against him was slight.[64] For example, the 2002 Department of State Human Rights Report on Haiti[65] does not mention Jean Tatoune a single time. It mentions Metayer a total of seven times, but never once can allege that he committed a single human rights violation in 2002.

To the extent that there were credible accusations of serious human rights violations by Metayer, the U.S. should have encouraged investigation and prosecution. If the U.S. had credible proof of those accusations, it should have supplied them to the justice system, or made them public. However, the insistence on demonizing Metayer, against whom there was little justiciable proof, while failing to condemn Jean Tatoune and Emmanuel Constant, both convicted of murder, gives the unmistakable impression that opposing Haiti's elected government is more important than establishing respect for human rights.

The appropriation of human rights issues to further political ends usually undermines both, long and short-term human rights objectives. In the case of Jean Dominique, it has diminished the mobilization among Haiti's poor, who are the government's prime constituency and therefore able to exert unique pressure.[66] In the case of Amio Metayer and Jean Tatoune, it politicizes, and therefore weakens, the pursuit of justice. In the long run, misappropriation of human rights discourse leads to cynicism about human rights in general. This is especially true when the appropriation is done by the U.S., a country that often rightfully takes a public leadership role in human rights.

## III. Human Rights and Elections

The pitfalls of *lave men, swiye atè* are no better illustrated than in U.S. policies towards elections and supporting a Haitian opposition. U.S. financial support for elections was critical to Haiti's first free and fair elections in 1990 and to several successful elections since 1994. The development of an opposition is an essential component of Haiti's democracy. Yet, much of U.S. support, both for elections and opposition parties, has been tied to influencing the policies of Haitian officials rather than supporting democratic development. The support for elections and for political parties has been closely tied to the candidates' willingness to comply with American policy dictates. The result is that U.S. electoral support has become divorced from the effective development of democracy, and there is no Haitian opposition with electoral credibility.

The most obvious form of *swiye atè* election policy has been support of brutal dictatorial regimes that ran sham elections, like the CNG and the Duvaliers, or promoting known human rights violators like Emmanuel Constant and Prosper Avril as political candidates. However the U.S. has worked against its avowed interest of promoting democracy more subtly, by undermining or co-opting democratic actors considered not sufficiently supportive of U.S. interests. The U.S. is currently combining both the obvious and subtle forms: in a single-minded and short-sighted attempt to undermine the *Lavalas* party, the U.S. has cobbled together a series of coalitions of people with both democratic and dictatorial credentials. The mere association with former dictators was itself enough to erode most of the democratic members' electoral support. Under U.S. patronage, the coalitions took increasingly unpopular stands, including support for the return of the hated army, and class-based attacks against *Lavalas* supporters. As a result, those in the U.S.-supported opposition who once had electoral support now have none, and there is no credible alternative to *Lavalas*.

The current incarnation of the U.S.-supported opposition is the *Convergence Democratique*, or CD. Parties now in the CD won a plurality in the legislature in the 1995 elections, which allowed them to name the Prime Minister and form the Government. They also did well at the local level, winning a majority of mayor offices, and a plurality of local councils. The most successful of these parties, *Organisation Politique Lavalas* (OPL) ran on a platform of eliminating the army and progressive economic and social programs. At the urging of the U.S., however, the OPL Government soon adopted the neo-liberal economic policies popular in the international community but unpopular in Haiti, including lowering tariffs on agricultural goods (now among the lowest in the world)[67] and privatizing state-owned enterprises. Those hurt by the policies exercised their newfound democratic right to protest, and by June 1997 the protests had become so widespread that the Government resigned.

The CD evolved out of the Haitian Conference of Political Parties (CHPP), a politically diverse assemblage including former communists, a convicted dictator, and ultra-right wing Duvalierists[68] forged by the U.S. International Republican Institute.[69] The CHPP included three candidates who had run in the CNG's January 1988 elections after the dictatorship had massacred voters two months before.[70] The CHPP evolved over the next eighteen months into the CD, which now includes the once-dominant OPL (since renamed *Organisation du Peuple en Lutte*). Neither of these coalitions has propounded a coherent political platform.[71] As Eugenia Charles, former Prime Minister of Dominica (and staunch supporter of the U.S. when it invaded Grenada) and the Caribbean Community's Representative to the CARICOM/OAS Mission to Haiti stated, "I had to ask them why they called themselves 'Convergence.' They were not converging on anything. They were not agreeing on anything. They cannot get together to form a plan."[72]

The CD's component parts did manage a consensus in three areas: the army should return, the popular Lavalas party should go, and the international community should continue its embargo on development assistance to the Haitian government. Haitian voters also formed a consensus on these same issues, but in the opposite direction: they hate the army, and support the Lavalas movement every chance they get. They believe that the aid embargo is aggravating the severe poverty of Haiti's majority, and cripples the government's ability to develop democratic institutions.

As the CD's policies diverged from that of the electorate, their electoral support plummeted. 1997's ruling parties garnered about 12% in the 2000 May legislative elections. A U.S.-commissioned Gallup Poll after the elections found a 4% credibility rating for the CD leadership, and also that President Aristide had by far the highest credibility rating of any politician. Sixty percent of those polled named Aristide the leader they trusted most and no one else received more than 4% support. Only 8% named Convergence as the party they most sympathized with.[73]

Under ordinary democratic rules, politicians who advocate unpalatable or undemocratic policies simply fade away. Yet as the CD's electoral support plummeted, its international support skyrocketed. In 1995, the U.S. sought to delegitimize the victory of current CD member OPL. After the party left the Lavalas movement, the U.S. financed it. Parties in the CD have received increasing funds from the U.S.: the IRI alone receives $3 million per year, most of it to support the opposition.[74] In 2001, when the CD refused to participate in an OAS brokered broad-based initiative to resolve the electoral crisis, the U.S. converted the 12% electoral support into a veto by declaring that any solution required CD approval.[75] One prominent Haitian economist and government critic opined that the "official" opposition "would be a joke if it were not so serious with its U.S. backers."[76]

Such foreign interference angers Haitian voters as much as it would Americans if it happened here. The anger is more justified, because Haitians know the consequences: from the lavish financial contributions to the brutal and corrupt Duvaliers, and military training during the 1991-1994 dictatorship, those who have terrorized ordinary Haitians often did so with help from the international community. Haitians also know that foreign support requires less accountability to domestic voters.[77] They doubt that the CD, if it succeeds in gaining power through undemocratic means, will exercise it in a democratic way.

The CD inspires fear of dictatorship by supporting the return of the hated army. The coalition's "Parallel President" Gerard Gourgue made the return of the army, and of civilians associated with former dictatorships, a central theme of his "inauguration speech." [78] Parties and individuals in the coalition frequently call for the army's return to fight common crime or counterbalance the elected authorities. Although some CD members are less enthusiastic, none publicly oppose the military's return. When two *Lavalas* senators broke ranks to oppose the army's abolition in September 2003, CD members hailed the move.

Haiti demobilized the army in 1995, soon after the restoration of democracy following the 1991-1994 dictatorship.[79] It is impossible to overestimate the impact of this accomplishment on the lives of average Haitians. It has been called the greatest human rights development in Haiti since emancipation, and is wildly popular. For once in their troubled history, Haitians are free to speak their minds and travel freely, without worrying about soldiers or informers in the market, on public transportation, and outside their doorway. The army's lion's share of the economy, extracted in small but regular amounts from peasants as bribes and protection money, and in large amounts from the state treasury, can now be diverted to healthcare, nutrition and education. Political succession for the first time obeys the calendar and the ballot: Haiti's only two transfers of power from one elected President to another were in 1996 and 2001, the only two elections without an army. President Rene Preval, when he left in 2001, became the first Haitian President ever to leave voluntarily after serving his entire term in the National Palace, no more no less.

To Haitians, the army's return means a return of brutality, spies, theft, corruption, coups and the dictatorships. It is no surprise that the vast majority of voters oppose it. It should also not be a surprise that Haitians fear and distrust anyone purportedly running for office on such an unpopular platform.

The CD has compounded this distrust by refusing to participate in any initiatives that risk leading to a test of electoral strength, and by associating with those trying to overthrow the government by unconstitutional means. The CD has systematically sabotaged every attempt by the Haitian government, by the OAS and by CARICOM to negotiate an end to Haiti's political crisis.[80] It also supplies more than tacit support to those seeking the violent overthrow of the elected government. In November, 2002 former Haitian army Colonel Himmler Rebu, who led an unsuccessful attempted *coup d'etat* in the 1980's, called for a popular uprising against the government, at a rally attended by CD leaders. He later became a visible member of the CD leadership. The CD representative in the Dominican Republic was arrested by Dominican authorities in a border town for plotting an armed attack against the government. CD leaders voiced support for escaped convict and convicted killer Jean Tatoune's violent anti-government movement in Gonaives.[81]

# CONCLUSION

The *swiye atè* component of U.S. policy imposes an obvious cost on Haiti. Our help may not have created the dictatorships and paramilitary groups, but it emboldened them and prolonged their existences, exposing more innocent victims to killings, rape and other torture. Beyond the human cost from the terror we supported is the opportunity lost by the democratic institutions we failed to support. If Haiti's elected governments had received for schools and hospitals the money that the dictatorships had received for guns and bullets; if the years citizens learned to struggle against and survive repression had been spent developing democratic civil society institutions; if the U.S. had set a good example by favoring human rights and democracy over short-term political and economic interests, then Haiti would today be more educated, healthy and peaceful, and less polarized and cynical.

The *swiye atè* policies impose a cost on the U.S. as well. We spent hundreds of millions of dollars on the military intervention to remove the *de facto* dictatorship and stabilize the country. From the Duvalier reign on, every dictatorship we supported has generated a flow of refugees to our shores. Today, the economic hardship to which our inadequate support for the democratic government contributes, forces even more desperate Haitians onto Florida-bound boats. Haiti's police force, chronically underfunded and overtaxed, is hard-pressed to intercept cocaine passing from Colombia through Haiti to U.S. consumers.

It is not too late for the U.S. to establish a more consistent policy on human rights in Haiti. Although we cannot recoup the wasted years, lives and dollars, we can make sure that from here on our money is invested wisely in developing Haiti's democracy and human rights. This means providing support to democratic actors, and only to democratic actors. We should help the Haitian government develop the justice system, police force and other institutions that provide a bulwark against human rights violations. Such support should be linked to realistic progress in democracy building, not to how much we like the government or its policies. We should support the development of civil society institutions, including opposition parties, but only to the extent that those institutions are willing and able to participate and succeed under democratic rules.

---

[1] This chapter will focus on civil and political human rights. Economic and cultural human rights are arguably more important, certainly in terms of numbers of people killed by violations of these rights (such as the development assistance embargo), and by the accounts of Haiti's poor majority, but are treated elsewhere in this book.

[2] Robert Heinl, Nancy Heinl and Michael Heinl, WRITTEN IN BLOOD, (1996) p. 696-702.

[3] *See* Patrick Lemoine, FORT DIMANCHE, DUNGEON OF DEATH (1996).

[4] Id. at 677-78. International investigators established that Jean-Claude Duvalier and his associates stole over $500 million from the Haitian treasury in the last few years of his reign (documents on file with author); Marjorie Valbrun, "U.S. to Pursue Torturers Who Flee Here," *The Wall Street Journal*, May 8, 2003.

[5] Id. at 678. But by 1982, the U.S. General Accounting Office had to admit that after $218 million in food aid and economic assistance over the previous eight years, USAID "is still having difficulty implementing its projects." United States General Accounting Office. *Assistance to Haiti: Barriers, Recent Program Changes, and Future Options.* Washington, D.C.: United States General Accounting Office, 1982; p. i.

[6] Americas Watch and the National Coalition for Haitian Refugees, *Haiti: Human Rights Under Hereditary Dictatorship*, p. 5, 1985.

[7] Id. p. 30.

[8] Id., p. 31.

[9] WRITTEN IN BLOOD, *supra* p. 700

[10] Amy Wilentz, THE RAINY SEASON (1989) p. 140.

[11] Id. p. 227.

[12] Paul Farmer, THE USES OF HAITI, 2003, p. 119; Robert Lawless, HAITI'S BAD PRESS, 1992 p. 166.

[13] Jim Mann, "CIA's Plan Would Have Undercut Aristide in 1987-88," *Los Angeles Times*, October 31, 1993; Tim Weiner, "Key Leaders Said To Have Been in the CIA's Pay," *New York Times*, November 1, 1993.

[14] Mann, "CIA's Plan Would Have Undercut Aristide" *supra*.

[15] WRITTEN IN BLOOD, *supra* at 726; Amy Wilentz, THE RAINY SEASON (1989) p. 363-64.

[16] He was removed quickly after a popular outcry against his Duvalierist past, THE RAINY SEASON, *supra* p. 324.

[17] Paul v. Avril, 901 F.Supp. 330, 335-36 (S.D. FL 1994). This case was a civil case, in which a default judgment was entered when Avril fled the U.S. after failing to have the claims dismissed.

[18] WRITTEN IN BLOOD, *supra* at 727-28.

[19] WRITTEN IN BLOOD, *supra* at 726-28.

[20] Douglas Farah, "U.S. – Haitian Relations Deteriorate; Disarmament Dispute, Contact with Ex-Ruler Infuriate Aristide," *The Washington Post*, Nov. 29, 1995.

[21] Author interviews with Haitian National Police Officers, 1996 and 2003.

[22] Prosper Avril, AN APPEAL TO HISTORY: THE TRUTH ABOUT A SINGULAR LAWSUIT (1999), p. 291-94.

[23] Id.

[24] Statements on file with author.

[25] Georges Fauriol, "Searching for Haiti Policy: The Next Ninety Days," HAITI ALERT, Vol. IX, No. 3 (June 2001).

[26] As of early 2004, Mr. Avril is still in prison. After a series of appeals, the torture case was dropped on a technicality. He was immediately re-arrested based on complaints filed by the victims of the Piatre Massacre, a March 1990 military/paramilitary attack on peasants. Because of concerns about transporting Avril from Port-au-Prince to St. Marc, where the Piatre Massacre judge sits (some raised by Avril's own lawyers), Avril was not brought before a judge within 48 hours for a review of his arrest, as is his right under Haitian law. That defect was eventually cured, in April 2003. On December 10, 2003, the investigating magistrate in the Piatre case issued his final report, charging Avril with murder.

[27] Declaration on file with author.

[28] Joseph E. Baptiste (National Organization for the Advancement of Haitians) and Robert Maguire (Georgetown University/Trinity College Haiti Program), *Intransigence is a Nonstarter*, South Florida Sun-Sentinel, June 11, 2001.

[29] Brian Concannon Jr., *Beyond Complementarity: The International Criminal Court and National Prosecutions, a View from Haiti*, COLUMBIA HUMAN RIGHTS LAW REVIEW, Vol. 32, n. 1 (2000) p. 203.

[30] Memorandum of Decision and Order by John F. Gossart Jr., U.S. Immigration Judge, in *In the Matter of Emmanuel Constant*, Case #A 74 002 009, September 1, 1995.

[31] *See*, Amnesty International USA, *United States of America: A Safe Haven for Torturers*, p. 33 (2002).

[32] David Grann, *Giving the Devil His Due*, THE ATLANTIC MONTHLY, June 2001 54, 59.

[33] Id. at 62.

[34] Department of Defense declassified intelligence report dated October 3, 1994, on file with author.

[35] Grann, *supra.*, at 64-66.

[36] Tracy Kidder, "The Trials of Haiti", *The Nation*, October 27, 2003, p. 28; Stan Goff, "The Longest Day" in *Haiti: A Slave Revolution: 200 Years After 1804,* Pat Chin, Greg Dunkel, Sara Flounders and Kim Ives, eds. (2004) p. 180.

[37] Id. at 63.

[38] Memorandum of Decision, *supra* at 13-14.

[39] CBS *60 Minutes*, December 3, 1995.

[40] Grann *supra* at 68. In contrast, the U.S. Justice Department now requires the incarceration of all Haitian asylum seekers who enter the country without documents, even if they establish a *prima facie* case for asylum, even if a judge finds them eligible for release on bond. Susan Benesch, "Haitians Trapped by War on Terrorism," *Amnesty Now*, fall 2003, p. 12-13.

[41] *United States of America: A Safe Haven for Torturers*, *supra* at 35.

[42] *Id.* at 75.

[43] Grann *supra* at 64.

[44] Training documents on file with author.

[45] Tim Weiner, "Key Haiti Leaders Said To Have Been in the CIA's Pay," *New York Times*, November 1, 1993.

[46] Id., Farmer The USES OF HAITI, *supra*, p. 161, 289.

[47] Michael Scharf, *Swapping Amnesty for Peace: Was There a Duty To Prosecute International Crimes in Haiti?*, 31 Tex. Int'l L.J. 1, 8 (1996). *See* Naomi Roht-Arriaza, *Conclusion: Combating Impunity, in* Impunity and Human Rights in International Law and Practice 300 (Naomi Roht-Arriaza ed., 1995).

[48] Brian Concannon Jr., *Beyond Complementarity: The International Criminal Court and National Prosecutions, a View from Haiti*, COLUMBIA HUMAN RIGHTS LAW REVIEW, Vol. 32, n. 1 (2000).

[49] Steve Fainaru, *U.S. Is a Haven for Suspected War Criminals*, Boston Globe, May 2, 1999, at A1 (15 high ranking former military personnel, including the entire high command except for Cédras and Biamby, emigrated to the United States).

[50] Immigration authorities have pursued Haitian human rights violators persistently since 2000. A third High Command member was arrested by the Department of Homeland Security in August, 2003. Alfonso Chardy, "Haitian Sought For Military's –94 Massacre Is Arrested" *Miami Herald*, August 27, 2003. Lower level Raboteau convicts have been deported as well.

[51] U.S. Embassy, Haiti, "Confidential Cablegram," April 12, 1994, on file with author, p. 2-3; Paul Farmer, PATHOLOGIES OF POWER: HUMAN RIGHTS AND THE NEW WAR ON THE POOR, 254 (2003) (rape victim called that seeing the dictatorship's lawyer denying the rapes on CNN "one of the most debasing moments of her experience").

[52] Grann, *supra*, p. 62.

[53] Sam Skolnik "Separating Cops, Spies" *Legal Times*, March 1, 1999.

[54] Id. The *Legal Times* reported CIA recruitment through ICITAP programs in other countries, including El Salvador. The ICITAP program has been investigated by the U.S. Office of the Inspector General for visa fraud, security breaches, contract abuses, hiring irregularities and workplace harassment. The investigation led to the downsizing of several ICITAP programs, and the elimination of the Haiti training program.

[55] Author interviews with U.S. Special Forces, 1995.

[56] Madison Smartt Bell, *Mine of Stones,* Harpers Magazine, January, 2004, p. 58.

[57] *Department of State Country Reports on Human Rights Practices*, March 2003, at www.state.gov.

[58] Some may not pause enough: as this chapter was in final edits in November 2003, Police Commissaire Honale Bonnet, the head of the Criminal Affairs Bureau and a collaborator with the BAI, was shot and killed while investigating a kidnapping.

[59] The official, Senator Dany Toussaint, was elected on the Fanmi Lavalas platform. He has been questioned several times by investigating judges, and the court formally requested the Senate to lift Sen. Toussaint's immunity. The Senate has not formally decided that issue. As Sen. Toussaint began breaking from the Lavalas movemnt in 2003 (primarily to oppose attempts to abolish the army), calls for his prosecution from the U.S. and its allies in Haiti declined, and since he joined the opposition in December 2003, have stopped.

[60] This is true of the Haitian press as a whole, but not of Radio Haiti Inter, the station founded by Jean Dominique, operated after his death by his wife, Michele Montas. Radio Haiti relentlessly criticizes what it considers to be defects in the investigation: political interference, inadequate support for investigating judges, and procedural irregularities, but does not engage in the broad anti-government rhetoric. Unfortunately, Radio Haiti suspended operations after a December 2002 attack against Ms. Montas, in which a security guard at her home was killed.

[61] Information from author conversations with members and leaders of grassroots organizations, 2000-2003.

[62] As this chapter went to final edits, the controversy over Metayer's liberty was, tragically, resolved by Metayer's assassination on September 21, 2003.

[63] Organisation of American States, *Report of the Commission of Inquiry Into the Events of December 17, 2001, in Haiti,* (June 2002), Sec. II(B)(2)(b)(1), p. 13-14 ("Mr. Amiot Metayer (alias Cubain) was identified as one of those who attacked").

[64] Even the arson charges against Metayer were soon dropped. The accusers had withdrawn their complaints even before Metayer's prison escape, so the prosecution dropped that case for lack of proof. The justice system should have pursued Metayer for the prison break, but even that case was not as strong as it might look from the Anglo-American legal perspective. Under the French system adopted by Haiti, an escape prosecution needs to prove not only the escape, but also that the escapee himself used or organized force or fraud in the attempt. Walking out through a hole in the prison wall is only punishable if the escapee helped create the hole.

[65] *Department of State Country Reports on Human Rights Practices,* March 2003, at www.state.gov.

[66] Grassroots pressure was the key to advancing the Raboteau Massacre, Haiti's most successful human rights case to date. Brian Concannon Jr., *Justice for Haiti: The Raboteau Trial,* THE INTERNATIONAL LAWYER, Vol. 35, No. 2, 641 (2001).

[67] According to an IMF "market openness test", Haiti was the second-most open market of those tested, slightly less open than Chile, but four times more open than the U.S. or the European Union. Oxfam Great Britain, DEUX POIDS DEUX MESURES: COMMERCE, GLOBALISATION ET LUTTE CONTRE LA PAUVRETE, (2002) page 144-5.

[68] Tom Reeves, "Still Up Against the Death Plan in Haiti," *Dollars and Sense,* September/October 2003, p. 38, 40.

[69] Avril, AN APPEAL TO HISTORY, *supra* p. 293.

[70] Leslie Manigat of the RNDP, who "won" those elections, Duvalierist Hubert de Ronceray of the MDN and Gregoire Eugene of PSCH. *Written in Blood supra* at 721.

[71] Alex Dupuy, "Who is Afraid of Democracy in Haiti? A Critical Reflection," *Haiti Papers*, Trinity College Haiti Program, No. 7 (June 2003) p. 5.

[72] Ross Robinson Associates, *Haiti Confidential,* August 2001

[73] Tracy Kidder, p. 29 THE NATION, October 27, 2003

[74] Reeves, *supra*, at 40.

[75] Dupuy, *supra*, at 5-6.

[76] Id., p. 44 (quoting Camille Chalmers of PAPDA).

[77] *See*, Dupuy, *supra*, at 8 ("the CD has emerged as the key power broker in the political conjuncture primarily because it is a willing servant of domestic and foreign interests that seek to impose an agenda on the Haitian people that is not of their choosing.").

[78] Gerard Gourgue, *De L'ouverture Des Etats Generaux Vers Les Grandes Assises Pour Un Nouveau Pacte National*, Speech delivered on Haiti's Presidential Inauguration Day, February 7, 2001.

[79] Although it has been demobilized for over eight years, the army is still recognized by Haiti's Constitution. In September 2003, Parliament began the process of amending the Constitution to formally abolish the army. Although both houses voted overwhelmingly in favor of abolition, the Senate's vote, which was unanimous with two abstentions, has been called into question because of the seven open seats.

[80] *See* Chapter IV *infra*; Dupuy, *supra*, at 6 ("At every turn in the process, the CD either refused to endorse agreements that were arrived at or issued new demands that it insisted had to be met before it could agree to endorse any proposed resolution.").

[81] *See*, Scott Wilson, "Armed Attacks Increase Pressure on Haitian Leader," *The Washington Post*, November 18, 2003 ("Opposition political leaders have declined to condemn the armed attacks, although they deny having political or financial connections to them").

# Human Rights and Justice in Haiti
*Mario Joseph, Esq.*

Born in a rural area and to a humble family, I witnessed first-hand the atrocities and repressive structures that oppressed poor people, peasants and women during the Duvalier era. I also witnessed and lived through the democratic transition after the fall of Jean-Claude Duvalier. This slice of history inspired me and reinforced my conviction to dedicate my professional life to dismantling this repressive structure, as an activist and as a lawyer, by defending human rights and representing the poorest and the socially excluded.

The repressive structures in Haiti have deep and extensive roots. Mentalities need to be changed. The Haitian judicial system suffers from chronic dysfunction and it would be no exaggeration to compare it to an engine that is able to crush all of those who dare to come too close. Therefore, dismantling the structures will necessarily take a lot of time and effort. Many initiatives have already been deployed. We need to go further and try to shape people's mentalities regarding the principles of the rule of law, the Constitution, the Universal Declaration of Human Rights, and human rights treaties.

Often I am asked, "How and why did you choose to become a lawyer, particularly a human rights lawyer?" The answer is not always easy, since I was not guided by anyone, nor did I have role models or a lawyer in my family. In fact, my parents are of modest means. Perhaps it is because I grew up in rural area where peasants suffered from all kinds of abuses, and was born in an area where the state fails to provide basic services, in a country where the public administration is centralized and inoperative, where going to school, having a hot meal everyday, dressing adequately and having electricity are not easy. I was brought up in an area where the *section chiefs*[1] have the power of life and death over the citizens, where women have nowhere to go for protection against men's atrocities and abuses. All that is lacking, these abuses and these human rights violations noted in my surroundings have motivated me.

Ironically, after my secondary education, which was often interrupted by a lack of financial resources, I had no thought of becoming a lawyer after graduating from the Teacher's College. On a scholarship from an evangelical organization, I was obligated to return to the countryside to work as a math teacher and manage the organization's schools. Fortunately, there was the School of Law and Economy in Gonaives. Yet, it was not within easy reach considering the distance between my home in Verrettes and Gonaives, the road conditions, and the difficulty of a beginner like me having a car while taking care of my younger brother and sister in particular, and my family in general.

After I defended my thesis entitled "The Haitian Penitentiary System and Human Rights," to finish my law degree in 1993, I set right to work defending human rights. First, during the September 30, 1991 coup period, I worked with the Justice and Peace Commission of Gonaives to train grassroots groups to monitor and denounce human rights violations, and to initiate legal proceedings on behalf of coup victims in the Artibonite Department. After the return of democracy in October 1994, working with the *Bureau des Avocats Internationaux* (BAI) "Bureau of International Lawyers," I helped the police with criminal investigations and supported the efforts of prosecutors and investigating judges in judicial proceedings for crimes committed during the coup period from September 30, 1991 to October 15, 1994. Likewise, I helped victims prepare complaints to start the litigation process. In this work, I continued and deepened my efforts to ensure that the victims' rights were respected by making sure that the cases were successful. The Raboteau massacre trial is proof of the commitment and continuous efforts of the *BAI* to work side by side with the victims in their fight against impunity. The cases of the December 27, 1993 arson in Cité Soleil, the Piatre peasant massacre of March 12 and 13, 1990 will justify this commitment in the near future.

Despite this, as an activist and human rights defender I was inadequately trained. I never took a human rights course in four years of law school (1986-1990). Yet, since I left Law School in 1990, I have been engaged in the service of my society's most vulnerable, defending their human rights.

## I. The Structural Nature of Impunity in Haiti

In Haiti, if there is one thing around which there is a consensus, it is the defense of human rights. It represents, without question, the very foundation of the rule of law in a democratic state. After many years of dictatorship, despite the resistance to change illustrated by multiple coups d'etat, the Republic of Haiti is on the path of democracy. As for the cultivation of respect for human rights principles, the Republic is confronted on one hand with the structural nature of impunity, and on the other with the requirements of the 1987 Constitution.

The struggle against impunity has always been a great concern of the Haitian people, particularly of the human rights defenders and organizations. The Haitian justice system was developed to reinforce the majority of the population's marginalization by establishing mechanisms that prevent any effective response to social conflicts. This is evidenced by its dysfunction and the lack of adequate services. Although the 1987 Constitution establishes minimal judicial guarantees, the habit has yet to enter our custom. It is necessary, in Haiti as elsewhere, to effect a long struggle against impunity for flagrant violations of civil, political, economic, social and cultural rights.[2]

Since the adoption of the Constitution of the Republic in March 1987, the Haitian people's will to build a democratic state has been subjected to numerous challenges which have weakened an already fragile process. The most important of these tests, and undoubtedly the most violent, was the September 30, 1991 coup. The overthrow of a president elected by universal suffrage, and the numerous violations and human rights abuses committed under the *de facto* regime which ran the country up to October 1994, are so many wounds that have marked the memory of a people who, to this day, have never seen their persecutors punished,[3] except for the trials of Carrefour Feuilles in July 2000 and the Raboteau Massacre in September 2000. The Haitian judicial system, like the state apparatus, reproduces the disjunction between the state and its citizens. It is essentially repressive and inaccessible because of the high cost of services and the excessive formalism of the procedures. In the public mind, the anarchy that derives from such a system encourages corruption and impunity.

As indicated above, the Haitian judicial system has yet to bring peace to its society. It does not propose solutions to the disputes that arise between individuals. Every society has conflicts and democracy requires the ability to manage social conflicts. It is evident that the chronic impunity that corrupts Haitian society requires one to call into question mechanisms that impede effective responses to social conflicts.

At the BAI, we consider impunity the central obstacle to efforts to improve the protection of human rights in Haiti. For example, the difficulties and obstacles that we overcame in preparing and conducting the Raboteau Massacre trial reveal that impunity has a multidimensional nature that resists a fair and honest trial, the establishment of truth, the distribution of justice, and the awarding of reparations to the victims. But our experience also shows that these obstacles can be overcome.

The Haitian Penal Code and the Criminal Procedure Code date back to 1835 and are very archaic; they also fall short of modern penal law. The formalism that prevails in the conduct of a trial gives the impression that the procedure is more important than the law, that justice can be reduced to a quarrel over rules. Thus, technical rules, procedural rules and bureaucratic opacity combine to derail the victim's quest for justice and reparation.

The lack of expertise of judicial authorities and police in criminal investigations is also an important aspect of impunity. Contrary to the obligations imposed by the law on the Prosecutor, public prosecutions have started automatically in very few cases. The Raboteau Massacre should have deserved the utmost attention from the judicial authorities at the time, but it was the victims' complaints prepared by our office in 1996 that pushed the judicial authorities to start the prosecution. It was the same for the Cité Soleil Arson and for all other cases of massive and systematic human rights violations committed during the coup period. Many cases stagnated with no follow-up in the Investigating Magistrate's office, or were simply lost in the file cabinets. For example, the case of the Piatre Massacre of March 12 and 13, 1990, spent about nine years in the file drawers of the Investigating Magistrate of the St. Marc trial court, Raphael Jean-Baptiste. Cases in preliminary procedures continue to be trivialized. The weaknesses in the search for truth, the absence of fair trials and the problems of moral and material reparation undermined the efforts of our office, and the hope and confidence of the victims.

In fact, during the dictatorship and coup periods, the judicial power was often associated with the phenomenon of impunity, because it either did not take action against human rights violators or it freed them. The reasons are of a political nature on one hand, and a socio-historical nature on the other.

Frequently, state security is put forward to justify the connivance between the judiciary and the government. The judicial structure makes judicial officials dependent on the central power and therefore the officials are likely to adhere to the government's ideology. Consequently, officials are more loyal to government officials than to the citizenry, because their careers depend on their membership, alliances or links with the government. Behind apolitical appearances, officials are always cornered by subordinate relations to politics.

The Haitian justice structure is the heritage of the Napoleonic model which articulates the judicial corps in a pyramidal structure similar to that of the Army. This vertical model automatically gives rise to a hierarchical justice structure. The right to reform a given judgment is legitimate. But the weak link is the connivance between the government and the judiciary that transforms the higher courts into political institutions. Law is used as a tool of social control.

All this contributes to making impunity a complex phenomenon. In addition, the Haitian penal system is not built to fight against criminality and human rights violations. Indeed, our work at the BAI with the victims of the coup of September 30, 1991 is confronted with obstacles of every kind. First, the laxity of official Magistrates in these cases centered on a dichotomy between officials and victims that in effect excludes the victims from the administration of justice. Then, the organization of the legal system in Haiti suffers from its own dysfunction and leaves a free range to the criminals. Finally, the mobilization of the victims on several occasions without satisfaction being given to them, which establishes an unfavorable climate for them to file complaints and a feeling of discouragement harms the advancement of our cases.

What is most troubling, up to now, is that there has been no real criminal prosecution associated with the old regime. Nor was there a trial of Jean-Claude Duvalier and his henchmen in Haiti. If, after the fall of Duvalier, the military government, known as the National Governing Counsil (CNG) organized some trials, according to most it was a smokescreen. The establishment of the truth on the events occurring during the thirty years of the dictatorial Duvalier regimes simply was not on the agenda. The violations of human rights committed under the Duvaliers remain unpunished. As Jean Léopold Dominique used to say: "the assassins are in the city" and circulate with complete impunity.

When considering my work at the BAI, more than one person has asked the question, "Why Raboteau?" It is necessary to underline the leading role of the BAI, which helped the victims in their efforts and collaborated with the judicial authorities in the realization of the Raboteau Massacre trial, the work done by the Justice and Peace Commission of the Gonaives Diocese which quickly collected witness statements and preserved forensic medical reports, and the National Truth and Justice Commission (CNVJ), which dedicated a chapter of its report to the Raboteau Massacre. In Haiti, legal assistance is not free. It is not easy for a poor peasant to go see a lawyer in his law firm. Moreover, lawyers provide services to those who can pay. Often, lawyers take part in the reproduction of undemocratic structures, which privilege repression and encourage corruption. Overall, the Raboteau Massacre case, Haiti's most complex ever, was heading towards the magic drawer of impunity and "the investigation is continuing."

As mentioned, the judicial apparatus has become an accomplice to the system of political repression. Today, although the political context has changed and the democratic transition is opening the way to judicial independence, we have not left impunity behind. The authors of the great massacres, such as: Jean Rabel, Piatre, Gervais, and Saint Jean Bosco are on the streets.

On July 23, 1987, in Jean Rabel (the Northwest Department), the Haitian Army and *Grandons* (large landowners) killed approximately 120 peasants, and buried them in a common grave following a so-called land conflict. Some of the people implicated in this horrible crime were the Lucas and Poitevin families and corrupt civil servants (judges, prosecutors, surveyors, notaries).

In Piatre (the Artibonite Department), there were reprisals for the death of Section Chief Bénissé Charles and his deputy St. Martin on March 12 and 13 1990. Charles and St. Martin were lynched by the population of Piatre for having killed one of its leaders, Samil Sainfacil, who led the lawsuit against the *Grandon*. A military commando from the Military District of Saint-Marc and from the Montrouis Substation was assisted by civilians from neighboring areas. Armed with revolvers, machetes, spades, sticks, gasoline and explosives and in the pay of the *Grandons,* they invaded the Piatre area and systematically plundered everything. The toll of damage was estimated at 11 persons killed, 375 buildings burned, including two schools, an incalculable quantity of cattle killed and carried off by the attackers, and numerous fields destroyed and burned.

On January 17, 1991, in Gervais (the Artibonite Department), while a group of peasants were claiming their land, the Section Chief Roger Charles and his assistants killed a peasant as a reprisal. The crowd, in a fury, lynched an assistant Section Chief. A military commando from the Military District of Saint-Marc invaded the region, 12 peasants were killed, their corpses devoured by local dogs and pigs, eight other peasants were reported missing, 20 were wounded and 494 houses were burned.

At the Church of Saint Jean Bosco, located in the lower class neighborhood of La Saline in the capital, on September 11, 1988, during mass celebrated by the Father Jean-Bertrand Aristide, men carrying red arm-bands, armed with machetes and other sharp weapons entered into the church courtyard and killed about ten people and wounded dozens of others. One of the victims was a pregnant woman who had her belly opened by one of the killers weapons. As if by a miracle, the mother's and her child's lives were saved and they survived their wounds.

A close look reveals a triad intervening in the majority of land conflict cases:
  a)  The great landowners or *Grandons;*
  b)  The Haitian Armed Forces, a repressive force par excellence;
  c)  The various corrupted civil servants of an exclusionary state: judges, prosecutors, clerks, surveyors, notaries.

These cases are examples of de facto impunity. Impunity does not arise only from legal impunity, which is a legal obstacle that prevents the distribution of justice. It also results from the structural and historical basis of the system. Therefore, the implementation of a systematic and coherent policy for criminal prosecution and compensation for victims of human rights violations is necessary. In addition, one of the principal causes of de facto impunity in Haiti was the army. In fact, the army produced, from January 1, 1804 to September 30, 1991, thirty-two coups d'etat, including four after the vote ratifying the 1987 Constitution. These coups never helped the establishment of the rule of law. For this reason, the prosecutor Roland Paphius declared in his testimony before the criminal court trying the Raboteau Massacre case, "during the coup d'etat of September 30, 1991 to October 15, 1994 justice was thrown in the trash," replaced by the Creole maxim "a constitution is paper, a bayonet is iron." Today the army is dissolved. A political initiative of criminal prosecutions to thwart impunity in all its aspects is imperative.

## II. The 1987 Constitution and Human Rights

The 1987 Constitution and its assumption of responsibility for democratic values requires the abandonment of the repressive tendencies of the state. It lays down the base and foundation of a new justice in Haiti. It obliges the Government to respect, promote and guarantee human rights. Indeed, article 173 of the 1987 Constitution consolidates the judicial power and affirms its independence. This independence requires the creation of a Judicial Academy and the installation of the High Council of the Magistrature. The Judicial Academy will play an important role in the transformation of the traditional behaviors of judges.

To achieve this, it is necessary to introduce into the training curriculum the following elements: a) sociology, in order to reinforce the relationship between judges and citizens and the adaptation of judges to social and cultural realities; b) human rights relating to the Constitution of 1987 and regional and international human rights treaties; and c) judicial ethics, to set out the rights and obligations of judicial officials and establish professional discipline.

In Title III of the Constitution, roughly fifty articles are devoted to the protection of rights and freedoms, and can modify the 1835 Code of Criminal Procedure based on the inquisitorial procedure. This renovation should contribute to the reinforcement of the independence of judicial power. As often happens in newly democratic countries, the use of legal codes before the 1987 Constitution still prevails in Haitians courts. It is indisputably necessary to apply the Constitution of

1987, which seeks to reform the exclusionary state, mired in the meanders of an authoritarian tradition. This reform should lean on pillars such as: democracy, human rights, the separation of state powers and the democratic participation of the people in state decisions. The preamble to the Constitution of 1987 declares:

> "The Haitian people proclaim the Constitution of 1987 to establish a governmental regime based on fundamental freedoms and the respect of human rights, social peace, economic equity, dialogue and participation of all the population in important decisions of national life, by an effective decentralization".

Haiti has signed a plethora of international conventions, most notably the International Covenant on Civil and Political Rights in 1991 and the American Convention on Human Rights in 1979. These conventions introduce elements of judicial guarantees that can trump all legislation incompatible with the rights guaranteed by the 1987 Constitution. As article 276-2 of the 1987 Constitution declares: "Treaties or agreements once sanctioned and ratified in the forms envisaged by the constitution, form part of the legislation of the country and repeal all laws which are contrary to them."

## II.a. Civil and Political Rights

Civil and political rights are guaranteed by the Constitution of 1987. Article 16 states *"The meeting of civil and political rights is the essence of citizenship."* Article 17 states *"All Haitians, regardless of sex or marital status, who have attained twenty-one years of age may exercise their political and civil rights..."* The right to life and safety, the prohibition against torture, cruelty, inhuman and degrading treatment arise from civil and political rights, and are also guaranteed. The Haitian judicial system, in particular the criminal law, was conceived as an instrument to serve the executive and makes the judicial official subservient to the political powers on which it is dependent. In such a context, the individual is relegated to the second tier and is sacrificed on the altar of "social order." Full civil and political rights, although formulated in the Constitution of 1987, remain, despite the efforts so far to implement them, wishful thinking.

*"The right to life is inherent to all human beings. This right must be protected by the law. No one can be arbitrarily deprived of life."* The Constitution of 1987 devotes its articles 19 and 20 to guarantee the right to life. In Haiti's recent history, death by electrocution of fifteen young people watching a basketball game in Petit-Goâve shows that the State does not respect human life. Indeed, the technicians of Electricity of Haiti were content to only repair a used electrical cable

instead of replacing it. Nothing was done to prevent this imminent danger. Such actions by the State with respect to its citizens are an insult to the Constitution of 1987, the Universal Declaration of Human Rights and the International Covenant for Civil and Political Rights.

The double murder of Jean Léopold Dominique and his guardian Jean-Claude Louissaint continues to draw attention. This case has progressed only slowly in pre-trial proceedings, thanks to the countless advocacy initiatives of *Radio Haiti Inter*, human rights organizations and certain members of civil society. As of this date, the Port-au-Prince Court of Appeals has annulled the indictment and remanded the case to the investigating magistrate for new pre-trial proceedings. Summary executions for political reasons have not ceased. The attempted murder of Duverger in Petit-Goave, the murders of the journalist Brignol Lindor, the Justice of the Peace of Lascahobas, Christophe Lozama, the events of July 28 and December 17, 2001, the recent violence of the fugitive from justice, Jean Pierre, a.k.a. Tatoune in Gonaives are part of a series of violence and repression that the police have not been able to prevent, or even punish. During the coup period from September 1991 to October 15, 1994, it was obvious that the summary executions had political motives. The process of transformation towards a democratic society requires that respect for justice and human rights must be engaged and consolidated. It will be necessary to go further, to transform mentalities to promote the respect of the principles of the rule of law, the constitution, the Universal Declaration of Human Rights, and Treaties.

*"Every individual has the right to freedom and to personal safety."* The Constitution of 1987, in articles 24, 25, 26 and 27 guarantees individual liberties and bodily integrity. Article 24 reads as follows: *"Individual liberty is guaranteed and protected by the State."* The right to freedom and bodily integrity imposes a limit on the State to apply its penal capacity in extreme cases and to punish only those actions which cause a serious wrong to society. Arrests that are without warrants and outside of the legal hours are often accompanied by ill treatment and torture. Some prisoners remain in prison for several days, even months, and most have served their sentence before they are brought before a judge, in violation of the 48 hour deadline set by the 1987 Constitution.

*"No one can be disturbed for his opinions."* Concerning the freedom of speech, article 28 of the Constitution establishes it in the following terms: *"Every Haitian has the right to express his opinions freely on any matter by any means he chooses."* Freedom of speech is one of the essential pillars of a democratic society founded on the rule of law, pluralism, tolerance, openness, justice, and mutual respect. Often under the dictatorships, repression was exerted on journalists and

broadcasting stations. During the period of the September 1991 coup, stations were closed by soldiers and others preferred to voluntarily close for fear of reprisals. In the countryside, those who tried to disseminate information on the exactions of the soldiers were persecuted, attacked and insulted.

Since the return of Constitutional order, people who are making use of their freedom of speech and opinion have abused this freedom, because they use it in a defamatory manner. With the political crisis generated by the legislative elections of May 21, 2000, freedom of opinion and speech are blocked by the actions of non-state actors. A journalist, apart from his or her penal and civil responsibilities, is obliged to respect professional ethics by article 28-2 of the 1987 Constitution. These ethics require a journalist to provide fair reporting. Journalists have the obligation to verify the accuracy of their information and sources and to find the subjects of their reports in order to give them the opportunity to respond to all allegations of misconduct. *"Analyses and commentary must be identified as such and must not distort the facts."* It is necessary in Haiti, indeed, to reconcile the freedom of the press on one hand, with the right of people not to have third parties damage their honor, their reputation and their private life on the other hand. It is to be noted, today, that the majority of media outlets are confirmed opponents of the governing authorities.

The Constitution of 1987 insists on the positive role of the state in development and the implementation of policies related to services in education, medical care, land distribution and other social and economic rights. Individual liberties are guaranteed (article 24). The Office for the Protection of the Citizens created by the Constitution of 1987 is implicated in the process of transforming the relationship between the State and its citizens in order to guarantee to some extent human rights in Haiti. This institution, therefore, is called to play an important role in Haitian public administration, by obtaining better protection for citizens experiencing difficulty with the public administration and by rectifying abuses strongly marked by the all-powerful character of the state and decisions that cannot be appealed. The local collectives, one of the great innovations of the Constitution of 1987, break the centralism of the State apparatus by instituting democratic participation in civic affairs through administrative decentralization. They allow the decentralization of the functions of public institutions through the principle of citizenship participation and democratic control. The 1987 Constitution granted local collectives the right to participate in the mechanism for nominating judges.[4]

Emphasizing this break from the dictatorial past, the 1987 Constitution requires the establishment of control mechanisms – the development of institutions to ensure the independence of their powers (Executive, Legislative, Judiciary). In addition, the Constitution recognizes the necessity to reform the Judiciary in order to combat human rights violations and to struggle against age-old impunity. Today, the rules and mechanisms for access to the courts must be clearly defined. There is therefore a fourfold challenge. The modernization of penal justice requires:

- The recognition and the obligations of the 1987 Constitution and those established by regional and international instruments;
- The adoption of penal law in the Haitian cultural context in order to ensure its effectiveness;
- The democratization of access to legal services as a means to realize the equality of individuals before the law;
- The re-appropriation of the right of victims to compensation in the context of a fair trial, that is, give back the law to the citizenry. Judicial independence is the spearhead of a justice system that is effective, accessible, fair, impartial, transparent, honest and at the service of the citizens.

## II.b. Implementing the 1987 Constitution

There was ample resistance to change illustrated inter alia by the successive coups d'etat, which removed, notably, the first democratically elected government. In response, several mechanisms were established to break the exclusionary state and construct the foundations of a democratic state that would protect and maintain individual rights and freedoms. One notes, although serious violations persist, we have seen notable improvements in the respect of rights and freedoms in Haiti. For the first time, after nearly two hundred years, on February 7, 1996 a democratically elected President transferred power to another one elected by universal suffrage. For the first time in our country, an elected President completed his mandate, from February 7, 1996 to February 7, 2001, voluntarily transferred power to his successor, and returned to his home region to resume the life of a citizen.

Not long after the return of the constitutional order, the authorities set up a complaint office to help victims of human rights violations during the September 30, 1991 coup period. Secondly, the government implemented the recommendations made by the National Commission of Truth and Justice. This meant creating what the Commission described as a model of courts based on impartiality, transparency, integrity and judicial independence and the installation of an authority to coordinate, energize and pursue legal reform.

The third major mechanism set up by the government was the Bureau of International Lawyers (BAI), which supports the efforts of judges and prosecutors in the pursuit of justice in crimes committed before, during and after the coup. Cases which pre-date the coup are: the Jean Rabel massacre of July 23, 1987 (still in pre-trial proceedings in Port-de-Paix); the Saint Jean Bosco attack of September 11, 1988 (still in pre-trial proceedings in Port-au-Prince); and the Piatre massacre of March 12-13, 1990 (indictment recently issued).

One of the crimes being investigated by the BAI which occurred during the coup is the December 27, 1993 Cité Soleil arson attack for which the indictment was recently issued, but was appealed to the Supreme Court. Another is the April 18 and 22, 1994 Raboteau Massacre. Over three years ago, on November 10, 2000, the Criminal Court of Gonaives decided the case, convicting 16 the 22 accused present and 37 by absentia; three of whom were deported from the United States and are in a national penitentiary, while the convictions have been appealed to the Supreme Court, which blocks the execution of the civil judgment. In the case of the assassination of Antoine Izmery on September 11, 1993, the Criminal Court of Port-au-Prince decided the case on September 25, 1995, by convicting 13 accused in absentia, one of whom, Captain Jackson Joanis, has been deported from the United States and is currently being questioned by judicial authorities. The assassination of Justice Minister Guy Malary on October 14, 1993, and the assassination of Jean-Marie Vincent on August 28, 1994 are also on the BAI's agenda. In the Vincent case the indictment was issued and appealed by ex-Captain Jackson Joanis to the Court of Appeals of Port-au-Prince.

In terms of crimes committed after the coup, the most prominent is perhaps the assassination of Jean Léopold Dominique and Jean Claude Louissaint. The indictment was issued but remanded by the Court of Appeals of Port-au-Prince to the investigating magistrate for additional investigation. The BAI is also working on the July 28, 2001 attack on several police stations, which is before the investigating magistrate of Port-au-Prince; the attempted coup of December 17, 2001 and violence committed in response which is before the investigating magistrate of Port-au-Prince; the Office of Prosecution and Follow-up, a body of the Ministry of Justice and Public Security, created at the beginning of 1997 which offered legal and financial assistance to victims of human rights violations.

In the struggle to resist regression or any arbitrary order, the human rights and victims' organizations play a critical role in denouncing the injustice and impunity that reign over the country. They bring another important element by demanding justice and compensation for their injuries. The adherence of Haitian governments to the principal regional and international human rights instruments would induce profound changes. A democratic state must take care to ratify the international treaties[5] that promote human rights. The nomination of members of the Permanent Law Reform Commission,[6] created in 1959,[7] is a significant step towards ensuring the transition of the penal system towards a modern and humane system responding to the obligations of the rule of law and to obligations established by regional and international treaties.

During the period of democratic transition and the valorization of human rights, the lawyer is well situated to apply the principles of human rights conventions in trial and appellate courts. Lawyers should invoke these principles in their discourses, and require consideration of the principles. The lawyer must also ensure that human rights, which are fundamentally guaranteed and recognized by the 1987 Constitution and international law, are respected. This should be undertaken in order to effect the modernization of legislation relating to the exercise of the legal profession.

A right is based on the concept of dignity, that is on the concept of "being" and not "having" or on the social and economic program of a government or a political party. A political program can and should be negotiated, whereas dignity is not negotiable. Political programs are necessary to honor human rights, but they cannot be a substitute for them. Political programs are subject to changes in the social and economic dynamic, and what is important today may not be so tomorrow. Dignity is immutable; it is the same at all times and in all places, and its essence transcends cultural, social, economical, political, racial and religious differences.[8] The human rights approach should neither attack nor support any particular form of government. Nor should it reinforce the existing system of exclusion and domination. The human rights approach implies an important alternate route towards the establishment of a new justice system. Moreover, the principal stake is none other than the establishment and consolidation of democracy.

## III. Government Action Against Impunity Since 1994

Haitian legal administration, strongly influenced by the official system of exclusion and repression, is characterized by ineffectiveness that involves, on one hand, a situation of uncertainty for people before the courts in ordinary disputes, and, on the other hand, a mistrust about the time required to resolve matters. As noted above, impunity is the trademark of the Haitian legal system.

Moreover, justice in Haiti has historically served money and power. Realizing this reinforced the conviction that the country's leaders must leave behind the old practices that ignored the people's claims. At stake is nothing less than the establishment and consolidation of the rule of law. The process of establishing and consolidating the rule of law after the return to the constitutional order needed to embrace, by action, the claims for justice by the victims of the September 1991 coup d'etat.

## III.a. The Raboteau Trial

The governmental authorities took steps to provide a response to the cries for justice of the coup victims and, at the same time, to eradicate age-old impunity. For example, the Raboteau Trial is a considerable step in the fight against impunity. This effort must continue, as much for the accused and the victims as for justice and all of Haitian society. The success of the trial was a necessary condition for the restoration of confidence in the judiciary, and, consequently, must be considered as part of the overall context of judicial reform and justice in Haiti.

Raboteau is a shantytown in Gonaives that from the very beginning opposed the September 30, 1991 coup d'etat. During the first trimester of 1994, the army undertook vast operations to counter all opposition to the de facto regime throughout the country. On Monday, April 18, 1994, the hostilities began, and culminated with the blood bath of April 22, 1994, commonly called the "Raboteau Massacre." According to the National Commission of Truth and Justice (CNVJ), "according to approximately thirty victims who filed their complaints with the CNVJ, the April 18, 1994 operation was primarily used as a training session in preparation for the massacre of April 22, to meticulously observe the flight patterns of people, which permitted better preparation and planning the technical details for the massacre's success."

On Friday, April 22, 1994, at dawn, soldiers of the Toussaint-Louverture barracks in Gonaives, in full battle gear, surrounded and encircled Raboteau, escorted by members of the paramilitary group, Front for the Advancement and Progress of Haiti (FRAPH), and *attachés*. The first shootings announced the terror. Several commandos were operating: some had the mission to operate on the ground; others embarked on boats and positioned themselves on the sea in front of Raboteau. They were deployed in such a way that the population had no way out, and was trapped, vulnerable to gunshots coming from both sides. These poor souls were forced to lie on the ground, and were then beaten, insulted and humiliated. Some were compelled to roll in open sewers or mud. The weakest, as well as the women and children, were kept prisoners inside their houses, subject to blows and mistreatment. The commandos ransacked, plundered, pulverized and left destruction in their wake. They stole money, jewelry and all valuable articles. The population, panicked and distressed in the face of such a terror, tried to flee to escape the carnage but was caught in a trap. Some young people were shot like animals and killed. Others who tried to flee by sea did not suspect the cruel trap that closed on them, making them the target of the commandos already posted on the sea, waiting for their prey.

At the beginning of the afternoon, when the shootings were ending and the city of Gonaives was holding its breath, the shantytown of Raboteau became a true desert, resembling a district destroyed after the passage of a fatal cyclone. The authorities blocked all judicial investigations and all investigation or even approach by journalists and human rights organizations, especially the Justice and Peace Commission of the Diocese of Gonaives. Nonetheless, the Justice of the Peace, Jean Baptiste Dorismond, a Raboteau native, began an investigation. The corpses of the young people killed on solid ground and those pushed back by the waves of the sea were not restored to their families. These corpses were simply thrown in a hole dug hastily and not too deep, at the mercy of dogs and pigs wandering in the neighborhood.

Any violation of human rights gives birth to a right to compensation in favor of the victim or his/her survivors. The victims of the Raboteau massacre, assisted by the Bureau of International Lawyers (BAI), took the legal path to assert this right, the right to obtain compensation, to rehabilitation and to see their torturers punished in accordance with the criminal law for the crimes and offenses they committed. Thus, in accordance with the legally guaranteed standards, the Criminal Court of Gonaives, sitting with a jury on November 10, 2000, after six weeks of intense pleading, convicted 16 of the 22 present on the dock. Among these, 12 were sentenced to life in prison. Top leaders of the army, such as General Raoul Cédras, commander-in-chief of the Army and Colonel Michel François were convicted *in absentia* and given life sentences but the Haitian Code of Criminal Procedure gives them the right to a new trial. A total of 37 were convicted *in absentia* and given life sentences. Out of the criminal trial came two civil judgments. The first, dated Thursday November 16, 2000 finds the 37 *in absentia* defendants jointly liable for one (1) billion gourdes, about $23 million. The second, dated December 18, 2000 finds the 16 convicted in person liable for two billion two hundred and fifty million gourdes, about $53 million.

It is necessary to note, unfortunately, that as of this writing the civil judgments have not been executed because the 16 convicted in person have appealed the case to the Supreme Court. Up to now, the Supreme Court has not issued a decision, which prevents the execution of the civil judgments. As remarked earlier, impunity is multidimensional.

Other cases are pending, such as: the Cite Soleil arson of December 27, 1993, the Piatre Massacre of March 12 –13, 1990, and the case of women victims of politically motivated rape and sexual assault during the coup. The Cite Soleil case is before the Supreme Court, as the accused appealed the indictment. In the Piatre case, the indictment was issued in December 2003. Fifty-three accused were ordered sent to a jury trial. Of the fifty-three indicted, nine are in prison, including former military dictator General Prosper Avril. The others are fugitives in Haiti, the U.S. and in the Dominican Republic. The Piatre indictment is not only a historic achievement by the Haitian justice system, but also the product of the tenacity and courage of the victims and their organization *(Tet Kole Ti Payizan Piat)*, who have struggled to obtain justice and to protect their land against the large landowners. The case of the women victims of politically motivated rape and sexual assault is in the preparatory phase.

### III.b. Judicial Reform Law

On May 8, 1998, the Haitian Parliament passed a judicial reform law that removed the statute of limitations for crimes and misdemeanors committed during the coup period from September 30, 1991 to October 15, 1994. Articles 466 and 467 of the Criminal Procedure Code set out the statute of limitations and are often invoked to impede the prosecution of human rights violators.

The Haitian justice system is "sick", the sickest of all the Republic's institutions. Contrary to the democratic rule of law that the 1987 Constitution proscribes, the judicial administration still follows the exclusionary model, resulting in justice that is inaccessible, ineffective, delayed, and disrespectful of basic rights. Judicial reform must bring a new conception of the administration of justice. It must make a clean break from the tradition of repression, exclusion and opacity. It is imperative that the fight for judicial reform and against impunity be inextricable.

### III.c. The National Commission of Truth and Justice (CNVJ)

The establishment of the National Commission of Truth and Justice by the decrees of December 17, 1994 and March 28, 1995 was a necessary preparation for breaking with the heritage of the past. The Commission was charged with establishing the truth about violations of human rights that took place between September 30, 1991 and October 15, 1994. Indeed, the March 28, 1995 decree stresses the need to establish the rule of law. The search for the truth is essential to national reconciliation: *"To establish the overall truth about the serious human rights violations committed between September 29, 1991 and October 15, 1994 inside and outside of the country."* On walls near the National Palace, the graffiti expresses clearly the popular demands regarding the thorny question of national reconciliation: "No reconciliation without justice."

### III.d. September 29, 1995 Decree
On September 29, 1995, President Jean-Bertrand Aristide issued an executive order that granted 20% of the Ministry of Justice budget to victims of the September 1991 coup d'etat,[9] in order to provide support and legal assistance. On July 15, 1996, the Haitian Parliament followed suit when it voted and allocated the sum of sixty million gourdes from the national budget to victims of the coup.

# CONCLUSION

In Haiti, human rights must become the object of a massive popular campaign in order to arrive at a shared understanding. Today human rights are helping to concretize the rule of law, and have become a two-edged sword in politics. For example, a crime committed against someone can be viewed as a human rights violation in one case and not be seen as such in another case, depending on who is making the claim. It is necessary to reshape the mentality of the people lawyers, judges, politicians, and litigants with respect to the principles of the rule of law, the Haitian Constitution, the Universal Declaration of Human Rights, and of human rights treaties and conventions.

Currently there is a perceived chasm between Port-au-Prince and the rest of the country, between the oligarchy and the rural peasants and urban proletariat. The lack of a culture of respect for fundamental rights, the lack of economic resources and the class conflicts generated by the inequality of access to resources must be added to this conclusion. At present, the Haitian government cannot fully play its citizen protection role. However, we must take into account that the efforts and will that the government has displayed run headlong into the defects from past dictatorships that still afflict the justice system.

At this stage of the democratic transition, the culture of the respect for human rights principles must remain the spearhead of the rule of law. Activists, victims organizations, human rights defenders and the international community must promote a wider and deeper interpretation of human rights in Haiti. Relevant government agencies must respect the obligations based on international treaties and other standards which human rights law imposes.

*You are always preoccupied with violence perpetrated by machine-guns and machetes. Nevertheless, there is also another form of violence that exists that you must be aware of.*

---

[1] Former rural Police and Haitian Armed Forces auxiliary. In an effort to decentralize and dismantle this system of oppression, section chiefs are replaced now by the Administration Council of the Commune (CASEC).

[2] International Civilian Mission in Haiti, OEA/ONU, The Struggle Against Impunity and for Reparation in Haiti p.147.

[3] Jean Bertrand Aristide, *Investir dans l'Humain,* Port-au-Prince, December 16, 1999, p. 158.

[4] 1987 Haitian Constitution, art. 175: "Supreme Court Justices are appointed by the President of the Republic from a list submitted by the Senate of three (3) persons per court seat. Judges of the Courts of Appeal and Trial Courts are appointed from a list submitted by the relevant Departmental Assembly; Justices of the Peace are appointed by a list drawn up by the Communal Assemblies."

[5] Mattarolo R." *Protection des droits de l'homme en Haïti et la ratification des traités"* Conférence, 7 May 1997, Académie Nationale Diplomatique et Consulaire, Port-au-Prince, Haïti.

[6] Decree of 12 December 2002 nominating the members of the *"Commission Permanente de Refonte des Codes Haïtiens"* (Permanent Code Reform Commission).

[7] Decree of 24 January 1959 creating at the Departement of Justice a mechanism called the *"Commission Permanente de Refonte des Codes Haitiens"* and Decree of 29 March 1977 creating and organizing the *"Commission de Refonte des codes Haitiens".*

[8] Jean Dreze et Amartya Sen: Economic Development and Social Opportunity, Oxford India Paperbacks 1998.

[9] Decree of September 29, 1995, art. 1 "Victims of the coup d'Etat of Septembre 30, 1991 or their families shall be provided with: a) legal assistance; b) compensation for damages, for which the amount and form will be determined by the appropriate authorities. Outside of other grants, 20% of the budget of the Ministry of Justice will be dedicated to this end."

# CHAPTER FOUR

*Manjèd ze pa konn doulè manman poul.*

The egg-eater does not know the pain of the mother hen.

# The Corruption of Democracy
## *Melinda Miles*

Haiti is a devastated place where poverty reigns and the majority of people do not have enough resources to eat even once each day. The devastation of today is the result of a deadly trend that has been underway since the beginning of the 20$^{th}$ Century. Steadily increasing poverty is not the only major characteristic of this trend; almost an entire century of governments controlled by the tiny Haitian elite and the military they largely controlled created the framework for the destruction of Haiti. Haiti's powerful neighbor to the North, the United States, dictated the terms of this destruction.

This ruinous trend began with the U.S. occupation of Haiti from 1915-34. Previously, the majority of Haitians lived decent lives as peasant farmers. The U.S. "treaty" government that ruled Haiti during the occupation restructured the country economically and politically to better serve U.S. business interests, setting the stage for a century long decline in the living conditions of most Haitians.

Haitians finally began to build democracy in 1990, after a popular movement dislodged the U.S.-sponsored Duvalier hereditary dictatorship and subsequent military juntas supported by the U.S. Voters elected the leader of the *Lavalas* popular movement, Father Jean-Bertrand Aristide, in Haiti's first democratic election. Eight months into his term, the U.S. supported the military and Haiti's business elite in a coup d'etat. Haitians were tortured, disappeared, killed and exiled every day for three years as the consequences for having dared to dream of a government that could serve the interests of the poor, while their elected government languished in exile in Washington, DC.

The United States finally bowed to the pressure from solidarity activists and residents of Florida, where thousands of Haitians were arriving on boats, and restored the government to power in 1994. However, the president the Americans returned to Haiti was weakened by the conditions of his return. The U.S. required him to leave office in 1995 even though he had served the bulk of his term in exile, and forced him to accept a structural adjustment program. His successor, Rene Preval, bore the brunt of the U.S. funded International Republican Institute's work to build "democratic pluralism" when the parliament stalled and refused to move forward with any of his policies. Preval's Prime Minister worked to usher through privatization, a linchpin of the structural adjustment program, until he fell into such disfavor with the population that he was forced to step down.

Privatization and lowered import tariffs were the primary economic policies forced on Haiti as collateral for the return of democracy in 1994. These policies hurt the very people who had fought for democracy by undermining local food production and workers' rights. Haitians had risked their lives because they believed that a democratic government would represent their interests. Instead, these economic policies destroyed the livelihood of peasant farmers and created the pool of cheap labor necessary for the advancement of sweatshop factories and free trade zones. Privatization, a pillar of structural adjustment in Haiti, threatened to rob the government of one of its only legal sources of income.

In the year 2000 Haitians had another chance to move forward on the path to democracy. Their old hero, Aristide, led the new Fanmi Lavalas political party to elections. Haitians took a chance and voted for this new party, only to have their mandate questioned by the international community. The controversy related to only .2% of the local and legislative elections.

With help from the United States, the political and business elite organized themselves into a coalition and blocked progress towards democracy. They boycotted presidential elections in November 2000 and set unrealistic goalposts for their participation in Haiti's political future. Disregarding the fact that these people had no support from the Haitian population (as evidenced by the elections in 2000 as well as U.S.-commissioned Gallup opinion polls), the U.S. granted this coalition a virtual veto over the electoral process. Attempts to force the Aristide government to comply came in the form of a U.S. embargo on humanitarian assistance. This accomplished the dual goal of handicapping the Haitian government and deepening the suffering of the Haitian people. True to form, the opposition coalition supported the embargo and began to call for the violent overthrow of the democratically elected government.

President Aristide has now served 60% of his term. One meaningful consequence of the protracted political crisis is that we will never know what his government may have accomlpished had they not been held hostage by the embargo.

Haiti is not an isolated case, but it is perhaps the most tragic one. As evidenced by the history of the U.S. relationship with Haiti, two of the fundamental principles of U.S. policy are to undermine democracy that can lead to a redistribution of money and power, and to promote compliant rulers. These leaders, many of them hand selected by the U.S. government, adhere to the status quo, deepening poverty for the majority of Haitians and limiting representation of these people in domestic policy decisions. More importantly, compliant rulers create an environment in which American economic interests can flourish – something unlikely to occur were it a true democracy.

As Haiti reaches the bicentennial of its independence, Washington and Haiti's opposition coalition continue to create obstacles to moving forward. U.S.-commissioned Gallup polls show that the U.S. strategy is working – the poor are getting poorer, and they are becoming disillusioned with the democracy they have wanted for so long, the democracy for which their mothers and fathers died.

It appears that the U.S. won't feel successful in Haiti until the popular movement for democracy is crushed and a compliant ruler is installed. The U.S. has gone so far as to occupy Haiti to accomplish this in the past. The current strategy is to hold the government hostage through negotiations and resolutions until the Haitian people become so disillusioned with their government that they are willing to accept any government supported by the U.S.

Then the corruption of democracy will be complete.

***

*"A very simple theory of democratization: the poor want democracy and the rich want nondemocracy, and the balance of political power between the two groups determines whether the society transits from nondemocracy to democracy (perhaps also whether democracy, once created, becomes consolidated or reverts back to nondemocracy later)."[1]*

This chapter analyzes U.S. policy towards Haiti, specifically the impact of U.S. policy on Haitian efforts to build a democracy that would serve the interests of its poor majority. By delving into the reality of the Haiti-U.S. relationship, it becomes clear that the U.S.'s economic objectives, systematized into programs advanced by international financial institutions, outweigh any good intentions to support a better Haiti. These economic policies are devastating to Haiti's economy and aggravate existing poverty. Moreover, the future of U.S. economic policy is being secured today by a campaign to weaken voter participation and confidence in the Haitian government through a series of destabilization efforts.

This chapter is intentionally focused on the effect of U.S. policies and hence does not fully analyze the domestic power-holders in Haiti or their positive and negative impacts on democracy building.

# I. The First U.S. Restructuring of Haitian Society and Economy

Before U.S. intervention and occupation at the beginning of the 20th Century, each of Haiti's eleven independent regions had its own oligarchy, with a landlord, military, administration, and merchants. The largest group of Haitians was (and still is) the peasant class, the vast majority of whom have never owned land. According to economics professor and historian Georges Werleigh, land was owned by three groups of people during colonial times: white, mulatto, and black slave owners. After the revolution, much of the free land was the private domain of the state. Landowners couldn't work their own land, and so by 1883 three classes of people existed: (1) the landowners, or bourgeoisie; (2) the land-less agricultural workers, or peasants; and (3) the rural bourgeoisie.[2]

The oligarchy that controlled each of the eleven regions usurped any surplus from economy for its own benefit, so even poor Haitians who owned their land remained impoverished. However, there was a railroad system operating in the country, and peasants were generally able to feed their families and live decent lives; Haitians did not yet know famine. The American occupation changed the system from eleven regional centers to one centralized capital of politics and commerce, a change that brought widespread poverty to Haiti for the first time.[3]

In 1915 American Marines were sent to occupy Haiti. The official reason was to end the widespread violence and to protect the lives and property of foreigners living in Haiti.[4] In the 72 years from 1843 to 1915, Haiti had experienced "102 civil wars, revolutions, insurrections, revolts, coups and *attentats* (assassination attempts)."[5] The occupation regime was created a by a treaty that the "U.S. insisted upon, [in which] it enjoyed sweeping powers, including control over customs receipts and the national budget."[6] Ending violence was not the only interest served by the occupation. Other major concerns revolved around European influence in the region. The Germans had a strong influence on the Haitian economy, and there was fear that the British would attempt to take power in the region once the Panama Canal was completed, making control of the Windward Passage strategically important if the U.S. was going to expand its hegemonic power in the hemisphere.[7]

At the time of the occupation, Haiti was operating under a Constitution drafted in 1889 that included a law banning foreign ownership of land. This law had been passed down from Haiti's first Constitution in 1801, written by Toussaint-Louverture before the end of the revolution. Louverture's Constitution systematized the rules of land and property rights, and the Code Rural of 1824 did the same. Other sets of rules for land ownership were introduced in 1848, and in the constitutions drafted during the 19th Century. In each of these, land ownership was restricted to Haitians.[8]

In 1917 the U.S. State Department drafted a new Haitian Constitution, and for the first time in its history, land ownership in Haiti was open to foreigners. When the Haitian legislature refused to approve it, the U.S. Marines suspended the legislature, a suspension that lasted twelve years. "A 'popular' plebiscite in which less than 5% of the electorate participated approved the U.S.-endorsed constitution."[9] This wasn't the only time that decisions in Haiti were made without voter participation.

Changing the land ownership law had a tremendous impact on Haiti's economy during and after the occupation. "With this industrial basis capitalism came to Haiti, and there was an attempt to reinstall colonial plantations."[10] By the 1920's, American firms were buying state lands for large agribusiness enterprises. One of these, the Haitian American Sugar Company (HASCO), cleared trees from fertile areas to make way for sugar production, marking the beginning of widespread deforestation and erosion.

To implement the radical changes in Haiti's economic structure, the U.S. Marines transformed the Haitian Guard (later the Haitian Army, or *Force Armee d'Haiti)*. The Guard was tasked with enforcing a relocation of the seat of political power. Before the occupation, each of the eleven regions had its own economic center, while most political decisions were made in the North. Occupation moved the political center to Port-au-Prince, and the return to large plantation agriculture also facilitated the centralization of economy.

Before long Haiti's society and economy had been drastically altered. As Brenda Gayle Plummer notes, "The development of a more highly organized, centralized state was a product of the occupation era... The expanding state sacrificed the regional centers to its own economic imperatives – concentrating capital and infrastructure in Port-au-Prince and leaving the hinterlands increasingly impoverished."[11]

The landowners, Haiti's traditional elite, and American business owners had little in common when the occupation began, except perhaps that "they all agreed on the task of exploiting Haiti's limited resources."[12] By the time the occupation ended, however, the relationship between the two forces had been forged. The 20th

Century would be characterized by the alliance between these two forces: Haiti's business elite and America's business elite.

The American occupation at the beginning of the 20th Century ended the armed uprising that threatened Haiti's stability and Marines built roads that strengthened Haiti's infrastructure. However, the occupation did nothing to halt the declining standard of living for the majority of Haiti's peasants, rather, the treaty government set into motion new economic policies that are the precursors of today's widespread poverty.

Even during the thirty-year Duvalier family dictatorship, the economic goals of the Haitian and American business elite would dictate Haiti's economy. Duvalier continued the trend towards centralization, and enjoyed the tacit support of the American government as he transformed the tiny villages of Haiti into a network of terror with his infamous *TonTon Macoutes* killing squads. Democratic organization and resistance during the Duvalier era were met with illegal imprisonment, torture and death. For more detail on U.S. relations with the Duvaliers, see Brian Concannon's contribution in Chapter III.

The next major U.S. intervention coincided with the advent of democracy in Haiti. Even during the darkest days of the Duvalier dictatorship and the military juntas that followed, the grassroots movement for democracy, better known as *lavalas,* grew like a flood from the grassroots. Haitian democracy would inevitably challenge economic policies that impoverished the majority of Haitians, and the U.S. would respond by challenging democracy's ability to alter the status quo.

## II. Democracy and the Death Plan

The story of the Lavalas movement for democracy and its first leader, Jean-Betrand Aristide, is well known to all who know Haiti. Aristide, a priest in the slums of Port-au-Prince, rose to national popularity through radio broadcasts of his fiery sermons. Based on liberation theology, Aristide's speeches frequently called for a new social order, one in which all of Haiti's people would be able to sit together at the table created from the country's resources. He called the poor, crouched on the dirt floor beneath the table, to overturn the social order.[13]

Lavalas was a grassroots movement that intended to change the face of Haitian politics, replacing the traditional political elite with democratically elected leaders who could represent the needs of Haiti's impoverished majority. "A transition to democracy shifts future political power away from the rich to the poor, thereby creating a credible commitment to future pro-poor policies and future redistribution."[14] As Alex Dupuy explains in *Haiti in the New World Order:*

> "Lavalas, in short, could be thought of as a broad popular front that aimed to dismantle the prebendary and discredited dictatorship and build a democratic state that made the demands of the excluded and exploited majority a priority and sought their full participation in setting the agenda of their communities and the nation."[15]

The Lavalas movement was up against forces more powerful than the tiny Haitian elite in their efforts to change Haiti's political and economic structure. The U.S. played a major role in creating the Haiti that produced the Lavalas movement, and had stakes in keeping things as they were. The Lavalas movement endeavored to create a moderate social democracy in Haiti[16] and was in direct contradiction to the imperatives of U.S. policy.

In 1990, Aristide won a landslide in Haiti's first democratic elections. The United States, United Nations, Organization of American States and many bilateral missions observed the 1990 elections, declaring them free and fair. Haiti's first democratically elected president took office in February 1991 with an ambitious and progressive plan. The three pillars of the Lavalas plan were:

> "Collectively characterized as components of 'a transition from misery to poverty with dignity,' they included (1) the decentralization of political structures to increase popular participation in decision-making at the rural, communal, departmental and national levels; (2) a literacy campaign; and (3) agrarian reform."[17]

As Haiti's first democratically elected president, Aristide needed to juggle the forces at play in Haiti: the impoverished rural majority, the urban poor, and the business elite. As Dupuy explains, "Occupying public office would necessarily place constraints on Aristide's actions."[18] The fiery sermons that characterized his priesthood would not serve him well as president, as they would surely alienate the most powerful and well-connected Haitians. Aristide also faced the expansive challenge of establishing democratic rule and building democratic institutions in a country where there were none. His political party, which attempted to encompass several small pre-existing political parties like the OPL, who backed his presidential campaign, and the millions of Lavalas constituents throughout the countryside, was weakly organized. "Despite its unquestionably democratic aspirations, Lavalas was not a democratically structured organization."[19]

In September 1991, conflicting powers within Haiti – Lavalas and its new government on one side, and the traditional elite with the backing of the United States on the other – came into confrontation. The traditional elite won, and a military coup d'etat on September 30 sent the Aristide government into exile and began a reign of torture, imprisonment and massacre for all those who had supported the democratic government. As is explored in detail elsewhere in this book, the U.S. government overtly called for the return of democratic rule while covertly supporting the coup regime and its paramilitary killing squads.

In 1994, as the level of human rights abuses escalated and thousands of Haitian refugees were arriving on Florida's shores, the United States was forced to return President Aristide to power in Haiti. Dupuy notes, "In the end, only a power bigger than the Haitian Army could veto the army's veto of the democratic process. And that power did not reside with Aristide or his Lavalas movement, but with the 'cold country to the North'."[20] Unwilling to let the Lavalas progressive agenda proceed, the U.S. returned Aristide with conditions that crippled his government. First, Aristide was required to conclude his five-year term as president in February 1996, regardless of the fact that he had spent most of that time in exile. Secondly, Aristide would implement certain economic austerity measures, known as structural adjustments, upon his return to power.

The power of the U.S. and the international financial institutions (IFIs) to usher in the era of structural adjustment came from the fact that the Aristide government couldn't proceed without the capital promised by these institutions. Two billion dollars was earmarked for Haiti for the period 1994-99.[21] This money came with many conditions, and the impact of these conditions has been immense.

## The Death Plan

In Haiti, the structural adjustment program (SAP) is referred to as the "death plan." Traditionally, SAPs are a series of formulaic economic reforms including decreased public services and a transfer of economic power to market forces. Although some of the elements of structural adjustment may be beneficial to the country in question, the universal application of the full set of adjustments has generally disastrous effects on the economies of developing countries. Where SAPs have generated economic growth for the economy as a whole, they have made the poor poorer and more numerous.[22]

SAPs are programs with a component from the International Monetary Fund (IMF), and in Haiti the IMF works hand-in-hand with the World Bank (WB). The U.S. has controlling power in both of these institutions.[23] At the same time, U.S. government-funded programs through the U.S. Agency for International Development furthered the same goals as the SAP. In Haiti the structural adjustment program:

> "Narrows the role of the state and controls government spending, privatizes state-owned enterprises (SOEs), maintains low wages, eliminates import tariffs and quantitative restrictions, and provides incentives for export-industries."[24]

The results of these policies in Haiti are crystal clear, from deepening impoverishment and destroying food security to undermining democracy. This section analyzes two of the pillars of Haiti's SAP: (1) lowering of import tariffs and the subsequent proliferation of food aid from the U.S. and (2) the privatization of state-owned enterprises.

## 1. *Food Aid and Food Security: The Lessons of Rice*

> *"For poor countries free trade is not so free, or so fair. Haiti, under intense pressure from international lending institutions, stopped protecting its domestic agriculture while subsidies to the U.S. rice industry increased. A hungry nation became hungrier."[25]*

In Haiti, 85% of the population survives through agricultural production. It has been noted that 80% of government revenues come from peasant farmers, and yet 90% of government expenditures are made in Port-au-Prince.[26] Unlike the Lavalas government's social plan, international donors/creditors have never given priority to investments in agriculture. Without attention and funding, the agricultural sector has been in steady decline since the 1960s[27], and rural peasant families make up Haiti's poorest and most vulnerable population.

Deepening poverty for farmers is not the only trend that can be seen in Haiti since the 1960's. Assistance from the U.S. and IFIs has an obvious pattern, which can be summed up as "turning Haiti into a low-wage, export-friendly economy" that could provide "profitable business opportunities for foreign investors."[28]

Creditors were well aware of the composition of Haitian society when they created Haiti's SAP in 1996. The SAP framework accepted on October 18, 1996 was characterized by a three-year structural adjustment credit (SAC) from the World Bank and loans from the Inter-American Development Bank. A Policy Framework Paper was developed by the IMF, World Bank, and Government of Haiti, in preparation for a loan from the IMF's Enhanced Structural Adjustment Facility (ESAF).[29]

A major focus of the SAP was market liberalization and reduction of agricultural tariffs and quotas. It is interesting to note here that this kind of economic policy directly contradicts the kinds of policies the United States, European countries, and others enacted during their own economic development. Liberalizing the market through reduced import tariffs brought a flood of American surplus grains, especially rice, into the Haitian marketplace. This, coupled with cuts in subsidies to domestic Haitian farmers, meant that peasant rice producers could not compete with the price of imported rice. These policies were in direct contradiction to the platform upon which Aristide's government was elected.

The IFIs knew the consequences their policies would have before they were implemented. "A 1987 report prepared for USAID warned that an export-driven trade and investment policy would relentlessly marginalize the domestic rice farmer unless rice remained protected behind high tariffs,"[30] yet the structural adjustment plan specifically called for the reduction of tariffs. As the U.S. began to export rice in greater quantities to Haiti in the mid-1980's, the U.S. Congress passed a protective subsidy bill for American farmers. The 1985 Farm Bill even created a loan program to make it easier for U.S. farmers to export their rice and other produce. So,

> "As the U.S. government stepped in to support American rice growers and exporters, it was helping – through the World Bank, IMF and USAID – to enforce policies that would stop the Haitian government from doing the same for its people, while opening the Haitian economy further to U.S. products. Haiti is now the largest market for U.S. rice in the Caribbean and the seventh largest importer of U.S. rice in the world."[31]

Through its USAID food aid programs, the U.S. took the destruction of native Haitian rice a step further. USAID's overall vision of development has always been based on the concept of "comparative advantage." The comparative advantage philosophy comes with the basic premise that the ideal situation is if "each nation produces only those things it can produce more cheaply than other nations."[32] Haiti's comparative advantages were identified by USAID to be its private sector, inexpensive labor force and its climate, which is good for industrial agriculture (not family level agriculture) and tourism.[33]

According to a Grassroots International report in 1997, the U.S. food aid program undermined local food production in a number of ways. First, U.S. aid was conditioned on reduced import tariffs. Rice from the United States, "Miami Rice", easily undercut the local rice prices, and it flooded the Haitian market. The price for local rice was necessarily lower when so much imported rice was introduced into the market, and this made growing rice a far less profitable endeavor for Haitian peasants. In this way food aid also shifted patterns of local consumption. Instead of relying on food produced in Haiti, the Haitian diet changed to include basic food imported from the United States.[34]

The SAP and USAID's food aid programs worked together to bring about the end of the era when Haitian farmers could survive by selling basic grains on the domestic Haitian market. In 1985, Haiti produced 125,000 metric tons of rice annually, and imported only 7,000 from the U.S. Today Haiti imports 225,000 metric tons from the U.S. Forty percent of Haiti's total hard currency is used to purchase food. Haiti now has one of the lowest food security levels in the world.[35]

These policies also contributed to widespread disappointment on the part of voters towards their new democratic government. The Lavalas government was forced to take steps to liberalize the market, contrary to the investment in agriculture they had promised. While there had been some significant investment in agriculture, particularly during the Preval presidency, it did not reach the levels Haitian voters had hoped for.

## 2. *Privatization of State Owned Enterprises*

The agreement with the financial instutions upon Aristide's return called for the privatization of Haiti's six major state-owned enterprises, which are: electricity (Electricité d'Haiti), telecommunications (Teleco), the port administration (Administration Portuaire de Port-au-Prince), the water supply (CAMEP), cement (Ciment d'Haiti), and the flour mill (Minoteri d'Haiti). Privatization is promoted by donors as a way to increase revenue in the short-term, provide an expanded tax base, and cut government expenditures.[36]

Contrary to popular belief, most of Haiti's public enterprises have been profitable. It is true, however, that some of them mainly serve the elite. For example, only 5% of Haitians have access to a Teleco telephone, and only 6% of the people have electricity. It is important to note that these enterprises were neglected due to the long years of government instability. During the coup, military leaders closed the cement company and the flour mill, choosing to rely on the water supply company to provide it with extra income. Teleco was very profitable, as calls made from the U.S. to Haiti provided $2 million each month in revenue.[37]

Although Aristide's successor, President Rene Preval, approved the privatization of some state-owned institutions, popular organizations and opponents of privatization challenged the notion that only by privatization would state enterprises become viable. They pointed to the seven months under President Aristide's government in 1991 when many failing institutions made noticeable improvement. For example, in less than three months, the cement factory went from a 4.5 million gourde loss to a 100,000 gourde profit. The flour mill went from a 2.76 million gourde loss to a 2.1 million gourde profit.[38]

In February 1995, the International Finance Corporation of the World Bank signed an accord to help the Haitian government study privatization at a cost of $2 million. By November, because of a delay in the process of privatization, USAID, IMF and the World Bank began to withhold over $100 million in aid to Haiti.

Two of Haiti's state-owned enterprises have now been privatized. The flour mill was sold to three companies, one Haitian and two from the United States: Sea Grain and Continental Grain. These three purchased 70% of the company for only $9 million, representing a near-liquidation. In addition, the Haitian government took over the debt of the company, which was $12 million. In 1984-85 the mill generated $15 million a year. At that time the market wasn't a quarter of what it is today.[39]

The state-owned Ciment d'Haiti, auctioned off by the Preval government on May 7, 1999, represented an opportunity to increase production because the raw materials needed for cement production were readily available in Haiti. The factory itself is located close to quarries that can supply 500,000 tons of cement for the next 125 years. A 1993 study observed that with a capital investment of $1 million the factory could be profitable.[40]

Therefore, the argument can't be made that the factory was sold because of money. Instead of upgrading the factory, it was closed so it could be sold more cheaply. The three companies that bought 65% of the company were the Swiss-owned UmarHolderbank, the Colombian-owned Colclinker, and the Haitian-owned National Cement Company. Haitian demand was 200 metric tons in 1990 but had risen to 700,000 by 1999. The balance is being supplemented by imported cement. Ciment d'Haiti, one of the largest factories in the Caribbean, could have satisfied the domestic need for cement as well as exporting to other countries.[41]

The Development GAP (Group for Alternative Policies) noted in its report, "Democracy Undermined, Economic Justice Denied," that:

> "USAID, by holding back the last US$4.5 million tranche of a US$45 million balance-of-payments support grant until the cement and flour mills were sold, confirmed the U.S. role as leader of the free market world and its willingness to use development assistance funds as a battering ram to further open the Haitian economy to foreign investors."[42]

## Privatization Stalled and International Aid Withheld

The first development assistance sanctions were applied when the Haitian government, bowing to grassroots pressure, failed to follow the IMF /World Bank calendar for privatization of state-owned enterprises. Although many believe that irregularities during the May 2000 local and legislative elections led to the withholding of aid to the Haitian government, it is important to recognize that this was already the position of the U.S. government going into the election year. The U.S. had been channeling aid through non-governmental organizations (NGOs) before the May elections, and reinforced this position after the OAS raised questions about the run-offs. The IMF and World Bank have been clear that re-engagement is contingent upon a renewed commitment on the part of the government of Haiti to follow the structural adjustment program.

In addition, the U.S. used its international influence to successfully prevent Haiti from receiving aid from other countries, most notably the European Union (EU). The EU made a statement that "since democracy had not been re-established in Haiti after the fraud of the May 2000 Senate elections... the EU renewed on January 10, 2003, the measures partially suspending its aid to Haiti."[43]

## USAID's Democracy Enhancement Program

Clearly, the structural adjustment program threatened to undermine democracy. As the Development Group for Alternative Policies explained in its 1997 report,

> "Designed without the input, understanding and consent of the Haitian people and implemented against rising protests from a

broad base of civil society, it will nevertheless determine the structure of Haiti's economy and direction of resource flows for many years to come."[44]

Structural adjustment wasn't the only policy undermining democracy during its early years. Through the U.S. Agency for International Development, the U.S. moved Haiti closer to its own version of democracy and further from the radical pro-poor democracy that Lavalas had intended to build. USAID's Democracy Enhancement Project "refers to collaborative, systematic efforts by an array of U.S. government agencies to further U.S. political and economic interests in poor countries – regardless of grossly negative impacts on the poor majorities in those countries – under the banner of building democracy."[45]

The project focused on Haiti's traditional political elite, instead of democracy's most important constituents: the marginalized rural poor. USAID Democracy Enhancement Project materials clearly stated

> "that Democracy Enhancement is aimed less at increasing the degree of awareness of democratic principles and more at increasing 'the number and types of institutions that can channel constructive competition into pluralistic endeavors.'"[46]

In its Investigative Report on Washington's "Democracy Offensive" the Inter-Hemispheric Education Resource Center explains that democracy enhancement is "especially pervasive in countries where Washington has determined that its democracy-promotion operations can play a critical role in shaping that nation's politics and bringing it closer in line with U.S. economic and political interests."[47] Certainly Washington wants to bring Haiti in line with its economic and political interests, but the Lavalas mass movement for democracy is unlikely to follow the U.S. economic agenda. Therefore, an important aspect of the USAID program has always been working with political parties. More specifically, the post-coup program required that political alternatives exist and pluralism was encouraged. Work with potential opposition parties was a fundamental part of the plan.

USAID doesn't directly fund political parties. Funding is channeled through two of the National Endowment for Democracy's four main grantees, the National Democratic Institute (NDI) and the International Republican Institute (IRI). These organizations both focus on political party building. Activities include research and polling, civic education, seminars and technical assistance. The IRI funds rightwing and conservative think tanks, research institutes, and civic organizations.[48]

The goal of the democracy program in Haiti is clear in the activities carried out by USAID during the 1990's. Funding and training for opposition political parties, financing for rightwing think tanks to produce "research" about the political and social situation in Haiti, and thinly veiled attempts to undermine the primacy of Lavalas through euphemistic encouragement of pluralism. The Democracy Enhancement Project promoted a different kind of democracy than the one that Haitians had been fighting for. It promoted a

> "narrow concept of democracy that bypasses or subverts pre-existing mass popular organizations and ignores the pressing need for structural changes, while concentrating on political parties, elections, elites, and gradualist change."[49]

These efforts to undermine democracy combined with the destructive economic policies of Haiti's structural adjustment program created an atmosphere of discontent among Haiti's voters. Peasants experienced deepening poverty and ecological devastation. Rural to urban migration escalated, filling Port-au-Prince's slums beyond capacity.

Elections for every post in local and national government in 2000 held great promise for Haiti's democratic process. However, as Haitians prepared to go to the polls, more trouble for democracy was brewing just a few hundred miles to the north in Washington, DC.

## III. Elections 2000

The year 2000 was a profound year in the Haitian political landscape. Perhaps the most notable phenomenon was the population's consistent will and motivation to participate in the country's nascent democratic process. Haitian voters overcame many obstacles, including a challenging voter registration drive. Months of struggle and intimidation preceded the May local and legislative elections. International discontent over the determination of winners in the May vote resulted in the withdrawal of aid and observers for the November elections. Even more violence and intimidation preceded the November presidential and partial senatorial elections, which suffered a near complete vacuum of "official" international attention.

# The 1999-2000 Provisional Electoral Council

According to the Haitian Constitution, Article 192, the Permanent Electoral Council consists of nine members chosen from a list of three names proposed by each of the Departmental Assemblies. In early 1999 the Departmental Assemblies had not yet been elected and put into place, therefore President Rene Preval undertook a process of selection that was political in nature. He called on the political parties to nominate people to become members of the CEP, and from this pool he made appointments.

As Georges Werleigh, a professor at Haiti's state university, points out, "The original sin of the CEP was choosing it from political parties."[50] Many within the human rights community felt that the CEP should have been chosen from civil society representatives. Political actors from across the spectrum accused the CEP of being partisan. In reality, several members of the 1999-2000 CEP had served on previous CEP's and represented diverse parties, not including the Lavalas party.

The creation of the 1999-2000 CEP had great impact on the electoral process that followed. Throughout the electoral season the CEP was accused of supporting various political agendas. The opposition accused them of being co-opted by the Fanmi Lavalas party and Fanmi Lavalas pointed the finger at the opposition. Some accused the CEP of being too beholden to U.S.-based agencies, while still others saw a CEP that was too independent of the Government of Haiti.

The CEP, according to the Haitian Constitution, is an autonomous body created to keep the electoral machinery out of the hands of both the legislative and executive branches of the government. The biggest challenge for the 1999 CEP was the organization of the election itself in a country with no infrastructure, an enormous rate of illiteracy, and a very young democratic tradition. In addition, as it began to create its plans for the electoral process, the CEP had to deal with political parties that could not reconcile enough to sit in the same room together. It was forced to work with international agencies that would not go through the Government of Haiti because of the legislative void. It was criticized by both domestic and foreign media for being incompetent, corrupt, and partisan. The role of the CEP was so politicized and challenged that the head of the National Democratic Institute mission stated, "No credible person would want to be on the CEP." [51]

By July of 1999, the CEP was ready to release the electoral law for 1999-2000. With the technical assistance of the International Foundation for Election Systems (IFES), a U.S.-based agency funded by USAID, the electoral law was published and distributed, and the process was ready to begin.

International organizations played a major role in shaping the electoral process as the May elections approached. The United States was directly involved in the creation and execution of the registration process itself through IFES. Furthermore, the U.S.-funded NDI was working with political parties and domestic observers. The U.S. was therefore able to influence the electoral process without having to answer to the Government of Haiti and without putting its resources into the hands of Haitian officials or Haitian government organizations.

In the period of time beginning with the OAS mission's arrival on February 23, 2000, through the termination of international support for Haiti's electoral process in July, meetings were held on a weekly basis in Port-au-Prince. In attendance at these meetings were the CEP, the OAS, the NDI, IFES and representatives from various diplomatic missions. During these meetings all significant policy for the electoral process was discussed and decided, allowing these international organizations influence over the entire process.

## Progress of Democracy Building Before May 2000 Elections

During interviews in the geographically distant communities of Jeremie in the Grande Anse, Gros Morne in the Artibonite, and greater Port-au-Prince, Haitians expressed universal discontent with the most "popular" political parties and actors.[52] All political actors, including Aristide, were the targets of disdain from groups of women, peasants and youth. People shared their disappointment that none of the members of this political scene felt it necessary to involve the populace in their discourses concerning the future of the country, its economy, and its social situation. Although the Fanmi Lavalas party produced a platform document in French, *Investir dans l'Humaine,* most average Haitians either could not access it or could not read it. Debate about the challenges facing peasants was relegated to local level campaigns.

Major disillusionment also stemmed from the inadequate registration process for the May elections, which suffered from organizational flaws and corruption. The most disturbing problem was the structural exclusion of poor rural and urban populations because of reduced numbers of registration bureaus. Some community groups in the North and the Artibonite claimed that as many as 60% of the poor population had been unable to register to vote. Many came to call the registration process an "electoral coup d'etat."[53]

Camille Chalmers of PAPDA described the situation going into the May elections as "a genuine political crisis, and the source is the split between the political classes and the popular movement." Many activists would agree and point to the fact that the "political class" is composed of the intellectual elite. According to Chalmers, the political base of the FL party is clearly large and important, but they follow a charismatic leader more than a political ideology. During a critical moment in Haitian history, political leaders had the opportunity to play a role in institution building but failed to do so. FL and OPL (Organization of People in Struggle), Chalmers explained, both had the opportunity after the coup ended to create parties with a strong base and organic relationships at a grassroots level. Although not a complete failure in the instance of the FL, a gap was nonetheless created between supporters and politicians. The population, according to Chalmers, is being forced to search for a political alternative in a process devoid of meaningful debate on the topics that affect the population.[54]

OAS observers pointed out that the election of local and legislative leaders was more important than any previous elections, because for the first time all political parties had the freedom to express themselves and campaign. But, as Alvaro Arciniegas, an OAS observer based in Jeremie, pointed out, the concept of sharing power is foreign to Haiti. There is a mentality that "if I'm not in control I disqualify everything that is beyond my control." Parties that were unable to control the whole electoral apparatus rejected it. Arciniegas said, "The culture of democracy has not taken root; it needs to be built. People need to believe in democracy and share power," because the concept of power-sharing and negotiation are essential to the participatory nature of the process.[55] Perhaps the fundamental problem in Haiti is not a power-sharing issue alone; the fundamental problem is one of elitism, where most leaders are not willing to empower the poor to make decisions.

Even though there was no meaningful discourse from political parties, the people of Haiti continued to grapple with the issues that affected their daily lives. The average Haitian does not have the luxury to ignore the failing economy, lack of health care and education. When weighing options for candidates some Haitians decided not to participate in the electoral process, because they could not clearly see how one candidate differed from the others.

The majority of Haitians, however, maintain a sophisticated understanding of the democratic process and know that their participation is key to making it a success. People looked at the candidates and parties and recalled the successes Aristide had while in power. Based on this, many people were planning to vote for his party again, in hopes that he would reemerge as a leader who fought for the good of the entire population. If not, the people understood that they would have the right to hold their leaders accountable, and the choice of not reelecting them when their terms were over.[56]

Spokespeople from the national peasant organization Tet Kole Ti Peyizan expressed their dissatisfaction with political parties by abstaining from participation in the May elections. Pointing at the proliferation of foreign products in Haitian marketplaces and the failing national product, Tet Kole noted that the whole question of elections was taking place in the context of neoliberal economic policies that were not favorable to the peasants. "Within the context of this grave situation, the question of elections comes up and those who have ransacked the nation appear as leaders in this new alternative. Those who have never participated in the struggle appear as candidates, and each says they will save the country. We ask, what good are these elections? Who should we vote for? No one represents the real needs of the country."[57]

As a movement, Tet Kole abstained from the elections because it couldn't see how any of the parties or candidates would address the needs of the country. An election needs to be based on a program and a structure. With the country in crisis, Tet Kole was frustrated to see that no one presented a new, alternative national program. Tet Kole based its analysis on concrete day-to-day experiences, and intended to continue reinforcing its community organizations and creating civic education programs to improve participation from the grassroots. This is the path to an alternative political program, one that is based on democratic participation.[58]

Tet Kole raised another important issue about democratic institutions and how they relate to Haiti's now disbanded military. Although Aristide was able to dismantle the overt structure of the military, former soldiers are at large throughout Haiti, and in many cases still hold significant power. The process of bringing these people to justice and bringing an end to impunity has just begun. In November 2000, Haiti's first large-scale human rights violation trial came to a close, and former military and paramilitary officers were punished for their crimes. By 2003 there was a constitutional amendment pending that would abolish the military permanently. However, Haiti's justice system is still evolving, and many of the perpetrators of violence in Haiti still walk free. As Tet Kole explained, it is difficult to have confidence in the government when murderers are at large.[59]

# May 2000: Local and Legislative Elections

On March 15, 2000 as the Provisional Electoral Council (CEP) began a three-day extension of the registration period, President Preval postponed local and legislative elections. No new date was announced, but many assumed the elections would be held on April 9, 2000. It was not until April 19 that Preval declared a new election day: May 21, 2000.

At a briefing in Washington, DC on March 31, the White House Special Coordinator for Haiti, Ambassador Donald Steinberg, referred to what grew to be called the "line in the sand" or "drop dead date" for the Haitian elections: June 12. If a new parliament was not seated by June 12, Haiti could expect to face consequences from the United States. This date, the second Monday in June, was the date Haiti's parliament was required to sit for its second session, after a recess, according to Article 92 of Haiti's Constitution. The date for the parliament to convene a new session, however, is the second Monday in January. The January date is the only Constitutionally mandated date for the seating of parliament.

Washington's insistence on this date for Haiti's elections was based on the premise that Haiti was technically ready to hold elections as early as April 30, and that any postponement beyond that date would be for political reasons. Many believed that Aristide and Fanmi Lavalas (FL) were trying to push the elections far enough back that they would need to be held at the same time as Presidential elections later in the year. By combining the two elections, FL was expected to have a landslide victory, because voters would simply vote for Aristide and his party in every position.

This theory implies that people in Haiti would not have chosen Fanmi Lavalas candidates otherwise, and that by adding Aristide to the election they would change their votes. Fanmi Lavalas did not ask for one election rather than two, and the party was deeply engaged in campaigning for elections throughout the beginning of the year 2000. FL was the party most prepared to participate in the elections. Whether or not it would have made their bids for positions in the senate and general assembly easier, the representatives of FL were making every necessary effort to prepare for separate local and legislative elections.

Ambassador Steinberg stated at the end of March that he was "firmly convinced an election can be held in relatively free and fair conditions in five weeks." A program officer from the International Foundation for Election Systems' (IFES) Washington office, Karen Seiger pointed out that from a technical standpoint the process was only 75% complete, and April 30 was not a technically feasible date. Steinberg responded that "all in all, these can be the best elections in Haiti's history, which may be a low standard."

The political repercussions for the "line in the sand" were first mentioned by the White House's top Security Council officer for Latin America, Arturo Valenzuela, during meetings with Steinberg in Haiti. They had "stressed the importance of holding these elections rapidly, in order to seat the parliament by the Constitutionally mandated date of June 12. Failure to constitute a legitimate parliament risks isolating Haiti from the community of democracies and jeopardizes future cooperation."[60]

Steinberg translated the statement above into clearer terms when he addressed a mixed group of academics and policy makers on March 31 at Georgetown University, in Washington, DC. "Isolating Haiti from the community of democracies" is a reference to a section of the Organization of American States (OAS) charter, known as the Santiago Declaration, or OAS 1080. The declaration calls for the hemisphere's foreign ministers to convene and determine if there has been a disruption of the democratic process in a member country and if so to take the appropriate measures. Such measures can include an embargo, and it was invocation of this declaration that was used to levy an embargo on Haiti during the coup. According to Steinberg, sanctions were not being considered by the U.S. government, because "keeping the dialogue going" was a policy goal. The U.S. government was being pressured by the Caribbean Community (CARICOM) on the question of whether or not Haiti would be allowed to participate in international forums. In other words, Steinberg clarified, there was a possibility of making Haiti an international outcast.

According to Steinberg, Haiti did not have the resources necessary to hold presidential elections on its own. He stated, "We can say to a particular individual planning to run for president at the end of the year that he can't have a credible and legal election without elections now because we won't support them. Aristide cares about credibility." The implications of a statement like this are great. Not only was Aristide accused of holding up the legislative elections, but Steinberg made it clear that the U.S. would be willing to sacrifice the legitimacy of Haiti's presidential elections in order to ensure that June 12, a purely political date, was upheld. Future assistance would be withheld and the ramifications of this would include the undermining of the presidential elections. Simply put, without U.S. assistance, the results of the presidential elections would not be considered credible or legitimate.[61] The humanitarian consequences of such sanctions were not discussed.

Three days before the elections took place U.S. Senator Michael DeWine made a statement that encapsulated the feelings of the U.S. Government. "I think it is a fair statement to say that future assistance, future aid from the international community, from the private sector, private organizations, as well as governments, as well as the U.S., will depend certainly to some extent on how these elections are conducted," he said. "Not on how they turn out, but on how they are conducted. The world will be looking on Sunday to see the amount of violence connected with these elections; to see whether or not the elections are fair, transparent and open; to see what kind of participation takes place among Haitian people."[62]

The Haitian elections would be judged, not on the winners, but on the conduct of the elections themselves. After the election, president of the CEP, Leon Manus, said, "We can say that this is perhaps the first time that so many people have gone to the polls to vote in legislative and local elections." He estimated that an impressive 60% of the population had participated. Congressman John Conyers, who had served as an official observer from the United States said, "It was really thrilling. What the Haitian people did was a success... Democracy is still strong in the hearts and minds of the citizens of this country."[63]

Haiti's opposition parties refuted official reports that the elections were free and fair. On Monday, May 22, opposition groups came together to form a new coalition called the *Group de Convergence* (later renamed the *Convergence Democratique*). At a press conference on May 27, this coalition declared the election fraudulent and called for a boycott of the runoff elections.

Other than the accusations of the opposition, it seemed for days that things had gone better than expected – than anyone had even hoped – and no shadows were cast over the victory of the Haitian people. But when the CEP announced results on June 1 that Fanmi Lavalas had won 16 of 17 Senate seats outright in the first round, as well as 28 of the 83 seats in the Chamber of Deputies, a controversy began. On June 2 the head of the OAS Electoral Observation Mission, Orlando Marville, stated that "according to the provisions of the Electoral Law the methodology used to calculate the vote percentages for Senate candidates, which were released earlier this week, is not correct."[64]

The letter in which Marville outlined his concerns about the calculations was printed in the Haitian press. In response, thousands protested in Port-au-Prince at the OAS, the UN, the U.S. Consulate and the U.S. and French Embassies. The CEP reconfirmed that its results were accurate. In a five page response to Marville, Leon Manus, president of the CEP, stated: "I consider the fact that a foreign observer published in the Haitian press a letter openly criticizing a national institution as an act of interference. The interference is more serious because this foreign observer, speaking in the name of a respected international institution, through reckless declarations, on questions of national importance, has induced the Haitian people to error and sought to discredit the CEP in the eyes of the nation."[65]

On June 15, as a continuation of their protests against the May elections, the opposition called for its members of the CEP to resign. In response, two of the three members of the CEP who represented the Espace de Concertation resigned from their posts.[66] In a shocking turnabout, Leon Manus fled Haiti on June 16 via the Dominican Republic. He was flown to the United States on a U.S.-leased helicopter that filed a false flight plan. Eventually, he met his children in Massachusetts. He claims he was facing death threats because of his refusal to sign election results.[67]

On June 18, Haitians protested in several major cities, calling for the publication of official election results. In the United States, the National Organization for the Advancement of Haitians (NOAH) released a statement calling the OAS criticisms an "attempt to tarnish the legitimacy of the victory of the Haitian people. Even if there is some remote validity in the arguments retained by the OAS Mission for calculating the percentages, the proper methodology should have been stipulated before and not after the elections." NOAH also noted that "the OAS and the international community were deeply involved in the preparation of these elections, therefore they were aware of the methodology used in the previous elections in Haiti and it should not be considered as a surprise or unprecedented action."[68]

On June 20, President Preval published the results of the May 21st elections, making them official. Runoffs were postponed until July 7. The CEP issued a Statement of Clarification on June 30, explaining the various reasons for its choice of methodology. The OAS stood by its criticism, and claimed that the methodology used by the CEP has no historic precedence.

In a statement before the U.S. House of Representatives, John Conyers stated: "We are holding Haiti to a higher standard than we are holding other nations including ourselves... Haiti's elections were relatively free of violence and we witnessed a firm commitment from Haitian citizens to have democratic elections. We observed great levels of voter participation and an overwhelming sense of civic pride, and concerted efforts toward the conduct of credible elections... Why are we so quick to condemn a country that has so little but is so important to our country...

Haiti is a fragile new democracy. This is only its third election since it rid itself of over fifty years of dictatorship rule. If only we could have been so perfect so early in our development as a full functioning democracy."[69]

## Negotiations and the November 26, 2000 Elections

On August 28, Haiti's parliament convened for the first time in more than eighteen months. Spokesperson for Fanmi Lavalas, Senator Yvon Neptune, was appointed president of the Senate. In response, the U.S. State Department told the press, "It is our view that Haiti's parliament has been prematurely seated, which calls into question the legitimacy of the new legislature. We are continuing to work with the OAS and others in pressing Haiti to resolve its electoral impasse."

On September 6, the U.S. representative to the OAS, Luis Lauredo, said: "The decision to install a parliament based on a flawed methodology for determining Senate winners and to prepare for the November 26 presidential elections with a compromised provisional election council indicated an unwillingness to cooperate with the international community regarding the most serious challenges facing democracy in Haiti. Absent new concrete steps to end the impasse, the U.S. will not be able to conduct 'business as usual' with Haiti." That same day the Clinton Administration vowed to impose economic sanctions against Haiti unless it "strengthens democratic procedures in advance of presidential and legislative elections." Canada and the European Union also raised the possibility of imposing sanctions against Haiti.

Without an accord between the opposition and FL, the U.S. would not give technical or financial support to the November elections, and would also withhold observers that could legitimize the election. "The parliament," stated political officer William Rowland, "is not a credible institution as long as the May electoral dispute remains unresolved, and therefore the U.S. would be keeping it at arm's length... Money from USAID is going directly through non-governmental organizations, and the U.S. would have a problem if any international financial institutions were to direct money to Haiti's government." [70]

During the October negotiations between the Convergence and FL, Erin Soto, Director of the Office of Justice, Democracy and Governance at USAID noted that the U.S. government would have to review its position if no agreement was made. "Either we maintain our position about fraud and basically side with the opposition," she said, "or we say there has been a good faith effort, the opposition is too unrealistic in the demands and FL is willing to concede on some points. There will be a constitutional crisis if we don't move forward and however mildly endorse the elections."[71]

With the U.S. decision to withhold aid and observers from the November election made public, almost all other international governments followed suit. Under pressure to organize and finance elections without outside help for the first time in Haiti's democratic history, the CEP surprised many by following its electoral calendar much more closely than it had before the May elections. Many of the necessary structures were already in place, and it appeared that the CEP would be prepared for the elections to take place on November 26.

According to Pierre-Antoine Lovinsky, "Before 1990 this illiterate majority of Haitians peasants did not know that they could choose their own leader. Now that they do, they are a new actor on the Haitian political scene." Lovinsky explained that Haiti had a parliament for three years with an opposition majority that did nothing. Instead of blaming the results of the May elections on fraud, as the opposition had, Lovinsky pointed to something truly democratic – the people didn't vote for these opposition parties again because of their ineffectiveness when in power. "Haitians have elected a parliament with a majority that can work with the Government of Haiti," said Lovinsky, "the irony is that those outside of Haiti won't work with it."[72]

Lovinsky declared the impasse at the OAS-chaired negotiations to be "a shame because it constituted a waste of time. Opposition is an integral part of the democratic process, and if the international community really wants to help the democratic process in Haiti it should work with the opposition. They need to consolidate, to get together and organize themselves into a real position. At the present time, the discourse of the opposition lacks continuity and has nothing to do with the reality of Haiti."[73]

The importance of the OAS negotiations was perhaps the fact that they represent a real effort on the part of the most powerful political party, Fanmi Lavalas, to enter into a dialogue with the opposition. It was an enormous step forward for the Haitian democratic process that a party with the backing of the majority of Haitians was still willing to make the necessary concessions to guarantee the participation of their opponents. Some critics pointed out that the negotiations were an effort on the part of FL to satisfy international interests more than national ones. However, any civil meeting between opposing parties in Haiti was a step forward.

The position of the Haitian population on the negotiations is of import as well. In the countryside people noted that this process had very little to do with their best interests. When given the opportunity to step up, accept concessions from FL and move forward with the process, the opposition stood fast on its demands and boycotted. Instead of offering the population of Haiti a political alternative, the opposition removed themselves from the democratic discourse and process entirely.

According to the Haitian Constitution of 1987, Article 134-2, "The presidential election shall take place the last Sunday of November in the fifth year of the president's term." Even though several rounds of negotiations ended without a compromise between Fanmi Lavalas and the opposition, the CEP accomplished the tasks necessary to hold elections on the constitutionally mandated date.

As the final days to the elections approached, Haitian voters still had serious obstacles to overcome. Violence erupted in the capital city during the first few weeks of November, and no governmental international election observers were there to witness the events of November 26. Donald Steinberg's statement at a policy briefing in Washington, DC on March 31 was once again a topic of discussion – without U.S. assistance, he said, the results of the presidential elections will not be considered credible or legitimate.

As promised, the United States, OAS, UN and other members of the international community withheld observers from the November 26 elections. The International Coalition of Independent Observers (ICIO), a coalition that included the Quixote Center, Global Exchange, Witness for Peace and Pax Christi USA Haiti Task Force, was the only officially accredited group of international observers in the country. Volunteers from three countries observed the elections with the non-governmental organizations in the ICIO.[74]

The reports of voter turn out on November 26 were consistent, with the exception of the opposition and CARICOM. The CEP released figures stating that over 60% of the registered voters had participated. Although no official report was readily available, the small CARICOM delegation declared voter turn out to be 15-20% nationally, even though they had only observed in Port-au-Prince.

The ICIO did not quote national turn-out figures, owing to the fact that ICIO observers were only able to observe in four major locations. However, the ICIO observed at 152 voter bureaus in four geographical departments. The ICIO stated: "Voter turn out varied in the places we observed. Our preliminary results based on our observations… average a 60% voter turn out."[75]

The national peasant organization KOZEPÈP, the largest member of the U.S.-supported National Observation Council (*Conseil National d'Observation,* CNO) deployed 5,842 observers nationwide on November 26. In their report to the press, they stated: "Based on KOZEPÈP's observation, participation was between 60-65%. People voted in peace and they had security. The small minor irregularities that we observed could in no way invalidate the results of the voting process."[76] This report also supported the results declared official by the CEP.

The bulk of reporting by international news agencies included numerous interviews and statements from the leaders of the opposition parties. Many papers quoted opposition leaders alleging that 95% of the population participated in their boycott of the elections. With 400 people registered at each polling station, the math would indicate that if true, this would mean no more than 20 people voted at each polling place. Haitian television, however, showed footage of lines as long as 40 people at any given moment during the day. With few exceptions, the foreign correspondents chose not to attend press conferences held by the various observer groups giving their accounts of what was witnessed in rural areas and towns other than Port-au-Prince.

On Wednesday, November 29, the CEP declared Jean-Bertrand Aristide the official winner of the presidency from the November 26 elections. He won approximately 92% of the votes cast, totaling over 2.6 million votes.

## Aftermath of 2000 Presidential Elections

The opposition coalition, the Convergence, had condemned the elections before they took place, so it was no surprise when they called the polling of November 26th fraudulent. Their estimates of voter turnout supported their statements that the majority of Haitians had followed their boycott by not participating in the elections. Within days of the announcement of official election results spokespeople for the Convergence began talking about constructing a "parallel government."

On December 13, the Convergence released what it called its Marlik Declaration. In it, leaders declared that "the elections of May 21 and November 26, 2000, form part of an electoral coup d'etat organized by Lavalas to the detriment of democratic pluralism, the stability of the country and the interests of the Nation." Later in the statement, the Convergence declared its intention to "construct a broad front for an alternative project to Lavalas..."[77]

Three U.S. Congressmen, Representative Benjamin Gilman, Senator Jesse Helms and Representative Porter Goss issued a statement which began: "November 26 marked a tragic day in Haiti's long and troubled quest for pluralism and representative democracy." It went on to allege that the elections had been a sham, with "the sole purpose of delivering absolute control over Haiti's government to Mr. Jean-Bertrand Aristide." Aristide cannot claim a popular mandate, in the opinion of these three legislators, and in addition, they refer to the "narco-traffickers, criminals and other anti-democratic elements" that surround Aristide.[78]

Many in Haiti saw this statement as proof of what they already believed to be true: Republicans in the United States were supporting the opposition parties. Facts were not presented in the statement from Gilman et al. to support their accusations against Aristide, and no sources were cited. Their statement is the most extreme example of the negative rhetoric directed at Haiti. In addition, it included threats to further isolate Haiti economically and exclude its participation in the then-upcoming Summit of the Americas.

Special Envoy for the White House Anthony Lake and the State Department's Special Haiti Coordinator Donald Steinberg traveled to Haiti with a small delegation the third week of December to meet with President-elect Aristide. The result of these meetings was a letter from President Aristide to President Clinton, outlining eight reforms demanded by the United States. Steinberg explained that in the meetings what "we made clear to President Aristide is that he needs to reestablish his relationship with the international community and to recognize that these steps are fundamental to building confidence."[79]

Included in the reforms outlined in Aristide's letter to Clinton were:

- Runoffs for the ten Senate seats awarded to the Lavalas Family in May;
- The inclusion of opposition members in Aristide's government;
- The establishment of a new electoral council;
- A semi-permanent mission of the OAS in Haiti to oversee domestic political negotiations;
- International monitoring of human rights;
- Working out an economic program with the World Bank and International Monetary Fund.

# The State of Democracy After the 2000 Elections

Erin Soto and Sharon Bean at USAID shared what they called a grassroots perspective on Haiti's democratic process. It was their observation that in Haiti, political will is everything, and it was this that allowed the CEP to pull off the elections on November 26. Frantz Faustin, *Chef du Protocole* for the CEP, stated that in his opinion, it was the training provided by the USAID-funded IFES that had equipped the CEP with the knowledge necessary to organize the elections.

The philosophy of the USAID Office of Justice, Democracy and Governance is that strengthening civil society to the point where members of communities can solve their community's problems would lead them to solving bigger problems and building coalitions. USAID staff members expressed that "Haiti was in transition mode but now was slipping back." Ms. Soto and Ms. Bean agreed that Haitians believe "democracy is anarchy and it means you can do whatever you want." They noted that it is difficult to "do democracy" with an illiterate population, and in Haiti 65-70% of the people are illiterate.[80]

This assessment raised concerns about the amount of funding USAID has poured into the democratic process and how little of it has been earmarked for civic education. If the obstacle to understanding democracy for Haitians was illiteracy, it would be logical for USAID to support more efforts to educate the Haitian populace about the democratic process.

The more than 60% voter turn out rates for both the May and November elections are evidence that one of the most basic tenets of democracy is understood by the majority of Haitians, whether literate or not. The idea of voting, and expressing your political will by electing representatives for your community, region and department is the foundation for understanding the entire structure of a participatory democracy.

Charles Suffrard, spokesperson for the national peasant group KOZEPÈP pointed out that because of Haiti's history of dictatorship peasants had more faith in individual people than governments. In an effort to build a more truly democratic structure, KOZEPÈP was preparing to work with elected officials at a local level throughout the country to ensure that they are faithful representatives of the people who elected them. KOZEPÈP was also engaged in civic education so that people will be better equipped to hold elected officials accountable.

In terms of official election results, only the opposition doubts that President Jean-Bertrand Aristide won a mandate from the people. In many places people spoke about Aristide's new government as key to the advancement of their community and the country as a whole. With Aristide it was expected that the government would be stable, and with the Fanmi Lavalas majority in parliament, laws would be passed and the country would advance. At a local level Aristide's new term as president created hope that justice would be a top agenda item, and that improving the lot of Haitian peasants would also be a priority. It appeared that on a national level the Haitian people were preparing for February 7, 2001, when they would welcome their new democratically elected and legitimate leader, President Aristide.

One thing is clear in looking back at the electoral process of 2000: the people of Haiti did not turn away in the face of great challenges. Rather, their voices were heard in a variety of forums, from national peasant and human rights organizations to small community based groups throughout the country. Their call for participation, their equal right to have representation in the government, and their consistent questioning of the process were in evidence at every important juncture of the electoral program. In spite of the historical realities of the country – one hundred and eighty-six years of independence passed before the first truly democratic election was held – there is an evident consciousness of the fundamental principles of democracy in Haitian society.

Perhaps the largest challenge still facing the Haitian democratic process is the accountability of political leaders to be representatives of the population. Throughout the election year, the Haitian people felt that political parties failed to present cohesive political platforms that outlined responses to the difficulties of everyday life for the Haitian peasant, market woman, student or urban dweller. Political parties and leaders needed to overcome the temptation to fall into traditional roles and corrupt practices, if democracy would have a chance.

The role of the OAS shifted in September 2000 to what it called "shuttle diplomacy." Assistant Secretary General of the OAS, Luigi Einaudi, began traveling to Haiti on a regular basis with the goal of brokering an agreement between the Haitian Government and the Democratic Convergence (CD). The Family Lavalas party had won strong majorities in both houses of Parliament, regardless of the contested senate seats. The negotiations focused on the issue of the disputed senate seats and how to resolve the situation effectively so that the CD could participate in future elections.

As the CD began to develop its agenda, it laid out a list of conditions required for its participation in the election process. These included declaring the May election fraudulent and re-running the entire vote, regardless of the fact that only eight of the senate seats were in question. Negotiations failed in 2000 and have continued to fail since. In the course of the OAS's diplomacy the elected Government of Haiti and the CD have been asked to meet certain requirements and have made demands themselves. The OAS has responded by making its own resolutions on the situation in Haiti which lay out conditions for all parties involved, including the international community and financial institutions.

## OAS Resolution 822

During the ongoing negotiations coordinated by Assistant Secretary General Luigi Einaudi, the Permanent Council of the OAS struggled to come to agreement on a resolution for Haiti. On September 4, 2002 the Council agreed to OAS Resolution 822. The Resolution set the guidelines for resolving the Haitian political crisis and straightening out the democratic process. Resolution 822 purportedly also attempted to de-link the political situation from the Haitian Government's ability to access international humanitarian aid loans and grants.

The issue that originally sparked the "election controversy," the eight contested senate seats, was resolved in July 2001. With the encouragement of President Aristide, seven of the senators whose first round victories were questioned resigned. The issue of the eighth senator was resolved by his re-election in November 2000.[81] However, despite eliminating the underlying controversy, between 2001 and July 2003, the Government of Haiti received no new multilateral humanitarian assistance from the Inter-American Development Bank (IDB), the International Monetary Fund (IMF) or the World Bank (WB). At the same time, bilateral aid from the United States drastically decreased. The U.S. State Department's reason for withholding aid during this time was the lack of a political accord between the Government of Haiti and the CD. Without a compromise that allowed the CD to participate in early elections, funding would not be released to the Haitian Government.

OAS 822 was accepted by the General Assembly even though Assistant Secretary General Einaudi made more than a dozen failed trips to Haiti to negotiate the compromise between the CD and the Haitian Government. The resolution reflects the sentiment among OAS member states that although a political compromise continues to be important, linking humanitarian aid to this compromise is having disastrous effects on the Haitian people.

The U.S. government and the European Union have said that their financial re-engagement with the Haitian Government hinges on the fulfillment of the commitments made by the government in the resolution. These are:

1. Strengthening of democratic institutions, especially the police and judiciary;
2. Formation of a new provisional electoral council (CEP);
3. Establishment by the CEP of an Electoral Guarantees Commission (CGE);
4. Development and implementation of a comprehensive disarmament program;
5. Reparations to victims and prosecution of perpetrators of violence on December 17, 2001 (when a violent attack on the National Palace prompted violent reprisal attacks);
6. Restoration of a climate of security;
7. Movement forward in investigations for politically motivated crimes.

In March 2003, the OAS sent a high-level delegation with members of the Caribbean Community (CARICOM) to review progress on the steps laid out in Resolution 822. Following their visit, they reported to the Secretary General of the OAS. This report came shortly after the "Third Report of the Secretary General on the Implementation of CP/RES. 822," and a month and a half before the Fourth Report. This section includes information from all of these reports.

The Provisional Electoral Council (CEP) was supposed to be created within 30 days of the adoption of Res. 822. Under Haiti's 1987 Constitution, the Permanent Electoral Council is entrusted with running all elections. The Permanent Council drafts the electoral code for the executive branch's approval, it oversees registration of candidates and voters, runs the election activities, announces the results and is the final arbiter of any electoral disputes. The nine Council members are named for nine-year non-revocable and non-renewable terms. Three members are chosen by each of the judicial, executive and legislative branches, from a list submitted by the Departmental Assemblies. A Departmental Assembly is formed for each of Haiti's nine Departments by the Department's Municipal Assemblies, which are in turn formed by each municipality's Sectional Assemblies. Sectional Assemblies are chosen by the voters in each municipal section.

The Permanent Electoral Council has not been chosen, because the Sectional Assembly system was never implemented. The 1987 Constitution provided for a Provisional Electoral Council to organize the first set of elections. The Constitution assumed that Sectional Assemblies would be elected during the first elections, and that a duly constituted Permanent Council would replace the

Provisional Council by the second election cycle. One Provisional Council member was chosen by each of: a) the Executive, b) the Catholic Bishop's Conference, c) the Consultative Commission, d) the Supreme Court, e) human rights organizations, f) the State University, g) the journalists' association, h) the Protestant Churches, and i) the National Council of Cooperatives. Their mandate was to end at the inauguration of the President. There is no provision in the Constitution for choosing subsequent Provisional Electoral Councils, as the Constitution expected that the Permanent Council would be chosen in 1987.

The first elections under the 1987 Constitution, in November 1987, were aborted when soldiers and paramilitaries attacked voting sites, massacring would-be voters. All subsequent elections were run by different Provisional Electoral Councils. With the exception of elections in December 1990, there were no free elections in Haiti until 1995. The 1990 and 1995 elections, although held for the executive and legislative branches and local government, did not include elections for Sectional Assemblies. Sectional Assembly candidates were on the ballot for the 1997 elections, but those elections were aborted due to controversy unrelated to the Sectional Assembly vote. Voters chose Sectional Assemblies again in the May 2000 elections, but the selection of municipal and departmental assemblies was delayed due to controversy unrelated to the Sectional Assembly vote.

The Sectional Assemblies are the foundation of Haitian democracy under the 1987 Constitution. Until they are properly functioning, along with Municipal and Departmental Assemblies, all elections will be ad-hoc, conducted by a Provisional Electoral Council, and subject to claims of illegitimacy by those who lose.

The Electoral Council issue is an interesting one. As previously explained, the Permanent Council's nine members are chosen by the executive, judicial and legislative branches, from a list proposed by Departmental Assemblies. As Lavalas party supporters constitute a majority of these assemblies and, like U.S. Republicans, Lavalas controls the executive and legislative branches, it is likely that a Permanent Electoral Council chosen by the Constitutional process will include a majority of government supporters.

In order to demonstrate its good faith to the international community and Haiti's opposition, the Government of Haiti sacrificed the potential advantages of a Permanent Electoral Council, and agreed to a provisional council (CEP) formed by nominees by groups from a broad spectrum of Haitian society. This extraordinary concession has not, however, yielded the hoped for results, as many of the sectors refuse to participate. The judiciary, and the Lavalas party have nominated council members willing to serve. The Democratic Convergence and the other opposition parties have refused to participate. The remaining five members have nominated council members, but instructed them not to participate in the CEP.

These five institutions originally requested a two-week delay in November, 2002. Their request also stated that they had finished the process of designating nominees, and conceded that it was their civic duty to contribute to the realization of the next elections. They said they were, however, not comfortable disclosing the names of the nominees until: a) Haiti and the OAS had negotiated the Terms of Reference for the technical cooperation requested by the Haitian Government in the areas of police professionalization, electoral security and disarmament; and b) the Haitian government had shown definitive progress in its disarmament program by addressing its concerns over heavy weapons carried by civilian security guards of local elected officials and parliamentarians.

The Haitian government moved quickly on both fronts. It negotiated terms of reference with the OAS in November 2002. President Aristide issued instructions that no civilian security guards of elected officials were allowed to carry heavy weapons. Neither the Group of Five (entities who would not nominate their CEP representatives) nor the OAS Special Mission expressed reservations about either of these steps. In response, the Group of Five did announce the names of five nominees, but then instructed them not to participate in the CEP.

Despite this lack of collaboration, the Government of Haiti has repeatedly made overtures to all those involved in Resolution 822 and the CEP. On January 30, 2003, the Minister of Foreign Affairs called a meeting of the nine naming sectors. On February 5, the President convened a meeting with the nine sectors and Ambassador David Lee, Chief of the OAS Special Mission. The two opposition coalitions refused to participate in either of these meetings, and the Group of Five maintained its refusal to allow its nominees to join the Council.

On February 7, 2003 the President issued a decree for the formation of the CEP, which includes the nominees of the Group of Five from civil society, Fanmi Lavalas, and the judiciary. The two vacant seats are yet to be filled with one candidate selected by Convergence, and one by political parties outside of Convergence. If they refuse to name candidates, a mechanism previously agreed to will allow for the naming of two additional council members.[82]

Obstacles to creating a CEP that could organize and hold elections before the end of 2003 constituted serious obstacles to Haiti's democratic process. As

Professor Alex Dupuy stated in, "Who is Afraid of Democracy in Haiti? A Critical Reflection,":

> "The failed OAS-CARICOM mediations throughout 2001 and 2002 made it clear that the CD was the main obstacle to a successful resolution of the conflict. At every turn in the process, the CD either refused to endorse agreements that were arrived at or issued new demands that it insisted had to be met before it could agree to endorse any proposed resolution." [83]

The Convergence's growing list of conditions for its participation in elections included some that are either unrealistic or impossible to demonstrate. For example, the Convergence insisted on "security", and used common civil disturbances as proof that the condition had not been met. The Haitian National Police (PNH) made many efforts to improve security, including changes in all top-level leadership, a disarmament program, and cooperation with the OAS Special Mission. Although both the PNH and the Special Mission have been hampered by financial constraints, the security situation improved considerably. As Dupuy noted,

> "The strategy, by both Convergence and the Bush administration that supports and directs it, then, is clear: to achieve by means of political and economic strangulation what they cannot achieve through the ballot box and then to call that a victory for democracy."[84]

## IV. U.S. Policy Deepens Suffering

> *We see politics wreaking havoc with people's lives. We know that the international community supported dictatorships in Haiti, that it winked and ignored the atrocities visited upon the people of Haiti. But now this international community has the audacity to say this isn't right. I'm not here to say there aren't problems in Haiti but my question is, are these problems enough to punish hundreds of thousands across the country? It is inhumane and it requires us to stand up and be counted. The only thing necessary for evil to triumph is for good people to do nothing. We are being called to speak for the people of Haiti who cannot speak for themselves, whose presentation in American media is undignified and humiliating and does not share the truth.[85]*

By the end of 2002, when OAS Resolution 822 became the roadmap for moving forward in Haiti, the U.S.-led embargo on humanitarian aid was well underway, including $146 million in withheld Inter-American Development Bank (IDB) loans. The victims of the embargo, a foreign policy weapon, have been the poorest Haitians in both urban and rural areas, because "when sanctions are leveled against an elected government, there is no collateral damage; ordinary citizens, who made the 'wrong' choice at the polls, are the targets. Their suffering and the social discord that necessarily ensues seem to be the intended result."[86]

## Humanitarian Crisis

One cannot fully understand the impact of U.S. policies towards Haiti in 2003 without exploring the real life situation of most Haitians. Haiti was a rapidly accelerating humanitarian crisis. Indicators for this situation are the vast poverty levels, HIV/AIDS rates, maternal mortality rates, extremely limited access to health care and clean drinking water, low levels of school enrollment and the general inability of families to find food each day. The statistics about Haiti paint a bleak picture:

- Haiti ranks 146 out of 173 on the Human Development Index.
- Life expectancy is 52 years for women and 48 for men.
- Adult literacy is about 50%.
- Unemployment is 70%.
- 85% of Haitians live on less than $1 U.S. per day.
- Haiti ranks 38 out of 195 for mortality rate under five years of age.[87]

One area in which funding has been withheld is rural road rehabilitation. It only takes a moment of reflection to realize just how critical this improvement would be. Two specific ways in which deteriorating rural roads affect Haitians are: access to markets and to potentially life-saving health care. Produce raised in rural areas requires transportion to urban centers for sale in markets. Due to deficient road conditions, peasant farmers are forced to walk for hours or pay large trucks in order to get their mangoes, avocados and other produce to the markets. Some produce is lost along the way and added cost and time for travel detract from the already meager profit.

In terms of health care, often patients die after traveling several hours over barely navigable roads only to arrive at the clinic too late for help. Pregnant mothers lose babies when traditional midwives encounter complications in rural areas. Some people have no option but to walk for hours while carrying a sick child in their arms. Repairing and rebuilding roads in rural areas will have a deep impact on access and mobility for peasants, who constitute the majority of Haitians.

Basic education is another area where funding is desperately needed. Haiti's governing elite has never invested in education for the majority. The democratic governments since 1994 have made great strides towards alleviating this historical injustice, but the withholding of the loans frustrates continued progress. Without the promised loans, the government must require user fees for many students, which their families cannot pay.

The significance of access to potable water cannot be overstated. Water is critically necessary for life. CAMEP is the semi-autonomous organization that oversees potable water for Haiti's capital, Port-au-Prince. Engineers explained in January 2003 that they have 32 wells, but of these only ten were functioning. These provided about 35 million gallons per day, which allowed CAMEP to serve 62% of the population. Their goal was to increase service to reach 80% of the population, 55 million gallons per day. Leaders at CAMEP stated that the IDB loan was necessary to enable them to deliver potable water:

> "We would like to do it with our own money but we can't. We started but the population can't pay for services so we don't have money. We've asked the Bank of Haiti for money because we don't have access to money from abroad. We would like to negotiate with foreign banks but we're blocked. We cannot increase the production of water...The embargo is having this effect: People can't pay for water so they get it clandestinely. The emerging statistics will show increased sickness from water borne disease."[88]

The area of perhaps the most desperate need is health care. Selena Mendy Singleton of TransAfrica Forum explained, "While the lack of international aid is not the sole cause of the dismal health services, the failure to release international aid certainly exacerbates an already dismal situation." The HIV/AIDS rate is one indicator of how truly dismal the situation is. The national infection rate rose to above 6% in mid-2003, the highest in the Caribbean. In real numbers that means 300,000 Haitians infected with HIV/AIDS. Three hundred of these people, or 0.1%, were receiving the anti-retroviral (ARV) treatment in 2003.

Beyond HIV/AIDS, another indicator of Haiti's health crisis is the maternal mortality rate. SOFA (Haitian Women's Solidarity Organization) has a clinic for women and small children in the Martissant suburb of Port-au-Prince. Martissant is a transitional neighborhood where peasants migrating from the countryside in search of jobs settle briefly. It is a very poor area where user fees for health care are prohibitive. Because women in Martissant have often just arrived in the city, most use traditional midwives for childbirth.

SOFA explained that it used to provide training programs for midwives. "Midwives used to come to the clinic to report on how many births they had overseen but we can't do trainings anymore. Some of the midwives need first-aid kits. We used to provide them with small kits of the things they need but we can't do that anymore."[89] SOFA has a limited capacity in terms of the level of health care provided at its clinic. A lot of referrals are made but because almost all health providers charge fees, referrals often go untreated. Staff explained that:

> "We refer deliveries of babies, TB, HIV, eye problem and dehydrated children. Each month we make 80-100 referrals. Some of the people we refer get care and some don't. Some won't even go. We do the consultation and offer medicine at low cost; many can't afford the places we refer them to. For example, we referred someone with meningitis to the hospital. He didn't go and he died."[90]

## Cutting the Petrol Subsidy

In the midst of its humanitarian crisis, the Haitian Government made efforts to release withheld international funds. The International Monetary Fund (IMF) had indicated that before it could resume lending to Haiti, the government needed to demonstrate its dedication to economic reform. The best way to do this would be to cut the government subsidy on petrol products.

In January 2003, the Haitian Government cut the petrol subsidy. The Charge d'Affaires at the U.S. Embassy in Port-au-Prince noted that "the Government of Haiti is between a rock and a hard place with the gas prices. They tried to keep the price of the kerosene down because of the environmental disaster that will come if people have to use charcoal."[91]

Suprisingly, Embassy staff agreed with the grassroots organizations that eliminating the petrol subsidy would have disastrous effects, even as the U.S. Government pressured the Haitian Government to cut the subsidy. The Haitian Government cut the subsidy, and prices for gas and kerosene for cooking went up about 70% in the first days. For weeks, transportation strikes were called to protest the high cost of public transportation.

One of the groups hardest hit by the rising gas prices was women working in the assembly factories of Port-au-Prince. Their daily wage had been 36 gourdes, but in response to the rising inflation, including the soaring petrol prices, the minimum daily wage was raised to 72 gourdes. Yannick Etienne of the workers' rights organization Batay Ouvriye explained that this small raise did not come close to keeping up with inflation. In real terms:

> "If a worker in the assembly factories lives in Kafou, it costs 10 gourdes for them to get downtown, 5 gourdes to the old airport and another 5 gourdes to get them into the industrial park. That is 40 gourdes each day for transportation. You have to eat as well! 10-15 gourdes will get you a little spaghetti and bread, and some coffee in the morning. That's 50-55 gourdes you've spent already. Lunch used to be 20 gourdes but now it's 25 gourdes and 5 more for a drink.... You will take home 2 gourdes of the 72 gourdes a day and that means no money for food for your children, school or health care."[92]

## The Free Trade Agenda

Another U.S. policy that has had tragic consequences for Haiti's poor is the promotion of free trade, and incentives for international corporations to set up assembly factories in Haiti. These assembly factories are basically sweatshops that take advantage of Haiti's high level of unemployment. The factories employ mostly women, and are known to regularly violate workers rights. The women are sexually harassed and do not have the right to organize.

The way business is done at these factories in Haiti is another problem. Some of the women who work in these factories explained that "the industrial park is a misery that is revisited upon the Haitian people." A recent development has been the use of a quota system for assembling pieces. Instead of having a certain number of hours to work to earn the minimum wage, women are offered a slighter higher wage for fulfilling their quota. This is having disastrous health effects for women who are skipping meals and working through the night to fulfill their quotas. According to reports, as many as three women died at their sewing machines between December 2002 and January 2003.

In the spirit of the North American Free Trade Agreement (NAFTA), U.S. Senator Michael DeWine and Representative Jim Kolbe introduced the Haitian Economic Recovery and Opportunity (HERO) Act during the 2002 and 2003 Congressional sessions. They will reintroduce it in 2004 and subsequent years until the Act is passed. The HERO Act has been presented as a way of increasing jobs and economic opportunity for Haiti, as well as giving a much-needed boost to the Haitian economy.

In truth, the Kolbe/DeWine HERO Act doesn't include strong enough provisions for labor rights. NAFTA has a provision for workers' rights but it does not actual protect them, according to Yannick Etienne. One of the Haitian women workers posed the question, "What kind of fight do the workers have to have in order to get their rights respected and their voices heard?" Women who work in the Port-au-Prince industrial park and labor organizers from the Batay Ouvriye organization shared:

> "This bill doesn't include anything for the Haitian people. We see enough from international governments that never moves us forward, only backward. This bill is in that group and should be opposed... the law is being discussed only in the U.S., not in Haiti. Maybe they've discussed it with ADIH (Assistance for Industrial Development in Haiti – an association for factory owners), with Madame Bayard (head of ADIH) – but they're not discussing it with the people. Of course she's pushing something advantageous for the bosses. In the U.S. they say it is good for the country but they didn't discuss it with the people here at all."[93]

A woman who has worked in the factory for many years spoke from her life experience about the "economic opportunities" these low-wage sweatshop jobs give to Haitian women:

> "I have a lot of experience in factories. It is a very grave and serious situation. I worked from 1979 – 1999 and my experiences were horrible. Especially because the workers work so hard and get nothing from that work. For example – the minimum wage no longer covers the cost of transportation to and from work – never mind housing, school and food. In this form we are still in slavery. That is why people are getting so deteriorated on the machines – they don't have enough to live. I don't work in the factory now. I can die. I don't see the future for my children. There is a pattern when you reach 35-36 years old where they cut you off and try to

take your first born. The majority of bosses will call the CIMO (riot police) if there are problems with workers instead of trying to work it out. After all these experiences I still haven't laid one cinder block for a home and the future. On pay day I have always tried to avoid food sellers so I could save the money instead of eating!"[94]

In addition to the HERO Act, a free trade zone is being established along the entire length of the border with the Dominican Republic (DR). The first factories have opened in the border town of Ouanaminthe. Charles Arthur of the Haiti Support Group reported:

> "The free trade zone on the Maribaroux Plain, in northeastern Haiti, is one of the first projects of the Hispaniola Fund, a debt-for-development initiative supported by the U.S. State Department... While supporters say that investments would benefit all sectors of society in both countries, the choice of a free trade zone as the first beneficiary of the fund has set off alarms. Haitian opponents argue that the free trade zone is a ploy to help Dominican manufacturers avoid potential problems with export quotas. They say that the zone will not create jobs for Haitians and they even object to the name. The DR's assembly sector is becoming a victim of its own success. With 200,000 workers in 52 free trade zones generating $4.7 billion worth of products, mainly garments destined for the U.S. market, Dominican companies have reached the textile import quota set by the U.S. to protect its own garment industry. This problem can be dodged if the final stitching on Dominican garments is done across the border in Haiti. The products would be considered Haitian-made, and could be exported to the U.S. without difficulty because Haiti is far from meeting its U.S. textile import quota."[95]

Pitobert is a 50,000 hectare section of the Maribaroux Plain, one of the richest plains in the country. A representative from the Committee to Defend Pitobert explained, "A study in 1995 said that with irrigation we could feed 500,000 people. It came as a total shock to us that they chose to build a free trade zone on this good soil."[96]

Interesting, but not surprising, was the news that the World Bank's private sector financing arm had approved a loan for the new free trade zone. This is the first loan from the World Bank to Haiti since 1998. Even as non-governmental organizations in Haiti, the Dominican Republic, and abroad campaigned against passage of the loan, $20 million was approved to finance the project through the

Dominican-based Grupo M Corporation.[97] By mid-2003, forty landowners and several hundred farmers had lost their livelihood to the 230,000 square meter plot for the free trade zone on the Maribahoux Plain, the second most fertile stretch of land in Haiti.[98]

# V. The Only Road Forward: Elections

As of this writing, the U.S. government and the Organization of American States (OAS) are facing a deadline for legislative elections that cannot be ignored. According to the Electoral Law of July 1999, the Senators and deputies who came to power during the May 2000 elections should be concluding their terms in January 2004. Even if one interprets the terms of the legislators based on the Constitutional mandate that they serve three-year terms, (in this case, the parliament was seated in August 2000) it is possible that elections will be held before the end of this legislature's term.

The opposition Democratic Convergence has hardly altered their demands since they first boycotted the May 2000 election results. They continue to call for a "compromise government," a plan that would allow President Aristide to remain in office until his term concludes in 2005 with the caveat that all ministerial positions be negotiated and new ministers selected in consultation with the opposition. Watching their choice for political leadership nullified by a compromise supported by the U.S. government and the Haitian opposition will alienate Haitian voters further. A "compromise" of this nature is hardly democratic, as it removes the most important players in Haiti's democracy from the decision-making role they have fought two hundred years to win – the people.

Holding elections for the parliamentary seats is the only democratic way to proceed. Elections are the only way to resolve Haiti's political crisis, which has dragged on too long and stunted the country's economic and political development. Elections place the resolution of the crisis where it belongs, in the hands of the Haitian voters. For these reasons, OAS Resolution 822 clearly stated that the elections should have happened in 2003.

The people who are most important to Haiti's democratic development, the impoverished majority, have been alienated and increasingly disenfranchised by current U.S. policies. They elected a government in 2000, but because of support given to the opposition coalition by the U.S., this government has been held hostage by a negotiation process and an aid embargo. The government has been unable to live up to its campaign promises, and the world will never know what the Aristide government could have accomplished if it had had access to international loans, and was unfettered by the political crisis.

While many in Washington, including the State Department and the OAS, have given priority to the ongoing battle between the party in power, Lavalas, and the coalition of those who wish to be in power, the Democratic Convergence, the voices of the Haitian people have been eerily absent from the debates on the democratization of their own country.

Spokespeople from the State Department have emphasized that elections will not be considered legitimate unless three things happen. First, the Provisional Electoral Council must be constituted according to the stipulations of OAS Resolution 822. Second, security conditions must be appropriate for holding elections. Finally, the Democratic Convergence must participate for the elections to be considered valid.

The Convergence has repeatedly proclaimed that security conditions necessary for holding elections do not exist in Haiti. Although better security makes for better elections, elections are too important to wait for perfect conditions. Civil unrest has often accompanied elections in the U.S., but the country has always persevered with the vote. The 1968 election year began with the assassinations of leading dissident Martin Luther King and presidential candidate Robert F. Kennedy. A summer of racial tension, rioting and police brutality in major cities culminated with a police riot against demonstrators outside the Chicago Democratic Convention, in which hundreds were injured. The unrest made holding elections difficult in the short run, but holding them despite this maintained the rhythm of consistent, regular voting that is a cornerstone of American stability.

If there is an example of conditions being less than perfect, it is Haiti in 1987, under the CNG dictatorship. In July of that year, landowners in the northern town of Jean-Rabel massacred more than three hundred peasants. In August a gunman attacked a church service near St. Marc, and a mob intercepted the fleeing priests and nuns down the road, in full view of a military checkpoint. Throughout the year, dozens of demonstrators and pro-democracy activists were gunned down by the military. At one point, the dictatorship stripped the CEP of its powers, and dissolved the labor unions. CEP members and facilities were attacked regularly. Despite this, the U.S. continued to supply generous military aid to the dictatorship. On election day, paramilitaries backed by regular soldiers attacked several polling stations, mowing down voters by the dozens.

Every Haitian election since democracy's arrival in 1990 has raised security concerns. The scale of violence never reached that of 1987 or the worst of U.S. elections, but each time someone, usually candidates without strong electoral support, claimed that conditions were not right for that vote, too. Still, Haitian voters showed that conditions were good enough by turning out, in percentages unheard of in the U.S.

Despite the talk of division and strife in Haiti, the voters are not only determined on election day, but remarkably clear and consistent. Candidates allying themselves with the Lavalas movement have won every single election since 1990. Those elections, like many of ours, are imperfect and must be improved upon. The dispute has always been over the extent of the Lavalas landslide, not that it exists.[99]

The final point of contention is the participation of the Democratic Convergence in any future elections. The parties in the Convergence did not win a popular mandate at the polls in 2000, and it is unlikely that they would now. They may have had more grassroots support before they inaugurated their own parallel president in February 2001. During his speech, he called for the return of the Haitian military, which in combination with the Convergence's position that the aid embargo continue, has eroded most popular support they once had.

One of the most important elements Haiti's democracy needs is regular elections that establish stability and respect for the Constitutional calendar. Postponing the elections for the reasons above will only deepen the suffering of the Haitian people by prolonging the political crisis and lengthening the aid embargo.

In order for Haitian democracy to fulfill its promise of a better life for Haiti's majority, democratic institution building must be a priority. These institutions will provide a check on the government that is needed to insure that future Haitian governments are accountable to the poor's desire for redistribution of the power and resources of Haiti. Haiti's protracted political stalemate has deepened the suffering of the Haitian people while undermining their confidence in participatory democracy.

It goes without saying that democracy building in a country without a democratic legacy is a long-term process. The only way to move beyond the paralyzing political standoff in Haiti is to put the decision in the hands of the Haitian electorate.

# CONCLUSION

The American foreign policy agenda has often been characterized as "safeguarding democracy" or "promoting human rights." As a country that freed itself from colonization more than two hundred years ago, the United States has cultivated an image as the champion of human rights and democratic governance. However, the true nature of U.S. foreign policy lies just below that facade. A survey of U.S. policy towards its Latin American and Caribbean neighbors in Chapter VI of this book aptly demonstrates that when it comes to U.S. policy, actions speak louder than words. In the case of Haiti it is also painfully clear that the goals professed by the U.S. are only a cover for an insatiable desire to create more markets and economic advantages for them.

During a dinner discussion on May 22, 2002, Ambassador Lino Guiterrez, Principal Deputy Assistant Secretary of State in the Bureau of Western Hemisphere Affairs shared the four official pillars of U.S. policy towards Haiti. He explained,

"The U.S. seeks to:

- Support efforts to strengthen democracy and improve respect for human rights;
- Provide humanitarian assistance to the most vulnerable Haitians, and actively promote sustainable economic development;
- Discourage illegal migration, which threatens maritime safety and the lives of those who risk dangerous sea travel; and
- Stem the flow of illegal drugs through Haiti to the U.S."[100]

These pillars of policy towards Haiti are completely appropriate, and if carried out would certainly lead to better lives for the majority of the Haitian people. In fact, building democracy and respect for human rights, while providing humanitarian assistance and promoting sustainable economic development, are exactly what a democratic Haitian government would be expected to do as well. Based on its stated foreign policy objectives, one would expect the U.S. to actively support the Haitian government enabling it to provide humanitarian assistance and economic development.

Encouraging the creation of truly democratic institutions and a culture of respect for human rights would lead Haiti towards the kind of democracy Haitian peasants have been struggling for – democracy leading to redistribution of power and resources, and promising a better life for the impoverished. In fact, a strong democracy would practically guarantee decreased numbers of fleeing Haitians. It is also likely that the training necessary for the Haitian National Police to become protectors of human rights would bring about a new vengeance against those who control the flow of cocaine through Haiti.

The U.S. has paid ample lip service to its noble policy goals for Haiti, but through this exploration of the reality of U.S. action and its impact on Haiti, it is clear that U.S. intervention serves different goals than those publicly stated. For more than a century, its own economic priorities have directed U.S. policy in Haiti.

***

Since Haitians had their first real chance at building a democracy in 1990, the U.S. has chosen its traditional allies and business interests over the needs of most Haitians. It is difficult to feel optimistic about Haiti's chances for building a real democracy. The powers that prevail against it are just too great.

The dream for which so many Haitians have been willing to give their lives is for a democracy that puts the needs of the poor first. Today Haiti needs strategic assistance for democratic institution building. This assistance must be delivered into the hands of Haitians themselves, through their own elected government. The Haitian people deserve our faith that they can handle themselves in a democracy – that they will closely monitor their own government and its institutions, that they will only vote for those who truly represent their needs, that if necessary they will rebel and raise their voices loud enough for the world, once again, to hear them.

Who are the Haitian people, if not the people we can most trust to rebel if they are not treated fairly by their government? In the last twenty-five years we have seen the overthrow of the Duvalier dictatorship, the creation of democracy, resistance to the military junta, rejection of the structural adjustment program, and record voter turnout. The Haitian people have never been complacent, and they have never sat idly by while their leaders destroyed their economy and country.

As President Aristide himself has explained, democracy in Haiti is not an abstract concept. In the United States, where democracy is a given, most Americans would be hard pressed to define democracy beyond pointing to its bureaucratic framework. Haitians can teach Americans a lot about what democracy is; during a meeting in a rural village, anthropologist Jennie Smith observed this exchange:

> "'What is democracy?' After a long pause, one man tentatively offered a definition. 'Democracy,' he said slowly and thoughtfully, 'is when every person is able to have enough food to eat – and good food – not just corn meal mush with no bean sauce.' A woman with a child nursing at her breast added, 'It's when everybody has the chance to give their children an education instead of having to keep them out of school because we can't afford shoes or books, or need them to work in the fields...Several other people continued: 'Democracy is having a bed to sleep on, instead of a pile of straw or rags heaped on the floor.' 'Some people shouldn't have to walk miles to get cruddy water while other people get ice in their glasses everyday.'"[101]

Haitians can also teach Americans a lot about the U.S. government's policies. The U.S. is not the great protector of human rights abroad. It is not the leading supporter of democracy in the developing world. In Haiti, the U.S. has undermined democracy for one hundred years while at the same time it demoralized, and quite literally killed, people who sought a better life.

It is difficult to feel optimistic about democracy in Haiti because the U.S. simply hasn't let a true democracy take hold. In an U.S.-commissioned CID Gallup Poll in March 2002, most of the Haitian respondents said that their country was headed down the wrong path. Widespread disillusionment with the political crisis was reported. Although the report states that "no other political party comes close to the support enjoyed by Fanmi Lavalas," it is clear that the entire political scene is becoming more irrelevant to people's daily lives. Perhaps the biggest problem is that three out of five of the respondents weren't eating enough every day, a greater concern than the protracted political crisis.[102]

The United States policy towards Haiti is clear: support for democracy will move forward when the government is willing to embrace the U.S. economic agenda. Widespread disenfranchisement of Haitian voters is an acceptable side effect of this policy. Even the humanitarian crisis gripping Haiti today is collateral damage. The U.S. will play hardball with Haiti's democratically elected government, either forcing it to accept the creation of a "compromise government" or simply waiting out Aristide's term as president. When he completes that term in 2006, he will be prevented by the Constitution to run again.

So far no viable Lavalas candidates for 2006 have emerged from the movement or the political party. The United States will continue to "assist" the parties that make up the Democratic Convergence in hopes that 2005 will be the year that the Convergence can beat their current 8% popular support and win the elections. As has been seen in the past, if the correct leader wins the election, the U.S. will accept flaws in the electoral process.

As stated at the beginning of this piece, the future of democracy depends on the ability of the population to tip the balance of power in its favor. With the U.S. on the side of the traditional elite in Haiti, the balance of power will never favor the average Haitian. The corruption of Haiti's young democracy will continue unabated until a mass movement of solidarity and diaspora emerges in the United States to say: *two hundred years is enough.* The U.S. cannot continue its current policies unchecked because those very policies deepen poverty, destroy lives, and threaten to shatter the dream of democracy in Haiti.

---

[1] *Political Origins of Dictatorship and Democracy.* Daron Acemoglu and James A. Robinson, http://socrates.berkeley.edu/~jamesar/

[2] Personal Interview, Georges Werleigh, Economy Professor, January 12, 2003.

[3] *Ibid.*

[4] *Haiti and the United States: The Psychological Moment.* Brenda Gayle Plummer, The University of Georgia Press, 1992. Athens, GA. Pg. 101.

[5] *Written in Blood: The Story of the Haitian People 1492-1995.* Robert Debt Heinl, Nancy Gordon Heinl and Michael Heinl, University Press of America, Inc., 1996. Lanham, MD and London. Pg. 385.

[6] *Haiti and the Great Powers: 1902-1915.* Brenda Gayle Plummer, Louisiana State University Press, 1988. Baton Rouge, LA and London. Pg.229.

[7] *Ibid,* pg. 194.

[8] Personal Interview, Georges Werleigh, Economy Professor, January 12, 2003.

[9] *Haiti and the Great Powers: 1902-1915.* Brenda Gayle Plummer, Louisiana State University Press, 1988. Baton Rouge, LA and London.

[10] Personal Interview, Georges Werleigh, Economy Professor, January 12, 2003.

[11] *Haiti and the Great Powers: 1902-1915.* Brenda Gayle Plummer, Louisiana State University Press, 1988. Baton Rouge, LA and London. pg. 244.

[12] *Haiti and the Great Powers: 1902-1915.* Brenda Gayle Plummer, Louisiana State University Press, 1988. Baton Rouge, LA and London., pg. 240.

[13] *In the Parish of the Poor: Writings from Haiti,* Jean-Betrand Aristide, Orbis Books, Maryknoll, NY. 1993, Pg. 9.

[14] *Political Origins of Dictatorship and Democracy.* Daron Acemoglu and James A. Robinson, http://socrates.berkeley.edu/~jamesar/

[15] *Haiti in the New World Order: The Limits of the Democratic Revolution.* Alex Dupuy, Westview Press, Boulder, CO. 1997, pg. 86-87.

[16] *Ibid*, pg. 101.

[17] *Ibid*, pg. 94.

[18] *Ibid*, pg. 83.

[19] *Ibid*, pg. 89.

[20] *Ibid*, pg. 34.

[21] "Democracy Undermined, Economic Justice Denied: Structural Adjustment and the Aid Juggernaut in Haiti," Lisa A. McGowan for the Development Group for Alternative Policies, Inc. (Development GAP), January 1997.

[22] *Ibid*, pg. 1. Also see website of the 50 Years Is Enough Network, http://www.50years.org/action/s26/factsheet2.html

[23] The World Bank Group is four individual bodies. The largest of these are the International Bank for Reconstruction and Development (IBRD) and the International Financial Corporation (IFC). Each member of the World Bank Group is a shareholder. Every shareholder is allocated a certain number of votes linked to the size of its shareholding. The United States has the largest percentage of the vote in both the IBRD and the IFC. For the IBRD the U.S. controls 16% of the total voting power. The second largest percentage is about 8% controlled by Japan, and Haiti controls .08% of the vote at the IBRD. The IFC is similar; U.S. controls 23% of the vote, Japan 6% and Haiti .04%. See www.worldbank.org. The International Monetary Fund (IMF) uses the same system for allocating voting power. At the IMF, the U.S. controls 17.14% of the vote, compared with Japan's 6% and Haiti's .05%. See www.imf.org.

[24] "Democracy Undermined, Economic Justice Denied: Structural Adjustment and the Aid Juggernaut in Haiti," Lisa A. McGowan for the Development GAP, January 1997. Pg. 1.

[25] *Eyes of the Heart: Seeking a Path for the Poor in the Age of Globalization,* Jean-Betrand Aristide, Common Courage Press, Monroe, ME. 2000. Pg. 11-12.

[26] "Democracy Undermined, Economic Justice Denied: Structural Adjustment and the Aid Juggernaut in Haiti," Lisa A. McGowan for the Development GAP, January 1997. Pg. 3.

[27] *Ibid.*

[28] *Ibid*, pg. 4.

[29] *Ibid*, pg. 13.

[30] *Ibid*, pg. 24.

[31] *Ibid*, pg. 25.

[32] "Feeding Dependency, Starving Democracy: USAID Policies in Haiti", Laurie Richardson for Grassroots Internaitonal, May 1997. Pg.8.

[33] *Ibid*, pg. 8.

[34] *Ibid.*

[35] Personal Interview, Camille Chalmers, PAPDA. January 13, 2003.

[36] "Democracy Undermined, Economic Justice Denied: Structural Adjustment and the Aid Juggernaut in Haiti," Lisa A. McGowan for the Development GAP, January 1997, pg. 19.

[37] Personal notes from economic justice meeting, Camille Chalmers, PAPDA, July 1999.

[38] *Ibid.*

[39] *Ibid.*

[40] *Ibid.*

[41] *Ibid.*

[42] "Democracy Undermined, Economic Justice Denied: Structural Adjustment and the Aid Juggernaut in Haiti," Lisa A. McGowan for the Development GAP, January 1997. pg. 20.

[43] "Declaration by the Presidency on behalf of the European Union on Haiti," March 7, 2003.

[44] "Democracy Undermined, Economic Justice Denied: Structural Adjustment and the Aid Juggernaut in Haiti," Lisa A. McGowan for the Development GAP, January 1997. pg. 2.

[45] "Democracy Intervention in Haiti: The USAID Democracy Enhancement Project," Washington Office on Haiti, March 1994.

[46] *Ibid.*

[47] "The Democracy Offensive," Resource Center Bulleting No. 18, Fall 1989 in "Democracy Intervention in Haiti: The USAID Democracy Enhancement Project," Washington Office on Haiti, March 1994.

[48] *Ibid,* pg. 19.

[49] *Ibid at 43.*

[50] Personal Interview, Georges Werleigh, Economy Professor,, April 7, 2000.

[51] Personal Interview, A. Cyllah, National Democratic Institute, April 13, 2000.

[52] Personal Interviews, April 2000, May 2000.

[53] For a detailed and thorough account of problems with the registration process, see "Elections 2000: Participatory Democracy in Haiti," March 2001, prepared by Melinda Miles and Moira Feeney. Available at: www.haitireborn.org.

[54] Personal Interview, Camille Chalmers, PAPDA, April 5, 2000.

[55] Personal Interview, Alvaro Arciniegas, Organization of American States in Jeremie, April 10, 2000.

[56] Based on various personal interviews conducted in April 2000.

[57] Personal Interview with leaders of Tet Kole Ti Peyizan, April 12, 2000.

[58] *Ibid.*

[59] *Ibid.*

[60] Miami Herald, March 27, 2000.

[61] Author's Notes, Donald Steinberg at Georgetown University, Washington, DC, March 31, 2000.

[62] Senator Michael DeWine, Congressional Record, May 18, 2000.

[63] Reuters, May 22, 2000.

[64] OAS, June 2, 2000.

[65] Haiti Progres, June 7, 2000.

[66] Agence Haitienne de Presse, June 15, 2000.

[67] Associated Press, June 18, 2000.

[68] National Organization for the Advancement of Haitians, June 18, 2000.

[69] Congressional Record, July 13, 2000.

[70] Personal Interview, William Rowland, Political Officer, U.S. Embassy in Haiti, October 19, 2000.

[71] Personal Interview, Erin Soto, USAID Haiti Democracy and Governance Program, October 19, 2000.

[72] Personal Interview, Lovinsky Pierre-Antoine, 30th of September Foundation, October 17, 2000.

[73] *Ibid.*

[74] For a complete list of ICIO participants, see: "Elections 2000: Participatory Democracy in Haiti," March 2001, prepared by Melinda Miles and Moira Feeney. Available at: www.haitireborn.org.

[75] *Ibid.*

[76] KOZEPEP Statement to the Press, December 4, 2000.

[77] Marlik Declaration, Democratic Convergence, December 13, 2000.

[78] Congressional Statement, December 8, 2000.

[79] Miami Herald, December 29, 2000.

[80] Personal Interview, Erin Soto and Sharon Bean, USAID Democracy and Governance, December 2000.

[81] Government of Haiti, Issue Paper on the Electoral Process, February 7, 2003.

[82] The analysis here was prepared by the Let Haiti Live Coalition, of which Miles is a founding member and spokesperson.

[83] See www.trinitydc.edu for the full report on the Trinity College Haiti Program website.

[84] *Ibid.*

[85] Njoki Njoroge Njehu, Director, 50 Years Is Enough Network at the Haiti Solidarity Annual Conference in Washington, DC, March 4, 2003.

[86] "Unjust Embargo of Aid for Haiti," The Lancet, by Paul Farmer, Mary C. Smith Fawzi and Patrice Nevil. 2003; 361:420-23.

[87] Statistics taken from UNICEF "State of the World's Children", the UNDP HDI Rating and the CIA World Factbook

[88] Personal interview, CAMEP Directors, January 16, 2003.

[89] Personal interview, Clinic Staff, SOFA, Martissant, January 13, 2003.

[90] *Ibid.*

[91] Personal Interview, Luis Moreno, Charge d'Affaires, U.S. Embassy, Port-au-Prince, Haiti. January 17, 2003.

[92] Personal Interview, Yannick Etienne, Batay Ouvriye. January 13, 2003.

[93] *Ibid.*

[94] *Ibid.*

[95] Latinamerica Press, Charles Arthur, June 18, 2002.

[96] Personal interview, Committee to Defend Pitobert, at the offices of PAPDA in Port-au-Prince. January 13, 2003.

[97] Reuters, October 10, 2003.

[98] "Rich Man, Poor Man: Ouanaminthe residents say Dominican business giant takes advantage of job-starves town," Amy Bracken for the Haitian Times, October 29, 2003.

[99] *Ibid.*

[100] "U.S. Haiti Policy," Remarks by Ambassador Lino Guiterrez, Principal Deputy Assistant Secretary of State, Bureau of Western Hemisphere Affairs, U.S. Department of State; Dinner Discussion at the Inter-American Dialogue Conference, "Haiti and Development Assistance," Washington, DC. May 22, 2002.

[101] *When the Hands Are Many,* Jennie Smith, Cornell University Press, copyright 2001 by Cornell University. Pg. 5.

[102] "Haiti Public Opinion Poll," March 2002 Final Report, CID Gallup. Copy on file with author.

# Enslaved by Debt

*Marie Clarke, Jubilee USA Network*

The external debt of underdeveloped countries has been one of the most efficient tools in modern history for maintaining what is tantamount to a system of global apartheid. It is a highly complex system that separates the rich from the poor. The poor are sentenced to life without health care, education, clean drinking water, and food. Their countries are burdened with debts so extensive that *"every child in Africa is born with a financial burden which a lifetime's work cannot repay. The debt is a new form of slavery as vicious as the slave trade."*[1]

Haiti provides a comprehensive illustration of the many uses of external debt. The players include the beneficiaries – a global minority of predominantly white creditors who control the resources – and the losers – mainly people of color throughout the developing world, or Global South. There is a wide spectrum of effects of debt, including the obvious: aggravation of existing poverty and erosion of national sovereignty.

Above all else, debt connotes dependence. For a variety of reasons, from lack of resources to corruption, leaders had to take loans from development banks and other governments. A core group of creditors, the wealthy countries known as the Group of 8, make loans and maintain the controlling stock in so-called "humanitarian" agencies like the World Bank and the Inter-American Development Bank, which also make loans. These same countries control the International Monetary Fund, the gatekeeper to international credit.

Each and every loan, bilateral and multilateral, comes with conditions that deepen poverty and human suffering. Perhaps this is where the case study of Haiti is particularly instructive; being in debt virtually since its independence, Haiti is a country whose entire history of development has been stunted by the weight and conditions of its debt. This section will explore the history of Haiti's debt and its effects.

\*\*\*

In 1804, the various Africans and Caribbean-born people enslaved in France's most profitable colony, Haiti, declared their independence. During the revolution, which began in 1792, the rebels burned fields and the homes of colonists and razed the capital of Cap-Haitien twice. All French plantation owners who were not killed were exiled to France.

Because it was a country of freed slaves, Haiti was treated to a sixty-year embargo by the United States. It was determined that Haiti was a bad example for the slaves of the American South, and therefore could not be treated as an equal sovereign nation. France had even more reason to fear and hate the new Republic of Haiti, especially a vocal group of former colonialists who demanded compensation for their losses in the colony. Haiti was allowed to participate in the world economy, but because it did not enjoy international recognition of its independence, its place in the system was at the bottom.

In 1825, in a desperate attempt to put an end to Haiti's alienation, President Boyer brokered a deal with Charles X of France. Haiti agreed to pay France 150 million francs over five years and granted France a 50% break in import tariffs in return for a unilateral declaration by France of Haiti's independence. One hundred and ten million francs would repay the former colonizers for their lost property (namely the Haitians themselves), and 35 million to the government of France for the loss of its public buildings. The second declaration of Haiti's independence was made on March 17, 1825.[2]

There is a twisted irony in freed slaves compensating their former owners; the transfer of capital was more a theft than payment of a debt. In order to make the first payment towards the indemnity, President Boyer was forced to seek loans from bankers in Paris. Haiti became formally indebted, and by 1830 Boyer was pleading with the French government for an alternative arrangement.

On January 23, 1838, Haiti was already deeply indebted when Boyer signed two new treaties. The first conceded without qualification that Haiti was, indeed, sovereign and independent. The second reduced the remaining debt for this independence to 60 million francs to be paid back without interest over thirty years.[3]

After making this new agreement with France, Haiti managed to maintain repayment. In 1915 the United States sent Marines to occupy Haiti, an occupation that lasted about fifteen years. The main goal of this occupation was to secure U.S. dominance in the country as part of its plan to achieve hegemonic control of the hemisphere. U.S. dominance was denoted mainly in economic terms, and the occupation gave the U.S. the opportunity to shift Haiti's economy towards the interests of the U.S.

In 1922, the United States consolidated Haiti's debt. For several years, the U.S. played the role of both creditor and debtor – a U.S. treaty government ruled Haiti and made debt repayment the top economic priority.[4] By 1947 external debt was no longer a problem for Haiti, but the U.S. occupation left a legacy of displaced peasants. The treaty government eliminated a Constitutional provision against ownership of land by foreigners. Fertile land was bought up by U.S.-based agro-industries, and Haiti's farmers watched their markets become flooded with produce from the U.S.

Throughout the second half of the 20th Century, Haitian peasants also watched the floor fall out under them. Produce prices plummeted, the land began to suffer the effects of overuse and widespread erosion, and Haitian staple foods were replaced by food aid from the United States. At the same time, the peasantry was being increasingly marginalized from the governance of their own country. The Duvalier family dictatorship and its supporters – Haiti's wealthy business elite – focused on increasing their profits at any cost, and Haitian peasants paid the price. "This elite did not hesitate to indebt the country internationally during the latter half of the 20th Century, by procuring loans, the proceeds from which primarily ended up in the pockets of politicians."[5]

Inspired by the economic growth spurred by assembly factories in the four Asian tigers, South Korea, Taiwan, Hong Kong and Singapore, international financial institutions (IFIs) made a series of loans to Haiti in the late 1970's intended to make Haiti the "Taiwan of the Caribbean." Money flowed with ease to the tyrannical regimes of the Duvaliers, and the military government that ruled Haiti in the late 1980's. By the time Haiti held its first democratic elections in 1990, elections that constituted a third declaration of Haitian independence, Haiti was deeply indebted, with very little development to show for it.

Haiti's first democratic government was overthrown by the military in a coup d'etat only seven months into its term. During the years of military control, Haiti's state institutions were looted, and the national treasury emptied. Although the U.S.-led multinational forces restored the democratic government in 1994, it also covertly supported the coup leaders.[6] By the time the U.S. publicly intervened, the military junta had destroyed Haiti's already weak and crumbling infrastructure and economy.

Instead of putting together funds for Haiti's reconstruction, the U.S. convened the group of international creditors and devised a series of loans that would lock Haiti into debt for decades to come, loans with conditions that would also put Haiti's new democratic government at odds with the needs of the Haitian population. The funding portfolio came with strict conditions including privatization of state-owned enterprises, cuts in spending for social services like health and education, and trade liberalization measures like lowering import tariffs.[7]

In addition to following the conditions attached to the new loans, the U.S. and other creditors expected the Haitian government to maintain payments on the loans made to the Duvalier dictatorship and the successive military juntas of the 1980's. Any casual observer of the progression of events in Haiti can see the illegitimacy of debts incurred by Haiti's dictators. Yet the institutions that knowingly lent money to thieves – and no one denies that the Duvaliers were thieves – insisted that Haiti make payments on these unjust debts while struggling to rebuild the country in the wake of the dictatorship's departure.

The irony of this scenario – where the victims of a dictator are forced to pay back the money borrowed to oppress them – brings echoes of the debt of independence the freed slaves were forced to pay France in 1825. In this case, Haitians are paying back the U.S. and the international financial institutions it controls, for money it needed to rebuild after the destruction wrought by a U.S.-backed regime.

During the presidency of Rene Preval from 1996-2001, Haiti made progress towards implementing the conditions of its reconstruction loans, (even though the conditions were aggravating already deep poverty), and it made timely payments on those loans. This progress was tempered by growing discontent in Haiti, as the popular movement demonstrated against the government to stop privatization. Haitians demanded the government invest in agriculture, a step that would bring quick condemnation from the IFIs.

As of 2003, Haiti was paying a $1.2 billion debt with payments of $50-80 million each year. To put this amount of money in relative terms, it was twice the public health budget, three times spending for education and four times the expenditures for agriculture.[8] Even as Haiti kept up its payments, the creditor institutions stopped disbursing loans in response to a series of obstacles to Haiti's democratic process. By the year 2000, when Haiti held local and national elections, Haiti's relations with its creditors were strained. Haiti stopped making payments on its loans in early 2001.

# Haiti and the Creditor Institutions:
## The International Monetary Fund (IMF), the World Bank and the Inter-American Development Bank (IDB)

Although its debt appears to be illegitimate for the many reasons detailed above, Haiti's primary creditors, the IMF, World Bank, Inter-American Development Bank (IDB) and the Paris Club, have not annulled Haiti's debt. On the contrary, Haiti is not even eligible for debt relief under the Heavily Indebted Poor Countries Initiative (HIPC).[9] Originally, this was because Haiti did not meet the eligibility criteria of 150% debt to export ratio. By the year 2000, Haiti had close to a 400% debt to export ratio. Once Haiti surpassed the HIPC threshold, Haiti was not eligible because then-President Rene Preval had not privatized national industries according to creditor deadlines.

## Haiti's Debt and Social Indicators at a Glance

| | |
|---|---|
| Total Debt | $1.2 billion |
| % of GDP spent on debt service | 35% |
| Annual debt service | $50-80 million |
| GDP per capita | US $400[10] |

*Haiti's Social Indicators compared to the average in Latin America and the Caribbean*

| Indicator | Haiti | Average for Latin America and the Caribbean |
|---|---|---|
| Rank in 2002 UNDP Human Development Index (out of 173 countries) | 146 | --- |
| People not expected to survive to age 40 (% of population) | 31.6 | 9.7 |
| Life expectancy at birth (years) | 52.6 | 70 |
| Infant mortality (per 1,000 live births) | 81 | 30 |
| Population without access to safe water (in percent) | 54 | 22 |
| Per capita health expenditure in U.S. dollars | 21 | n.a. |
| Physicians per 100,000 people | 8 | n.a. |
| Adult illiteracy (in percent of age 15 and above) | 50.2 | 11.7 |
| Primary school net enrollment (% of relevant age of population) | 80 | 93.3 |
| Percentage of population below the national poverty line<br>Percentage of population living on less than $1 a day | 65<br>85 | n.a.<br>n.a. |

**Sources:** UNDP Human Development Report 2002, IMF SMP Paper 2003, UNICEF "State of the World's Children."

## Haiti and the IMF

The International Monetary Fund characterizes Haiti's economy as being a "critical situation".[11] Haiti has had negative GDP growth, growing external and domestic debt, and rising inflation for several years. In an attempt to re-engage the

IMF, the Haitian government began 2003 by eliminating the subsidy on petroleum products and implementing a flexible pricing mechanism. As a result, fuel prices rose by 130% in a matter of days. Combined with a tightening in monetary policy at the central bank, which resulted in a sharp rise in market interest rates, the subsidy cut stabilized the foreign exchange and inflation began to ease. However, the impact on the poor of Haiti was devastating. Suddenly the cost for the average worker to get to his or her job climbed to 40 Haitan gourdes. These same workers made only 36 gourdes, or less than one dollar per day.

The IMF considered the measures taken by the Haitian government "progress" and to build on such initiative, the IMF re-engaged with Haiti late in 2003 with a Staff-Monitored Program (SMP). If Haiti complied with IMF conditions and completed a successful SMP, it would be eligible for a Poverty Reduction and Growth Facility supported program. Haiti would then prepare an Interim-Poverty Reduction Strategy Paper that would outline the conditions for new loans. In other words, Haiti would be eligible for new concessional loans, and the IMF would give Haiti approval, allowing it to re-engage with the entire donor community.

In order to pass out of the SMP, Haiti needs to implement key structural reforms in the public and banking sectors. Some of these radical reforms include cutting the fiscal deficit by half, creating a sizable reduction in discretionary spending, refusing to grant any public sector wage increases, reducing inflation and stabilizing the exchange rate, addressing governance issues in the public and private sector, raising taxes, and clearing out Haiti's external arrears.[12] However the IMF recognizes in their SMP paper that Haiti will not be able to pay their arrears on debt service without taking out new loans. Thus, Haiti is caught in a catch-22 as they need to accomplish their SMP – which includes clearing their arrears: they need to loans to pay their arrears to get more loans.

In describing the overall context in which Haiti exists the IMF SMP paper adds that Haiti will need "a resolution to the current political stalemate" in order to provide "a credible basis for the implementation of policies."[13] This political analysis may seem out of place in an IMF paper, but it is likely due to the American influence at the institution. The International Monetary Fund (IMF) gives each shareholder a certain number of votes linked to the size of its shareholding. The U.S. has the largest percentage of the vote with 17.14%, compared with the second largest shareholder, Japan who controls 6%. Haiti has 0.05% of the vote at the IMF.[14]

# Haiti and the World Bank and IDB

The World Bank is also controlled, in large part, by the United States. The World Bank Group consists of four individual bodies. The largest of these are the International Bank for Reconstruction and Development (IBRD) and the International Financial Corporation (IFC). The United States has the largest percentage of the vote in both the IBRD and the IFC. In the IBRD the U.S. controls 16% of the total voting power. The second largest percentage is about 8% controlled by Japan, and Haiti controls.08%. The IFC is similar; the U.S. controls 23% of the vote, Japan 6% and Haiti.04%.[15]

The World Bank (WB) is Haiti's largest creditor, followed closely by the Inter-American Development Bank (IDB). Together they claim 75% of Haiti's debt.[16] Although the WB and the IDB are the largest creditors, they follow the lead of the IMF in their relationships with indebted nations.

Haiti's largest and final commitment to the World Bank was made in 1996, when it was credited US$293.6 million. Disbursements of funding to the Haitian government were suspended in January 2001, "due to the accumulation of arrears to the World Bank."[17] As a result, a health project closed on schedule in March 2001 and $16.5 million in credit for road rehabilitation and forest protection were canceled in June 2001. All operations were shut down by December 31, 2001.

In a Country Assistance Evaluation (CAE) published in February 2002, the World Bank found that its own development impact had not been significant and that its strategy was predominantly unsatisfactory, with little impact on poverty reduction. Although the World Bank had been lending to the government of Haiti, in January 2003 the board of the Bank authorized a small grant program of U.S. $4.7 million to international organizations and non-governmental organizations (NGOs) for health, economic governance and institution building.[18]

The World Bank has linked its full re-engagement in Haiti to the government's demonstrated commitment to macroeconomic stability, including good economic governance and progress on reforms. In order to facilitate this, in early 2004 the World Bank was providing advice on a comprehensive arrears clearance plan. The World Bank will only be able to re-engage when Haiti is in an IMF program.

The Inter-American Development Bank (IDB) interrupted its lending for one year because Haiti could not pay its debt service and had accumulated "arrears." The withholding of loans earmarked primarily for health, education and infrastructure sparked significant criticism both in Haiti and among Haitian solidarity groups. Haiti was forced to spend 90% of its reserves to pay the arrears and enable the IDB to re-activate lending. At the end of 2003 the IDB activated $362.45 million in loans and $0.95million in grants.[19]

# Haiti's Debts Must be Cancelled

Today Haiti is facing devastating problems, some of which can be clearly linked to France and the United States, and the creditor institutions in which they are major shareholders. Debt has meant that national resources have been sent to rich creditor countries and institutions instead of being used to improve basic sanitation, health care and education in Haiti. American agro-industry and the peasants they displaced have destroyed Haiti's forest and arable farmland.

Yet, the U.S. still takes no responsibility for events in Haiti. As Dr. Paul Farmer noted in testimony about Haiti before a European Union Commisssion:

> "Much of the analysis [of Haiti], most notably those of French and America journalists, presents Haiti's current problems as if they have nothing to do with slavery, with racism, with war and two centuries of interior and exterior hostility to popular democracy."

In 2003, President Jean-Bertand Aristide launched a national campaign for restitution of the independence debt from France. The demand for more than $21 billion represents the indemnity repayment with interest. Farmer has called this "giving Haiti back the price of its blood." The independence debt is not a debt but a theft, and a historical exploitation that should be immediately repaid with an abject apology.

Cancelling the other debts of Haiti is an obvious way to give the Haitian people a chance at survival. The debts are illegitimate and inhumane, especially in consideration of the price Haitians have already paid in human suffering. The United States should feel a special responsibility to cancel the debts of the Duvalier dictatorship of terror, which was well funded under the U.S. watch.

Unfortunately debt cancellation alone will not solve all the problems in Haiti. If Haiti continues to borrow from international financial institutions and creditor countries, Haiti will still be subject to the harmful economic conditions attached to the loans. It is therefore imperative to cancel the debt without attaching potentially harmful conditions.

---

[1] All Africa Council of Churches.

[2] *Written in Blood: The Story of the Haitian People 1492-1995.* Robert Debt Heinl, Nancy Gordon Heinl and Michael Heinl, University Press of America, Inc., 1996. Lanham, MD and London. Page 162-63.

[3] *Ibid.* Page 164.

[4] Lundahl, Mats. *The Haitian Economy: Man, Land and Markets.* St. Martin's Press, NY. Copyright 1983. Page 33.

[5] *Ibid.* Page 44.

[6] This statement is well supported by the contribution of Brian Concannon, Jr. in Chapter III and by Tom J. Driver in Chapter II of this book.

[7] For a complete treatment of the post-coup loan program, see "Democracy Undermined, Economic Justice Denied: Structural Adjustment and the Aid Juggernaut in Haiti," Lisa A. McGowan for the Development GAP, January 1997.

[8] Personal interview, Camille Chalmers, PAPDA. January 2003.

[9] HIPC, the Heavily Indebted Poor Country Initiative, is the current debt relief program created in 1996 by the World Bank and IMF to provide limited debt relief for the poorest countries with a goal of bringing countries to a "sustainable" level of debt.

[10] Statistics from "HAITI: Why is it necessary to relieve Haiti of its debt burden?" A report by Jubilee 2000 Haiti, Ricot Jean-Pierre, June 2002

[11] International Monetary Fund, Staff-Monitored Program, Prepared by the Western Hemisphere Department June 13, 2003, page 3

[12] International Monetary Fund, Staff-Monitored Program, Prepared by the Western Hemisphere Department June 13, 2003

[13] ibid page 4

[14] See www.imf.org.

[15] See www.worldbank.org.

[16] This fact was spoken by Gerard Johnson, Haiti's Resident Representative for the IDB in a personal interview on January 16, 2003.

[17] International Monetary Fund, Staff-Monitored Program, Prepared by the Western Hemisphere Department June 13, 2003, page 41 Appendix III

[18] ibid

[19] International Monetary Fund, Staff-Monitored Program, Prepared by the Western Hemisphere Department, June 13, 2003, page 42 Appendix IV

# CHAPTER FIVE

*Lamizè fè chen monte kayimit.*

Misery makes the dog climb the tree.

# Haitian Refugees: A People In Search Of Hope[1]

*Cheryl Litte, Esq.*

The United States prides itself on being a nation of immigrants. Its very existence is, after all, the result of the collective effort of those who emigrated to its shores. And in the course of building a great democracy they embraced the cultures that made up their diversely rich population. Along the way to becoming the most powerful and the richest country in the world, Americans also pledged to protect those who fled political persecution.

Asylum should not depend on politics. Asylum seekers do not ask for special treatment, only fair and just treatment. To flee from persecution is not a crime; it is a basic human right and one the U.S. government has recognized since it declared its own independence more than two hundred years ago.

Haitian asylum seekers -- including women and children -- have been singled out by the U.S. government and denied the fundamental protections that are promised to refugees of virtually every other nationality. A series of measures, including prolonged detention, fast-tracked adjudications, interdiction, summary return and third country resettlement, have been put in place to deter and prevent the arrival of Haitian asylum seekers.[2]

Haitians have uniquely been subjected to higher standards, unjustified hardships, and discrimination. While Haiti has never once been cited as a threat to the security of the American people, this government has argued that releasing Haitians who have reached U.S. shores in their quest for freedom, encourages terrorists to use Haiti as a staging point for invasion. Therefore, it concludes, Haitians should remain in detention during the course of their court proceedings, while asylum seekers from any other nation have been allowed to go free.

The first boatload of Haitians seeking asylum from persecution in Haiti arrived in the U.S. in September, 1963. All 23 were denied asylum and deported, signaling the wave of rejection to come. Forty years later, very little has changed. Haitians continue to take boats to flee persecution, only to find discrimination in the very country they hoped would liberate them. Instead of having the opportunity to improve their lives, the lives of their families and their community, the asylum seekers are held as prisoners; families are separated; hopes of freedom are shattered; and many asylum seekers are forced to return home to face the possibility of even greater persecution than that which they had fled.

The most recent high profile case of Haitians fleeing their homeland is a poignant example of our flawed asylum system. On October 29, 2002, South Florida and the world watched in disbelief as 212 Haitians took drastic measures to secure asylum in the United States. Scenes of proud, frightened Haitian men, women and children jumping from the ship that had carried them were broadcast around the world. Shocked Americans watched Haitians, just yards from shore, toss their children overboard into the waiting arms of their fellow asylum seekers, whom they hoped would transport them to safety.[3] Rather than processing them in the usual manner, U.S. immigration officials rounded up the Haitians like criminals and carted them off to detention. Even small children were handcuffed during transport.

Although they came here seeking a better life, harsh reality soon confronted the Haitian refugees. Following their processing at Miami's Krome Detention Center, families were broken up. Parents were forcibly separated from their children and many spouses and siblings separated from each other. The men remained detained at Krome, while many unaccompanied children and women with children were confined in a local hotel, virtual prisoners in their rooms. Some other women were taken to a Broward County location.[4]

One 13-year-old boy whose father was hospitalized following his arrival went for days without knowing that his father had been transferred to Krome. A 17-year-old girl detained in the hotel went for weeks without knowing that her father had been moved from the hotel to Krome. Detainees in one facility were unable to call family members detained in others.[5]

While many Americans who watched the scene unfold were awed at the emotional courage and determination of the Haitians wading to shore that October day, most did not know about their own government's secret policy directed toward Haitians, which had gone into effect eight months earlier.[6] Following the December 3, 2001 arrival of 167 Haitian refugees who had made it to Florida's shore by boat,[7] the INS adopted a secret policy directed solely at Haitians, prolonging the detention of virtually all Haitian asylum seekers in South Florida, regardless of whether they arrived by boat or by plane, and despite the fact that all but two of the 167 had convinced Asylum Officers they had a credible fear of persecution upon return to Haiti.[8]

While adopting the Haitian policy, the INS (now the Department of Homeland Security's Bureau of Immigration and Customs Enforcement) made no changes regarding asylum seekers of other nationalities in the Miami District and continued to routinely release those who had passed their INS Asylum Officer "credible fear" interviews.[9]

The effect of this policy was dramatic and immediate. The release rate for Haitians who had passed their Asylum Officer interviews dropped from 96% in November 2001 to 6% between December 14, 2001 and March 18, 2002.[10] Even Haitians who had been granted asylum and could no longer be legally detained by INS were not immediately released. Only after persistent efforts from immigration lawyers and advocates to determine this sudden change in policy was it revealed that in fact a secret policy did exist, and Acting Deputy INS Commissioner, Michael Becraft, took responsibility for issuing the directive to keep the Haitians in detention (Becraft Policy).[11]

On March 15, 2002, the Florida Immigrant Advocacy Center (FIAC), along with other non-profit legal agencies, filed a class action lawsuit in the Southern District of Florida on behalf of the Haitians.[12] Although the Court found that the INS detention policy differentiated between Haitians and non-Haitians, on May 17, 2002 the judge summarily dismissed the case on the basis that the INS has virtually unfettered statutory and constitutional authority to discriminate and that it is up to politicians in Washington, not the courts, to determine the Haitians' fate.[13] In her ruling, the judge wrote: "Petitioners' cry for freedom needs to be directed to those representatives of the political branches responsible for enacting immigration laws and policies."[14] The Eleventh Circuit Court of Appeals affirmed the lower court's decision and FIAC is appealing to the United States Supreme Court.[15]

## Access to Legal Counsel

Navigating the complex legal system is, at best, complicated and daunting; doing so from detention is exponentially more difficult. Officials created a special Haitian docket to expedite the hearings of the Haitian detainees and additional Immigration Judges were detailed from their downtown Miami courtrooms to detention centers to rush these cases forward. Many of the hearings were scheduled for only 30 to 60 minutes, including time needed for translation, whereas non-Haitian cases are routinely set for three to four hours. Judges have held as many as five merit hearings in a single day. Requests for continuances to prepare the cases for detainees fortunate enough to have legal counsel -- including children -- have routinely been denied.[16]

Both the United Nations High Commissioner for Refugees (UNHCR) and the Lawyers Committee for Human Rights (LCHR) have emphasized that detention severely hinders an asylum seeker's ability to access legal services and effectively present an asylum claim.[17] A study conducted by Georgetown University found that asylum seekers in detention are more than twice as likely as those who aren't detained to be without legal representation and that persons with attorneys are four to six times more likely to be granted asylum.[18]

The vast majority of Haitian asylum seekers speak only Creole; yet in detention, they have been forced to complete complex asylum applications in English. Many Haitians were ordered removed by immigration judges simply because they couldn't properly complete their asylum applications.[19]

Released asylum seekers in South Florida generally have a year or more to find lawyers and prepare their cases. The Haitians, however, have had only weeks to prepare and most are without attorneys. Few agencies are able to provide legal help to the Haitians.[20]

Ironically, at a time when more attorney access than ever was needed to assist the Haitians, there has been less.[21] Since December 2001, attorneys have faced increased restrictions in meeting with their detained clients, including waiting hours, lack of adequate visitation space, and outright denial of access.[22] Attorney access is made even more difficult because the Haitians in South Florida are being housed in four different facilities, miles apart from each other.

## Conditions of Confinement

On March 9, 2002, Congressman Conyers visited the Haitians in three Miami facilities: the Krome Service Processing Center (Krome), a large Department of Homeland Security (DHS) detention center which houses hundreds of men, including those seeking asylum; Turner Guilford Knight Correctional Center (TGK), a maximum security Miami-Dade County jail; and a local hotel which holds asylum seeker children and families. Conyers found "serious deficiencies" in all three facilities.[23] Such conditions of detention further compromise the Haitians' ability to seek asylum.

From December 3, 2001 until August 26, 2002, the Haitian women were held at TGK and subject to frequent invasive strip searches, lockdowns and hourly interruptions of sleep during the night.[24] The Women's Commission for Refugee Women and Children (Women's Commission) twice assessed conditions at TGK and found that the women were living in deplorable conditions and that incarcerating them there seriously interfered with their access to legal assistance and thus jeopardized their ability to successfully pursue their asylum claims.[25] FIAC issued its own supplemental report about conditions at TGK, focusing on the dehumanizing nature of the Haitian women's detention, including inadequate medical care and the lack of translation services, which routinely led some officers to misunderstand, berate and humiliate them.[26] On October 1, 2002, Marie Jocelyn Ocean passionately testified before Senator Edward Kennedy's Subcommittee on Immigration about her detention experience in Florida:

> "On behalf of all the asylum seekers still in detention, I would like to thank you for honoring me with the opportunity to speak to you today about our experience and the treatment we have received here in the United States....

> I came to the United States for peace, freedom and protection. And because I am speaking to you here today, you know that I have found freedom here, and for that I am grateful. On May 31, 2002, the Immigration Judge granted me asylum here in the United States because of the persecution I suffered in Haiti. I am the lucky one though. I am the only Haitian woman from TGK that I know of who has been granted asylum so far, although I know that many of the other women I was detained with also suffered terribly in Haiti. Yet they continue to suffer because they are still detained.

> Like me, all the other Haitian women came here seeking freedom from oppression. We did not leave our homes because of hunger or lack of food, we left because of the political violence in Haiti. So when we first arrived we thought the Americans would treat us with dignity and that they would protect us after what we had suffered....

> So I was shocked by how they treated us. Instead of finding freedom, we were thrown in jail. We were treated worse than nothing, we were treated as criminals.... Even though the laws were too complicated for us to understand alone, our detention made it very difficult for us to get access to lawyers and we had to go to court very quickly. Being detained made it so much harder for us to even have a chance in court.

> At first I was taken to a local hotel in Miami with many of the other women.... One day the officer yelled, "Ocean, court!" and I left thinking I had a hearing. But they did not take me to court. They took me to jail, to TGK. They took my picture and they strip-

searched me. I was so afraid I was about to be deported. I was completely humiliated, and it seemed so unnecessary to treat us like that. But they do this to all the women, not just me.

I never understood what was happening until I got an attorney. At night when I would try to sleep at the jail they would flash lights in our eyes and bang on our doors, and it would startle me terribly. Sometimes it made me remember bad things that happened in Haiti. Many of the officers yelled at us a lot and we didn't understand why. They scared me a lot. Whenever I tried to tell my lawyer about my experience in Haiti, it was difficult to concentrate because we were in a place that was only adding to our misery.

It was at the jail that I met staff from FIAC and they were able to help me and represent me in court. If I didn't have a lawyer I would never have been able to tell the judge my story because the laws are very difficult to understand here. We were supposed to fill out our asylum applications in English, but none of us speak English and many of us cannot read or write.... If it had not been for FIAC, no one would have helped us at all. Most of the women had to go to court and speak to the judge by themselves.... [M]y heart cries for the women that are still there and who did not have a lawyer to help them speak to the judge... it has been almost ten months for them now. They came here because they were afraid for their lives. I cannot understand this because everyone else from every other country was quickly released while the Haitians have stayed in detention. This has made it even more difficult for us, to watch so many other women from other countries come in and quickly get released.

I didn't think the United States would treat people differently just because of the place they were born, I thought everyone was equal here. But we were not treated like everyone else, even though we are all human and we all have the same blood. It became clear to us that the only reason we were in jail indefinitely is because we are Haitian. But I still cannot understand why the Haitians are kept in detention and all the others are released.

I pray that my words today will somehow help the Haitians that are still imprisoned. Thank you for listening to me today."[27]
In late August 2002 the women at TGK were moved to the Broward

Transitional Center (BTC), a minimum-security facility located in Pompano Beach, Florida.[28] While a much more appropriate setting for asylum seekers,[29] Haitian women at BTC complain that certain staff there have yelled at them and told them they smell.[30] There are no counseling services available to the women at BTC.[31] In May 2003, one of the Haitian women suffered a mental breakdown and was taken to a psychiatric hospital.[32] One Haitian woman at BTC used a Creole phrase, "N'ap manje prizon. N'ap bwe prizon," to describe their suffering: "We are eating prison. We are drinking prison."[33]

Krome, which houses most of the male Haitian asylum seekers, has been terribly overcrowded since the Haitians' arrival in December, 2001. In May 2002 the population was over 800 even though officials say the maximum capacity is 485. Haitian men have complained that certain Krome guards call them "terrorists" and otherwise psychologically abuse them.[34] Some complain they have been physically abused.[35]

One of the Haitians at Krome attempted to hang himself in June 2002, and another in April 2003.[36] A statement from one of the young Haitian detainees taken earlier this year illustrates the extent of their suffering:

> "I am 24-years-old. I fled Haiti and arrived on the boat with my brother and his son....

> ...I came to save my life because I thought I would be killed if I stayed in Haiti. I remember I always thought that America is a good and powerful country and that if people fled here for refuge they would be helped. But we have been imprisoned since we arrived, for almost four months now....

> ... My brother Alfred and his son were granted political asylum and they've been released from detention.... When I talk to Alfred, he often cries on the phone with me, because he knows what we suffered in Haiti, he knows the terrible journey we took by boat to get here, and he knows that we continue to suffer in detention....

> There are guards here that say we only came because we are hungry.... The guards look down on us. I told one of the guards that I came here for refuge and didn't expect to be treated the way we are; that if this is how we are going to be treated, they might as well send us back to be killed. The guard said what do we want; we have food and beds, what more do we want.... We can't communicate

with most of the officers though because of the language, although there is one Haitian officer that is nice to us.

What hurts the most is to watch the other nationalities get released. I feel I've seen at least 500 different people come and go from all over the world in these many months I've been here. Only the Haitians stay detained. The people from Guyana, Colombia, China, everywhere you can think of, they all stay for generally a few days and then they are out. Many of the Cubans stay less than a day. But not the Haitians; we stay.

After visitation with our families, we are strip-searched. It is so humiliating....

Sometimes I feel like I'm going crazy in here and that I would rather die than continue facing this mistreatment at Krome.

My dorm is so full of people that sometimes you can't walk without bumping into someone. They had to bring in cots for the people to sleep on. Right before the big group of officials came from Haiti though they moved many people out of my dorm. I don't know where they went, but they haven't come back. It's getting full again though, there are too many people.

...But it's hard to have hope here because... I know there are Haitians from the boat that came in December before us and they are still here 14 months later."[37]

Of all the detention facilities where the Haitians on the October boat were sent, the most egregious is the Comfort Suites Hotel in Southwest Miami, where women and children have been virtual prisoners.[38] Armed, uniformed guards and plain clothes INS guards with handcuffs dangling from their waists monitor the hallways of the fifth floor of the hotel where the mothers and their small children are locked up 24 hours a day, this despite a pool and fitness center located on the premises.[39] Adults and children have gone weeks, even months, without a haircut, comb, change of underclothes, and deodorant.[40] One Haitian mother said she had to bite her 2-year-old's nails because detainees at the hotel had no access to nail clippers or scissors. [41] None of the detainees with whom FIAC has spoken have been able to make any international calls from the hotel, even at their own expense.

Immigration officials issue only adult-sized T-shirts, not pants, to the young children. Detainees are not permitted to wear socks and shoes, only flip-flops, unless they are taken to Krome for court. On random trips to and from Krome some children have been handcuffed with plastic restraints. When taken to court children often miss their regular meals and have to go all day without eating. For over a month earlier this year, the children detained at Boystown -- the non-secure juvenile care facility in Miami -- were forced to wait for court at Krome outside in the hot sun for hours, without shade or any chairs to sit on, due to construction at Krome.

Attorney access at the hotel is more restricted than at any other detention facility in South Florida.[42] Despite repeated requests by FIAC and other immigration attorneys to meet with the Haitian women and children who arrived last October, INS withheld information about them for days. It was only on November 8, 2002, a full ten days after their arrival, that INS finally granted FIAC permission to visit children and families at the hotel.[43]

Once inside the hotel, FIAC learned that six of ten unaccompanied Haitian children being held there had been taken to Krome for court hearings earlier in the day without having any opportunity to speak with an attorney and without legal representation.[44] The remaining children told FIAC that they had no idea what was happening to them and that since their arrival they were unable to contact family members and let them know where they were. The children also said they were told to sign papers they didn't understand. Several of them, including two three-year-olds, had not had a change of clothing, including underwear, since their arrival.[45] The inability of the Haitians at the hotel to communicate with anybody from INS makes it extremely difficult for them to communicate even their most basic needs.

Children ranging in age from seven to seventeen were denied access to education until mid-December 2002, following FIAC's efforts to have them transported from the hotel to the Boystown shelter for classes (primarily English classes). Children younger than six and those eighteen and older continue to be denied access to education, recreation and fresh air. Mothers of children both able to go to Boystown and those not permitted to do so report the troubling effects on those left behind. One child taken to Boystown said he didn't want to return there because they have no deodorant at the hotel and people at Boystown told him he smelled.[46]

Family visits almost never occur. Even legal resident fathers of children and legal resident spouses of detainees have not been permitted to visit or speak with their loved ones. During court appearances, they are generally forced to sit in the back, unable to give their spouses, sons or daughters a hug or kiss.

In March, 2002 FIAC staff accompanying Congressman John Conyers on a tour of the hotel observed a family of five in one room, which included an ill seventy-nine year old Haitian woman and a nineteen month old baby. Those in the same hotel room are often unrelated, forcing families to share their small room with others and sleep two to a bed. Although INS officials have claimed that the hotel is for temporary detention only, a number of Haitian detainees have been held there for months.

Detainees at the hotel spoke to FIAC about the terrible toll conditions there have taken on them and their families. Guilene Silien summarized the particular hardships experienced by women with young children:

> "I arrived on the boat on October 29th with my husband and our six children. My oldest son is 18-years-old so he and my husband are detained at Krome. My other five children and I have been detained here at the hotel since we arrived. We are having such a hard time.
>
> My children who are here with me are ages 5, 8, 12, 14, and 16. We are all in the same room together. I sleep in a bed with my two daughters, two of my sons sleep in another bed, and my 16-year-old sleeps on the sofa bed.
>
> I never knew the United States would imprison children, especially under conditions such as these we live in here.
>
> I never leave our room except for court or to walk down the hall to use the phone. About two months ago, they started taking four of my children to school during the day during the week. But they said my 5-year-old is too little for school, so he and I just stay here locked up in our room all the days.
>
> We never get outside; we never breathe the fresh air. It's especially difficult for my little boy because he's just five, and he cries all the time. And when he cries, I begin to cry too, because I don't know how to console him. He's just a child, he's five years old, he shouldn't be locked up like this. He should be able to go outside and play and be a child. But here they won't even let him out in the hallway, much less outside.
>
> During the day when we're just locked in here alone, I try to teach him things like the alphabet and I try to play with him. But right

now we have no pencil or paper because an officer took them away from us. When my other children came back from Boystown once, they had homework to do, but the officers took away their paper and pencils. We've had toys donated at different times that he plays with. My children that go to school at Boystown got toys on Christmas from a Haitian radio station. But some officers have taken the toys away and given them to the white kids at the hotel. My children cried and asked for their toys back but the officers shooed them away.

We have no way to call my husband and son at Krome. We never have visitation with them and it's so hard not to be able to talk to them. The only time we see each other is when we're taken to court but we can't hug each other or really talk then.

Usually they wake us up at 4 am. It's so cold in the morning but we only get one gray t-shirt. My little girls are especially cold. They got warmer clothes at Boystown, but when they got back from school there the officers took them away. The officers put the clothes in a box and I guess they sent them to Krome.

They even took away the sandals they got. Here they only allow us to have rubber flip-flops.

We can only wear these gray clothes they issue us here. It's like a prison uniform. Imagine my five-year-old little boy isn't allowed his own clothes; he has to wear this prison uniform. And why? Why? He's a child!

We've seen many other people who look like they're from all over the world who are detained here, but they don't stay here. We know now it's only the Haitians who stay detained so long like we have. It's been almost four months now. We are not treated the same as the others.

Visitation is terrible. I've filled out the request paper to visit my family so many times and I haven't been able to see them once. I don't think any of the Haitians have gotten visitation. What's worse is that four times - FOUR times - we've been taken to Krome for visitation. But then we don't get to see our family. We're there. They're there. We ask the guards what's going on, but we just stay there waiting all day until they eventually bring us back to the hotel. I don't know why, it doesn't make sense. Four times we've been taken to Krome for nothing. It's not like we could even see my husband and son. They didn't even know we were there....

We only get to use the phone once a day for five minutes. And it depends on the officer because sometimes it's more like three minutes. Not being able to use the phone when we need to is a serious problem. For example, my attorney needed my children's birth certificates and a friend of my family is going to Haiti and I needed to call that person at 5 pm before he left. I went out to start trying to use the phone at 4 pm, but a guard was on the phone. The guard saw I was waiting for the phone. But then she left, without letting me use the phone.... When she returned, the guard went and got another woman, a white woman, who needed to make a call but I know I was waiting before her.... So in the end, I wasn't able to call the person going to Haiti in time, and I don't know what to do about the birth certificates now.

What I don't understand is why the Haitians are treated different; why are we treated worse than everyone else? Why are we blamed for everything?

One time when my children and I were at court, the judge brought markers and papers for them to color because she knew they were stressed and upset and the kids didn't have anything to do.... When one of the officers left the room, a white man, I think he spoke Spanish, who was also in the room took a Coke from the small refrigerator and drank it. When the officer came back, he went to get his Coke and he got angry. He yelled at my children and me; and then he took their markers and paper away. He brought a Haitian guard who asked us in Creole if we took the Coke. We didn't! My children were crying, and it was the day of our hearing so we were already feeling stressed. That guard still thought we took his Coke. Later on, he found out who really took his Coke and that he was wrong, I don't know how. He did come and apologize to us, but it wasn't necessary, it shouldn't have happened in the first place. He blamed us because we're black and because we're Haitian. And my children suffered for it."[47]

Medical care for detainees at the hotel is terribly inadequate. The manager of the hotel acknowledged in July 2003 that when one of his cleaning staff knocked on one of the Haitians' bathroom door, she found the Haitian woman "in position to give birth." This woman had to be taken to the hospital where her baby was delivered.[48]

Sometimes requests for medical care are ignored. On April 10, 2003 FIAC staff observed Lormise Guilaume carrying her 2-year-old son, Jordan, who was visibly ill. FIAC requested immediate assistance and officers called 911. Jordan was rushed to the emergency room of a local hospital. His health had been deteriorating for some time and medical attention repeatedly requested was inexcusably delayed.[49] On April 3, 2003, a week before Jordan was rushed to the hospital, Lormise stated:

> "I fled Haiti with my two-year-old son, Jordan, by boat. Our boat landed here on February 17th.... My husband is here in the United States..."

> I am very worried about my son here at the hotel. We never go outside. Recreation does not exist for us, we only see the outside world through the glass window, we cannot breathe the air. It's very difficult for my little boy. Sometimes he wakes up screaming in the middle of the night, banging his head on the bed and the walls. He cries much more here. I feel helpless because I don't know what to do for him.

> We have no exercise. My body aches all over from not moving about. I know it's even worse for Jordan. He was much healthier before we came here.

> My son has been sick for weeks. A doctor finally did come and see us here at the hotel and prescribed him some medicine, but the medicine has not worked and it's been well over a week since he saw the doctor. The problem was that I don't speak English and the doctor didn't speak Creole. He did not use an interpreter, so I couldn't tell the doctor about all of my son's symptoms.

> Jordan doesn't eat the food they give us here. Mostly, he just drinks juice; he won't eat much at all. I don't know what to do. I'm very worried about his health, because they give the children the same food they give adults. It's terrible food and we're not used to it, and

it does not seem nutritional to me. Sometimes Jordan can't sleep because he's hungry, but I have nothing to give him....

Sometimes there aren't even enough diapers for him. He didn't have anything at all for the first couple of weeks we were here. As a result, sometimes he urinates on the floor and then I have to clean up the mess....

At first we were in a room with the other Haitian woman and her 2-year-old daughter when we arrived. There are two beds and a sofa in our room. Now we're in a room with a [unrelated] pregnant lady.

It's just so hard to be locked up all day and to never get out. My little boy is bouncing off the walls. There's nothing for us to do. The only time we've gotten out is when they take us to the van to go to Krome for court....

I never imagined the United States would treat us like this."[50]

Lormise and Jordan were finally granted humanitarian parole on April 17, 2003, following media coverage about the case.[51]

Prolonged detention at the hotel is also causing psychological harm to young children. Milia Auguste, who was detained at the hotel for over two months with her two-year-old daughter, perhaps best described the problem:

"I fled Haiti by boat with my two-year-old daughter, Fara, because of political problems. Our boat made it to shore and we were picked up by Immigration on February 17, 2003. My father lives in Miami and he's a U.S. Citizen.

I know we are in a 'hotel,' but it's really a prison. They have no pity, no mercy, on us, not even on the children....

Our children cannot play outside in the sun, they can't breathe the air. This is no way to treat a child....

Fara, my daughter, has started acting out here. She is constantly running to the window and trying to pull down the curtains. She gets excited looking at the cars and the people outside but she doesn't understand why she can't go outside too. She jumps on the bed and sometimes she's tried to break things. She tries to take the sheets off the bed. She never acted this way in Haiti. I think she's suffering because she's locked up.

She also cries all the time here. I don't have enough diapers for her. I usually get two a day, but it's not enough. If she stays wet her skin gets very irritated. She already has rashes all over her body here... you can see them....

Fara only has a big adult-sized t-shirt. She has two of them so I wash one each day. She has three pairs of boy's underwear that are about five sizes too big. She has no pants and no socks. Only when we go to Krome can she get her shoes she came with. She can't have them here at the hotel....

We do our hair in small braids because it's the cleanest way we can be. The only combs are from detainees who have left so everyone's using the same combs. You can't get a haircut here. Another woman asked for a haircut for her two-year-old son and was told no.

We don't have nail clippers. I bite my nails to trim them. I bite Fara's nails for her to trim hers. They treat us like animals.

Fara can't eat the food here.... I can't force Fara to eat. She's hungry all the time. She only eats the cereal and milk and drinks juice. But for two weeks we didn't even get the juice. They give the children the same food they give the adults. It's not healthy for children. Sometimes she's had diarrhea because she's eating so poorly here.

There is a woman here with a six or seven month old baby. They don't even give her special food for the baby. Sometimes she gets a banana that she tries to feed him, otherwise she's just breastfeeding. The mother told me that's about all her baby boy gets.

The children are starving. What hurts the most is when the guards come in with their own food. Fara loves fried chicken and the guards will come in with Kentucky Fried Chicken. The children smell it, and they're hungry so they go to the doors and stare at the guards eating. The guards just yell at them and make them go back in their rooms.

Why can't they allow our families to at least bring us food so our children can eat?...

When they take us to court they come for us at 6:00 a.m. I don't know why it's necessary to take us so early since we didn't have to be in court until 1:00 p.m. When we had court last, Fara didn't eat all day. She had a little cereal in the morning but she wouldn't eat anything at Krome and they didn't bring us back here until 11:00PM at night. We had to just sit in processing at Krome for all those hours.

I told the guards at Krome about Fara's rashes but in all that time while we were waiting they didn't take us to the doctor. They said the doctor would come this week to the hotel. Then Monday they took us to Krome again supposedly to see the doctor. We left at noon and came back around 5:00p.m. But the doctor never saw us....

Not all of the guards are mean though. But some really are, maybe they just don't have children themselves, and they don't understand how much it hurts that the children can't go outside to play....

Some guards allow the children to play in the hall and will let us go to other rooms to visit. But other guards will yell if we stick out necks out of our room for just a second. There is one who is especially mean and orders all the guards not to let us out of our rooms. He yells at us a lot and I cry when he comes.

Fara doesn't understand which guard is which and sometimes when she gets too excited she'll try to run in the hallway when there's a guard who doesn't allow the children out. Guards have told me more than once that if I can't control my little girl they will take her away from me and give her to someone who can. I've heard them say that to other mothers too.

I'm so scared they'll take Fara away from me....

She doesn't want to stay in the room. She wants to go outside and play. One day she was playing by the door, and not all of the women officers knock when they come in our rooms. She opened the door on Fara and it hit her head. I know the officer didn't mean to and it was an accident and she gave Fara ice. But they don't have consideration for children at all.

But other officers are nice.... And others have said they don't understand why we're still here if my father is a U.S. citizen.... They guards said it's not Immigration, it's our attorneys who are keeping us here....

Even my two-year-old daughter understands that we're being treated differently. The others get released and we stay. Some women come to say good-bye and it makes Fara cry so much because she doesn't understand why we can't go too. I can't explain it to her....

We live in a room with two other adult women. I sleep with my daughter in one bed, one woman sleeps in the other bed, and the other woman sleeps on the sofa-bed. Fara needs another child to play with though. She has no one....

Some of the women who were here and had been here for a longer time than we have talked about wanting to hurt themselves and die. This place drives people to want to kill themselves....

My father is a U.S. citizen. It's not hunger that drove us to leave Haiti... We came because we have real political problems.... We did not come to be a burden to the American people. We have families willing and able to take care of us.... I never expected this from the United States. This is a very powerful country. How can they treat children this way? Why are they punishing us so? Why are they treating my baby this way?"[52]

Not surprisingly, the vast majority of the Haitians are increasingly anxious, depressed and despondent, which has adversely affected their ability to articulate their asylum claims. Many have said they feel pressured by U.S. officials to abandon their asylum claims; it has been hard for them to remain focused after months of detention, lack of contact with their family and friends, and restrictions that make them feel as though they are criminals. Many Haitians have engaged in a number of hunger strikes to call attention to their plight.[53]

Despite these obstacles, more than 25% of the Haitians who arrived on October 29, 2002 have been granted political asylum, which speaks to the strength of their claims. Several Haitians granted asylum have languished in detention simply because the INS filed an appeal in their case, a harassment that seems particular to the Haitian detainees.

For example,18-year-old Ernesto Joseph was granted asylum while at Krome. Immediately following his asylum grant, the immigration judge advised the INS trial attorney she hoped the case would not be appealed. INS, nonetheless, decided to do so and kept Ernesto in detention.

Ernesto, a soft-spoken young man who looks much younger than his age, told FIAC during one of their visits with him:

> "I arrived on the boat on October 29th with my little brother. But I made it to land and he didn't, they picked him up in the water. He was deported to Haiti."

> I said I was 17 when I arrived and all of the kids were sent to the hotel. I was in a room with my two cousins who were about my age and they were also on the boat.

> After a couple of weeks my finger was infected because I got a nail stuck in it on the boat. I was taken to the clinic at Krome to fix my finger and they just never took me back to the hotel. My cousins and the other kids went to Boystown. I just stayed here at Krome even though I was still 17...

> I don't know why I haven't been released. My uncle and aunt are here. I can't talk to them on the phone very often though because I don't have any money to call. Sometimes another detainee let's me use a few minutes of their card to call, but that's it. I know my family in Haiti has my birth certificate but I think they haven't found anyone to bring it here yet.

> Jack is my attorney from FIAC. When I went to court on January 29, 2003 I was granted asylum. But since then, I've been very confused about what is happening to me because I'm still detained....

> I feel so alone....

I cry every day at Krome. I'm very sad because I don't understand why I'm still detained. Even before I won my case, I watched all the other nationalities get released except the Haitians.... I don't understand why this is all happening to me. It troubles me a lot.

Some of the guards say we just came here because we're hungry.... They mistreat us by yelling at us....

I just keep wondering, why me? What did I do? I'm so confused and down and depressed. It doesn't make any sense."[54]

Amnesty International took up Ernesto's case[55] and FIAC contacted a Trauma Specialist who diagnosed Ernesto with Post Traumatic Stress Disorder (PTSD), and extreme depression. She concluded that his prolonged detention was causing Ernesto "irreparable harm" and that he was in need of immediate therapy, which he was not receiving at Krome.[56] A psychologist contracted by DHS also evaluated Ernesto on two occasions and his findings confirmed this evaluation.[57] Ernesto was released almost 5 months after being granted asylum.[58]

A father and son detained in the hotel were also among a group of Haitians forced to remain in detention after being granted political asylum. Alfred Selmo tearfully reported:

"I arrived on the boat on October 29, 2002, with my 13-year-old son, Angelo. Our lawyer is Christina [at FIAC]. The judge granted us political asylum... but we're still detained here at the hotel. I don't know when we'll be released but I don't see how they can hold us here anymore since the judge said we can stay. I couldn't sleep all night last night because I was thinking about how we got asylum, but we're still here, and I'm so confused...."[59]

The Board of Appeals (BIA) has upheld decisions in cases where immigration judges granted asylum to Haitians, forcing INS to release them.[60] The BIA has also reversed immigration judges' denials of asylum to Haitians (such as the case of one 27-year old who spent nine months in Krome following his October 2002 arrival by deciding that "Lavalas members [in Haiti] have terrorized and executed members of opposition parties.)"[61]

One family was tragically torn apart when certain members were granted asylum and others denied. Ernest Moise, along with his two children, his common law wife and her two adult children from a prior relationship, arrived off the coast of Florida on December 3, 2001. The family was detained in three separate locations; initially, INS placed the father and the two teenage sons in a secured hotel room, and the mother in a separate room at the hotel before moving her to TGK. The adult daughter and the adult son were placed in TGK and Krome, respectively.[62]

Mr. Moise convinced the Immigration Judge that he and his two sons should be granted political asylum. But because INS reserved the right to appeal the case before the BIA, Mr. Moise was forced to return to the locked hotel room with his two sons following the judge's decision in his favor. Only after Representative Conyers met with the Moise family, and FIAC filed a lawsuit in federal court, did INS finally decide that they would not appeal Mr. Moise's case. INS therefore had to release Mr. Moise and his two sons.[63]

However, because Mr. Moise and the boys' mother were never legally married, she could not benefit from his asylum status. Another Immigration Judge heard her claim and that of her two adult children. He denied that case, refusing to take into account the asylum status of her other children and common law husband.[64] The mother and daughter were detained at TGK and then BTC for over a year before being forcibly removed to Haiti.[65]

## Treatment of Unaccompanied Minors Detained At Boystown

Several of the more than thirty children from the October boat were unaccompanied minors. These children should have been quickly taken to the Boystown shelter because there was ample room for them there. Instead, they languished at the hotel for days.[66] Indeed, one Haitian girl was detained at the hotel for six months before being moved to Boystown.[67]

While it is reasonable that sponsors for these children are subject to background checks and suitability assessments, the government should make prompt and continuous efforts to secure their release but this has not been done. On the contrary, even though most of the unaccompanied Haitian children who arrived in October 2002 had family in the United States, their detention was delayed and the release process put unreasonable demands on their families.[68]

Chimene Noel, the legal resident sister of 16-year-old Jimy Noel, spent weeks gathering the required documents for Jimmy's release and had to travel to Haiti to attempt to secure his original birth certificate.[69] Due to the enormous time spent to satisfy INS' demands, Chimene was fired from her job. She had also been denied permission to visit Jimmy at the hospital shortly after he arrived in October 2002, and burst into tears when she was forced to leave the hospital:

> "I called Haiti and found out that Joseph, my 15-year-old brother, came to Miami on the October 29, 2002 boat. I found out that he was taken to Jackson Hospital. When I went to the hospital and into his room, there was an immigration Officer there. I was about to go in to hug my brother and see how he was doing, but the officer would not let me in. I tried to plead with the officer and begged him to let me see my brother, but he started screaming at me and did not let me in the room. It had been six years since I had seen my brother. I had to leave the hospital in tears without being able to talk to him and see how he was doing."[70]

Because Chimene spoke to the press about her concerns, Jimmy was advised while at Boystown that he could be deported because his sister was "making problems."[71] Jimmy was finally released on Christmas Eve, 2002.[72]

At times the INS delays seemed deliberately cruel. Kervens Bellot, who was 16 when first taken into immigration custody, won his asylum hearing on January 28, 2003, but was kept in detention solely because his family in Haiti had provided documentation in excess of what INS was requiring. His family's letter from Haiti gave his Miami aunt permission to "adopt" him, rather than simply take "custody" of him. The Miami aunt was forced to obtain a modification of the original letter and send it back to INS, significantly delaying Kervens' release.[73]

Particularly egregious was the prolonged detention of a 17-year-old girl who arrived in October 2002. Although pregnant at the time of her arrival, she was detained at Boystown for 3½ months. She told FIAC "I can't stay here much longer. I am suffering so in this place."[74]

All unaccompanied children taken into custody by immigration enforcement officials are placed in removal proceedings and have the right to a hearing before an immigration judge who will determine if the child will be allowed to remain in the United States.[75] In the past, unaccompanied Haitian children, like many others who have appropriate caregivers in the U.S., have generally been released fairly quickly and therefore spared the trauma of having to prepare their legal cases while in detention. FIAC represented all of the unaccompanied children who arrived on the October 2002 boat.[76] Since they languished in detention, virtually all were forced to go forward with their cases while in custody at

Boystown, in the same expedited manner as the adults. The INS' Miami Juvenile Coordinator acknowledged that "no Haitian [child] at Boystown has ever [before] had to go forward with their [court] proceedings in detention."[77]

Trying to prepare a case for someone in detention is a serious challenge, if not a penalizing handicap, and for children it is even more so. Unaccompanied minors often are intimidated and confused upon arrival, unable to make informed decisions. Children, like adult detainees, have little if any understanding of the American legal process and have to overcome language and cultural barriers, too. For children who have fled persecution and may be suffering from post traumatic stress disorder, getting the true history with accurate and verifiable details takes time, something the U.S. government will not afford them.

Of particular concern was the government's decision to send to foster care in New York and Virginia certain children who had family in the United States willing to raise them. In many of these cases, the government insisted that the proper paperwork had not been provided, ignoring the persistent and deliberate efforts of family members to comply with stringent requirements and the extreme difficulties the families faced in attempting to do so.

One such relative told FIAC:

> "The worst thing is that INS told my cousin that if she doesn't give them what they ask, they're going to send her nephew to a family he doesn't know in New York. How can they do that? They're going to give the kid to a family he doesn't even know when he has family right here.... I would do anything to take care of my family. I love my family so much. I can't believe they treating them like this, just because we're not like them."[78]

Ironically, many children without family or other sponsors who should have been quickly sent to foster care remained in INS custody for months.[79] A process that should have taken no more than a few weeks took months.[80]

In addition, children who should have been released to family in the U.S. were instead kept at Boystown until they turned 18 and then transferred to Krome.[81] Ovide Paul is the father of one such child. His statement on December 13, 2002, reflects the devastating affects of this cruel policy:

"The INS is detaining my son in Miami. On November 1,2002, my brother left me a message from the Krome Detention Center, letting me know that he was on the October 29th boat...

A few days after my brother's call, a caseworker from Boystown called me and put my son on the phone and let me talk to him. The next day I went to Boystown to visit my son. I was told to bring in several documents in order for my son to be released to me. I took all of the documents with me and gave them to the caseworker.

I was told that my son would be released to me before his eighteenth birthday, which was on December 3rd. On December 1st, I called and was told that I would get a call letting me know when to pick him up.

On my son's birthday, when I did not get any call, I again called Boystown. But this time I was told that he had been transferred to Krome, where they hold adult men. I was devastated by the news. I did everything I was asked to do and do not think that it was right of INS not to release my son. The situation is very hard for me. He is my oldest son and I love him so much. I am very disappointed by INS' actions.

My son would have not come unless he was scared and desperate. I thought that INS would take the cases of the children into consideration and release them, but they did the opposite. I know that many other families are in the same situation as myself; that they are troubled, depressed and worried because their relatives not being released, especially those who have children that are being detained. I pray that INS will do the right thing and release these children and people to their families."[82]

Little has changed, even though the Office of Refugee Resettlement (ORR) is now responsible for the care, custody, and placement of unaccompanied minor children through provisions of the Homeland Security Act. Children's advocates are concerned that DHS is dragging its heels in turning cases over to ORR. Gilbert Alcenor was approved by the ORR for foster care placement in Michigan while still a minor, but instead was kept in DHS custody until he turned 18, and then transferred to Krome, where his status changed from an unaccompanied minor to an adult. The program in Maryland was expecting Gilbert to be transferred there on June 6, 2003, and was fully prepared for his arrival.[83] Following his transfer to Krome Gilbert told FIAC:

> "Last Friday [June 6th] my social worker at Boystown told me Washington approved me for a foster home in Michigan. She said even if I was turning 18 on Monday, it was not a problem, Washington agreed to send me to the foster home. I was so happy and excited. I had so much hope. But I never went to my foster home.
>
> Then Krome came for me on my birthday, on Monday. At about 2:00 pm they came and got me out of class. I was frightened. They said Krome came for me. No one told me anything except that. I didn't see my social worker again. I told the Krome people I want to speak to my Deportation Officer C I want to know why C for what reason did he do this to me? I still haven't spoken to anyone and no one [official] has told me anything.
>
> I couldn't call my family to say I was sent here and not to Michigan. I don't know if my family knows I'm here. I don't have a phonecard. No one told me how to get one, and no one let me call anyone to say where I am. I still don't know why I'm here. I mean, they said Washington agreed for me to go to a foster home, but I'm not there, I'm in jail. I just been crying all the time. I thought I was going to a foster home, and this is what happened to me. They locked me up. I keep thinking they must hate me, they must really want to get rid of me. But why? Why tell me I'm going to a foster home and then take me to a jail? It hurt me a lot, a lot. I feel so alone here.
>
> All I want is to be given a chance. I can't go back to Haiti. I wouldn't last a day. I got real problems there. I just want to be free from all that. I don't want to cry all the time. I can't take it here. I feel like I'm dying here.
>
> What they did to me was very wrong. They give me hope and then they took it away."[84]

Children who claim to be minors with vaild birth certificates have been placed in adult facilities based on dental exams requested by DHS. Kenier Tima, for example, says he is sixteen. His uncle in Dania Beach, Florida, swears it's true. A birth certificate confirms this. But Kenier has been confined in an adult jail in Louisiana for months, 650 miles away from his FIAC attorney and U.S. relatives.[85] Tima's uncle can't believe what's happened to his nephew: "He's only sixteen, he's supposed to go to school. He can't. I'm very worried about him. They treat him like a criminal."[86]

Kenier arrived in Miami on a boat in February 2003. His uncle said his nephew stopped calling him after Kenier was transferred to the New Orleans jail in April. A New Orleans deportation officer told FIAC that Kenier's relatives in Haiti would have to travel to the American Embassy there to provide further evidence of Kenier's age. According to the South Florida Sun-Sentinel, the Miami-Dade dentist who evaluated Kenier's x-ray for the federal government admitted, "at best it's a guesstimate."[87]

Two Haitian children who arrived in October and were initially mislabeled adults based on dental exams were eventually transferred from adult facilities to Boystown. Still, the children suffered needlessly for months. Groups such as Amnesty International and Physicians for Human Rights have criticized the frequent use of dental exams conducted in cases of children where the government doubts their age.[88]

Still other children have been unable to win release because DHS officials have labeled them "accompanied" since they arrived with older siblings. These siblings, however, were placed in immigration custody in adult detention facilities. This is an inescapable quandary. The release of the siblings from Boystown is contingent on the release of the older sibling, except those young men are being detained indefinitely at Krome and thus unable to even communicate with their younger siblings much less care for them.

Miami-Dade County Commissioners were so outraged by the treatment of both unaccompanied and accompanied Haitian children who arrived in October that on December 17, 2002 they passed a resolution calling for their immediate release.[89] In March 2003 Senator Bob Graham urged the Department of Homeland Security to release all the Haitian children.[90]

Sister Jeanne O'Laughlin, President of Miami's Barry University, even offered to sponsor the Haitian children, but DHS officials repeatedly and mistakenly claimed they were unaware of such a request.[91] Sister Jeanne's offer was not made lightly. In 1982 she successfully helped sponsor over 300 Haitians following their release from detention.[92]

## Government's Justification For Its Haitian Policy

Despite repeated requests from immigrant advocates, politicians and leaders in the Haitian community, INS did not feel it had any responsibility to provide justification for its Haitian policy. In March, 2002, following FIAC's lawsuit, INS officials claimed they adopted the policy in order to save Haitian lives because there was evidence of a "mass exodus" of Haitian boat persons that could rival the tens of thousands who fled Cuba and Haiti in the 1990's or the Cuban Mariel Exodus in 1980.

The U.S. Coast Guard's statistics clearly belie this claim. The only evidence INS offered in support of its initial claim of a mass migration were Coast Guard statistics which showed that 350 Haitians were intercepted in November, 2001 as compared to 96 during the preceding three months. However, such patterns are not unusual and Coast Guard statistics have shown such patterns in the past yet no mass migration followed.[93]

Moreover, although there were fewer interdictions in the first half of 2002 than there were in the first half of 2001, the drop cannot be attributed to the Haitian detention policy because the INS denied it even had such a policy until mid-March 2002. A secret policy clearly cannot have a deterrent effect. Indeed, although no Haitians were interdicted in January or February of 2002, when this policy was still a secret, in the months *after* this policy was made public the number of interdicted Haitians increased considerably.[94]

According to the Coast Guard's own figures, more Ecuadorians were interdicted at sea last year than Haitians. And this year, it has interdicted more Dominicans than Haitians.[95]

Most importantly, INS' claim that absent the current Haitian detention policy we were likely to see a Haitian exodus rivaling the Mariel Boatlift or the number of Haitians and Cubans who were detained in Guantánamo in the mid-90's is absurd. Only 1,391 Haitians were interdicted at sea by the Coast Guard in FY 2001 and only 1486 in FY 2002. These numbers are significantly smaller than the

Mariel Boatlift in the spring of 1980, during which 125,000 Cubans arrived in the United States, or the relatively large flow of refugees in 1994-1995 consisting of 25,069 Haitians and 37,191 Cubans.

History suggests that Haitians who are desperate to flee political violence in their country will not be deterred from coming to the United States by threat of detention; they know full well the risks they face when they take to the high seas in flimsy boats. The vast majority are interdicted by the U.S. Coast Guard and forcibly returned. Others, even less fortunate, lose their lives at sea. For many Haitians, however, the only option is to flee by sea. Indeed, Haitian refugees have repeatedly claimed: "the sea is our embassy."

At FIAC's request, the United Nations High Commissioner for Refugees wrote an advisory opinion on April 15, 2002 concluding that using detention as a deterrent to asylum seekers is a violation of international law and amounts to arbitrary detention.[96] They also concluded that detaining asylum seekers of a particular nationality while releasing those of other nationalities violates international norms of refugee law.

Following the very public arrival of Haitians in October 2002, our government suddenly insisted it must detain the Haitians for purposes of "national security."[97] This justification followed decisions by immigration judges to release many of the Haitians on bond. One such Haitian is David Joseph, an 18-year-old who fled Haiti with his younger brother. Attorneys from FIAC represented David at his bond proceedings and after carefully considering the facts, an Immigration Judge concluded that David was not a flight risk or a danger to the community and granted him a bond of $2500. His uncle, a permanent legal resident of the United States, willingly paid. However, at the bond hearing INS invoked a new regulation created post 9-11 which prevented David's release.[98] FIAC filed a brief with the BIA -- the highest immigration court in the U.S. -- in support of the Immigration Judge's decision to release David. The BIA upheld the judge's decision, calling into question the legitimacy of the detention policy applied to virtually all Haitians who arrived by boat in October 2002.[99]

On March 20, 2003 Under Secretary for Border and Transportation Security, Asa Hutchinson, urged the Attorney General to deny not only David Joseph's release but that of all similarly situated Haitians.[100]

On April 17, 2003, John Ashcroft did just that. In a 19-page decision he ordered the indefinite and arbitrary detention of David Joseph and all Haitian asylum seekers granted bonds, even though Mr. Ashcroft recognized that neither

David nor any of the other Haitians themselves posed a risk to national security. General concerns about conditions in a particular country were sufficient reason, he claims, to deny release to individuals such as David.[101] Haitians were to be kept in detention, in other words, simply because they were Haitian.[102]

More specifically, the Attorney General concluded that releasing the Haitians would cause a "surge" in other aliens attempting to reach the United States by sea and that there were insufficient resources to adequately screen such persons who might "contain aliens seeking to threaten the homeland security of the United States." He further noted that the State Department has "noticed an increase in third country nations (Pakistan, Palestinians, etc.) using Haiti as a staging point for attempted migration to the United States."[103] Releasing Haitians, therefore, would encourage terrorists to use Haiti as a staging point to invade our shores.

Such arguments are clearly a pretext for discrimination and set a dangerous precedent. In a declaration submitted to the District Court on March 18, 2002, the Acting Deputy INS Commissioner never once mentioned national security reasons for keeping the Haitians in detention. He argued that it was the threat of a "mass migration" and the desire to prevent Haitians from risking their lives on the high seas that drove the policy.[104] Moreover, by including airport arrivals in its initial directive to detain the Haitians, it was clear that saving lives on the high seas was merely a cover for a more discriminatory purpose.

In a White House briefing on October 30, 2002, Press Secretary Ari Fleischer said that "the Coast Guard determined that the [Haitians'] vessel did not present a threat to the homeland security of the United States."[105] And even Intelligence experts have questioned the Justice Department's tactics. The former head of counter-terrorism for the CIA, Vincent Cannistrana, has said that Haiti is not a favorable environment for terrorists.[106] Similarly, Harry "Skip" Brandon, former head of counter-terrorism for the FBI, said of the expanded use of expedited removal, that "this is not a national security measure per se and may be a misapplication of the national security rubric."[107] One would also think that U.S. government officials would be able to discern between a black, Creole-speaking Haitian refugee and a true terrorist.[108]

DHS' purported rationale is further undermined by the fact that DHS does not seek to detain Cuban nationals who arrive by sea. Cubans represent one of the two largest ethnic groups who arrive in the United States via water craft. U.S. Coast Guard interdiction statistics since 1995 indicate that Cubans are interdicted about as frequently as Haitians and represent one quarter of the individuals coming to the United States by sea.[109] If DHS officials actually believed that detaining sea arrivals would deter sea migration, save lives, and free up Coast Guard anti-terrorism resources, surely DHS would not have exempted one of the two largest populations arriving in the U.S. by boat from their detention policy.

Ironically, although Haiti has *not once* been cited as posing a threat to the security of the American people, Cubans who flee by boat and make it to the United States continue to be quickly released on a regular basis, even though Cuba *is* on the list of seven countries that the Administration designated as state sponsors of terrorism.[110] In a July 16, 2002 Fact Sheet, the White House states "[t]he Cuban government rightfully remains on the State Department's Terrorist List due to its continued support for terrorism, including the fact that it continues to harbor fugitives from justice wanted in the United States for terrorism-related offenses." It strains credibility that the Administration, on the one hand, claims that Haitian boat people might be detained for purposes of national security while it exempts those from the only country in the region that appears on the Administration's List of State Sponsors of Terrorism.

The former U.S. Ambassador to Haiti, Brian Dean Curran, acknowledged that "we have a double standard, but it's legislated."[111] Still, our government cannot justify its differential treatment of Cubans today solely on the basis that Cubans are automatically eligible for lawful permanent residency soon after they reach our shores. The Cuban Adjustment Act of 1966 (CAA) only applies to Cubans who have been "inspected and admitted" or "paroled." If Cubans were denied parole, as are the Haitians, they would not be eligible to become lawful permanent residents under the CAA.[112]

This is not to suggest that Cuban boat people should be treated as poorly as Haitian boat people, but rather to suggest that if DHS maintains that illegal migration by Cuban nationals does not represent a threat to national security, then there is no legitimate basis for arguing that Haitian boat people do. To imply, as DHS does, that Coast Guard resources expended in the rescue of Cubans is money well spent, but that Coast Guard resources expended to rescue Haitians is a waste of money, is plainly discriminatory.

Cubans have typically been described as "political refugees" and Haitians as "economic migrants." In its resettlement plan for FY 2003, the State Department described Haitian migration as being largely "economic" in nature.[113] Yet the State Department's own annual human rights report raises serious concerns about the deteriorating political situation in Haiti, citing "extrajudicial killings" by members of Haiti's police and increasing attacks on journalists and political dissenters.[114] In August 2003 the State Department concluded that "Haiti has experienced an alarming rise in civil and political unrest," that "there are no 'safe areas' in Haiti" and that "U.S. citizens who must travel to Haiti should exercise extreme caution throughout the country."[115] Public statements from high-level U.S. government officials, including Colin Powell, reports from Amnesty International, and other reputable human rights organizations, also paint a dismal picture of Haiti's political landscape.[116] The characterization of Haitians as economic immigrants ignores the fact that Haiti's economic problems are intrinsically tied to its political instability.

It is notable that the Office of Inspector General (OIG), the Justice Department's internal oversight unit, released a report on June 2, 2003 that seriously questions the U.S. government's current detention policies.[117] The 198-page report is highly critical of long-term "preventative" detention of immigrants swept up in the aftermath of 9-11.

Those concerned about the Haitian policy became extremely frustrated in attempting to learn exactly how the Haitian policy was developed and who had final authority for revising it.[118] In remarks to the Senate Immigration Subcommittee last fall, Senator Bob Graham wrote: "[be]cause the decision-making process has been shrouded in secrecy, with no person or agency seemingly accountable, the feelings of unfairness, discrimination and disparate treatment have deepened..."

On November 7, 2002, in response to a question about the U.S. government's Haitian policy, President George W. Bush said that Haitians should be treated fairly and raised hopes that the government was finally going to do the right thing.[119] Yet the following day INS announced that in the future all asylum seekers who fled by boat and made it to land on their own (except Cubans) would be subject to mandatory detention, expedited removal, and would no longer be entitled to bond.[120] This was a directive clearly targeting Haitians, as they are almost exclusively the only group of asylum seekers to reach American shores by boat, other than Cubans.[121] Before this, detained boat people who made it to dry land on their own had the right to request a bond, as was the case of the October 2002 boatload of Haitian refugees.

Government officials argue that this new policy will further prevent mass migrations that could divert the Coast Guard from its national security duties.[122] However, as the Executive Director of Amnesty International, USA, Dr. William Schultz, has pointed out, this is a "specious argument," using national security as an excuse for jailing asylum seekers and putting them into fast-tracked removal proceedings.[123]

Since December 2001, the U.S. government has locked up Haitians for as long as 15 months, while quickly releasing asylum seekers from other countries.[124] Well over nine months since his arrival, David Joseph remains behind bars, working the 5:00 am to 9:00 am shift in the Krome cafeteria. With an average national detention cost of $85/day,[125] David's detention alone has already cost U.S. taxpayers nearly $25,000. When asked why the United States thinks the Haitians might be dangerous, David responded: "When you talk about an 18-year old kid here you talk about a big person who could do any bad thing. Maybe [Ashcroft] doesn't realize that I'm a small guy."[126] On August 22, 2003 the BIA sent David's case back to the immigration judge who denied him asylum to hear further evidence.[127]

## Other Measures Designed To Keep Haitians Out

The Attorney General's decision is the latest and most dangerous in a series of measures the Bush Administration is using to prevent and deter Haitian refugees from coming to the United States, despite the rapidly deteriorating human rights situation in Haiti.

Other measures include summary return by the U.S. Coast Guard of interdicted Haitians with no routine screening of their asylum claims unless a person loudly and explicitly expresses a fear of return.[128] This is the so-called "shout test" whereby Haitians on a crowded boat who are most likely hungry, thirsty, exhausted, and traumatized must step forward and inform a uniformed U.S. official on board the cutter that they fear return to Haiti. Not only is this improbable, in all likelihood there is no official Creole speaker on board to help the Haitians do so.

Even those courageous enough to aggressively express their fear of return face tremendous obstacles in eventually making it onto United States soil. It is up to the discretion of the Coast Guard whether an immigration Asylum Officer will fly out to the boat to interview them. And Haitians who successfully convince Asylum Officers they have a credible asylum case are transferred to Guantánamo Bay Cuba for a second refugee interview by yet another Asylum Officer. Those few who are then found to have a well-founded fear of persecution if returned to Haiti and who therefore qualify for refugee status, are still not brought to the United States, even if they have close family here, but instead are processed for resettlement to Guatemala, Nicaragua or Australia.

On November 15, 2002 President Bush issued an executive order allowing the Attorney General to maintain custody of any interdicted person at any location he deems appropriate, including Guantánamo Bay.[129] It allows the Attorney General to conduct any screening he deems appropriate, including most importantly, no screening at all. It also authorizes third country resettlement.[130]

Haitians also have great difficulty entering the U.S. legally. Although Attorney General Ashcroft, in deciding that Haitians should not be released, issued a statement urging Haitians to enter the U.S. legally,[131] those attempting to do so, routinely face obstacle after obstacle imposed by U.S. government officials. For example, a number of children eligible for family-sponsored visas were stranded in Haiti for months following the 1991 coup d'etat, while their applications were subject to heightened scrutiny imposed only on Haitians. This group included children who had lived with their parents in the U.S. for years, attended school here, and had little familiarity with Haiti or its language.[132]

Additionally, the Bush Administration has rejected the recommendation that it provide in-country refugee processing in Haiti.[133] Haitians in fear of their lives typically have only one option left, risking their lives on the high seas in order to seek protection.

Since the fall of 2002, the U.S. Attorney in Miami has been criminally prosecuting asylum seekers who arrive by air without legal travel papers, even though the nation's highest immigration court has recognized that the use of fraudulent documents may be the only means to escape persecution.[134] Thus far the policy has most directly affected Haitians.[135] Persons convicted on a document-fraud charge may face severe consequences, including denial of asylum. Even those granted asylum may be precluded from ever gaining permanent resident status.[136] All Haitians with criminal convictions are automatically jailed by Haitian authorities in Haiti upon return, under horrific conditions.[137]

Unfortunately, the failure to treat Haitians fairly is not limited to the United States. In August 2002, the Women's Commission, in collaboration with the National Coalition of Haitian Refugees (NCHR) and FIAC, sponsored a delegation to evaluate the treatment of Haitian asylum seekers in the United States and the Dominican Republic. Their assessment revealed that hundreds of Haitian asylum seekers have been in legal limbo in the Dominican Republic for years and suffer abuses from both the Dominican authorities and the community at large.[138]

The Miami Herald reported on November 25, 2002 that the United States is giving the Dominican Republic's 23,000 member army 20,000 m-16 assault rifles to help seal the border with Haiti as well as rotating as many as 900 U.S. soldiers every 15 days as part of joint military training exercises with the Dominican Army.[139]

# History of Discriminatory Treatment

The extraordinary effort to which the U.S. government has recently gone to keep Haitians out is nothing new. Indeed, the current Haitian-only detention policy is a surreal repetition of past discriminatory policies targeting Haitians that have been repudiated by our courts time and again.[140]

In July 1980, a landmark lawsuit was filed on behalf of over 4000 Haitians whose asylum applications had been denied. The trial court held that U.S. government agencies had set up a "Haitian Program" designed specifically to deny these claims in wholesale fashion and as quickly as possible, a program which "in its planning and executing [was] offensive to every notion of constitutional due process and equal protection." The court found that the INS was engaging in scare tactics by encouraging government attorneys to point out "THE DIMENSIONS OF THE HAITIAN THREAT," calling Haitians a threat to the community's social and economic well-being. The judge also concluded that the discriminatory treatment of the Haitians was part of a pattern of discrimination, which began in 1964.[141]

Despite the federal court's absolute condemnation of the U.S. government's Haitian policy, the government began to systematically detain Haitians entering the U.S.. In a case filed on behalf of Haitians indefinitely detained at Krome in the early 1980's, the trial court noted the INS' callous disregard for the rights of Haitian refugees and ordered the release of over 1,000 Haitians who were improperly denied access to their attorneys and faced overcrowded conditions and illegal transfers. The Appeals Court in this case rejected the government's claim that there was a massive influx of Haitians coming to the United States and noted that Haitians at the time represented no more than 2% of the illegal immigration flow into the U.S.. The Appeals Court concluded that the Federal Government had engaged in a "stark pattern" of discrimination against the Haitians.[142]

In 1990, a District Court Judge in Miami concluded that "INS is routinely engaged in underhanded tactics in dealing with Haitians seeking asylum in this country, and has singled them out for special discriminatory treatment.[143]

Despite these and numerous other rulings clearly chastising our government for its discriminatory treatment of the Haitians, following the 1991 coup d'etat in Haiti U.S. officials once again claimed they had reason to keep the Haitians out. They were successful, in part because they had Kenneth Starr, then Solicitor General of the United States, argue the case for the government. Even at its earliest stages in a Miami District Court. Solicitors General usually only argue cases in particularly important United States Supreme Court cases.[144]

Lawyers for the Haitians had filed a class action lawsuit in this case on behalf of Haitians on board U.S. Coast Guard cutters who were about to be forcibly repatriated. Their goal was to ensure that the Haitians received fair screening interviews before repatriation continued.[145]

On January 28, 1992, the government filed an emergency petition with the Eleventh Circuit, alleging that 20,000 Haitians "were massed" on the Haitian beaches and ready to head to Guantánamo, and that Guantánamo could not accommodate those Haitians.[146] Three days later, even before the Eleventh Circuit had ruled, they went to the Supreme Court with the same allegations.[147]

Attorneys for the Haitians believe that legal issues in that case took a back seat to political maneuvering and that Government lawyers deliberately misled the courts with false claims of a national emergency. For example, under sworn deposition, Undersecretary Bernard Aronson admitted that the term "massing" was ambiguous and that he was quite unsure of the number of Haitians preparing to leave. Independent observers, including the Coast Guard attaché in Port-au-Prince who frequently flew over the point of departure for Haitians, concluded there was no threat of mass migration. In its brief to the United States Supreme Court, the Government relied on the declaration of Robert K. Wolthuis, whom they presented as the Assistant Secretary of Defense. Mr. Wolthuis had assumed that position for one day only - the day he signed the declaration. He readily admitted that most of the facts sworn in his declaration were dictated by the lawyers who had drafted it told him. The declaration was so defective that attorneys for the Haitians filed a separate memorandum concerning it. Moreover, during 1994-1995, Guantánamo held over 30,000 Cubans and over 20,000 Haitians and United States officials claimed they could facilitate an endless number of arrivals.[148]

The Supreme Court, in a brief two-sentence order, issued without comment, permitted the Government to repatriate the Haitians. Justice Blackman alone wrote that if the Haitians were to be repatriated, such a ruling from the highest court in the land should only come "after full and careful consideration of the merits of their claims."[149]

On May 24, 1992 President Bush issued an executive order, ordering INS to repatriate Haitians interdicted at sea without any investigation into the likelihood of their persecution in Haiti ("Kennebunkport Order").[150]

It is worth noting that while the 1981 interdiction agreement between the Reagan Administration and Baby Doc Duvalier clearly specified that legitimate refugees were not to be returned to Haiti, INS determined that only 28 of the 23,000 Haitians intercepted in the decade following the program's inception were qualified to apply for asylum in the U.S.[151] In its 1996 Annual Report, the Inter-American Commission on Human Rights, Organization of American States, concluded that the U.S.'s interdiction and repatriation policy toward Haitians violated the following provisions of the American Declaration of the Rights and Duties of Man: the right to life, the right to liberty, the right to security of the person, the right to equality before the law, the right to resort to the courts, and the right to seek and receive asylum.[152]

Groups such as the Women's Commission have documented the very real human cost that the restrictions and measures adopted by the Administration carry.[153] In a report issued in January 2003, the Women's Commission highlighted the story of Rigmane, a Haitian woman who arrived in the U.S. as part of the October 2001 boat.[154] Rigmane suffered eight months of detention in a maximum-security prison in Miami before she was deported. According to the Women's Commission, Rigmane was awakened at 2:00 am by the INS on July 29th, taken to the airport, and handcuffed and shackled throughout the trip back to Haiti. There she was turned over to the Haitian authorities who imprisoned her for two days. She was housed in a cell with 60 women, some of whom were sick or pregnant, one of whom was accompanied by her newborn infant. There was only one cot for every three women. There was no food or water. There were no toilet facilities. Rigmane told the Women's Commission that the smell was unbearable.[155]

Rigmane's family finally got her out of prison, at which point she returned to her home in Gonaives, one of the most troubled areas in Haiti. But her problems did not stop there. The Women's Commission reports that after her return, her mother's restaurant was sprayed with gunfire. Rigmane and her brother-in-law were later attacked by forces aligned with the Lavalas party, who beat her on the back and chest with rifles. Rigmane ended up in the hospital and was still spitting up blood when the Women's Commission interviewed her.[156] She went into hiding after that, from where she told the Women's Commission,

> "We were living in a nightmare in Haiti before we left, then we lived a nightmare in the United States of America and we are living

a nightmare again in Haiti. I still have the scars of the shackles on my ankles they put on us when they deported us because they were so tight... Why are we being treated this way? Doesn't anybody care about our lives? The next time that you call, I might be dead. I will do whatever it takes to get out."

And sadly, the U.S. government appears intent on doing whatever it believes it takes to keep Rigmane and others out.[157]

# CONCLUSION

Haitian asylum seekers -- including women and children -- have been singled out by the U.S. government and denied the fundamental protections promised to refugees of virtually every other nationality. As Wendy Young, Director of Government Relations and U.S. Programs for the Women's Commission, recently remarked, "In effect, the U.S. asylum system exists ONLY on paper only if you are Haitian."[158]

The longer the Haitians are detained, the more desperate their situation becomes. This is a sorry response to Haitians fleeing a fragile democracy. Reputable human rights organizations as well as the U.S. State Department have expressed grave concern regarding the escalating political instability and human rights abuses in Haiti. The shame continues here in the United States. In June 2002 a Haitian asylum seeker at Krome attempted to hang himself. He told advocates, "I thought I wanted to die rather than stay here in Krome being humiliated everyday... It looks like they are just going to send us all back anyway. We always feel pressure to just give up. So what am I to do?"[159]

His statement is eerily reminiscent of a letter written more than ten years ago, by a group of detained Haitian asylum seekers in Krome: "We wish to emphasize... that right now we are living in the most difficult and painful times of human life.... We prefer to die than to live in the uncertainty that drowns our thoughts."[160]

While advocates for the Haitians recognize the U.S. government's responsibility to protect Americans from terrorists acts, and support real reasons for doing so, it seems misdirected, if not racist, to indefinitely detain Haitian asylum seekers who have committed no crime and treat them differently than any other group for "national security" reasons. This is a shocking abuse of power that does little to serve U.S. national interests. The Bush Administration should focus its attention on the real criminals of the world, not innocent Haitians.

As the United States seeks to protect the safety of the American people, it is also inexplicable that the government is wasting our limited resources on the prolonged detention of Haitians. Most of the Haitians who arrived in the United States these past few years seeking asylum have family lawfully residing in the U.S. who are ready, willing and eager to care for them. The Haitians themselves want nothing more than to work and be self-supporting during the course of their court proceedings, rather than be a burden on taxpayers. The cost for detention is $85 per detainee per day; tens of thousands of taxpayer's dollars are diverted for this unjust and arbitrary policy.

This is not a local South Florida issue – it affects the entire nation and deserves national attention. While public attention and criticism of the Haitian policy has been relatively short-lived, a number of human rights and national non-governmental organizations have repeatedly decried the treatment of Haitians and urged the U.S. government to end its discriminatory policy.[161]

On June 21, 2002 FIAC and the America Civil Liberties Union (ACLU) co-hosted an informal briefing with the United States Commission on Civil Rights. Testimony focused on the fact that the war on terrorism had become a war on immigrants and that Haitian asylum seekers had become the scapegoats for a flawed Administration policy that treated freedom-seeking Haitians like common criminals and terrorists.[162] Members of the Commission later met with Haitian women detained in a Miami maximum security jail, as actor Danny Glover had on July 27, 2002.[163]

On October 1, 2002 Senator Edward Kennedy's Subcommittee on Immigration held a hearing on the treatment of Haitian asylum seekers.[164] Representative Ileana Ros-Lehtinen's Subcommittee on International Operations and Human Rights held a briefing on the issue that same day.[165]

On May 27, 2003 the Haitian women detained in Miami wrote a letter to members of Congress. Their letter eloquently reminds us of the urgent need to double our efforts to help the Haitians:

"We did not leave our country because of economic problems, but because of political problems. The trip to Miami was a very dangerous one, but our hopes of reaching a land where we would be truly free and safe from oppression gave us courage to hold on...

Why are we, Haitians, being detained? What horrible crime have we committed to be treated this way? Why are we being treated differently than all the other asylum seekers?... We are not criminals. We did not come to the United States to commit any crimes. We came here to save our lives... All we are asking is to be treated fairly, to be treated like human beings, not by which country we come from.

If we thought that we could have survived in our country we would have stayed there.... Listen to our cries for help.... Treat us according to what the U.S. stands for: the Land of the Free. Please dry the tears from our eyes. May God bless you."[166]

---

[1]The title of this chapter is the title Ms. Little used for a paper she wrote about Haitian refugees while in law school. Ms. Little is extremely grateful to Kathie Klarreich for her careful editing of this article and for the endless hours spent by Sharon Ginter and Charu Newhouse Al-Sahli in assisting with the endnotes.

2.For a comprehensive review of the discriminatory treatment of Haitians, see "Refugee Policy Adrift: The United States and Dominican Republic Deny Haitians Protection," Women's Commission for Refugee Women and Children (January 2003); Cheryl Little, "Inter-Group Coalitions and Immigration Politics:The Haitian Experience in Florida," The University of Miami Law Review, p 717 (July 1999).

3.Dana Canedy, "Haitians Dash from Stranded Boat to Florida Shore," New York Times (October 30, 2002); Charles Rabin, Jacqueline Charles, and Martin Merzer, "A Desperate Voyage to Miami," The Miami Herald (October 30, 2002); "Haitians Jump Ship Off Miami," Reuters (October 29, 2002).

4.Andres Viglucci, "Legal Groups Meet with Haitian Migrants," The Miami Herald (November 1, 2002). Due to overcrowding resulting from the Haitians' prolonged detention, some Haitians were sent to facilities far removed from family and pro bono attorneys. One Haitian woman and her infant child were transferred to rural Pennsylvania following their arrival by boat in October 2002, where they have been unable to secure free legal help.

5.See Statement of Alfred Selmo (January 16, 2003); Statement of Guilene Silien (February 14, 2003). All statements and documents cited in this chapter are on file at the Florida Immigrant Advocacy Center (FIAC). Names of detainees and former detainees only used in this article when they have already been revealed publically in the media or where explicit permission was obtained by Florida Immigrant Advocacy Center from the individual. Otherwise, the detainees' identity is protected by using pseudonyms.

6.Alfonso Chardy, "Detentions are political, attorneys say," The Miami Herald (January 18, 2002); Alfonso Chardy, "INS is detaining Haitians rescued at sea last month," The Miami Herald (January 18, 2002); Max Rameau, "Hear the Haitians' claim for asylum," The Miami Herald (January 18, 2002); Jody A. Benjamin, "166 Haitians who arrived Dec. 3 face deportation, immigration group says," South Florida Sun-Sentinel (December 20, 2001); "INS moves to deport Haitians saved at sea," The Miami Herald (December 17, 2001); Jody A. Benjamin, "Haitians rescued from grounded boat await ruling on status," South Florida

Sun-Sentinel (December 11, 2001); Joe Mozingo, "18 of 185 Haitians released by INS," The Miami Herald (December 10, 2001).

7.Luisa Yanez, "Haitian migrants taken ashore," The Miami Herald (December 4, 2001). The Haitians who arrived on December 3, 3001 called their boat, "Si m'ap viv se Jesus" ("If I'm still alive it's because of Jesus").

8.After a federal lawsuit was filed, pointing out the illogic of this policy, the INS began releasing some Haitian asylum seekers who arrived by plane. However, even these cases were subjected to "enhanced scrutiny" and sponsors required to submit countless documents, such as payroll stubs, bank statements and notarized affidavits of support from approved sponsors and reporting requirements not required in non-Haitian asylum cases. See Memorandum from Johnny Williams, Executive Associate Commissioner, Immigration and Naturalization Service, "Parole of Haitians Arriving by Regular Means at a Designated Port of Entry in South Florida" (April 5, 2002).

9.Declaration of Clarel Cyriaque (March 13, 2002); Declaration of Cheryl Little (March 14, 2002); and Declaration of Evenette Mondesir (March 12, 2002).

10.Declaration of Howard Gitlow, Ph.D, School of Business, University of Miami (March 14, 2002); Declaration of Charu Newhouse al-Sahli, Detention Advocacy Coordinator, Florida Immigrant Advocacy Center, (March 13, 2002).

11. Declaration of Peter Michael Becraft, Acting Deputy Commissioner, Immigration and Naturalization Service (March 18, 2002).

12.Jeanty, v. Bulger, Civ-Lenard (S.D.Fla 2002); Alfonso Chardy, "INS sued over detention of 240 Haitian refugees," The Miami Herald (March 16, 2002); Jody A. Benjamin and Madeline Baro Diaz, "Haitian detainees sue INS, demand release," South Florida Sun-Sentinel (March 16, 2002); "Center to file suit for asylum-seekers," The Miami Herald (March 10, 2002).

13.Jeanty v. Bulger, 204 F.Supp. 2d 1366 (S.D. Fla. 2002).

14.Id. at 1368.

15.Moise v. Bulger, 321 F.3d 1336 (11th Cir. 2003).

16.Declaration of Cheryl Little, Florida Immigrant Advocacy Center (March 14, 2002), supra. See also, Letter to Steven Lang, Executive Office for Immigration Review, from Mary Kramer, South Florida Chapter, American Immigration Lawyers Association (February 19, 2002); Letter to Florida Immigrant Advocacy Center from Steven Lang, Executive Office for Immigration Review (February 13, 2002); Press release from Executive Office for Immigration Review (February 13, 2002); Letter to Steven Lang, Executive Office for Immigration Review, from Cheryl Little, Florida Immigrant Advocacy Center (January 18, 2002); Letter to Gail Padgett, Assistant Chief Immigration Judge, Executive Office for Immigration Review, from Cheryl Little, Florida Immigrant Advocacy Center (February 12, 2002); Letter to John Mata and Gail Padgett, Executive Office for Immigration Review, from Cheryl Little, Florida Immigrant Advocacy Center (December 13, 2002). See also, "Unease grips rescued Haitians, Activists Decried Lack of Counsel," The Miami Herald (January 19, 2002).

17. See Lawyer's Committee for Human Rights, Brief of Amicus Curiae in Support of Petitioners'–Appellants and Reversal of the District Court's Decision Motion (May 9, 2002), and United Nations High Commissioner for Refugees Advisory Opinion on

Detention of Asylum Seekers (April 15, 2003).

18. "Asylum Representation, Summary Statistics," prepared by Dr. Andrew I. Schoenholtz, Director of Law and Policy Studies, Institute for the Study of International Migration, Georgetown University (May 2000).

19.Declaration of Cheryl Little, Florida Immigrant Advocacy Center (March 14, 2002); Press release, Florida Immigrant Advocacy Center (December 16, 2002); see also Jacqueline Charles and Jennifer Maloney, "Judge Denies Haitians' Asylum; First Setbacks Worry Activists," The Miami Herald (December 17, 2002); Dana Canedy, "Haitian Detainees Being Treated Unfairly, Advocates Assert," New York Times (December 18, 2002). Florida Immigrant Advocacy Center attempted to assist hundreds of Haitians in filing their briefs with the Board of Immigration Appeals (BIA). However, the BIA is now streamlining decisions and a number of Haitians have received summary affirmances of the judges' decisions without explanation. Florida Immigrant Advocacy Center even received a BIA denial for a Haitian whose appeal brief was not yet due.

20.See Letter to Steven Lang, Executive Office of Immigration Review, from Mary Kramer, South Florida Chapter, American Immigration Lawyers Association (February 19, 2002), supra (outlining concerns that the expedited processing of Haitian asylum cases was discriminatory so American Immigration Lawyers Association attorneys reluctant to participate in any effort that would somehow lend it credence and referencing fact that their pro-bono resources were already stretched thin).

21.Although INS officials have acknowledged they lack adequate space to meet the needs of attorneys and others trying to assist the Haitians at Krome, in February 2002, they restricted weekend and holiday visitation there to just four hours, between 7:00-11:00 am. Also, FIAC was notified in late December 2002 that staff had to quickly vacate the small Krome office they shared for six years with other pro bono groups. See e.g., "Legal aid center folds Krome Office," The Miami Herald (January 12, 2003); Jim DeFede, "INS harasses legal-aid agencies," The Miami Herald (January 9, 2003; "Access Denied, Justice Denied," The Miami Herald (Editorial) (January 6, 2003); "Ros-Lehtinen opposes closing of legal center at Krome," The Miami Herald (January 6, 2003); "Graham backs immigrant rights advocate," The Miami Herald (January 4, 2003); Alfonso Chardy, "Advocacy group for immigrants to leave Krome," The Miami Herald (January 3, 2003); Letter to Donald Kerwin, Executive Director, Catholic Legal Immigration Network, Inc. and others from David Venturella, INS Assistant Deputy Executive Associate Commissioner, Office of Detention and Removal Operations (response to January 21, 2003 sign-on letter) (January 29, 2003); Sign-on Letter to Michael Garcia, INS Acting Commissioner from Catholic Legal Immigration Network, Inc. on behalf of 31 co-signers (January 9, 2003); Letter to Wesley Lee, INS Transition Field Coordinator, Headquarters Detention and Removal from Florida Immigrant Advocacy Center (January 7, 2003); Letter to Wesley Lee, INS Transition Field Coordinator, Headquarters Detention and Removal from Florida Immigrant Advocacy Center (January 2, 2003); Letter to Congresspersons and Seven Lang, Pro bono Coordinator, Executive Office of Immigration Review from Florida Immigrant Advocacy Center (January 2, 2003); Letter to INS Acting Commissioner Garcia from Senator Graham (January 3, 2003); Letter to INS Acting Director Jack Bulger from Congresswoman Ileana Ros-Lehtinen(January 2, 2003).

22.See Letter to Gail Padgett, Executive Office of Immigration Review, from Cheryl Little, Florida Immigrant Advocacy Center (February 12, 2002), supra.; Letter to Steven Lang, Executive Office of Immigration Review from Mary Kramer, Esq. (February 19, 2002), supra.; Letter to John Bulger, Acting District Director, Immigration and Naturalization Service from Cheryl Little, Florida Immigrant Advocacy Center (May 30, 2002); Letter to Daniel Vara, INS District Counsel, Cheryl Little, Florida Immigrant Advocacy Center (August 2, 2002); Letter to John Bulger, Acting District Director, Immigration and Naturalization Service, from Cheryl Little, Florida Immigrant Advocacy Center (September 20, 2002) supra.; Letter to John Mata and Gail Padgett, Executive Office of Immigration Review from Cheryl Little, Florida Immigrant Advocacy Center (December 13, 2002).

23."Congressman decries treatment of Haitians," The Miami Herald (March 10, 2002).

24.See e.g., Jody A. Benjamin, "Awaiting Asylum, 'I Don't Know Why I Am In Jail'," South Florida Sun-Sentinel (April 22, 2002).

25. "Innocents in Jail: INS Moves Refugee Women from Krome to Turner Guilford Knight Correctional Center, Miami," Women's Commission for Refugee Women & Children (June 2001); "Freedom Denied: Middle Eastern Asylum Seekers Caught Up in U.S. Immigration Sweep," Women's Commission for Refugee Women & Children (December 2001).

26.See Cheryl Little and Charu Newhouse Al-Sahli, "INS Detainees in Florida: A Double Standard of Treatment," Florida Immigrant Advocacy Center (December 2001), Supplement (January-April 2002).

27.Testimony of Marie Jocelyn Ocean, before the Senate Judiciary, Subcommittee Immigration (October 1, 2002).

28.Statement on New Detention Facility in Broward County, Immigration and Naturalization Service (August 12, 2002). See also Jacqueline Charles, "INS Plans to Move Female Haitian Detainees," The Miami Herald (August 16, 2002); José Dante Parra Herrera, "Detainees Will Move From Jail to Work Center," South Florida Sun-Sentinel (August 16, 2002); "INS to Move Haitian Asylum Seekers," Associated Press (August 16, 2002).

29.The women were moved from Krome to TGK following allegations that women at Krome were sexually abused by officers there. Only after its own internal investigation and pressure from the Miami community, local service providers such as Florida Immigrant Advocacy Center, and national immigrant and refugee advocacy organizations to release the women or place them in an appropriate alternative to detention, did the INS agree to remove the women from Krome.

30. Statement of Violette Lincifor (March 11, 2003).

31.Ibid.

32. Statement of Marie (pseudonym) (July 3, 2003).

33.Susan Benesch, Refugee Advocate, Refugee Project, Amnesty International, USA, "Haitian Refugees Trapped by War on Terror," Amnesty Now (Fall 2003).

34.Statement of Evens (April 26, 2002); Statement of Emmanuel (July 12, 2002); Letter from detained Haitian asylum seekers at Krome (March 25, 2002); Statement of detained Haitian asylum seekers on hunger strike at Krome (July 9, 2002); Statement of Robert (July 11, 2002); Statement of Roland (April 30, 2002); Statement of Loussaint (July 11, 2002).

35.Ibid.

36.Statements of Casimir (June 7 and 12, 2002); Florida Immigrant Advocacy Center interviews with Haitian asylum seekers (April 2003).

37.Statement of Frantz (February 21, 2003).

38.The Department of Homeland Security rents all 30 rooms on the hotel's fifth floor to hold children and families. Single adults are sometimes held there as well, due to overcrowding in other facilities.

39.Since mid-July 2003 certain detainees at the hotel have been bused to Krome to get fresh air and limited exercise. Detainees report they can't go to Krome unless they sign up to do so but they're not given details about how to sign-up. Only a limited number can be bused to Krome on any given day.

40.Statement of Yvrose (June 5, 2002); Statement of Laura (June 5, 2002); Statement of Linda (June 5, 2002); Statement of Livernie (June 5, 2002); Statement of Magda (June 5, 2002); Statement of Maryse (June 5, 2002); Statement of Alfred Selmo (January 16, 2003), supra.; Statement of Guilene Silien (February 25, 2003), supra.; Statement of Milia Auguste (April 10, 2003); Statement of Lormise Guillaume (April 3, 2003). See also, Letter to Marion Dillis, Acting Officer-in Charge, Krome Service Processing Center from Charu Newhouse al-Sahli, Florida Immigrant Advocacy Center (March 7, 2003).

41.Statement of Lormise Guillaume (April 3, 2003), supra.

42.Following a visit in February 2003 by prominent film director Jonathan Demme, Congresswoman Carrie Meek, Congressman Kendrick Meek and prominent Haitians including radio journalist Michele Montas and author Edwidge Danticat, Florida Immigrant Advocacy Center was told they could no longer visit clients at the hotel. Fortunately, about two weeks later the attorneys were let back in. Florida Immigrant Advocacy Center was not allowed to give Know Your Rights presentations to the hotel detainees until early August 2003.

43.In April 2002, the INS was holding 113 men, women and children at the hotel. Letter from Cheryl Little, Florida Immigrant Advocacy Center, to John M. Bulger, Immigration and Naturalization Service (May 30, 2002).

44.Memorandum from Charu Newhouse al-Sahli, Florida Immigrant Advocacy Center (November 8, 2002). A number of Haitian women with children detained at the hotel were also forced to go before an immigration judge without first speaking to an attorney. FIAC's initial requests to meet with these families were denied.

45.Letter to Marion Dillis, Acting Officer-in-Charge, Krome SPC from Cheryl Little, Florida Immigrant Advocacy Center (November 15, 2003).

46.Statement of Claude (pseudonym) (January 16, 2003).

47.Statement of Guilene Silien (February 14, 2003), supra.

48.Interview with Charu Newhouse al-Sahli, Florida Immigrant Advocacy Center (July 22, 2003).

49.See Letter to Marion Dillis from Charu Newhouse al-Sahli, Florida Immigrant Advocacy Center (March 7, 2003), supra.; Letter to Marion Dillis from Jack Wallace, Florida Immigrant Advocacy Center (March 31, 2003); Letter to Deportation Officer Morales from Jack Wallace, Florida Immigrant Advocacy Center (April 9, 2003); Letter to Deportation Officer Morales from Charu Newhouse al-Sahli, Florida Immigrant Advocacy Center (April 11, 2003).

50.Statement of Lormise Guillaume (April 3, 2003), supra.

51.Jacqueline Charles, "Officials Release 3 Haitian Families," The Miami Herald (April 18, 2003); Jacqueline Charles, "Advocates for Haitians: Free boy, 2, from hotel," The Miami Herald (April 12, 2003).

52.Statement of Milia Auguste (April 10, 2003), supra.

53.Rachel Swarns, "Haitians Are Held in U.S. Despite Grant of Asylum," New York Times (July 25, 2003); National Briefing: Washington, New York Times (August 12, 2003); Tanya Weinberg, "Haitian teen enjoys freedom after 7 months of detention," South Florida Sun-Sentinel (June 13, 2003).

54.Statement of Ernesto Joseph (February 21, 2003).

55."Haitian Teenager Granted Asylum is Still in Detention," Refugee Action, Amnesty International USA (March 14, 2003); Urgent Action, "Free Ernesto Joseph Now," Florida Immigrant Advocacy Center (February 26, 2003).

56.Teresa Duskily, Psychological Evaluation of Ernesto Joseph (May 2, 2002).

57.FIAC believes that most, if not all, of the Haitians -- and especially the children -- are suffering from PTSD and other chronic conditions. A report released by Physicians for Human Rights in mid-June 2003 concluded that there was a steady deterioration in the psychological well-being of asylum seekers facing prolonged detention, with severe physical and mental consequences. See "From Persecution to Prison: The Health Consequences of Detention for Asylum Seekers," Physicians for Human Rights (June 2003).

58. Editorial, "Free the Children," The Miami Herald (February 23, 2003); Tanya Weinberg, "Advocates Blast Teen's Detention," South Florida Sun-Sentinel, May 23, 2003; "Free Ernesto Joseph,"LIRS Urgent Action, Newsletter of the Forgotten Refugees Campaign (Spring 2003); Amnesty International Refugee Action (March 14, 2003), supra.

59.Statement of Alfred Selmo (January 16, 2003), supra.

60.In August 2003, for example, the BIA upheld an immigration judge's asylum grant to Gabriel Joseph. Gabriel was kept in detention for several months following the judge's favorable decision. FIAC represented this Haitian before the BIA.

61.In re Dauphin Jacnel, A# (July 23, 2003)(unpublished). FIAC represented this Haitian before the BIA. In some cases the BIA has reversed immigration judges grants of asylum to Haitians.

62."U.S.: Detention of Haitian Asylum-Seeker Jesiclaire Clairmont," Amnesty International Refugee Action (January 15, 2002).

63.Testimony of Randolph McGrorty, Catholic Charities Legal Services, before the U.S. Commission on Civil Rights (June 21, 2002); Jody A. Benjamin, "Haitian Mother Detained in Maximum Security Jail Has Little Contact with Children," South Florida Sun-Sentinel (May 20, 2002).

64. Testimony of Randolph McGrorty, Catholic Charities Legal Services, before the U.S. Commission on Civil Rights (June 21, 2002), supra.

65.Recent press coverage addressed the plight of children in detention, including the Haitian children. See e.g., Bob Dart, "Rights Advocates decry conditions under which immigrant children held," The Atlantic Journal-Constitution (June 19, 2003); Holly Hickman, "U.S. Handling of Young Immigrants Criticized," The Associated Press(June 19, 2003).

66.Stipulated Settlement Agreement, Flores v. Reno, Case No. CV85-4544-RJK (C.D. Cal. 1996) at 14 and 18, General Policy Favoring Release.

67.This Haitian girl had been labeled "accompanied" while at the Miami hotel because she arrived with an 18 year old sibling who was detained at Krome.

68.Letter to Carmel Clay Thompson, Office of Refugee Resettlement, and John Pogash, Office of Juvenile Affairs, from Cheryl Little, Lisa Frydman, Jack Wallace, and Charu N. Al-Sahli, Florida Immigrant Advocacy Center (March 17, 2003); Jacqueline Charles, "Haitians struggle to unite families," The Miami Herald, December 12, 2002; Statement of Chimene Noel (December 3, 2002). See also, Thalif Deen, "50 Million Children Lack Birth Certificates, Says UNICEF," Inter Press Service, June 4, 2002.

69.Even the Haitian Consul General acknowledged that, due to past corruption in Haiti, not all Haitian nationals had their birth certificates registered in the National Archives and that about 50,000 children who were abandoned by their parents in Haiti have never had their births registered. Still, families are required to produce original birth certificates for the children seeking release. Other documents have to be notarized in Haiti, even though many of the children's families there live hours away from a notary.

70.Jacqueline Charles, "Haitians struggle to unite families," The Miami Herald (December 12, 2002); Statement of Chimene Noel (December 3, 2002).

71.See Letter to Carmel Clay Thompson from Cheryl Little (March 17, 2003), supra.

72. Alfonso Chardy, "Young Haitian migrant released," The Miami Herald (December 25, 2002); "Christmas Present for Noel," Washington Post (December 26, 2002).

73."USA (Florida): Haitian Child Granted Asylum is Still in Detention," Amnesty International Refugee Action (February 12, 2003).

74.Interview with FIAC Attorney Lisa Frydman (January 15, 2003).

75.In 1998, the INS adopted guidelines for use in adjudicating children's claims that draw heavily on international law and standards to better protect children.

76.Two children unfairly labeled "accompanied" by INS were not initially represented by FIAC.

77.See Charu Newhouse al-Sahli, Chris Kleiser, Cheryl Little, " 'I running out of hopely...' Profiles of Children in INS Detention in Florida," Florida Immigrant Advocacy Center (October 2002).

78.Statement of Simon (February 6, 2003).

79.Jacqueline Charles, "Haitians struggle to unite families," The Miami Herald (December 12, 2002); Statement of Chimene Noel (December 3, 2002).

80.In a recent report, Amnesty International noted that organizations have criticized the INS "for not following any set criteria or guidelines for determining whether a child should be placed in foster care and often do so on an ad hoc basis, usually following lengthy detention." Amnesty also noted that "[c]hildren should be confined and imprisoned only in exceptional circumstances or as a last resort, and then only for the shortest possible time." "Why Am I Here?," Amnesty International (June 18, 2003).

81.Letter to Marion Dillis, Acting Officer-in-Charge from Jolie Justus, Shook, Hardy & Bacon (June 27, 2003).

82.Statement of Ovide Paul (December 13, 2002).

83.Letter to Marion Dillis, Acting Officer-in-Charge, Krome Processing Center from Jolie Justus, Esq., Shook, Hardy & Bacon (June 27, 2003).

84.Statement of Gilbert Alcenor (June 11, 2003).

85.Tanya Weinberg, "Critics say faulty INS procedure often lands children in adult jails," South Florida Sun-Sentinel (July 21, 2003). See also Tanya Weinberg, "Tests showed refugee to be an adult," South Florida Sun-Sentinel (May 24, 2003).
86.Ibid.
87. Tanya Weinberg, "Critics say faulty INS procedure often lands children in adult jails," South Florida Sun-Sentinel (July 21, 2003), supra.
88."From Persecution to Prison: The Health Consequences of Detention for Asylum Seekers," Physicians for Human Rights (June 2003); "Why am I here? Children in Immigration Detention," Amnesty International USA (June 2003).
89.Miami-Dade Legislative Item File Number 023546, "Release Detained Haitian Children" (December 17, 2002).
90.Rachel Swarns, "Haitians Are Held in U.S. Despite Grant of Asylum," New York Times (July 25, 2003).
91.Letter to Congresswoman Carrie Meek, U.S. House of Representatives from Sister Jeanne O'Laughlin, Barry University (April 26, 2002); Letter to Sister Jeanne O'Laughlin, Barry University, from Anthony S. Tangeman, Immigration and Naturalization Service, (September 30, 2002); Letter, to Commissioner James Ziglar, Immigration and Naturalization Service, from Sister Jeanne O'Laughlin, Barry University (August 19, 2002); Jody Benjamin, "Barry U. Educator Wants to Lead Effort to Free Haitian Detainees," South Florida Sun-Sentinel (April 30, 2002).
92.For a general overview of the treatment of Haitian children and families, see "INS Discriminatory Treatment of Haitian Children and Families: Backgrounder," Florida Immigrant Advocacy Center (November 20, 2002) (updated, January 30, 2003); see also Tanya Weinberg, "Dozens Fast to Protest detention; Haitian Children Have Been Held Since Refugee Boat Arrived on October 29," South Florida Sun-Sentinel (December 17, 2002).
93.Coast Guard statistics show that they were routinely interdicting more than 300 Haitians a month at various times during the last 5 years (for example, 395 in January 2000, 477 in October 1998, 428 in September 1998, and 421 in November 1997). Each of these monthly interdictions represented substantial increases over total interdictions from the preceding three months, yet no mass migration followed. U.S. Coast Guard, "Migrant Interdiction Statistics" (July 25, 2003) (available on-line at: http://www.uscg.mil/hq/g-o/g-opl/mle/amiostats1.htm).
94.INS also claimed there was evidence of a "mass migration" because 264 Haitians were interdicted shortly after the October 2002 boat made it to shore, in November of 2002. They stated that whenever a boat successfully landed in the U.S. it encourages others to leave. Yet in December 2002, the month following the highly publicized announcement of President Bush's latest measures to deter Haitians from fleeing, the Coast Guard captured more Haitians than it did the previous month. In re D.J -, 23 I:N Dec.572, 578 (A.g. 2003).
95. Ibid.

96.United Nations High Commissioner for Refugees, "Request for Advisory Opinion on Detention of Asylum Seekers" (April 15, 2002).
97.Leaders in the Haitian community, immigrant advocates and local politicians in South Florida took advantage of the media's coverage of the October 2002 boatload of Haitians by

asking Florida Governor Jeb Buts to urge his brother in the White House to allow for their release. See e.g., "Protecting Jeb?," The Wall Street Journal (April 26, 2002); Marjorie Valbrun, "Bush to Face Florida Protests Over Move to Detain Haitians," Wall Street Journal (April 29, 2002); Advocacy efforts were later directed at Jeb Bush's brother, President George W. Bush. See e.g. Liz Balmaseda, "Haitian refugees turn eyes to Bush," The Miami Herald (May 20, 2002); Jody A. Benjamin, "Haitians protest immigration policy during President Bush's Visit," South Florida Sun-Sentinel (May 21, 2002); "Florida Governor urges fairer treatment," CNN (October 30, 2002); Maya Bell, "Gov. Bush assures Haitians of 'fair and decent treatment," Orlando Sentinel (October 30, 2002); Larry Lebowitz, Alfonso Chardy and Andres Viglucci, "Haitian Fury Grows; 6 held in plot; The Miami Herald (October 31, 2002);

98.Brian Bandell, "INS Appeals Bond Issued to Haitians, Citing National Security Threat," Associated Press (November 7, 2002); see also Alfonso Chardy, "Holding Haitians a Security Issue, INS Brief Details," Miami Herald (November 13, 2002); Andrea Elliott, Larry Lebowitz, and Jennifer Maloney, "INS Appeals Bonds, Calls Detained Haitians a Threat to National Security,"Miami Herald (November 7, 2002). The policy of keeping the Haitians in detention for purposes of national security was criticized by countless groups across the country. See e.g., Press Release, "Justice Department To Use Detention To Keep Refugees Out of Country, Amnesty International Charges," Amnesty International (November 13, 2002); Press Release, "Advocates Express Bitter Disappointment Over Latest INS Directive and Demand Fair Treatment of Haitians," Florida Immigrant Advocacy Center and National Coalition for Haitian Rights (November 13, 2002); Press Release, "Immigration Judge Granted Haitians Bonds But INS Invokes National Security Rule To Keep Haitians Detained," Florida Immigrant Advocacy Center (November 6, 2002); Press Release, "Parole the Haitians Now," Florida Immigrant Advocacy Center (October 31, 2002).

99.The BIA specifically rejected as irrelevant the government's argument that "the release on bond of additional alien passengers from [the October 29] vessel will cause a 'surge' in other aliens attempting to reach the United States by sea" and that "there are insufficient resources to adequately screen the passengers of these vessels, which may contain aliens seeking to threaten the homeland security of the United States." In re D-J-, I & N Dec. 572 (March 13, 2003).

100.Asa Hutchinson, "Referral of Decision to Attorney General" (March 20, 2003). See also Press Release, "Recent Victory for Haitian Refugees Thwarted by DHS; Major Refugee Organizations Decry Decision," Florida Immigrant Advocacy Center, Lawyers Committee for Human Rights and Women's Commission for Refugee Women and Children (March 21, 2003); Letter to Attorney General John Ashcroft from Cheryl Little, Florida Immigrant Advocacy Center (January 28, 2002).

101.In re D-J-, 23 I&N Dec. 572 (A.G. 2003).

102.Ashcroft claims he is "broadly authorized" to keep Haitians like David Joseph in detention without the detainees' having any right to parole or review by a judge,"based on any reasonable consideration." Indeed, Ashcroft declared himself the final word on all immigration law.

103.The Coast Guard, the Department of State, and the Department of Defense submitted declarations to the immigration court arguing that Haitian migration constitutes a threat to national security. They based their position on: 1) concern that a mass migration from Haiti would require the diversion of Coast Guard and military resources away from national security to interdiction and detention efforts; 2) fear that the use of Guantánamo Bay to detain Haitians would undermine efforts to extract intelligence information from the AlQaeda members held there; and 3) allegations that third country nationals, such as Palestinians and Pakistanis, might use Haiti as a staging point. See Declaration of Captain Kenneth Ward, U.S. Coast Guard; Memorandum to Stephen E. Biegun, National Security Council, from Maura Harty, Department of State; Declaration of Joseph J. Collins, Department of Defense.

104.Declaration of Peter Michael Becraft (March 18, 2002), supra.

105.Ari Fleicher, White House Press Briefing (October 30, 2002).

106."America's Challenge: Domestic Security, Civil Liberties, and National Unity After September 11," prepared by the Migration Policy Institute (June 30, 2003). (Available at http://www.migrationpolicy.org/pubs/americaschallenges.pdf ).

107.Donald Kerwin, "Undermining Antiterrorism," America Magazine (June 23, 2003).

108.As an Amnesty International official recently wrote, "It is hard to imagine a would-be terrorist heading for the United States on a Haitian boat -- since that would likely lead either to drowning or a face-to-face encounter with U.S. authorities. It is also hard to imagine U.S. officials unable to distinguish a Pakistani or Palestinian from a Haitian." Susan Benesch, Refugee Advocate, Refugee Project, Amnesty International, USA, "Haitian Refugees Trapped by War on Terror," Amnesty Now (Fall 2003), supra.

109.U.S. Coast Guard, "Migrant Interdiction Statistics" (July 25, 2003), supra.

110."Patterns of Global Terrorism," U.S. State Department (May 21, 2002).

111.Carol J. Williams, "Haitians Continue to Brave Seas Despite U.S. Barriers to Entry," Los Angeles Times (June 28, 2003).

112.See News Release, "Clarification of Eligibility for Permanent Residence Under the Cuban Adjustment Act," Immigration and Naturalization Service (April 26, 1999).

113.See "Proposed Refugee Admissions for Fiscal Year 2003: Report to Congress," submitted on Behalf of the President of the United States to the Committees of the Judiciary of the Senate and House of Representatives by the Departments of State, Justice, and Health and Human and Services (September 2002).

114.Bureau of Democracy, Human Rights, and Labor, "Country Reports on Human Rights Practices, 2002: Haiti," U.S. State Department (March 31, 2003). According to the report, "the Government's human rights record remained poor, with political and civil officials implicated in serious abuses. There were credible reports of extrajudicial killings by members of the HNP. Police officers used excessive -- and sometimes deadly - - force in making arrests or controlling demonstrations and were rarely punished for such acts. Attacks on journalists and political dissenters by Fanmi Lavalas supporters continued.... Legal impunity remained a major problem, and police and judicial officials often failed to respect legal provisions or pursue and prosecute suspected violators.... From July through December, several radio stations closed down temporarily due to intimidation and threats. Abuse of children and violence and societal discrimination against women remained problems." See also U.S. Department of State, "Country Reports on Human Rights Practices

-- 2001" (March 4, 2002); Jim DeFede, "Is U.S. Policy Subverting Haiti?," The Miami Herald (December 15, 2002); Arthur C. Helton, "Price of Indifference: Refugees and Humanitarian Action in the New Century" (2002).

115.U.S. Department of State, Bureau of Consular Affairs, Consular Information Sheet (August 21, 2003).

116.Ellen Ratner, Interview with Secretary Colin Powell, Talk Radio News (October 30, 2002); Amnesty International Report on Haiti (August 21, 2003).

117. Office of the Inspector General, "The September 11 Detainees: A Review of the Treatment of Aliens Held on Immigration Charges in Connection with the Investigation of the September 11 Attacks," U.S. Department of Justice (June 2003).

118.Written testimony of Senator Bob Graham, before the Senate Judiciary Subcommittee on Immigration (October 1, 2002); "Who's Responsible for Unfair Policy on Haitian Refugees?" Miami Herald (October 3, 2002).

119.White House Press Conference (November 7, 2002); President George W. Bush, "President Outlines Priorities," White House News Release (November 7, 2002); see also Alfonso Chardy and Jacqueline Charles, "President: Treat Haitians Just Like Other Immigrants," The Miami Herald (November 8, 2002).

120."Notice Designating Aliens Subject to Expedited Removal under Section 235(b)(1)(A)(iii) of the Immigration and Nationality Act," Federal Register (Order No. 2243-02)(November 13, 2002); "INS Announces Notice Concerning Expedited Removal," U.S. Department of Justice (November 8, 2002).

121.A number of human rights organizations submitted written comments opposing the proposed notice designating aliens subject to expedited removal. See e.g., Comments to Director, Regulations and Forms, Services Division, INS from Bill Frelick, Director, Refugee Program, Amnesty International, USA (December 13, 2002); Comments to Director, Regulations and Forms, Services Division, INS from Guenet Guebre-Christos, United Nations High Commissioner for Refugees Regional Representative (December 2002); Comments to Director, Regulations and Forms, Services Division, INS from Cheryl Little, Executive Director, Florida Immigrant Advocacy Center (December 13, 2002).

122."Notice Designating Aliens Subject to Expedited Removal under Section 35(b)(1)(A)(iii) of the Immigration and Nationality Act," Federal Register (Order No. 2243-02)(November 13, 2002).

123.News Release, "U.S. Justice Department to Use Detention to Keep Refugees Out of Country, Amnesty International Charges," Amnesty International (November 13, 2002). See also "INS Announces Expedited Removal for Migrants Arriving By Sea," Media Alert, Lawyer's Committee for Human Rights (November 12, 2002).

124.As of August 7, 2003, one Haitian who arrived by boat on December 3, 2001 remained in detention. 14 Haitian males who arrived on the October 29, 2002 boat were still at Krome and six of the women who made that journey were detained at BTC. Two unaccompanied Haitian children from the October 29, 2002 boat languished at Boystown while six of the Haitian men charged with smuggling the October boatload of Haitians into the U.S. remain in federal custody. 102 of the Haitians who arrived on October 29, 2002 were deported and 53 of them were granted asylum.

125.Office of the Federal Detention Trustee, "Statistics," U.S. Department of Justice (Fiscal

Year 2002) (available at http://www.usdoj.gov/ofdt/statistics.htm).

126.Susan Benesch, Refugee Advocate, Refugee Project, AIUSA, "Haitian Refugees Trapped by War on Terror," Amnesty Now (Fall 2003), Supra.

127.Jacqueline Charles, "Haitian gets another chance to stay in U.S.," The Miami Herald (August 12, 2003); Tanya Weinberg, "Haitian teens who landed in Biscayne Bay win review of asylum claims," South Florida Sun-Sentinel (August 12, 2003).

128.Rescue at sea, does not necessitate repatriation. Just as maritime law requires boats to offer assistance to those in peril, refugee law requires that a country refrain from returning bona fide refugees to life threatening persecution. Article 33, Principle of non-refoulement, United Nations Convention Relating to the Status of Refugees, 189 UN Treaty Series 137 (opened for signature July 28, 1951); United Nations Protocol Relating to the Status of Refugees, 606 UN Treaty Series 267 (opened for signature January 31, 1967).

129.Executive Order, "Delegation of Responsibilities Concerning Undocumented Aliens Interdicted or Intercepted in the Caribbean Region" (November 15, 2002).

130.Human rights organizations decried this latest Administrative directive. See e.g., Amnesty International, USA Analysis of President Bush's Nov. 15 Executive Order on Interdiction in the Caribbean Region, by Bill Frelick, Director, Refugee Program, Amnesty International, USA; Press Release, Women's Commission for Refugee Women and Children, "Latest Bush Executive Order Further Erodes Haitians' Ability to Gain Refugee Protection" (November 18, 2002).

131.Statement of Attorney General John Ashcroft regarding the Haiti Migrant Situation in Miami, Florida (October 30, 2002) (available at www.USDOJ.gov).

132.Letter to Senator Bob Graham from Cheryl Little, Esq., Florida Immigrant Advocacy Center (September 19, 2000); See also Cheryl Little, "Haitian Children Awaiting Visas: A Plea for Help," Florida Rural Legal Services (April, 1994).

133.The Department of State responded to a congressional inquiry about the feasibility of in-country processing by stating: "We do not believe that the extraordinary remedy of an in-country refugee processing program for Haitians is appropriate at this time. Given the level of economic desperation in Haiti, an in-country program is likely to attract many more ineligible than eligible applicants. We believe that existing protection options for Haitians who may be at risk of persecution or torture are sufficient." "Responses to Congresswoman Ros-Lehtinen's Refugees," Submitted by Paul V. Kelly, Assistant Secretary for Legislative Affairs, U.S. Department of State (November 22, 2002).

134. See e.g. Letter to Marcos Jimenéz, U.S. Attorney for the Southern District of Florida, from Cheryl Little, Esq., Florida Immigrant Advocacy Center (March 14, 2003); Sign-on Letter to Marcos Jimenéz from Refugee Council USA, with 43 signatories (May 29, 2003); Sign-on Letter to Attorney General John Ashcroft and DHS Secretary Tom Ridge from Refugee Council USA, with 59 signatories (July 23, 2003).

135. See e.g., Catherine Wilson, "Advocates challenge prosecution of Miami asylum seekers," Associated Press (August 3, 2003).

136. Despite being sentenced to "credit for time served" in exchange for a guilty plea, some female Haitian asylum seekers are being held in a maximum security jail in Miami due to their "criminal alien" status.

137.See Letter to Marcos Jimenéz, U.S. Attorney for the Southern District of Florida, from

Cheryl Little, Esq., Florida Immigrant Advocacy Center (April 1, 2003); "Haiti's Prisons: Inside the Gates of Hell," Miami Herald (March 25, 2001); Statement of Michelle Karchan, Executive Director of Alternative Chance, (August 30, 2000); Andy Kershaw, "Haiti's Desperate Deportees," BBC News (December 8, 2000); "Mother of Two, Deported to Haiti, Dies in Haitian Jail," Haiti Progress, Vol 18, No. 28 (September 27-October 3, 2000).

138."Refugee Policy Adrift: The United States and Dominican Republic Deny Haitians Protection," Women's Commission for Refugee Women and Children (January 2003), Supra.

139.Nancy San Martin, "Dominican Army Tightens Watch," Miami Herald, p. 6A November 25, 2002.

140.Cheryl Little, University of Miami Law Review, Supra.

141.Haitian Refugee Center v. Civiletti, 503 F. Supp. 442 (S.D.Fla,1980), aff'd as modified sub nom.Haitian Refugee Center v. Smith, 676 F. 2d 1023 (5th Cir. 1982).

142.Jean v. Nelson, 711 F.2d 1455, 1462 (11Cir. 1983), dismissed in part & rev'd in part, 727 F.2d 957, 978-79 (1984) (enbanc), aff'd, 472 V.S. 486 (1985).

143.Molaire v. Smith, 743 F. Supp.839, 850 (S.D.Fla. 1990).

144.Cheryl Little, The University of Miami Law Review, supra.

145.For a comprehensive review of the discriminatory of the Haitian children detained at Guantánamo, see Cheryl Little, "Not In Their Best Interest: A Report on the U.S. Government's Forcible Repatriation of Guantánamo's Unaccompanied Haitian Children," Florida Rural Legal Services (May 1995); "Not In Their Best Interest: A Report on the U.S. Government's Forcible Repatriation of Guantánamo's Unaccompanied Haitian Children," Karla Pearcy and Cheryl Little, "Unaccompanied Haitian Children Repatriated from Guantánamo: Stories of Trauma and Despair," Florida Immigrant Advocacy Center (September 1996); see also Bob Herbert, "Suffering the Children," New York Times Editorial (May 27, 1995).

146.Haitian Refugee Center, Inc. v. Baker, 112 S. Ct. 1245 (February 24, 1992); see also "Supreme Court Lifts Ban on Forced Repatriation of Haitians,"Interpreter Releases, p. 149 (February 3, 1992); Interpreter Releases, supra (February 24, 1992).

147.Three times the District Court judge in HRC v. Baker ruled in favor of the Haitians and each time the Eleventh Circuit Court of Appeals stayed or vacated the judge's orders. The Appeals Court found that the Haitians had no legally enforceable rights in the United States because they were outside United States territory. The "catch-22" nature of this finding was not lost on Judge Hatchett, the one African-American judge on the Appeals panel, who remarked in a dissenting opinion: "Haitians, unlike other aliens from anywhere in the world, are prevented from freely reaching the continental United States." Haitian Refugee Center, Inc. v. Baker, 953 F.2d 1498, 1520 (11th Cir. 1992) (J. Hatchett, dissenting).

148.Cheryl Little, The University of Miami Law Review, supra.

149.Haitian Refugee Center, Inc. v. Baker, 112 S. Ct. 1245 (February 24, 1992).

150.President George Bush, Executive Order 12807 (May 24, 1992); "Bush Orders Coast Guard to Return All Haitians," Interpreter Releases, p. 672 (June 1, 1992).

151.In response to public criticism of what became known as the Alien Migrant Interdiction Operation and a legal challenge to permissibility of the Haitian Interdiction program under international law, the program was revised in January 1991 to better inform interdicted

Haitians about their right to apply for asylum and to improve the pre-screening interviews conducted on Coast Guard cutters. See Immigration and Naturalization Service, Memorandum from Asylum Branch, "Procedural Changes in the INS Asylum Pre-Screening Component of the AMIO" (March 1, 1991; "INS Revises Policy for Screening Haitians Interdicted at Sea," Interpreter Releases, p. 793 (July 1, 1991. See also, Cheryl Little, The University of Miami Law Review, supra. Twenty of the 28 Haitians "screened in" between 1981-1991 were brought to the U.S. after INS agreed to improve the interdiction process, which took effect after President Aristide took power.

152.Haitians who were "screened-in" at Guantánamo in 1991 and 1992 were only allowed to come to the United States after a federal judge issued a temporary injunction prohibiting their forcible return. Several interpreters at Guantánamo provided sworn statements detailing a pattern of heavy pressure by U.S. State Department Officials on asylum officers to decrease the number of Haitians "screened-in". A 1992 Harvard Law School report on the asylum process expressed concern that "special foreign policy pressures" had been influencing treatment of the Haitian cases. In addition, the more than 10,000 Haitians "screened-in" the United States from Guantánamo, after INS officials found they had a credible fear of persecution continued to be in real danger of being denied asylum. Even before asylum officers had interviewed many of them after their arrival in the United States, the INS Deputy Commissioner publicly stated that 90 percent of these cases would probably be denied, a self-fulfilling prophecy. Indeed, preliminary assessments by asylum officers in Miami recommended grants of asylum in thirty-three of the first forty-three Haitian cases. Yet, in a May 26, 1992 memorandum to the Associate Deputy Attorney General, the Director and Assistant Director of the Asylum Policy and Review Unit ("APRU") in Washington disagreed with eighteen of the recommendations to approve, but with only one recommendations to deny. He also expressed concern that the grant rate was "higher than expected." To combat this, special incentives were given to asylum officers to deny these cases, specifying that the "INS could be encouraged to. . . [count] a completed denial as a double case completion and a completed grant as a single case completion for the purposes of . . officer evaluation." Cheryl Little, University of Miami Law Review, pp. 729-730, supra.

153.The vast majority of the Haitians who arrived by boat on December 3, 2001, were from Raboteau, an impoverished seaside neighborhood outside of Gonaives. Gonaives and Raboteau were in turmoil in August of 2002, following a massive jailbreak that resulted in the escape of 159 prisoners, including Amiot "Cubain" Métayer, a former Aristide ally whom the government had arrested in connection with the December 2001 unrest, and former soldiers convicted for 1994 massacre of civilians in Raboteau. See e.g., Nancy San Martin, "Turmoil Spreads In Haiti: Aristide foes stoke rebellion," The Miami Herald (August 9, 2002). Michael Norton, "Haitian Protesters take over City," The Miami Herald (August 6, 2002); Press Statement, U.S. Department of State (August 5, 2002); Nancy San Martin, "Haitian Police Break Up Residents' Street Protest," Miami Herald (August 6, 2002); "Protesters Seize Control of Haiti's Fourth-Largest City," CNN.com (August 6, 2002); "Thousands Protest in Haiti," Combined News Services (August 6, 2002); "Haitian City remains Tense After Jail Break," Reuters.com (August 6, 2002).

154."Refugee Policy Adrift, The United States and Dominican Republic Deny Haitians

Protection," Women's Commission for Refugee Women & Children (January 2003). See also, Press Release, "Women's Commission Gravely Concerned About the Plight of Haitian Refugees," Women's Commission for Refugee Women and Children (October 31, 2002).

155.Ibid. pp. 29-30.

156.FIAC met with Rigmane a number of times during her detention in Florida and arranged for the Women's Commission to interview her upon her return.

157.Ibid.

158.Presentation by Wendy Young, Director of Government Relations, Women's Commission for Refuge Women and Children, Church World Service Conference on Haitian Refugees (February 5, 2003).

159.Statements of Casimir (June 7 and 12, 2002).

160.Cheryl Little, The University of Miami Law Review, supra.

161.These groups include the American Immigration Lawyers Association, Amnesty International, Asia America Law Group, Catholic Legal Immigrant Network, Inc., Church World Service, Colombian American Service Association, AFL-CIO, Florida's Catholic Bishops, Immigrant and Refugee Rights Project, Lutheran Immigration & Refugee Service, NAACP, National Immigration Forum, TransAfrica Forum, National Coalition for Haitian Rights, Physicians for Human Rights, U.S. Committee for Refugees, Washington Lawyers' Committee for Civil Rights, and the Women's Commission for Refugee Women and Children.

162.Jody Benjamin, "U.S. panel to press Bush," South Florida Sun-Sentinel (June 22, 2002); Alfonso Chardy, "Agency to probe Haitians' detention," The Miami Herald (June 22, 2002).

163.A resolution passed by U.S. Mayors at a national conference in June, 2003 also called for the fair treatment of Haitians. The Mayors, who met in Denver, unanimously approved a resolution that calls for an end to the detention policy. The City Commission of Key West, Florida has likewise passed a resolution urging President Bush to rescind its Haitian immigration policy. The Greater Miami Chamber of Commerce and Miami-Dade County's prestigious Beacon Council not only issued resolutions last summer calling for fair treatment of the Haitians but their leaders traveled to DC with Congressman Kendrick Meek to discuss their concerns with high-ranking government officials. In early June 2003, a delegation of over 40 community activists traveled to Washington, DC with Congressman Meek and Miami-Dade County elected officials, to protest the Haitians' treatment. A relative of one of the detained Haitian women also testified at a post 9-11 public forum before the U.S. Senate regarding the discriminatory detention of Haitians on the unjustified basis of national security. See National Conference of Mayors, "A resolution urging President Bush to Rescind the Immigration Policies Against Haitian Immigrants and Calling for the Equal Treatment of All Immigrants," Adopted Resolution 71st Annual Meeting (June 2003); City Commission of the City of Key West, Florida, Resolution No. 03-228 (July 2, 2003); Resolution, "Haitian Immigration Issues," Greater Miami Chamber of Commerce (July 1, 2002); Resolution, "Support for Haitian Immigration Justice," Miami-Dade County Beacon Council; Jacqueline Charles, The Miami Herald (July 10, 2002); Frank Davies, "South Florida delegation pushes Haitian causes in D.C. mission," The Miami Herald (June 5, 2003). See Testimony of Kerline Phelizor, Public Forum at the U.S. Senate, "Justice For All: Selective Enforcement in Post-911 America," (June 4, 2003); Julia Malone,

"Immigrants tell of swift, harsh actions during anti-terror sweep," Atlanta Journal-Constitution (June 5, 2003).

164."The Detention and Treatment of Haitian Asylum Seekers," U.S. Senate Judiciary Committee, Subcommittee on Immigration (October 1, 2002) (Testimony available on-line at: http://judiciary.senate.gov/hearing.cfm?id=483). Senator Kennedy also made a compelling case against the Haitian detention policy in early 2003. See remarks of Senator Edward M. Kennedy, Conference on the Current Haitian Migration Crisis (February 5, 2003).

165.Briefing before the Subcommittee on International Operation and Human Rights (October 1, 2002). Florida Senators Bob Graham and Bill Nelson, as well as Florida Congresspersons Ileana Ros-Lehtinen, Lincoln Diaz Balart, Carrie Meek, and Kendrick Meek have all called for fair treatment of Haitian asylum seekers, as has the Congressional Black Caucus, among others. See e.g. letter from Congresswoman Ileana Ros-Lehtinen to INS Commissioner James Zigler (January 28, 2002); letter from Congresspersons Hastings, Meek, Christiensen, Towns, Conyers, McKinney, Clayburn and Johnson to U.S. Attorney General John Ashcroft (January 31, 2002); letter from Congresswoman Carrie P. Meek to INS Commissioner James Zigler (April 26, 2002); Elaine De Valle, "Haitian Advocates, Rep. Meek meet to push for release of asylum seekers," Miami Herald (April 30, 2002); Letter from Senator Bill Nelson to INS Commissioner James Zigler (May 2, 2002); Press Release, Congressman John Conyers, Jr. (October 30, 2002); "Haitian advocates, Rep. Meek to push for release of asylum seekers," The Miami Herald (April 30, 2002).

166. Letter from detained Haitian women seeking asylum at the Broward Transitional Center to Members of Congress (May 27, 2003).

# The Treatment of Haitian Refugees in the U.S.: A Travesty of Justice
*Marleine Bastien, MSW, LCSW*

## Marleine Bastien and the Founding of FANM

I completed secondary school at College Bird, and I was unable to enter medical school because I did not have a *parenn* (sponsor). I taught and worked at the Haitian Art Museum for a year but grew so dissatisfied with the overall situation in Haiti that I became more vocal about it. After an interview at Radio Haiti Inter where I criticized the Haitian government for their lack of sensitivity vis-à-vis the plight of Haitian students, my father, fearing for my life, sent for me.

I entered the United States on September 23, 1981. Two days after my arrival, my father brought me to meet Father Gerard Jean-Juste, and I started volunteering with the Haitian Refugee Center (HRC). I accompanied the HRC lawyers to Krome Detention Center a week later, and what I saw changed my life forever. Hundreds of Haitian detainees were jailed for months at a time, in the most restricted environment. They were victimized for the simple fact that they failed to understand a command made in English. Many were physically abused and placed in solitary confinement for minor violations. Although the men had a hard time coping with the long-term detention, the women's situation was ten times worse. Children were kept together with adults in one big compound with no supervision and no one to advocate on their behalf. Pregnant women had no access to medical care and their complaints were ignored for days, sometimes with grave consequences.

At about the same time, I started to volunteer at HACAD (Haitan-American Community Association of Dade). I worked closely with lawyers who represented newly arrived Haitian families in landlord-tenant disputes. In my capacity as a social worker's aide I visited the Haitians, assessed their home situations and reported back to the lawyers. Once again, I was shocked to see the level of desperation, abuse, and repression to which the Haitians were subjected. These experiences reinforced my desire to become a social worker to help these families. More importantly, I wanted to be a voice for the voiceless since I could speak English and could get my message across.

As a social worker, I don't believe in "giving handouts to people," I believe in empowering them so that they can organize and make decisions that will guarantee their families a better future. I am one of the founding members of the Haitian Coalition on Health, which stood up against the FDA's inclusion of Haitian on the high-risk list for HIV. I played an instrumental role in organizing the biggest demonstration in the history of the Haitian community in Miami against the FDA (Federal Drug Administration). Moreover, I advocated for women with HIV/ AIDS who lacked access to proper treatment and those who were excluded from the many medication protocols that were made available to men.

During the Haitian refugee crisis in the 1990s, I traveled several times to Guantanamo Bay, Cuba to advocate for the rights of Haitian detainees. As a result, I founded the "Justice Coalition for the Haitian Children of Guantanamo" to fight for the release of the children who were incarcerated. Then I received tremendous support from my supervisors at Jackson Memorial Hospital who saw my work in the field as an extension of my day-to-day duties as a clinician. A few years later, I founded FANM[1] *(Fanm Ayisyen Nan Miyami,* Haitian Women of Miami) which is now a leading advocacy group for the rights of Haitian immigrants and refugees in the U.S.

When I was going to school in Haiti, I learned that the United States was a great democracy, a place where human rights are respected. Needless to say, I was greatly disappointed when I saw the way Haitians were treated. Even under the Duvalier dictatorship, which used the worse kind of repression against the Haitian people, the U.S. Justice Department was arbitrarily deporting Haitian refugees in complete denial of their most basic right. The Haitians' right of due process was violated under the premise that they were economic refugees and not political refugees. Haitians were jailed for months and sometimes years, and later released into the community without any guidance or support. Unlike Cubans, who received housing and education subsidies, Haitians were left to fend for themselves.

I decided to develop an organization that would advocate for the rights of women refugees and their families, and facilitate their adjustment to life in South Florida. As a result, I founded FANM in 1991, to work for the "social, political and economic empowerment" of Haitian women. Its founding coincides with a critical turning point in the history of the Haitian community in the United States, which was the transition from the activism typical of an exile community, focused on politics inside Haiti, to an activism focused on the needs of Haitians self-defined as immigrants. Haitians are as deserving as other groups to receive fair treatment. If there is a policy to regulate refugees' entrance into this country, it has to be implemented equally across the board. There cannot be a policy for white refugees and another one for black refugees. The United States has an obligation to respect international conventions and the basic human rights of the Haitians.

During the Duvalier years, grassroots organizations in Miami's Little Haiti were a vibrant part of the struggle for democracy and human rights in Haiti. The refugees' battles against discriminatory U.S. immigration laws and practices were a powerful school for organizing and coalition building in the United States. But in recent years, with many activists having returned to Haiti, a new generation of community leaders is struggling to reshape existing organizations and build new ones to address the long-term needs of Haitians in the United States.

FANM was initially led by a cadre of strong Haitian women who volunteered their time and efforts. These women represented a new generation of leadership, devoted to the welfare of the Haitian community as a whole but sensitized to the particular needs of Haitian women. The beginnings were very difficult for FANM. I was accused of "breaking the Haitian families" when I began to use the airwaves to educate women about domestic violence, and other pertinent issues. I received death threats from some Haitian men, and I was even shunned by some Haitian women.

At present, FANM's activities include both a strong advocacy and service component. FANM provides:

- Advocacy for equal treatment of Haitians under U.S. immigration laws.
- Advocacy for worker rights and respect.
- A micro-loan program for women starting their own small businesses.
- Outreach to inform and refer immigrants/low-income people to free/low-cost health insurance programs for children.
- Breast cancer education and awareness program: seminars, transportation to screening/follow-up appointments, translation.

Today, FANM continues to be concerned with some of the same issues that sparked its inception, and the organization addresses them through these programmatic areas:

## 1. Immigration Advocacy and Citizenship

The Immigration, Advocacy and Citizenship program focuses on public policy issues surrounding Haitian detainees, entrants, refugees, and asylees. It entails (1) meeting with the media, elected officials, INS staff, and other ethnic groups and organizations that share our views and concerns surrounding unfair treatment of entrants into the United States, especially Haitians; (2) educating the community about the current state of immigration via radio; (3) assisting entrant-asylees-refugees with completion of INS forms; (4) conducting workshops and presentations on immigration issues and citizenship procedures; and (5) teaching citizenship classes with an English literacy component to a Creole speaking audience.

## 2. Community Economic Development

The Community Economic Development (CED) program focuses on creating income and benefits by organizing Haitian women to create their own businesses. To accomplish this, FANM trains Haitian women with job and business skills such as inventory, marketing, customer service, and sales. CED also advocates for a living wage in the county and nation, and empowerment of women workers which focuses on service workers (primarily employed in nursing homes), to build organization and leadership skills. The third component is community education via community meetings where topics of common concern are discussed with local experts and government officials.

## 3. Family Intervention and Empowerment

Family Intervention and Empowerment focuses on providing case management, mental health counseling, social services, referrals and other economic assistance, and parenting classes. FANM facilitates discussions on crime; capacity building with families; advocates in the courts, schools, and the department of children and families; and provides links and access to health care.

In 1998, FANM took the lead in South Florida in working for the passage of the Haitian Refugee Immigrant Fairness Act (HRIFA) Enacted into law in October 1998, the legislation allows 50,000 Haitian families who arrived in the U.S. prior to December 31, 1995 to apply for residency. I was chosen by Congresswoman Carrie Meek to make presentations to members of Congress and their staff, in an effort to educate them about the issues most urgently faced by Haitian immigrants. FANM helped organize several busloads of Haitian Americans to go to Washington to participate in demonstrations demanding the passage of HIRFA. For the first time in Haitian American history, Haitians in large numbers from South Florida joined those from Boston, Chicago and Connecticut to lobby for fair and equal treatment of Haitians. In addition, FANM helped to build the Haitian American Grassroots Coalition, consisting of some 15 Haitian organizations.

# Haitians in the United States

It is estimated that over one million Haitians reside in the United States[2]. The largest number live in the New York Metropolitan area. Other states with a large concentration of Haitians include: Florida, Connecticut, California, Illinois, Massachusetts, and New Jersey. Haitians have immigrated to the United States since the American Revolution. Many Haitian nationals have made significant contributions to the social, political, and economic fabric of this country. For example, Jean Baptiste Pointe du Sable built the first permanent settlements for what is now known as Chicago. Haitians fought in the battle of Savannah, Georgia and died to make this country what it is today. When Haitians defeated the powerful Napoleon army in 1803, they derailed France's dream of conquering the United States. The U.S. would probably be completely different today had it not been for Haiti's victory, which forced Napoleon Bonaparte to change his domination plans.

Haitians began to experience difficulties in the U.S. when they reached critical mass. There was a strong fear that this "sea" of Black Haitian immigrants would be contributing to the "browning of America". Between 1972 and 1981, The United States Immigration and Naturalization Services (INS) reported that about 55,000 boat people arrived in South Florida. INS believed that probably more than half that number arrived undetected while a significant number died while attempting to reach the U.S. in non-seaworthy vessels. Successive U.S. administrations have tried to curb this continuing flow of refugees. "Between 1981 and 1991, the U.S. Coast Guard interdicted and forcibly returned only Haitians. During those 10 years, out of 24,558 interdicted Haitians, INS shipboard screeners allowed only 28 persons to pursue their asylum claim in the United States. Those Haitians who managed to register for asylum during the 1980s had the lowest asylum approval rate of any nationality – 1.8%. By contrast, Soviet and Cuban asylum approvals were at that time 74.5%. In May 1992, for the first time in American history, the United States began forcibly returning interdicted asylum seekers to Haiti wihtout any screening whatsoever.[3] In contrast, from the 1960's to the present, hundreds of thousands of Cubans have been paroled in and after a year have been automatically adjusted to permanent resident status in the U.S.

# Waves of Haitian Refugees

Many of the first refugees in the 1950s and 1960s were urban middle-class families fleeing the brutal dictatorship of Francois Duvalier. Throughout the 1970s however, an increasing number of rural and lower-class urban Haitians also immigrated to U.S. The first wave of refugees came primarily because of direct political oppression during the first decade of the rule of Francois Duvalier (1957-1967) as he eliminated all opponents, real or perceived. The second wave of refugees consisted of skilled craftsmen who came to the United States for better living conditions.

After Francois Duvalier's death in 1971, he was succeeded by his son Jean-Claude Duvalier. The younger Duvalier continued the harsh political repression and waste of natural resources. The third wave of Haitian refugees consisted of peasants who had been dispossessed of their land or were unable to make a living on the deteriorated soil. These refugees arrived in Florida in late 1970s to early 1980s; at around the same time Cubans were also arriving en masse. The fourth wave of immigrants came in 1991, after the coup that overthrew Haitian President Jean-Bertrand Aristide. These refugees were mainly young students, members of grassroots organizations/coalitions, women, peasants and human rights advocates.

## Treatment of the Haitian Refugees

In September 1981, the United States entered into an agreement with Haiti to interdict Haitian boats and return refugees to Haiti. Under the agreement, 3,107 refugees were returned by 1984. A decision was made by the Justice Department to stop the Haitian boat people at all costs. Haitians intercepted by the U.S. Coast Guard were returned to Haiti without even a cursory attempt to identify those who might be at risk, a direct violation of international rules and the obligations of the United States under Article 33 of the 1951 Convention relating to the Status of Refugees. The United States government claimed that while some Haitians deserved political asylum, most attempted the difficult 750 mile voyage for economic reasons, and furthermore, allowing them to remain in the U.S. would encourage others to risk their lives coming to the U.S. in search of better economic opportunities.[4]

In a collective letter written by a group of refugees detained at Fort Allen Puerto Rico, in 1981, the anguish, the desperation, and the frustration of the refugees who felt rejected by mother liberty were articulated. The refugees wrote:

> "Since we arrived on American soil, we have been mistreated. We have been made to suffer and we have accepted it all, we have endured it all... We are Christians, we have blood in our veins and thoughts like every other people yearning to be free. We have been

suffering for months, we asylum seekers, in prison, we need to be set free. Our situation is pitiful. We have been locked up behind barbed wires from Miami to Puerto Rico. The days are always the same... We don't know what the date is... sometimes we are hungry, and we cannot eat. We have needs and cannot satisfy them. Is this the better life we were seeking? We took refuge in the United States in the hope of filling our voids...Can we not fill them? Now, we cannot stand it anymore, if we have not been released by November, a good number of us are going to commit suicide. Because we have sworn to die in the United States... we are asking why you treat us this way...Is it because we are Negroes? Why are you letting us suffer this way, America? Don't you have a father's heart? Haven't you thought that we are humans that we had a heart to suffer with, and a soul that could be wounded? Give us back our freedom! Why among all the nations that emigrate to the United States have only Haitians known such suffering?"[5]

In 1992, President George Bush issued an Executive Order stating that all Haitians intercepted at sea outside U.S. territorial waters would be returned directly to Haiti, without any consideration of their asylum claims. When President Bill Clinton took office in January 1993, he continued this policy despite campaign promises to end it. For two years, while the policy was in force, this arbitrary decision was often fatal for returned refugees who had been supporters of President Jean-Bertrand Aristide.[6]

The case of Oman Desanges is an excellent example. Oman Desanges was the founder and President of the *Association des Jeunes Progressistes de Martissant* (Young Progressive Association of Martissant, a neighborhood committee) and a supporter of President Jean-Bertrand Aristide. He was returned to Haiti after requesting political asylum in the U.S. in 1993. On January 26, 1994, Oman Desanges' body was discovered near the international airport in Port-au-Prince, with his arms bound, a cord around his neck and a red handkerchief around his arm reading "president of the Red Army and indigent (destitute)". His eyes had been gouged out, an ear cut off and his stomach split open.[7]

# The Old is Still New

Thirty-one years later, Haitian refugees are still being detained, even though they have committed no crime. Haitian asylum seekers detained by INS can be found in Immigration Processing Centers, facilities run by private corporations, U.S. Bureau of Prisons Facilities, local jails and maximum-security prisons. In a depressed economy, prisons are still big business. Westinghouse, AT&T, Sprint, MCI, Smith Barney, American Express, General Electric and Corporation of America operate 48 correctional facilities in 11 states, Puerto Rico, the United Kingdom, and Australia. They are raking in billions of dollars by cutting corners, which harms prisoners. Some of the corners cut include sub-standard diets, extreme overcrowding, and abusive and often racist prison guards.[8]

Asylum seekers suffer more from poor conditions in the prison system than anyone else. They have no criminal background, yet they are housed with criminals. Often criminals and prison guards take advantage of the detained Haitians. They harass them mentally and physically. The majority of Haitians are unable to communicate in English, which only increases their torment. Haitians are often traumatized and scarred for life in these horrible prison cells.

No logical standards to regulate the placement of asylum seekers exist. In 1998, INS issued standards for its own facilities. They promised to use these new standards for county jails and other centers that have contracts with INS. Under the new standards:

- Detainees are entitled to eight hours of uninterrupted, private, legal visitation seven days a week. Meals will be provided to detainees who are meeting with their legal counsel during mealtimes.
- Detainees will not be strip-searched after attorney visitation without reasonable suspicion of contraband. However, the INS makes an exception for a few non-INS facilities that mandate strip-searches after visits. Under the new guidelines, persons held in facilities that mandate strip-searches may request a "non-contact" visit with their attorney to avoid being strip-searched, otherwise, they may be strip-searched.
- Detainees can make free, unmonitored, private phone calls for *pro bono* representation and to confer with consular officials through pre-programmed phone technology. However, most non-INS facilities do not have this technology.
- Detainees are entitled to at least one hour daily to use law libraries equipped with immigration and asylum-related materials and typewriters. The relevant

forms and copying will be available to detainees to help them prepare their cases. Detainees will be allowed to assist one another in preparing their cases.

- Family, including children and friends can visit detainees for at least thirty minutes per visit on weekends and holidays.
- Detainees may practice their religion and participate in group religious activities. The INS plans to set up chaplain programs at the 18 INS service processing centers and contract facilities to provide detainees with access to religious services and individual counseling
- Attorneys will be allowed to provide "Know Your Rights" presentations to groups of detainees every day to educate them about their legal rights and other issues related to their cases.
- Attorneys can call ahead to a facility to ascertain whether an actual or prospective client is detained at the facility.

But INS has failed to implement these standards in its own facilities let alone those outside its control. According to Lewelyn G. Prichard, the new standards have not been issued as federal regulations and therefore do not have the force of law. Judy Rabinovitz of the American Civil Liberties Union Immigrants' Rights Project said: "Advocates have been pushing for national regulations for a long time because of the horrendous conditions in INS facilities. Conditions may not improve even after the standards are in place because they do not have the weight of law and could prove impossible to enforce."[9]

On December 3, 2001, in an unprecedented move, INS decided to keep the Haitians who arrived on U.S. shores detained even after they passed their credible fear interviews. The Haitians were submitted to accelerated legal proceedings that made it impossible for the them to secure legal representation or even to give the lawyers adequate time to prepare them for their asylum hearings.

Under FANM's leadership, meetings were held with INS District Administrator John Bulger and Assistant District Director John Schwairy in December 2001 and again in January 2002. The officials assured the advocates that the "refugees will soon be released". At no point did INS admit a change in the policy. However, during a meeting with Congressman John Conyers, Jr. at the Krome Processing Center, INS finally admitted that there was indeed a change in the policy and that there was an "order from Washington to keep Haitians in detention pending a determination in their cases."[10]

On October 29th, 2002, another group of Haitian refugees ran aground in a rickety boat in Key Biscayne. The tragic images shown all over the world told the story of a desperate group of people: men, women, and children as young as 3 years old, some in their Sunday best, jumping overboard to run toward freedom and liberty! They were rounded up like animals, handcuffed, and taken to detention centers by INS. Ten months later, these desperate refugees are still detained; children and their mothers are held at especially great expense to taxpayers. Children as young as 3 years are held at area motels which are believed to be worse than Krome and other detention centers. Children under six are confined to a motel room with their mothers for months with no access to recreation or even fresh air. For the first time, INS has begun detaining Haitians even after immigration judges have granted them political asylum, while the U.S. government holds their cases in appeal.

## Condition of Haitian women in INS Detention

Haitian women in INS detention, especially at the Turner Gilford Knight Center (TGK), complained of many problems including but not limited to: lack of access to lawyers, language barriers, lack of access to telephones, inability to communicate with family members in Haiti, inadequate visitation opportunities, lack of activities and medical care, and inedible food. [11]

## Access to attorneys

Attorneys trying to interview their clients at the TGK and other detention centers where women are incarcerated face numerous problems and difficulties. Not only is there a long-waiting period to see clients but oftentimes visits are cut short due to arbitrary head-counts, lockdowns, arbitrary policy changes, and unexplained emergencies.

## Telephone Access

Haitian women have a lot of problems communicating with their family members in the U.S. and Haiti adding to their sense of isolation and betrayal. Some have difficulties communicating with their lawyers. Most of them can only make collect calls, the cost of which are extremely high. Additionally, most families do not have telephones that are set up to receive collect calls. Also, Haiti has automatic blocks that prevent exchange among the detainees and their family members. Some detainees have gone for months without knowing if their family members are dead or alive. One detainee was able to call home after spending months in detention only to find out that her mother had died. When she called four weeks later (with a donated calling card from a Haitian doctor) to find out about her mother's funeral, she was given the news about her father's death. She was inconsolable, and she then became suicidal.

# Visitation

Women detainees at TGK are only allowed one contact visit per month and two non-contact visits a week. The contact visits are often conducted in the hallway and there is constant interruption of guards and other personnel entering and exiting the area. Non-contact visits are horrible. Women detainees are able to see their relatives through a window of Plexiglas but, since the small holes that allow the detainees to communicate with family members are below the glass and at waist level they have to bend and twist their head in order to hear each other. The women interviewed by FANM advocates indicated that they feel "ashamed, dehumanized, and undignified by the process". These women are still luckier than the ones in the motels who have no access at all to recreation or visits. All will undoubtedly be scarred forever by these horrible experiences.

# Recreation and Other Activities

Women detainees at TGK and other facilities around the U.S. lack access to even the most basic activities. At TGK, the outdoor recreation area only consists of a small concrete wall space exposed to the elements. The women supposedly have access from 8 AM to 7 PM, but due to frequent lockdowns and other unexplained emergencies, they cannot take advantage of even that small space. When interviewed by FANM employees, the women complained that they feel "useless, helpless and hopeless sitting around all day with nothing to do". Many expressed suicidal thoughts. A Haitian woman interviewed by a delegation of businessmen headed by the chair the Greater Miami Chamber of Commerce said, "We came here in search of freedom and liberty. If I knew I would be treated so bad, disrespected and humiliated, I would have thrown myself overboard".

# Food Service

One of the biggest complaints about TGK and the other detention centers is the food. Most of the women said that they have lost weight because they have not received proper nutrition and the food is for the most part inedible, spoiled, uncooked, cold, and very scarce. FANM has offered to seek contracts with area Haitian restaurants to provide more culturally sensitive foods to the detainees, but the offer was rejected.

During several visits at TGK, the women indicated that they are woken to eat breakfast at 5 AM and served dinner at 4 PM. Consequently, they get hungry often and they have to spend money at the vending machines which most of them do not have.

# Medical Care

Haitian women detainees lack access to medical care. Medical complaints often go unreported for days, and the center staff intervene only after the woman's lawyers complain to authorities higher up. FANM and other advocacy groups have complained about these practices many times to no avail.

# Abuse, Harassment and Illegal Lockdown

Many women detainees are victims of abuse and racial slurs by guards. Women are punished, punched, pushed around and placed in isolation or lockdown for minor offenses such as asking repeatedly for an item like sanitary pads, not readily reacting to commands due to lack of understanding/language barriers.

The United States of America, the champion of human rights is supposed to lead developed and under-developed nations in the protection of women and refugees' rights yet, right here in this country, women who have made it here through great sacrifice find themselves incarcerated all over the country in detention centers and jails that house the worst types of criminal elements. Haitian women refugees are held at Krome, TGK, area motels and hospitals, in Sarasota County jails, Palmetto Mental Health Center, Federal Detention Center in Miami, in Fort Lauderdale jails, Stockade and Palm Beach County Jail, Hernando County Jail, and

Monroe County Jail. The conditions in all these institutions mimic each other: they all lack the basic infrastructure to treat these women in a humane and dignified manner.[12]

## Impact of Detention on Women Detainees

Long-term detention has physical and psychological impacts on women detainees. Many have already suffered great tribulations in Haiti and therefore are experiencing post-traumatic stress disorders. Incarceration in maximum-security prisons and jails worsen their conditions. In Hawa Abdi Jama vs. INS, a New Jersey federal district court's finding of the inhumane and abusive condition that detained asylum seekers face in detention authorize them to sue the federal government for damages under the Alien Tort Claims Act. The court claimed that the "alleged treatment suffered by the plaintiff in the above-referenced case violated the international human right to be free from cruel, inhumane, or degrading treatment." The Universal Declaration of Human Rights adopted by the General Assembly of the United Nations on December 10th, 1948 also provides protection for refugees:

> "**Article 1:** All human beings are born free and equal in dignity and rights. They are endowed with reason and conscience and should act towards one another in a spirit of brotherhood.
>
> **Article 2:** Everyone is entitled to all the rights and freedoms set forth in this Declaration, without distinction of any kind, such as race, color, sex, language, religion, political or other opinion, national or social origin, property, birth or other status.
>
> **Article 10:** Everyone is entitled in full equality to a fair and public hearing by an independent and impartial tribunal, in the determination of his rights and obligations and of any criminal charge against him."[13]

We are the Women of the world
Lost in a foreign land
Shamed, denied, violated, tortured,
lapidated, maimed, intimidated
crushed, victimized, abused

we are the wives, fiancées, sisters
daughters, mothers forced to leave

our motherland in conditions
not fit for human beings
we risk our lives in non-seaworthy vessels
after many trials, adversities, tribulations
we make it to the land of the free
during out worst nightmare
the dream of being comforted
by the sweet arm of mother liberty
keep us going, hoping
then reality sinks in
our dreams are shattered
steel hug our ankles
leave scars deep in our flesh
scars that last a lifetime
oh yes, we are wide awake now
cold feel of handcuffs
leave bruises, shame, hurts
the thumping of heavy metal doors
takes away our last hope
what crimes have we committed?
we are the women of the world
in search of a safe haven
yet jailed...treated like criminals
who have we killed... who have we robbed?
is it a crime to seek protection
safety for our children
respect, dignity, humanity?
Is a crime to fight death, desperation
Is it a crime to want a future
Is it a crime to want to live?
Is it a crime to dream?[14]

## Condition of Haitian Children in U.S. Detention

Of all the refugee groups that come to the U.S., the case of Haitian children is the most compelling. The world witnessed how children as young as 3 years old, dressed in their Sunday best, were dropped in the water with the hope that they would make it to shores on October 2002. The children who were with their parents were sent to area motels where they remain locked up for days and days without access to education, recreation, or even fresh air. Many of the children in the motels suffer from post-traumatic syndromes, loss of their appetites and even their smiles. Three year-old Cherlande has spent six months of her life in one of those motel rooms with her mother and 14 year old sister. Immigration cannot legally place refugee children in prison but the hotel is actually worse. Unlike Cherlande, detainees at Krome have daily recreation and outdoor activities. The first time I visited Cherlande, I was appalled by the sadness in her eyes. She did not respond to any stimuli, and her mom expressed fear for her mental status. She had no toys, not even crayons, because there was fear that she might color on the walls. The first year of a child's life is the most important for healthy psychological adjustment and development. The long-term incarceration of Cherlande can cause irreparable damage and it is inconceivable that the U.S. – a country which dictates to other countries about human rights – would treat children this way.

The unaccompanied minors are sent to a detention center named Boystown where they are submitted to all kinds of emotional abuse. Some of the children complained that the deportation officer threatened to send back to Haiti, and prevented them from communicating with their family members and legal advocates. Some were called derogatory names and were severely disciplined for minor violations. When little children stop smiling, playing, or eating and are involved in destructive behaviors (such as bumping their heads on the wall) the world needs to care. The U.S. is committing gross child abuse in the way they treat the littlest refugees in its custody: the children. The world needs to wake up and rise up to its moral obligation to condemn this hypocrisy and mistreatment of children.[15]

## Prosecution of "airplane arrivals"

In a departure from at least twenty-two years of practice, the Justice Department has begun arresting and criminally prosecuting Haitian "airplane" asylum seekers. This is unprecedented, unnecessary, and hypocritical. Haitians flee in one of two ways: by boat or by air. In 1981, President Ronald Reagan initiated Coast Guard interdiction and repatriation of Haitian "boat persons". Bona fide refugees who had problems with Haiti's military knew that fleeing by boat would only guarantee them arbitrary deportation back home, so they elected to enter the U.S. with altered documents. Until a few months ago, INS routinely paroled them pending their asylum hearings. After all, asylum law recognizes that in order to save their lives, refugees have to flee with altered documents.

In an abrupt change, however, the Justice Department is now prosecuting Haitian "airplane people" in the United States District Court for the Southern District of Florida, taking up the time, staff, and resources of the federal court, the U.S. Attorney's office, and the Federal Public Defenders office. These refugees are branded as criminals, and if – or rather when – they are deported to Haiti, they will be treated like criminals and placed in Haitian jails where conditions are horrendous. It is a waste of taxpayers' money. Surely, this nation, and its federal judges, prosecutors, public defenders, and detention officers have more important things to do!

Since Haitian boat people began arriving in Southern Florida, successive U.S. governments have been trying to return them as expeditiously as possible. The U.S. government contends that while a few deserve asylum, the vast majority of Haitians are economic and not political refugees. They are not fleeing persecution but rather are coming to partake of vastly better U.S. economic opportunities. Most Haitian asylum seekers now in detention in the U.S. have passed their credible fear interviews. They have met the burden of proving bona fide cause for political asylum in the U.S. Refugees from any other country who meet that criteria are automatically released into the community once the process is completed, but not Haitians. INS has reverted to the same policies it used over 25 years ago.

As previously discussed, the policy consists of arbitrarily detaining Haitian refugees in complete denial of their rights and speeding up their deportation to Haiti. All the refugees have loving family members in the U.S. willing and able to support them. INS justifies the indefinite detention of Haitian asylum seekers as a "deterrent to prevent future boat exodus and to protect lives" (John Schawairy at a meeting with Congressman Conyers and Haitian advocates at Krome on March 9th, 2002). This justification lies in the face of truth! Cubans also risk their lives on small boats and rafts to make it to the U.S., and yet, they are welcomed and allowed to stay. Is the U.S. government more concerned about Cuban lives than Haitians? How are they protecting Haitian lives, by jailing them indefinitely? The most recent explanation is that "Haitians constitute a threat to National Security… and that terrorists could use Haiti as staging point to enter the U.S. as boat people."[16] This is ludicrous since Haiti has never been on the list of countries that harbors terrorism. Cuba is, and yet Cubans are allowed in the U.S. on a regular basis. Because Haitians are incarcerated, they are unable to secure legal representation, and their deteriorating mental conditions resulting from long-term incarceration and mistreatment have prevented them from presenting the best legal defense in court. Both Amnesty International and the United Nations High Commissioner on Refugees indicated that the "U.S. is violating international laws that protect refugees' rights by keeping Haitians in jail and not affording them the right of due process in a court of law."[17]

# CONCLUSION

U.S. government policies harm Haitians in many ways, ways which FANM seeks to redress. This includes advocacy against the inhumane policy of indefinitely detaining asylum seekers, even children, and the need to publicize this grave injustice. The U.S. treatment of Haitian refugees including women and children is inhumane, immoral and racist at best. Haitians have contributed for centuries to building the social, political, and economic fabric of the United States of America. Instead of recognizing these lasting contributions, it has gone over and beyond to curtail Haiti's progress by creating the Haitian army to represent its interest and repress the Haiti's citizen. Consequently, for 200 years, the majority of the Haitian people have been kept at the margin of society with no access to education, health care, nutrition, or even clean water. The peasants were dispossessed of their land and other vital economic capital: the black pigs, which the U.S. claimed were diseased and dangerous to the population. Left empty-handed, the peasants were unable to cultivate their land and feed their families. They moved to the Haitian capital with the hope of emigrating to the U.S.

When they arrive in the U.S. today, these same Haitians are jailed, mistreated, abused, humiliated and arbitrarily deported back to Haiti. Oh heartless and cruel punishment! In the meantime, the U.S. continues to undermine Haiti's young and fragile democracy by refusing to release badly needed funds for health, the building of roads and hospitals, police and anti-violence training. Meanwhile, the majority of Haiti's consumed goods come from the U.S., the free-market economy is flourishing while Haiti's poor get poorer and see no hope for the future. Haiti's political crisis is augmented daily by so-called friends who have an interest in its never-ending drama. Haiti will live and breathe again when its children in the diaspora and Haiti realize that its future is in their hands, and that as long as the majority of the Haitian people are kept at the margin of society, things will not change. A space has to be created for them to partake in the social, economic, and political processes of the country. Programs need to be implemented to fortify grassroots organizations in all Haiti's nine departments so this fragile democracy can at last grow and blossom without foreign interference and meddling

---

[1] FANM has received the following awards and recognition:

- 1997- Best Non-Profit of the Year – Miami-Dade Chamber of Commerce (Haitian Unit)

- In 1998, New Times named FANM "Best Champion of Dade's Powerless" in its yearly edition: The Best of Miami (5/14/98).
- October 31, 1998 FANM was honored by The South Florida Haitian Businessperson Achievement Award as the *Non-Profit Organization of the Year*.
- March 8, 1999, was proclaimed *Haitian Women of Miami Day* in Miami-Dade county by Mayor Alex Penelas for FANM's contribution to enrich the fabric of life in the county.
- 1998 - FANM was chosen by *La Reine Entertainment* as the nonprofit of the year
- In the Company of Women Award, 1998
- 2000 – Appreciation Award from North Miami Chamber of Commerce
- October 2000 – Fanm Ayisyen Nan Miyami, Inc., Executive Director, Marleine Bastien, received the "Human Rights Award" from the Miami chapter of Amnesty International.
- December 2000 – "Torch Award"(highest award given to Alumni) to Marleine Bastien, Executive Director, from Florida International University's Alumni Association.
- December 2000 – the "Service Medallion Award" was awarded to Marleine Bastien during Florida International University's commencement ceremony in front of thousands of students, faculty and their families.
- NAACP "W.E. B. Dubois Award, 2001
- Eta Phi Beta Sorority, Inc. "Public Servant Award"
- Ford Foundation "National Leadership For A Changing World Award"

Florida Memorial College "Pioneering Woman Award", 2003

[2] The Haitian- American Democratic Club is a well-known group established in Miami 2. . (Haiti: The Society and Its Environment, Haitian Information Resource, December 1989) 3. Kevin Drew (CNN, Atlanta), U.S. policy on Haitians, Cuban differs, June 15, 2003, Bill Frelick, Senior Policy Analyst, U.S. Committee for Refugees, "Most Favored Refugees?, "Washington Post, April 20, 1998, Stepick, Alex (1981) Haitian Refugees in the U.S., Miami, Florida Minority Rights Group. 3) Kevin Drew (CNN, Atlanta), U.S. policy on Haitians, Cuban differs, June 15, 2003, Bill Frelick, Senior Policy Analyst, U.S. Committee for Refugees, "Most Favored Refugees?, "Washington Post, April 20, 1998, Stepick, Alex (1981) Haitian Refugees in the U.S., Miami, Florida .

[3] Human rights abuses qualitatively and quantitatively worsened in months directly following the coup on September 30, 1991. Soldiers and armed thugs staged almost nightly raids on neighborhoods where many Aristide supporters lived, raping the wives and children of political activists and critics of the regime, abducting young people, and disfiguring victims' faces. Raids were conducted on clergy, fires were set in private homes, and the bodies of men shot with their hands tied behind their backs appeared on the streets of Port-au-Prince, part of a new practice designed to terrorize the people.

[4] In a landmark case, Haitian Refugee Center vs. Civiletti filed by the Haitian Refugee Center in 1979, Haitian advocates successfully argued that the so-called "Haitian program violated the most basic rights of the Haitian refugees and that it was both unconstitutional and illegal". Between 1977 and 1991 at least ten federal court decisions in class actions described our violations of their rights. Haitians were unlawfully denied their statutory and treaty rights to a hearing before an immigration judge in exclusion proceedings on their claims for political asylum. Sannon v. United States, 427 F. Supp. 1270 (S.D.Fla. 1977) vacated and remanded on other grounds, 566 F.2d 104 (5th Cir. 1978). They were unlawfully denied their right to notice of the procedures that the government intended to use against them in exclusion proceedings. Sannon v. United States, 460 F. Supp. 458 (S.D.Fla. 1978). They were unlawfully denied the right to work while their asylum claims were pending. National Council of Churches v. Egan, No. 79-2959-Civ-WMH (S.D.Fla. 1979). They were unlawfully denied access to information to support their asylum claims. National Council of Churches v. INS, No. 78-5163-Civ-JLK (S.D.Fla. 1979).

[5] Excerpt of letter written by a group of refugees in Fort Allen, Puerto Rico, published by Dr. Alex Stepick in "Haitian Refugees in the U.S"., 1981.

[6] AMR 36/33/94 (August 19940, pp.1-25): "repression reigned in Haiti during the years following the coup d'etat that toppled President Aristide.

[7] "How U. S. error sent Haitian to his death," Miami Herald, April 18, 1994. Dr. Alex Stepick, "Haitian Refugees in the U.S." Amnesty International, "Haiti: On the Horns of a Dilemma, Military Repression or Foreign Invasion?" In 1994 president Clinton explained: "They are chopping people's faces off, killing, and mutilating innocent civilians, people not even involved in politics...." A delegation from the IACHR (Inter-American Commission on Human Rights) has identified 133 cases of extrajudicial killings between February and May 1994 alone, and

attributed full responsibility for those and other atrocities to the de facto authorities, i.e. the military and their supporters.

[8] Heather Cottin: U.S. substitutes jails for schools, reprinted from the Sept. 12, 2002, issue of Workers World Newspaper.

[9] Judy Rabinovitz, American Civil Liberties Union, Immigrant Rights Project. Added Andrea Black, a Soros Justice fellow at the Florence Project "The standards lack teeth, stating that any facililty violating the rules will loose its federal contract, or will be forced to pay steep fines would have made a difference." The INS issues Detention Standards Governing the Treatment of Detained Immigrants and Asylum Seekers, by Llewelyn G. Pritchard, Chair of the American Bar Association´s Immigration Pro Bono Development and Bar Activation Project www.refugees.org.

[10] See "Illegal Aliens Can Be Held Indefinitely, Ashcroft Says," New York Times, April 26, 2003; "More Illegal Immigrants Can Be Held," Washington Post, April 25, 2003 .9. Of about 214 Haitian boat persons caught October 29, 2002 off Key Biscayne in Florida, about fifty-three (53) – about one in four – have won their asylum claims, an unprecedentedly high rate, indicating the importance of counsel in these cases. 9. Delegation to see change in Haitian migrant policy, Daphne Duret, Miami Herald, June 4, 2003. Haitian Activists Protest Bush Administration Immigration Policy, Haitian Times, June4-10, 2003, Leaders appeal to Congress on behalf of Haitians: Plight of Haitians discussed at Capitol, The Miami Times, June 11-17, 2003. South Florida Delegation urges Haitian Policy change, Raphael Lorente, Sun Sentinel, 2003. 10. Of about 214 Haitian boat persons caught October 29, 2002 off Key Biscayne in Florida, about fifty-three (53) – about one in four – have won their asylum claims, an unprecedentedly high rate.

[11] Amnesy International, "I'm not an inmate. Why should I be treated as one? Women asylum punished for state's failure to protect," AMR 51/028/01 (March 2001). "Behind Locked Doors: Abuse of Refugee Women at the Krome Detention Center", Women's Commission for Refugee Women and Children (October 2000). See also letter from John Bulger, Immigration and Naturalization Service, to Barbara Carey-Schuler, Miami-Dade County Board of County Commission (May 30. 2001)

[12] Special thanks to FIAC for well documented reports on the conditions of women at TGK. FIAC letter of Concerns and Recommendations regarding conditions at TGK, January 8th, 2002.

[13] Convention relating to the status of Refuees, 189 U.N.T.S. 150, entered into force April 22, 1954

[14] Marleine Bastien wrote this poem on September 9, 2002 while waiting her turn to speak at a conference sponsored by the Woodrow Wilson International Center for Scholars and the Migration Policy Institute titled: Women Immigrants in the United States. The Conference was supported by a grant from the Ford Foundation. Leaders from Protestant, Roman Catholic, Jewish and Muslim communities who visited a detention center run by the Wackenhut Corrections Corp. which contracted with the Immigration and Naturalization Service wrote to the Bush administration to express their discontent " We are deeply troubled by the way our country is treating people who come to our shores fleeing persecution in their homelands . Said Rev. Robert Edgar:" I was shocked at what I saw, imprisoned criminals have more freedom, access, and opportunity"....If it looks like a jail and acts like a jail, it´s a jail said Archdeacon Michael S. Kendall of the Diocese of New York. In the name of God, let´s open our arms and treat these people as human beings". The detention center had no indicating signs and according to Rev. John L. McCullough, executive director of Church World Service:" even the entryway had no windows, you must pass through security checks and heavy steel doors. The air is immediately stagnant"...added Richard Parkins, executive director of Episcopal Migration Ministries :" . Catholic Legal Immigration Network, the Needless Detention of Immigrantsin the United States: Why are we Locking Up Asylum Seekers, Children, Stateless Persons, Long-Term Permanent Residents and Petty Offenders? (2000).Women's Commission For Refugee Women and Children, "Behind Locked Doors: Abuse of Refugee Women at the Krome Detention Center, October 2000. Women's Commission for Refugee Women and Children< "Liberty Denied: Women Seeking Asylum in the United States, April 1997. Miami Herald: detention condition criticized, Al Chardy, February 8, 2001. INS Women Detainees, Miami Herald Editorial, December 18, 2000. Convention relating to the Status of Refugees, 189 U.N.T.S. 150, entered in force April 22, 1954.Article 1 . All human beings are born free and equal in dignity and rights. They are endowed with reason and conscience and should act towards one another in a spirit of brotherhood. Article 2 . Everyone is entitled to all the rights and freedoms set forth in this Declaration, without distinction of any kind, such as race, color, sex, language, religion, political or other opinion, national or social origin, property, birth or other status. Article 10 Everyone is entitled in full equality to a fair and public hearing by an independent and impartial tribunal, in the determination of his rights and obligations and of any criminal charge against him.

[15] Florida Immigration Advocacy Center demands the "Immediate Release of Haitian Children, December 13, 2002. Miami Herald "Delegation to seek change in Haitian Migrant Policy, June 4th, 2003. Florida Immigrant Advocacy Center " INS Discriminatory Treatment of Haitian Children and Families"., November 26, 2002.

[16] "My Clients Are Not Terrorists", Candace Berg, Lawyer, Catholic Charities, Miami, Florida NACARA granted residence to Nicaraguans present in the U. S. before December 1995. HRIFA restricted eligibility to those paroled in, or who had filed for asylum, in both cases before 1996. All of the otherwise-eligible Haitian "airplane refugees" therefore by definition fled Haiti before that date, the vast majority ten to fifteen years ago. "Haitian Parents of U. S. Kids Deserve to Remain Here Together," Miami Herald lead editorial, May 4, 2000; "Protect 5,000 American Children, Don't Deport Parents", op-ed, Miami Herald, May 5, 2000.

[17] Advisory Opinion, United Nations High Commissioner for Refugees, 2002.

# CHAPTER SIX

*Kote y'ap plimen kodenn, poul pa ri.*

In the place where they pluck
the turkey's feathers,
the chicken does not laugh.

# U.S Low Intensity Conflict and Haiti: Lessons from the U.S. Campaign against the Sandinistas
### *Tom Ricker*

# INTRODUCTION

In mid-July 1979 U.S. backed dictator Anastasio Somoza Debayle fled Managua, Nicaragua for a safe haven in Miami. The insurrection that led to Somoza's downfall was characterized by a multi-class alliance. Traditional elite opposition to Somoza joined with mass mobilization under the banner of the Frente Sandinista to topple the hated dictator.[1] Nicaragua and the rest of Latin America celebrated the downfall. But in the U.S., the new government was viewed with immediate skepticism.

The socialist character of the Sandinista majority on the Junta for National Reconstruction,[2] close ties with Cuba, and renewed revolutionary activity in El Salvador and Guatemala set off alarms in the minds of the cold warriors of the Carter and Reagan administrations. Pulling out the simplistic Vietnam-era domino theory from the file of justifications for intervention, the U.S. began beating the drum against this new "communist wedge" forming just south of the border. Carter criticized the Sandinistas. Reagan would seek to destroy them.

Between December of 1981 and February of 1990 the Reagan and Bush administrations created, trained, funded, and gave political cover to an army of terrorists operating from across Nicaragua's northern border with Honduras. As this "Contra" force gained in strength, the death toll rose in the countryside. Clinics, schools, Sandinista mayors and minor party officials, cooperative farmers, and children all became targets of Reagan's proxies. In the international arena the Reagan administration sought to isolate the government in Nicaragua, blocking multilateral loans, private credits, and finally imposing an embargo on the country in 1984.[3]

Thirty thousand Nicaraguans died as a result of this game. In the end, though the Contras were defeated militarily, the Sandinistas were voted out of office in 1990. The irony of the Sandinista government holding internationally recognized fair elections in 1990 (and in 1984), thereby giving lie to the public depiction of the government as a totalitarian monster, was lost on a devastated people.

In 1986 Jean-Claude Duvalier fled Haiti bringing to an end a 29-year family dictatorship that had been supported by several U.S. administrations. Following five years of military governments and the writing of a new constitution, Aristide was elected by an overwhelming majority, riding the tide of the popular Lavalas movement to office in 1991. Aristide came into office committed to changing the status of Haiti's impoverished majority. A commitment that ran counter to the goals of the wealthy class (1% of the population controlling 45% of all wealth)[4]. Aristide was ousted in a coup within seven months, and was replaced by U.S. trained Haitian military Colonel Raul Cedras.

Since the return of the Lavalas in 1994, consecutive U.S. administrations have made life difficult for Haiti's government. Aristide returned as a weakened president, who agreed to transfer power in 1995, essentially foregoing the 3 years his exile cost him. Aristide toned down his reformist rhetoric and shifted his energies to securing a base for Lavalas, efforts that included the disbanding of the military.

Since the electoral controversy of 2000, this campaign has escalated. While there are many legitimate concerns about the conduct of the election, no one except a handful question that Aristide's re-election, with 92% of the vote, represents the will of the Haitian majority.

Yet, the U.S. government has thrown its support behind a small collection of opposition parties, the Democratic Convergence (CD), and has sought to further isolate Aristide in the international community. The Convergence can not win popular elections, and continue to be players only because of U.S. backing. Alex Dupuy writes, "because Washington has made it essential to the crisis, the CD's strategy is to force Aristide to resign or to block any democratic resolution that relegitimizes him."[5]

There are many parallels between the Reagan/Bush campaigns against the Sandinistas and the current Bush administration's efforts in Haiti. Two themes in particular that stand out as parallels between U.S. campaigns against the Sandinistas and current policy toward Haiti are U.S. support for a constructed opposition, that absent U.S. patronage would be marginal, and U.S. efforts to isolate the governments in the international arena. I touch on both of these below, and conclude with some discussion of the shifting geo-political context that suggests continuity in U.S. policy from the 1980s to today in the Caribbean Basin. Unfortunately for the people of Haiti, the Sandinista example does not bode well for a peaceful resolution to the current crisis in Haiti. The U.S. then, as now, will be intent on keeping the pressure on the country until the Lavalas movement and Aristide are forced to the sidelines.

# Supporting the "Opposition"

One of the parallels between the Nicaragua and Haiti cases is U.S. support for an opposition party, or movement that would otherwise be a marginal player within national conflicts. In Nicaragua this support was given to the Nicaraguan Democratic Front (Contras), the Nicaragua Democratic Coordinating Committee, or *Coordinadora,* and later the National United Opposition, or UNO. In Haiti this support has been most recently extended to the *Convergence Democratique*, or Democratic Convergence. In these cases the coalitions brought together forces that shared little in common other than opposition to the governments that were also targets of U.S. policy.

In the Nicaragua case there can be little doubt that the Contras began life as a U.S. creation. Edgar Chamorro, leader with the Nicaraguan Democratic Front, the vanguard of the Contra organization, wrote of the contras, "We were a proxy army, directed, funded, receiving all intelligence and suggestions from the CIA. We had no plan for Nicaragua, we were working for American goals."[6]

The "plan" was in fact to topple the Sandinsta government. It is not clear that the contra army was ever prepared to achieve this goal by itself, as a military venture. Rather the Contras played a part in a complex campaign that sought to cripple the country and undermine Sandinista governing capacity, thereby forcing a change of government. The Contras worked their violence in rural areas, while opposition leaders, funded by the U.S., provided political cover.

In the 1984 elections in Nicaragua, the U.S. government did its best to manipulate the process. One of the lead opposition coalitions was the Nicaragua Democratic Coordinating Committee, or the *Coordinadora*. The *Coordinadora's* candidate, Arturo Cruz was later discovered to have been a CIA agent, receiving $6,000 a month from Washington.[7] At U.S. urging Cruz withdrew from the election citing unfair treatment at the hands of the Sandinistas, though it is clear now that the real reason was that the opposition was sure to lose. The New York Times ran a story in October of 1984, in which a senior administration official was quoted as saying, "The Administration never contemplated letting Cruz stay in the race... because then the Sandinistas could justifiably claim that the elections were legitimate, making it much harder for the United States to oppose the Nicaraguan government."[8]

Rather than supporting an election process that would be transparent, but that might achieve results inimical to U.S. policy, the Reagan administration chose to support efforts to delegitimize the process itself. "Like the Contras, [the Coordinadora] eventually called on Nicaraguans to abstain from voting. This was also the position of the major opposition newspaper La Prensa, which, apart from biased and often inaccurate reporting, even refused to run paid party advertisements in its pages and became the principal media conduit for Coordinadora and Reagan administration views."[9]

The elections proceeded without the *Coordinadora*. Seven parties ran candidates in the election. International observers declared the election fair. The Sandinistas won 67% of the vote for the presidency and for the assembly.[10]

The Reagan administration response to the November elections in Nicaragua was to manufacture a crisis. The Office of Public Diplomacy, under the direction of Otto Reich, planted a story in the press claiming the Soviet Union was sending a shipment of MiG fighter jets to Nicaragua. The story appeared on November 4, just before Nicaragua's election. The story was also used to further bully Nicaragua. "[T]he Reagan administration... used this blatant case of disinformation to launch a successful 'psy-op' against Nicaragua."[11] Military operations in Honduras were announced, and the administration approved surveillance flights over Managua, "deliberately causing a series of sonic booms that thousands of Nicaraguans mistook for bombs falling on their city."[12]

Following the 1984 elections the new government in Nicaragua began the process of drafting a new constitution. Assemblies were held throughout the country in order to invite popular participation in the process. Again, the U.S.-dominated *Coordinadora* refused to participate. The new constitution crafted a government that "established a separation of powers among four branches of government: executive, legislative, judicial, and electoral. The Supreme Electoral Council broke a certain amount of new ground while the other principles of presidential government, proportional representation, and an independent judiciary drew heavily from existing Western European models."[13] The new constitution was ratified in 1987.

By the time George Bush took office in 1989 the Contras, though still active, had been more or less neutralized as a military threat. The Bush administration would put its energies toward strengthening the internal political front in the form of the National Opposition Union (UNO) in preparation for elections in 1990. The contra war had been devastating for the country. Thirty thousand Nicaraguans had died, and damages from the war totaled $12 billion.[14] The economy had been severely weakened as the war ate up important resources. With limited resources for elections, the Sandinistas were vulnerable to the well-funded opposition.

In 1989 the U.S. Congress appropriated $9 million in overt funding for the opposition.[15] Through the National Endowment for Democracy, the Bush administration funneled $5.6 million of this directly to UNO, while keeping the threat of a renewed war over the heads of the people of Nicaragua should the FSLN win.

The UNO coalition was an amalgamation of opposition groups, including members of *Coordinadora*, as well as opposition from far-left parties. Violetta Chamorro was the UNO candidate. Chamorro was the widow of La Prensa Editor Edgar Chamorro whose assassination in 1978 had been one of the sparks leading to the revolution. Chamorro had taken part in the original Junta, though she stepped down in 1980. Chamorro was the U.S. choice, and with U.S. backing edged out Enrique Bolaños, the favorite of the business community, for the UNO nomination.

U.S. scholar Harry Vanden, who served as an election observer in the 1990 elections, wrote "As the United States helped to fashion the programme and campaign thrust for the UNO, the economy and the claim that the US-supported candidate was the only one who could improve economic conditions (by enlisting U.S. support and stopping the US-backed Contras) became increasingly prominent." Further, "[o]nly with the election of the U.S. sponsored candidate –it was suggested – could the Nicaraguans hope to begin to recover from the unbearable economic conditions they were experiencing, or end the Contra attacks."[16]

The U.S. funded propaganda campaign worked. The Sandinistas lost this second election to the UNO coalition, receiving 40.8% to the UNO's 54.7%.[17] After 10 years of violence and economic hardship the people of Nicaragua were ready for a change. The UNO coalition, however, would fall apart. By 1992 political crises emerged as the hardline elements of the UNO coalition openly criticized Chamorro's efforts at power sharing with the FSLN, and even staged a walk out from the National Assembly in 1992.[18] U.S. policy had elevated hardliners to positions of power they would not have otherwise held, and the result was more turmoil.

Throughout the 1990s the U.S. has continued to back the most staunch anti-Sandinista candidates. The U.S. government backed the very corrupt, former Managua mayor, Arnoldo Aleman in 1996, and during the 2001 presidential elections, the George W. Bush administration threatened the country with retribution should Sandinista candidate Daniel Ortega win. Ortega, ahead in the polls in June of 2001when these threats began, lost to Enrique Bolaños in October.

In Haiti the current Bush administration has placed its support behind the Democratic Convergence (CD). Much like the UNO coalition, the CD represents small parties that share only a distrust, if not outright hatred of Aristide and the Fanmi Lavalas. U.S. funding for the CD comes from the partisan International Republican Institute.

The CD is playing the same game played by the *Coordinadora* during the 1984 elections in Nicaragua. They refuse to participate in efforts at reconciliation, for to do so would legitimate an electoral process in which they can not win. The U.S. is backing this power play by continuing to insist on CD participation in any new institutional reforms to the disputed Provisional Electoral Council (CEP) before the CEP can be viewed as "legitimate." The result is a stalemate that is only deepened by U.S. policy.

U.S. support for opposition to Lavalas, however, goes back to the 1990 election itself, when the Bush administration put the resources of the U.S. behind Marc Bazin, a former official with the World Bank. Bazin lost the 1990 elections, garnering only 14% of the vote to Aristide's 67%. After the generals took charge in Haiti following the September 1991 coup, Bazin became Prime Minister (June 1992-August 1993). While the Bush administration accepted an OAS declared embargo, they were not committed to it. Exceptions were made for U.S. companies, and in 1992 U.S. trade with Haiti was at the pre-coup level.[19] So, despite public opposition, the Bush administration was willing to engage with, and even support coup leaders. For example, reports surfaced in October 1994 in *The Nation*, "that as the State Department and National Security Council were working for Aristide's return, the CIA and Pentagon financed and encouraged Emmanuel Constant, an instructor with the CIA-linked National Intelligence Services, to launch the notorious paramilitary organization FRAPH to 'balance the Aristide movement' and conduct intelligence work against it."[20] Balancing the "Aristide movement" meant violence against the Lavalas base. More than 5,000 people died at the hands of the military and FRAPH (Front for the Advancement and Progress of Haiti).

With the Lavalas movement devastated by the violence, Aristide was returned to power in 1994 – but, as mentioned before, only after agreeing to give up office in 1995. The elections took place under UN and OAS monitoring, and with the U.S.-led peacekeeping mission on the ground. First round parliamentary elections took place in June with a virtual sweep (75% of seats) for Lavalas.[21] Criticism of the Provisional Electoral Council, which oversaw the election, erupted immediately from the opposition. KONAKOM's (Congress of National Democratic Movements) leader, and presidential candidate, Victor Benoit, said of Lavalas, they "took all of the political space....That is not democracy."[22] KONAKOM threatened to boycott the run-off elections as well as the presidential elections that were held in December of 1995. Aristide made some adjustments to the CEP, and the U.S. reluctantly accepted the election results. The Clinton administration was feeling heat from House Republicans over U.S. involvement in Haiti, and thus, the seeking of an annulment of election results, conducted under de facto U.S. occupation, would have been very embarrassing for the administration. In the end, the Lavalas candidate, Rene Preval, won 86% of the vote in December 1995 elections.

The December 1995 election indicated that Lavalas remained a powerful popular force. However, a split in the party, fomented by Aristide's creation of the Fanmi Lavalas, alienating much of the party's middle class leadership, would create problems for Preval. Members of the parliament moved into opposition to the Fanmi Lavalas as the OPL (Organization of People in Struggle), and from that position blocked Preval on several fronts, including the rescheduling of parliamentary elections.[23]

U.S. support for the Convergence since the election controversies of 2000 has helped polarize an already tense situation. The point, however, is that several U.S. administrations have been suspicious of Aristide and the Lavalas movement from the beginning. So, current support for the Convergence must be placed in this context. Even while Aristide has softened his populist rhetoric dramatically since 1990, it seems clear that the current Bush administration remains committed to creating a non-Lavalas power base within Haiti that can challenge Aristide's continuing prestige amongst the country's poor majority. The Convergence is only the current vehicle for achieving this goal.

## Isolation in the International Arena

All U.S. administrations of recent memory have employed a variety of tactics to isolate governments that the U.S. finds problematic. From the 40-year old embargo of Cuba, to more recent efforts to isolate North Korea, to threats of isolation issued to El Salvador and Bolivia in 2003 should populist/leftist candidates win in elections, U.S. administrations have strived to use their influence in the international community to pressure governments into compliance with the current U.S. world view. Such tactics were employed with mixed success against the Sandinista government during the 1980s, and are currently being applied to Haiti. The most common form of "isolating" a government in the third world is to go after the flow of money and inhibit trade. Make the poor even poorer and the government will quickly lose legitimacy.

When Somoza fled Nicaragua in 1979 its external debt stood at $1.6 billion. Capital flight in the final months of the Somoza regime had exceeded $1.5 billion, and the insurrection itself had left the country with $500 million worth of damage to its infrastructure.[24] The Junta of National Reconstruction, which replaced Somoza in July of 1979 immediately set about renegotiating debts and trying to ensure that, as scarce as resources in the country were, that the new government would have the support of international donors. In 1980 the Junta approved payment of arrears to the International Monetary Fund (IMF) – even after the IMF extended a bridging loan to Somoza in May of 1979; money that never made into the country's coffers.[25]

In addition to establishing good relations with the world's creditors, the Sandinista government's foreign policy also sought to reach out to other third world countries and popular movements. In particular the Sandinistas sought the support of the "non-aligned movement," and the Group of 77, as well as other Latin American governments.[26] The non-aligned movement was formed as a coalition of poor countries seeking to craft foreign policies independent of both the United States and Soviet Union during the Cold War. The Group of 77, with much overlap to the non-aligned movement, was, and remains, a coalition within the United Nations that grew out of the United Nations Commission on Trade and Development in, and the call for, a New International Economic Order. Both forums were important vehicles for third world states seeking power in numbers to confront the two superpowers of the cold war. As the Sandinsta government was committed to an independent foreign policy, these were important alliances to make.

The Reagan administration would respond to these initiatives toward a new internationalism by the Sandinista government with disdain, and efforts at isolation. The U.S. became the only major bi-lateral creditor to refuse to renegotiate Somoza's debts with the new government in 1981.[27] The U.S. would use its influence at the IMF and the World Bank to cut off assistance to Nicaragua, and less successfully attempt to cut Nicaragua off from regional institutions like the Inter-American Development Bank. The Reagan administration also attempted to disrupt Nicaragua's international trade. The now famous incident of CIA mining of

Nicaragua's harbors in 1984 was tied to this goal. Lt. Col. Olliver North, released documents that revealed the CIA had taken this scheme so far as to suggest sinking an oil tanker in the Gulf of Fonseca. The goal being to make trade with Nicaragua so dangerous that ships would not be able to get insurance.[28] The tanker-sinking scheme was cancelled after the CIA mining operation was made public, however, not before ships from Japan, Britain, and the Soviet Union had been damaged.

In 1980 the United States was the destination of 30% of Nicaragua's exports. This number declined dramatically by 1985 when the Reagan administration formerly announced an embargo against Nicaragua.[29] As Nicaragua increased economic ties with other countries in Latin America, Western Europe, and socialist countries, the Reagan administration sought to pressure these states to back off from supporting the Sandinista government. The only region in which the U.S. had much success was in Central America, where U.S. presence in El Salvador, Guatemala, and Honduras was strongest. Indeed, aid from Western Europe and the rest of Latin America outpaced aid from socialist countries throughout most of the 1980s. Nevertheless, the squeeze on Nicaragua's economy was effective. International trade fell dramatically for the country throughout the 1980s putting extreme pressure on the country's foreign currency accounts. By 1990 the country was saddled with an international debt of $11 billion!

On the political front, Nicaragua's support for the non-aligned movement was scoffed at. Reagan consistently painted the Sandinistas as tools of Castro (an important figure in the non-aligned movement) and granted the new government no credit for being an independent player seeking a sovereign foreign policy. Even after the elections in 1984, the U.S. refused to admit that the Sandinistas were anything but "Marxist" regime bent on serving as wedge for a socialist take over of Central America.[30] Sounding much like George W. Bush today, Reagan's foreign policy team took the stand that states were either with us or against us. A non-aligned foreign policy was tantamount to support for the Soviet Union in this mindset.

What is clear in hindsight is that there is nothing that the Sandinistas could have done other than remove themselves from office that would have satisfied the Reagan and Bush administrations. These administrations had demonstrated utter contempt for any notion of an autonomous foreign policy by such an impoverished state in "its own backyard." The international squeeze placed on Nicaragua's economy had a devastating impact. More than any other reason, the economic collapse in Nicaragua that accelerated dramatically in 1987 and 1988, led to the UNO victory in 1990.

In Haiti, the poorest country in the Western Hemisphere, the use of international assistance and poverty-alleviation monies as leverage to achieve political goals has become the cruelest sort of hypocrisy. The government is being asked to provide stability before any negotiated settlement can be reached, while being denied the resources to achieve this. Adjustment has forced hundreds of thousands of peasant farmers off their land, as the country is flooded with imported subsidized rice from the United States. The continued blockade on assistance from multilateral creditors is denying desperately needed money for health, education and infrastructure. Again, these pressures have been applied to Haiti in various forms since Aristide was first elected in 1990.

Labeled a "radical firebrand" by the Bush administration, Aristide would see little support from the U.S. when first elected in 1990. "Though the United States could not deny Aristide's legitimacy, it never trusted or supported him, and much of the aid monies promised by the international financial institutions was never delivered."[31] As mentioned, the Bush administration had put its support behind a former World Bank staffer, Marc Bazin; someone they felt sure would pursue a pro-U.S. economic policy. Aristide's platform of reform, on the other hand, was not "pro-U.S." and was also a threat to the "Duvalierists" and the military in Haiti. Thus, "no one was surprised, then, when the military, supported by the wealthy business class, overthrew Aristide and sent him into exile in September 1991."[32]

When Aristide was reinstated in 1994 the conditions included Haiti's implementation of far reaching structural adjustment reforms. "Structural adjustment" refers to a package of policy changes that include privatization of state enterprises, lowering tariffs, marketizing currency valuations, and cutting public spending. The goal of these programs is to free foreign exchange for servicing debt, while "rationalizing" the state – a euphemism for de-regulation and cuts in social services. Aristide followed through on these policy reforms initially, under the auspices of a joint United Nations/U.S. peacekeeping mission.

After Rene Preval was elected in 1995, however, popular organizations reacted strongly to the privatization of state services. "In late 1995 the new Haitian Parliament, responding to vehement popular opposition to privatization, refused to authorize the privatization of state-owned industries as mandated by donors."[33] The result was a suspension of assistance from multilateral donors and the United States. In October of 1996, Rene Preval signed a new structural adjustment agreement with international financial institutions that "Outlined his government's commitment to cut government workers, increase taxes on the poor, provide subsidies to assembly industries and export agriculture, decrease tariffs to near zero (including those which provide some protection to domestic food production), and partially privatize nine state enterprises."[34]

Though two of Haiti's state-run enterprises were privatized, Preval did not meet deadlines for further sales. Aid was suspended again. While attention has been drawn to U.S. cutting off assistance to the Haiti government since the 2000 election, the suspension of aid was already a tool being used to force Haiti into compliance with economic reform demands before the elections were even held.

U.S. efforts to embargo development and humanitarian assistance reached new heights following the electoral controversy of 2000. Much of this story is told elsewhere in the book. Concern about an illegal method of counting ballots in eight senatorial districts, where the Fanmi Lavalas candidates had clear pluralities, but not absolute majorities as required to avoid a run-off, was elevated by the opposition in an effort to discredit the entire election.[35] The Organization of American States and the U.S. government refused to recognize the results of the May legislative elections. Opposition parties, which would later reform as the Convergence Democratique (CD), boycotted run-off elections and then the general election of November 2000. Aristide would win the November elections with 92% of the popular vote. However, the CD refuses to acknowledge the elections as legitimate.

Since this stalemate began the U.S. has tried to force Aristide's hand by cutting Haiti off from loans from multilateral lenders. The Inter-American Development Bank is withholding $317 million dollars in assistance, already approved, for vocational training, basic infrastructure, health and agriculture. Some IDB monies were released in July of 2003 after the government of Haiti paid arrears to the IDB totaling $32 million. Monies from the World Bank, and the International Monetary Fund are also being held back. Finally, assistance from the European Union is being withheld as well, including over $300 million for education and infrastructure programs.

In September of 2002, the OAS, under U.S. leadership, passed Resolution 822 to establish a framework to resolve the political crisis. Key components of the resolution include:

- Restoring a climate of security by implementing a comprehensive disarmament program;
- The creation of a new Provisional Electoral Council (CEP) with nine representatives drawn from various sectors of Haitian society;
- The new CEP will organize elections in 2003;

- The OAS will provide support and technical assistance to the government of Haiti and political parties
- Normalize relations with international financial institutions.

Points one and two have proven to be the sticking points, and U.S. policy has only contributed to the impasse.

The level of violence in Haiti continues to be high. Armed gangs, often assumed to be tied to Aristide, have wreaked havoc throughout the country. But the reality of the *chimeres*, as the gangs are called, is more complex. Alex Dupuy writes, "The *chimeres* are primarily hired thugs with no ideological commitment or political objectives, and they are willing to do anyone's bidding. Thus they can, and have been, used by both the government and the opposition, and they can switch allegiance whenever circumstances warrant."[36] In addition, armed groups of former Haitian military have been making incursions into Haiti from the across the border with the Dominican Republic attacking police stations and power stations. Ira Kurzban, an attorney with the Haitian government says of the groups, "This is a small group of people with no popular support in Haiti but which is well armed and well financed."[37] Shortly after attacks in May of 2003, a U.S. missionary was arrested near the Dominican border on suspicion of gun running. While there is no direct evidence linking these groups to either the Dominican government or any U.S- sponsored operation, the delivery of 20,000 M-16s to the border zone by the Bush administration in December of 2002 only fuels speculation of a Contra like operation, and certainly has done little to encourage "disarmament."[38]

The construction of a new Provisional Electoral Council has proven to be the primary issue holding back implementation of the Resolution 822. The Aristide government has sought to create a new CEP, but the *Convergence* still refuses to participate, and has taken the position that they will not until Aristide resigns. The U.S. has made clear that a CEP that does not include the Convergence is not acceptable. Though not mentioning the CEP by name, U.S. policy statements consistently say that a new CEP, that is "credible, neutral and independent,"[39] must be created before elections can proceed. "Neutral and independent," seems to mean a CEP that makes significant space for members of the *Convergence*. As of September 2003, Aristide's government was planning on moving ahead with elections for the Haitian legislature. Two-third of the legislators' terms will expire in January 2004. If elections are not held, Aristide will be faced with a no-win situation in which he either violates the constitution by extending the terms, or refuses to extend the terms and be subject to accusations of "disbanding the parliament." The *Convergence* strategy, with U.S. backing, seems aimed at creating such a situation. At this point candidates from the *Convergence* say they will boycott the election.

As a result of the ongoing violence – much of which is clearly beyond Aristide's control - and the refusal of the Convergence to take part in a new CEP, implementation of OAS Resolution 822 has not taken place. Without implementation of 822 Haiti will remain effectively isolated by the international community. Marc Grossman, Under Secretary of State for Political Affairs, testified before the Senate Foreign Relations Committee on July 15, 2003, "Hemispheric patience is running out. OAS Resolution 1959, adopted by the OAS General Assembly in June, calls for the Secretary General to provide an assessment by September of the ability of the OAS Special Mission to fulfill its mandate under the circumstances of delay and resistance."[40] Yet, the only object of accusations of "delay and resistance" referred to in this testimony is the Aristide government. The *Convergenc*e is not mentioned.

While the Bush effort to confront the Aristide government in Haiti has not reached the level of the Reagan campaign against the Sandininsta government, it is still, in essence, blackmailing a regime to comply with a U.S. imposed settlement. In some ways the Bush campaign has been more effective in cutting Haiti off from assistance. It is interesting to point out that the 2000 elections in Peru were also contested. But in this case the winning candidate, Fujimori, was a valued U.S. ally in the drug war (and also a brutal ruler, who had ruled the country through Presidential decree for several years after disbanding Peru's legislature). The loser was a populist candidate with a strong base among Peru's indigenous majority. The U.S. recognized the election results immediately. When Venezuelan President, Chavez was overthrown briefly in a coup in 2002 the Bush administration was openly celebrating, and recanted only after it became clear that the coup had been a failure. These cases contrasted with Haiti's situation where Aristide's electoral victory was clear, providing little legitimacy for the Bush administration's position.

# CONCLUSION

This chapter has compared current U.S. policy toward Haiti with the campaigns conducted against Nicaragua during the 1980s. I have chosen to focus on two specific themes: U.S. support for opposition coalitions to project U.S. interests into a domestic conflict, and U.S. efforts to isolate and otherwise pressure the two governments in the international arena. There are differences in the cases that have not been explored. The geopolitical contexts are significantly different, for example. The Nicaragua campaign was conducted within the context of heightened tensions between the Soviet Union and the United States in the early 1980s, while current policy takes place within the context of United States global supremacy, at least in terms of military power. Nevertheless, the goal of this chapter is to demonstrate continuities in U.S. foreign policy, and to draw lessons from the Nicaragua case for the current crisis in Haiti, which is the central concern of the *Let Haiti LIVE* book, and coalition. This is not meant to be a definitive comparison by any means, but suggestive of areas of concern.

With this limited goal in mind, I conclude this chapter by arguing that the United States government will likely not let up on its current campaign in Haiti absent some public outcry. This is, perhaps, the hardest lesson to draw from the Nicaragua case. The Reagan administration set in motion a policy with the goal of crippling the Sandinista government, thereby forcing a regime change. They pursued this goal even after the Sandinsitas held elections, drafted a constitution, and, early on, sought to appease international creditors. The Sandinista government offered Nicaragua an alternative path – an independent foreign policy and a restructuring of domestic economic and political relations: Both of these efforts were seen as threats by the U.S. government. In the end, the economic democratization project failed, while the political democratization project had some success; the Sandinista constitution of 1987 is the framework under which Nicaragua has been governed through four election cycles.

Similarly, Aristide was elected on a platform of reform in 1990. The Lavalas movement was, and remains, rooted in the aspirations of Haiti's impoverished majority. This is taken as a threat to U.S. interests in Haiti, which have historically been based on maintaining relations with Haiti's small wealthy class. The United States has demonstrated little in the way of historical commitments to democracy in Haiti, and that is not the concern driving policy today. The controversy surrounding Haiti's legislative elections in 2000 emerged from what would be viewed as relatively minor issues were such irregularities to have surfaced in a pro-U.S. government. Indeed, the real threat to U.S. interests in Haiti is a functioning democracy that would ensure representation to the 80% of Haiti's population living in poverty. A government advocating for land reform, for protections to Haiti's small agricultural producers, fighting for the enforcement of workers' rights, and seeking to build a thriving public sector would challenge U.S. policies which seek to erode all of these. As long as Aristide retains the respect and support of the poor, Fanmi Lavalas will be a threat to U.S. interests. The goal of U.S. policy is not democracy, it is eroding the popular base of the Lavalas movement.

This is not to suggest that Aristide has retained his popular vision. Aristide has made many compromises to his vision of widespread economic and political reform since reinstated in 1994. He has compromised this vision, in part, because of U.S. policy, and in part to build coalitions which provide Lavalas a more secure base. In other words, he has compromised like all political leaders have in order to govern and retain power. Of course, there are serious concerns about corruption, and it is clear that Aristide bears some responsibility for the ongoing violence in the country. But none of this justifies U.S. policy, especially when contrasted against other governments in Latin America that suffer similar if not worse deficiencies, yet receive unchecked support from the Bush administration. Allowing elections to move forward and de-linking foreign aid from stringent adjustment policies would be the best antidote for the current crisis. Let Haitians find their own path to democracy. This may well mean that U.S. corporate interests will be challenged with regulations, with minimum wage laws, and tariffs on imported agricultural products. But that is a choice that Haitians have the right to make as a sovereign people. The current policy of holding up elections and multilateral assistance in the name of a small coalition, that is not representative of the Haitian people and committed to the removal of Aristide from office is an unjustified abuse of power.

---

[1] There are many resources on the history of the insurrection that toppled Somoza. E.g., John Booth's (1981) *The End and the Beginning*, Boulder, CO, Westview Press, and Thomas Walker's (1981) Nicaragua: *The Land of Sandino*, Boulder, CO: Westview Press. For a more academic, comparative study, see Timothy Wickham-Crowley (1992) *Guerillas and Revolutions in Latin America*, Princeton University Press. Wickham-Crowley argues that the success of the insurrection had much to do with Somoza's alienation of all of society, including the traditional business class, coupled with the U.S. withdrawal of support for Somoza late in the game. The multi-class nature of the insurrection is important for understanding the early years of the revolution, as this "alliance" of opportunity broke down fairly quickly, even as the FSLN continued to reach out to the business sector throughout the 1980s. Of course, as in most multi-class alliances, the poor did most of the dying during the conflict.

[2] Formally, the Governing Junta for National Reconstruction (JGRN). The JGRN operated as the executive of the new government from 1979 until elections were held in 1984. The composition of the JGRN was mixed. Originally composed of five members – the JGRN included 3 FSLN representatives, and 2 traditional elite, including Violetta Chamorro. See Andrew Reding (1991) "The Evolution of Governmental Institutions," in Thomas Walker, ed. *Revolution and Counterrevolution in Nicaragua*, Boulder, CO: Westview Press.

[3] On the Contra War there are many sources. Some used extensively here, are Peter Kornbluh (1987) *The Price of Intervention* Washington, D.C., Institute for Policy Studies and Thomas Walker, ed., (1991) *Revolution and Counterrevolution in Nicaragua*, Boulder, CO: Westview Press. See also, Holly Sklar (1988) *Washington's War on Nicaragua* Boston, MA: South End Press. Peter Davis (1987) *Where is Nicaragua*, New York: Simon and

Schuster. Peter Kornbluh and Malcolm Byrne, eds. *The Iran-Contra Scandal: The Declassified History*, A National Security Archive Reader, New York, New Pres.

[4] Jean-Bertrand Aristide (2000) *Eyes of the Heart.* Common Courage Press, p. 20.

[5] Alex Dupuy (2003) "Who is Afraid of Democracy in Haiti" *Haiti Papers, No 7.* Trinity College

[6] Edgar Chamorro (1987), *Packaging the Contras: A Case of CIA Disinformation*, New York: Institute for Media Analysis. Cited in Peter Kornbluh (1991), "The U.S. Role in the Counterrevolution," in Thomas Walker, ed. *Revolution and Counterrevolution in Nicaragua*, Boulder, CO: Westview Press.

[7] See Andrew Reding (1991) "The Evolution of Governmental Institutions," in Thomas Walker, ed. *Revolution and Counterrevolution in Nicaragua*, Boulder, CO: Westview Press, p 27. Arturo Cruz's son has written about CIA involvement in the election process and with the resistance more broadly. See his (1989) *Memoirs of a Counter-Revolutionary*, New York, Doubleday.

[8] *New York Times*, October 24, 1984 as cited in Kornbluh (1991), "The U.S. Role in the Counterrevolution," in Thomas Walker, ed. *Revolution and Counterrevolution in Nicaragua*, Boulder, CO: Westview Press.

[9] Harry Vanden and Gary Prevost (1993), *Democracy and Socialism in Sadninista Nicaragua*, Lynne Reiner Press p 77.

[10] Ibid., p 81.

[11] Peter Kornbluh (1987) *The Price of Intervention* Washington, D.C., Institute for Policy Studies, p 149.

[12] Ibid.

[13] Harry Vanden and Gary Prevost (1993), *Democracy and Socialism in Sadninista Nicaragua*, Lynne Reiner Press, p 85.

[14] See Kornbluh (1991), "The U.S. Role in the Counterrevolution," in Thomas Walker, ed. *Revolution and Counterrevolution in Nicaragua*, Boulder, CO: Westview Press, p 344-345.

[15] Harry Vanden (1997), "Democracy Derailed: The 1990 Elections and After," in Gary Prevost and Harry Vanden, eds. *TheUndermining of the Sandinista Revolution*, New York: St. Martin's Press.

[16] Ibid, p 53.

[17] Summary of elections results and analysis in Harry Vanden and Gary Prevost (1993), *Democracy and Socialism in Sadninista Nicaragua*, Lynne Reiner Press, pp 129-151.

[18] See Harry Vanden (1997), "Democracy Derailed: The 1990 Elections and After," in Gary Prevost and Harry Vanden, eds. *TheUndermining of the Sandinista Revolution*, New York: St. Martin's Press pp 63-65.

[19] An interview with Noam Chomsky by David Barsamian from *Secrets, Lies and Democracy*, published in 1994 Odonian Press, Tucson, AZ.

[20] U.S. Policy in Haiti Volume 2, Number 3, January 1997, by Lisa McGowan

[21] Report from Haiti Information Bureau in Haiti Info, volume 3, number 21, July 30, 1995

[22] Ibid.

[23] For some analysis of this split see Alex Dupuy (2003) "Who is Afraid of Democracy in Haiti" *Haiti Papers, No 7.* Trinity College.

[24] See Richard Stahler-Sholk (1987) "Foreign Debt and Economic Stabilization Policies in Revolutionary Nicaragua," in Rose Spalding, ed. *The Political Economy of Revolutionary Nicaragua* Boston: Allen and Unwin, Inc.

[25] Ibid.

[26] See Harry Vanden (1991), "Foreign Policy," in Thomas Walker, ed., *Revolution and Counterrevolution in Nicaragua*, Boulder, CO: Westview Press.

[27] See Richard Stahler-Sholk (1987) "Foreign Debt and Economic Stabilization Policies in Revolutionary Nicaragua," in Rose Spalding, ed. *The Political Economy of Revolutionary Nicaragua* Boston: Allen and Unwin, Inc.

[28] Kornbluh (1991) "The U.S. Role in the Counterrevolution," in Thomas Walker, ed. *Revolution and Counterrevolution in Nicaragua*, Boulder, CO: Westview Press, p 337. Kornbluh cites extensively from a memo written by Oliver North and Constatine Menges to McFarlane outlining the scheme. From the memo: "It is entirely likely that once a ship has been sunk, no insurers will cover ships calling in Nicaraguan ports."

[29] For study of Nicaragua's trading relations during the Contra War see Michael Conroy (1987) "Patterns of Changing External Trade in Revolutionary Nicaragua: Voluntary and Involuntary Trade Diversification," in Rose Spalding, ed. *The Political Economy of Revolutionary Nicaragua* Boston: Allen and Unwin, Inc.

[30] Reagan and his staff continual referred to the Sandinsta government as a Marxist government, and even denied that elections had taken place in 1984, see Peter Kornbluh (1987) *The Price of Intervention* Washington, D.C., Institute for Policy Studies.

[31] Alex Dupuy (2003) "Who is Afraid of Democracy in Haiti" *Haiti Papers, No 7*. Trinity College.

[32] Ibid.

[33] McGowan 1997.

[34] McGowan, 1997

[35] A report by the International Coalition of Independent Observers, notes that a similar methodolgy had been employed in the 1990 elections, and that the CEP defended its choice in 2000 based on the same logic as the decision in 1990 – a decision that was not challenged.

[36] Alex Dupuy (2003) "Who is Afraid of Democracy in Haiti" *Haiti Papers, No 7*. Trinity College., p 7

[37] Canute James "Links between Haiti and Dominican Republic cool" Financial Times, May 28, 2003.

[38] On arm shipments to D.R., See Haiti Progres, December 3, 2002, "Republic Dominicaine: Base de lancement d'une intervencion"

[39] See, for example, statement by Peter DeShazo, U.S. deputy permanent representative to the OAS, in "U.S. Urges Haitian government to Create Conditions for Free Elections," January 30, 2003 in *Washington File*, U.S. State Department, International Information programs.

[40] Marc Grossman, "U.S. Policy Toward Haiti" Testimony before the Senate Foreign Relations Committee, Washington, D.C., July 15, 2003.

# The Effects of U.S. Foreign Policy in Latin America and the Caribbean

*Larry Birns, Director, Kanisha Bond, George Dorko III, Curtis Morales, Charles Willson, Council on Hemispheric Affairs*

Perhaps the most momentous statement ever made in shaping the relationship between the United States and the rest of the hemisphere was not intended at the time to be historically grandiose. On December 2, 1823, in the midst of the various wars of independence being waged throughout Latin America against Spain, President James Monroe declared to Congress that the Americas would thenceforth be free from further European colonization.[1] His words have been variously interpreted in the nearly 200 years since, but historians commonly credit them with entrenching the idea – first proposed by early American thinkers, including Thomas Jefferson and Henry Clay – of an American hemisphere free from the influence of outside states, with its relations largely determined by Washington. The Monroe Doctrine subsequently became the definitive assertion that the affairs of the Western Hemisphere were to be of primary concern to the United States. Further, this proclamation conferred upon Washington the right to intervene in the affairs of its neighbors in order to protect their internal stability or to further U.S. commercial and strategic interests.[2] In substance, the Monroe Doctrine was the first overt signal of Washington's aspiration for regional preeminence, which initiated a longstanding prescriptive U.S. policy for Latin America. The sweeping promise of U.S. security responsibilities embodied in the doctrine all but overshadowed any recognition of the sovereignty of the hemisphere's newly independent states.

More than a century later, the advent of the Cold War led to a revival of the spirit of the Monroe Doctrine as a statement of policy goals, with Soviet communism replacing European colonialism as the external stimulus. As Washington watched Soviet influence spread quickly across the Eastern Hemisphere, fears of a similar putative expansion to the Americas motivated the hemisphere's lone superpower to interfere repeatedly in the political processes of various Latin American countries, all in the name of security. With nearly all of Latin America and the Caribbean firmly under its influence, Washington would see to it that no country in the hemisphere would be allowed to even flirt with Moscow, at the risk of drastic repercussions. Furthermore, the Cold War provided a welcome smokescreen for U.S. efforts to advance its economic goals in the region. Conveniently, Latin America provided not only a wealth of raw materials in Washington's own backyard, but also the added economic benefits of cheap labor and untapped consumer markets. Geostrategic goals and the quest for economic development, not for the first time became inextricably intertwined in the formulation of U.S. foreign policy.

However, while isolating Latin America and the Caribbean from the communist threat was expected to provide positive national security dividends for the United States, it actually served to heighten already acute ideological and political tensions in the region, and largely perpetuate its persistent economic underdevelopment. The socioeconomic inequalities that had plagued Latin America for decades continued unabated under the "development" schemes proposed by its northern neighbor, and social, political and economic cleavages were further deepened by the market distortions, corrupt authoritarian regimes and often counter-productive social patterns favored by Washington.

\*\*\*

## THE COLD WAR'S LEGACY IN LATIN AMERICA

Washington's Cold War strategy was effectively a continuation of Monroe Doctrine geopolitics. It sought to contain the spread of communism at any cost, and aimed to inoculate the region against the threat through the infrastructure of capitalism and democracy – and, when needed, chicanery on the part of U.S. military and intelligence agencies. The reality for Latin America was that the large-scale regional development plan promised by the United States would take its executive orders from the additional imprimatur of the international lending agencies that were also largely controlled from Washington.

Unfortunately, during most of the postwar period Washington saw Latin America as a function of its national security interests, with much greater primacy given to a government's anti-communist bona fides than to its fidelity to democratic processes and human rights. The result was a blatant indifference to democratic principles and processes, which only pushed the region closer toward instability and revolution. "Humanitarian capitalism," the moniker given in recent years to the advancement of neoliberalism as a remedy for socioeconomic crises, proved to be simply a euphemism meant to lend credibility to free enterprise-oriented development prescriptions that ultimately did little to broadly enrich the Latin American societies in which they were applied. Bilateral aid and carefully choreographed diplomacy between Washington and various responsive regional strongmen occurred against a backdrop of some of the most egregious human, civil and political rights abuses that the Western Hemisphere has ever experienced. This willingness to actively prop up regional dictatorships on national security grounds reflected a conscious choice of repressive but stable political regimes over pluralistic and democratic – but potentially recalcitrant – governments that might on occasion question the direction of U.S. policies.

## The Caribbean Basin

Due to their proximity to the U.S. mainland, the islands of the Caribbean basin were of special importance to U.S. foreign policymakers during the Cold War era. Abounding with "micro-states" still adjusting to a postcolonial existence, the Caribbean also has been particularly vulnerable to influence from outside of Washington. The geographic insulation and cultural fragmentation of the island nations, combined with the influence of non-state actors such as drug traffickers, multinational corporations, and illegal immigrants, have led to a history of instability punctuated by numerous literal and figurative foreign interventions.

Because of their generally insignificant sizes and economies, the individual countries of the Caribbean have not merited repeated acquisitive policies from Washington, aside from U.S. efforts to limit their relations with Cuba or the massive intervention in the Dominican Republic (1965) or Grenada (1983), and Haiti (1994). While Latin America as a whole was for long periods of time relegated to the back-burner by U.S. policymakers in the post-Cold War era, the Caribbean countries particularly have lost much of their strategic significance to their powerful northern neighbor, who now seems interested only in their increasing role in international drug trafficking and their torpid economies and growing emigration woes. This has led to a highly idiosyncratic, and at times nonexistent, foreign policy toward the region.

## The Dominican Republic: Fair Weather Friendship

Washington policymakers traditionally have often had a special interest in the Dominican Republic, and since its independence from Spain in the nineteenth century, the small island republic has been subject to repeated U.S. interventions. Because of its proximity to both the United States and Cuba, in recent years political developments on the island also have been awarded disproportionately high priority in European capitals. Washington has often used the Dominican Republic as a model for how U.S. foreign policy works in the hemisphere, and as a testament to the rest of Latin America that cooperation with U.S. policies is beneficial.

Despite its lofty rhetorical goals, however, Washington's policies consistently have endorsed a legacy of notoriously squalid Dominican presidents, who cumulatively have immiserated much of the Dominican population. At the outset of the Cold War, Washington willfully abetted the repressive and violent dictatorship of Rafael Trujillo, who was considered "the best friend of the United States in Latin America" because he was willing to assume an unrelenting anti-communist stance. After Trujillo's grip on power began to loosen, however, the Kennedy administration changed tactics and began to support a liberal democrat named Juan Bosch, with hopes of avoiding further Trujillo-style repression.

This change in policy was conducted more for regional political stability than for the sake of the abused Dominican populace; another overbearing dictator like Trujillo might have invited the same sort of broad-based opposition that emerged in Cuba during the 1950s leading up to the Castro Revolution. However, Washington's "experiment in democracy" was less than resolute, and it soon crumbled in the mid-1960s, when a military coup overthrew the Bosch government, with the Johnson administration backing the military out of the fear of danger on the left.

In 1965, when the coup plunged the Dominican Republic into revolution, the United States intervened to avoid the sort of outcome seen in Cuba after 1959. Joaquín Balaguer, a self-proclaimed pro-American moderate "democrat," emerged from the revolution as the next Dominican president. Balaguer's ascension to power, in spite of his notorious corruption, cruelty and incompetence, pleased Washington, and his rightist disposition ensured that the communist threat could be forestalled with relative ease. However, while Balaguer was placating Washington, he was actively consolidating his power on the island, and in 1978, when the Carter administration intervened to ensure a fair presidential election, the Dominican president was defeated by his mildly left-leaning opponent, Antonio Guzmán of the Partido Revolucionario Dominicana (PRD). Washington's acceptance of Guzmán indicated that it now considered the possibility of a dormant communist threat to be remote. This conclusion was subsequently validated by a long parade of U.S.-friendly presidents, fueled by the Reagan administration's Caribbean Basin Initiative and the aid that it brought to the island throughout the 1980s.

However, after a decade of top-heavy growth funded by the U.S.-led international financial institutions, the Dominican economy is now under considerable stress. Privatization efforts completed under the auspices of the lending agencies often have backfired, subsequently raising energy prices and causing frequent blackouts. A floundering Dominican currency and weakened economy have increased the island's dependency on remittances from hundreds of thousands of expatriates now living in the United States. Perhaps related to the country's adverse economic situation, the current government of Hipólito Mejía has joined the "coalition of the willing" in the war on Iraq, working hard to maintain Santo Domingo's warm relationship with Washington, in order to ensure the continuance of U. S. investment. While the U.S. has not intervened militarily in the Dominican Republic in the last two decades, Dominican democratic institutions remain somewhat undermined by Washington's past efforts at manipulating its political processes to guarantee its conformity to U.S. foreign policy goals.

## *Haiti: Tenuous Stability*

U.S.-Haiti relations during the post-World War II period have been characterized by Washington's support for two major dictatorships and a string of minor ones. Coupled with this diplomatic support has been a long history of "assistance packages," which have been used to ensure Port-au-Prince's cooperation in the Cold War's offense against communism in the Caribbean – particularly as it relates to Cuba. While the U.S.-Haiti relationship was particularly informed by U.S. assumptions that Haiti shouldn't be held to the same standards as other Caribbean nations – a notion that carried racist overtones – Washington nevertheless, at least in one respect, viewed Haiti much as it did the other Caribbean states: as a necessary stronghold in the fight against communism. Consequently, the most important U.S. foreign policy initiative toward Haiti became the prevention of any indication of pro-Soviet activity, particularly as it related to Castro's Cuba. Put concisely, Washington's goal in Haiti was stability at any cost. To this end, Washington tolerated corrupt governments and brutal police forces in Haiti, even if they practiced various forms of economic, political, and social repression.

Port-au-Prince habitually had turned its anti-communism to Washington when it sought economic assistance to deal with poverty and to ward off internal threats to the island's oligarchic political system. In exchange, it was willing to sell its acquiescence to U.S. foreign policy desiderata as it did in the early 1960s, when it provided the key vote to suspend Cuba's membership in the OAS in exchange for a new airport at Port-au-Prince. In 1953, Haiti became the first Caribbean republic to sign a treaty with Washington encouraging private U.S. investment on very favorable terms. Once Francois "Papa Doc" Duvalier had begun his decades of venal rule, Washington was quite satisfied with the status quo because it promised stability. However, Duvalier's tenuous, self-serving and opportunistic diplomatic sorties, on one occasion ostensibly seeking closer relations with Fidel Castro, soon alarmed containment-obsessed Washington. In hopes of silencing Duvalier's furtive courtship of Castro, Washington responded with even more public aid and 'development assistance' funds, which in reality were hijacked by Papa Doc – and by his son Jean Claude "Baby Doc" Duvalier – to strengthen the *tontons macoutes* (the government's extra-constitutional terror squad), as well as to finance the family's private financial dealings centering on huge defalcations of public funds.[3]

The Duvaliers were shrewd politicians who used an intimate understanding of the average Haitian's psyche, and a persistent willingness to play chicken with the United States, to cement their political primacy and to generate Washington's sympathy for the increasingly tyrannical policies that they pursued. Although so-called 'development aid' from the U.S. was relatively substantial, topping $15 million in one year at the height of the Cold War conflict, the island's population suffered woefully from a lack of basic social services – a potable water supply, adequate education systems and health services. The plight of illegal immigrants from Haiti to the U.S. has worsened in recent years, serving as painful evidence that the levels of U.S. economic assistance being earmarked for Haiti during a series of military dictatorships were either ill-conceived or misappropriated. In either instance, the Haitians' plight may have been abated somewhat by making certain that U.S. allocations would be kept out of the pockets of the nation's corrupt leaders. Such initiatives would have represented a dramatic departure from Washington's Cold War paranoia at the time, a departure that Washington simply refused to even consider.

As long as Haitian politics were dominated by authoritarians with good anti-communist bona fides, Washington remained reluctant to abandon its standard policy tools of military and economic assistance. If the current government seemed immune to any form of radical fervor, Washington considered Haiti to be 'stable,' and that was all that was asked of the country's leadership at the time.

Historically, Washington has shown a disturbing indifference to the aspirations of the Haitian population and its bitter trials. Tens of thousands of Haitian refugees have undertaken the perilous 500-mile journey to Florida's shores, with many of them never making it. Some have been political refugees, while others have been simply fleeing the poverty and chaos of their everyday lives. For these refugees, rampant human rights abuses perpetrated by Papa and Baby Doc were one of the few government products of U.S. economic and technical assistance to Haiti.

In the early 1980s, U.S. federal prosecutor Rudy Guiliani's inflammatory statements, which minimized the urgency of the Haitian refugee crisis and the political and economic factors which were bringing it about, went as far as to call the Duvalier government "friendly," and asserted repeatedly that "political repression is not the major reason for [refugees] leaving Haiti."[4] This sort of blind ignorance of Haitian reality has continued beyond the Cold War and into the present period, in which the United States has made itself complicit in one of the more tragic eras to befall the Caribbean nation.

In 1990, after a series of harsh and corrupt military regimes, Father Jean Bertrand Aristide was elected president by two-thirds of the nation's voters. After assuming office in 1991, he was ousted in a matter of months by a military coup, which eventually was headed by Colonel Raul Cedras. Isolated in Washington, where he sought political asylum, Aristide was seen by the Clinton administration as a radical and provocative figure whose aspirations were more akin to Fidel Castro's than Clinton was prepared to accept. Consequently, rather than viewing him as the one figure who could unite most Haitians behind him and exact the sacrifices which were necessary to build solid political institutions and a functional economy, the Clinton administration eyed Aristide as an unguided missile who, if given the opportunity, would provoke a confrontation with the island's tiny financial elite as well as tolerate massive numbers of desperate Haitians to try to flee the island to improve their lives.

In 1994, after years of human rights abuses by the military junta, which were benignly tolerated by Washington, the U.S. led a military force to the island to overthrow the Cedras-led military junta and restore President Aristide to office. This was after Washington policymakers had maintained pressure on Aristide to share power with the military and Haiti's discredited political establishment, something that the Haitian president refused to do while he was in exile and for which he was later vindicated by events.

### *The Caribbean Basin: Central America*
At the height of the Cold War conflict efforts to stymie putative leftist takeovers in Central America were also of paramount importance to Washington. As a region especially ravaged by the economic inequities and sociopolitical tensions plaguing the rest of Latin America, Central America struck the United States as the area most likely to become communism's next foothold on the continent, perhaps mirroring Cuba's role in the Caribbean. Once the U.S. had laid the mantle of its Cold War strategy over the area, many of the dangerous aspects of the region's political economy were allowed to fester unaddressed, if not entirely overlooked. Washington's lack of focus on the social and economic realities of such countries as Guatemala, El Salvador and Nicaragua often led to inconsistent and detrimental policies. When human rights abuses became commonplace as brutal authoritarian regimes peppered the region during the 1980s, Washington's national

security strategy toward Central America sanctioned such policies as one of the unfortunate by-products of its strategy, rather than using its leverage to demand solid democratic institutions in these countries.

## *El Salvador: Repression from All Sides*

The October 1979 coup in El Salvador was a welcome development for Washington at the time. Following President Carlos Romero's renouncement of U.S. aid in 1977, the threat of a possible resurgence of leftist activities was of the highest concern to Washington. The growth of popular support for the radical left in the country had expanded significantly throughout the mid-1970s, inciting an equally radical reaction from the far right that severely threatened the country's fragile political balance. With the intention of bolstering a centrist alternative to leftist political forces and members of the far right, U.S. economic and military aid flowed freely to the post-coup junta governments in order to maintain the greatest degree of stability possible. Washington's chosen ally within El Salvador was the center-right Christian Democratic Party. At the time, the political successes of the *Frente Sandinista de Liberación Nacional* (FSLN) in Nicaragua were beginning to unnerve Washington and increased the urgency of preventing a similar development in El Salvador.[5]

Despite this ostensibly centrist approach, however, a series of ill-conceived initiatives resulted in Washington's growing relationship with the country's right-wing political forces, and the military and paramilitary figures associated with them. As the decade came to a close these developments led to further increases in the levels of economic assistance flowing to the country. By 1980, El Salvador had become the largest recipient of U.S. economic aid in the hemisphere. Meanwhile, economic disparities and social discontent stewed beneath a thin veneer of stability.

The Carter administration supplied economic assistance to El Salvador until the end of 1980, when a largely fabricated incident in which a Nicaraguan Sandinista military shipment allegedly was made to Salvadoran guerrillas provided justification for the authorization, for the first time, of "lethal" U.S. military aid to the country.

Throughout the 1980s, the Reagan administration systematically downplayed the extent of the human rights abuses committed or ignored by the Salvadoran government. Meanwhile, large U.S. assistance packages were being designed to maintain El Salvador's general economic infrastructure and increase its military firepower, as guerrilla attacks and social discontent continually threatened both the country's political and economic institutions as well as its international credibility. Painfully absent was a consideration of the impact of those attacks on the Salvadoran population, which bore the brunt of many ill-fated guerrilla raids and overzealous military responses, which targeted civilians as much as the FLMN. In 1983, the Reagan administration certified that El Salvador had registered "significant human rights improvements." This vote of confidence caricatured the country's abysmal human performance, because it came at the very time that four cases involving the rape and murder of U.S. religious figures by Salvadoran military personnel were still pending, and the toll of extra-constitutional deaths was rising exponentially.[6]

Despite the continuous flow of "development aid" into El Salvador, the majority of its citizenry remained extremely marginalized and all but ignored by its own government. In 1975, average achievement figures regarding three of the UNDP's most commonly recognized indicators of human development—"a long, healthy life, knowledge and a decent standard of living"—were scraping the bottom.[7] The obvious conclusion is that development as such was not the primary goal of either U.S. or Salvadoran authorities, but that a military defeat of the leftist FLMN was Washington's overriding mission.

### *Noriega and Panama*
In the 1980s, Washington's relationship with Panamanian General Manuel Noriega became one of the most emblematic examples of the shifting priorities in its Latin American diplomacy. While maintaining a powerful grip on his country's politics for most of the decade, Noriega was once one of the White House's most important covert allies in its declared fight to save Central America from communism. Washington was unwilling to go after the unscrupulous general until he became a political embarrassment to the first Bush administration (in spite of the fact that he had become a prime U.S. intelligence asset), when he was turned into Washington's most reviled opponent in the escalating war on drugs. After attacks against Noriega by the U.S. Senate that centered on his drug trafficking role, Noriega's usefulness to the Reagan-Bush administrations was ended, and his repressive rule and drug-related criminal behavior were no longer tolerable. This occurred in the larger context of the post-Cold War during which Washington's priorities had shifted as foreign policy goals moved away from the containment of communism and toward stemming the inter-American drug trade.

Pressured by legislation and U.S. public opinion, a reluctant President George H.W. Bush mobilized U.S. troops in Panama to remove Noriega in an effort labeled *Operation Just Cause*. Although the operation was an immediate military success–apprehending its man in less than two weeks–the fact remained that Bush's decision to invade Panama had been a "final admission of U.S. failure." The move came only after years of irresolute diplomatic maneuvering plainly had failed to oust Noriega.[8] While applauded by the Panamanian middle-class, who hated the strong-arm figure, Washington's pyrrhic victory did nothing to clean up the country's drug and money laundering operations or to deal in a broader manner with Panamanian corruption. Due to its featuring mostly urban combat, the invasion also saw the deaths of scores of innocent civilians and considerable property destruction.[9]

Upon his graduation from the U.S.-run School of the Americas in the late-1960s, Noriega proved to be a capable intelligence resource during the Nicaraguan Contra- Sandinista conflict in the 1980s. Even though his involvement in the drug trade had troubled the White House since the early 1970s, he remained on the U.S. payroll throughout those decades. While serving as head of the Central Intelligence Agency in 1976, George Bush (senior) even hosted Noriega in Washington and gave him a tour of the CIA.[10] As the civil conflict in Nicaragua intensified in the 1980s, Noriega served as an important source of intelligence for the CIA on Nicaragua's Daniel Ortega and Cuba's Fidel Castro. He allowed Oliver North and other Washington operatives to expand surveillance efforts in Nicaragua from Panamanian bases, as well as to use his country as a base for supply and training operations for the Nicaraguan Contra forces.[11] As Washington's ties to Noriega grew stronger, he became more repressive and more prone to tighten his control. Panama's 1984 presidential elections were almost universally denounced as having been rigged by U.S. operatives at Noriega's behest, with Washington hardly questioning the victory of the general's hand picked candidate.[12] In 1985, low-level U.S. drug enforcement officials began an investigation into Noriega's connections to the drug trade, but the White House was so entrenched in its partnership with the Panamanian strongman that he remained officially on the federal payroll, until at least 1986.[13]

In 1988, Noriega declared himself head of state after a series of fraudulent elections. After surviving an attempted coup that had been half-heartedly backed by the White House in 1989, Noriega left Bush with no other choice but to oust the general by the use of massive U.S. force.[14] Once Noriega was transported to Miami to await trial, however, Bush's rhetoric, which first had accused Noriega of "poisoning our children"[15] with drugs, now became more muted.

Three years after the U.S. operation, Panama's President Endara's neoliberal economic reforms had brought a six percent annual growth to the Panamanian economy, but had failed to slash a level of unemployment that had reached almost 30 percent. Nor did the U.S.-backed government do much to stem the growth of money-laundering and the level of contraband activities in the country. The drug-trafficking rate once again became as high as in Noriega's heyday, if not higher. Washington's priorities had shifted across the globe, and a rally for democracy staged to mark the occasion of Bush's five-hour visit to Panama in 1992 was disrupted by 3,000 demonstrators protesting the United States' treatment of their country as an afterthought.[16]

## South America

While the Caribbean Basin countries attracted sustained attention from the U.S. during the Cold War period, the rest of Latin America was not ignored. Beginning with the Reagan presidency, the United States periodically became involved in various attempts at regime change on the continent. U.S. intelligence sources also provided information on a number of instances to repressive regimes, intent as Washington was on squelching revolutionary activity that could threaten the region's "stability". Washington also cooperated with opposition parties, as during the presidency of Salvador Allende in Chile as well as Hugo Chávez in Venezuela, when the parties in power were considered threats to U.S. interests. Washington derived its traction in the region from the fact that many South American governments were entirely deferential to U.S. policies, in part because of Washington's domination of the international lending agencies that were vital to their financial health.

## Chile

The CIA began to seriously involve itself in Chilean politics beginning in 1958.[17] The United States, particularly under the Kennedy administration, viewed Chile as a potential model of the Latin American state embarking upon the path to democratic development with U.S. guidance. In 1964, Washington supported the presidential candidacy of Eduardo Frei Montaya and later became involved in funding the Frei government's urban and rural reforms.[18] U.S. support of Frei led to considerable resentment on the part of both the conservative Chilean upper class and the Marxist left.[19]

In 1970, the U.S. plan to aid a centrist Chile was derailed by the election of Socialist Salvador Allende as the country's president. An avowedly leftist Chile would not only pose a direct threat to U.S. interests there, but would also present a problem for U.S.-South American relations on the whole. It could also serve as a vehicle for the further expansion of Soviet influence in the Western Hemisphere, and carry with it global significance in the context of the Cold War.[20]

In response to Allende's attempts to move toward a socialist economy, President Nixon and his National Security Advisor, Henry Kissinger implemented a covert economic blockade against the country. This was based on freezing new financial assistance and blocking vital loans to Chile.[21] Nixon gave CIA Director Richard Helms "the marshal's baton" to carry out covert activities in Chile in order to prevent Allende's inauguration in November 1970.[22] These included attempts to bribe the Chilean Congress not to swear in Allende as President if a clear majority was not initially gained, along with enlisting the military. Right-wing paramilitary groups were hired to ambush members of Allende's government, including Chief of Staff General René Schneider.[23] When these efforts failed to prevent Allende's inauguration, Washington focused on provoking economic sabotage, social instability and violence by launching smear campaigns against Allende and nonstop efforts to asphyxiate the Chilean economy.[24]

On September 11, 1973, with the accompanying support of U.S. intelligence agencies, the Allende government was overthrown in the bloodiest coup experienced by Latin America in the 20th century. While heavy tank and air attacks pummeled the presidential palace, U.S. Navy ships were stationed off the coast in the event of a loyalist faction rising up to challenge the coup plotters.[25] The coup brought to power General Augusto Pinochet, who shortly before had been named commander of the army. He quickly established himself as the leader of the brutal dictatorship that would rule unchallenged until 1990.[26]

Much to Washington's delight, Pinochet immediately began dismantling Allende's socialized Chilean economy. Market and trade liberalization were among the first transformations, as was the stripping of trade union rights from workers, as Chile was re-integrated into the world market economy. Bolstered by White House support, the Pinochet regime quickly became an absolutist dictatorship, and its command-and-control leadership soon squelched all attempts at dissent in the country. Nevertheless, for Washington, Pinochet's undesirable leadership traits were more than neutralized by the rapid implementation of neoliberal economic policies, even if this meant the banning of legal opposition and the use of water cannons, tear gas and mass arrests to quell street protests.[27] Furthermore, the Pinochet regime promptly dissolved the Congress, suspended the Chilean Constitution and outlawed opposition parties.[28] Pinochet's ruling military junta began a systematic terror campaign that arrested, tortured and murdered hundreds of "suspected subversives."[29] All told, nearly 4,000 people disappeared or were murdered for political reasons during Pinochet's rule, including 1,200 of his victims who "disappeared" after having been known to be detained by government forces.[30]

### *Justice Sought*
The effort to clean up the damage that Pinochet had done to Chile has included only minimal U.S. cooperation, despite the superpower's extensive involvement in fomenting the situation. In recent months both Spanish and Chilean

judges requested that Henry Kissinger, Nixon's National Security Advisor at the time of the coup, testify in response to the accusations that he had helped facilitate *Operation Condor*—a coordinated effort of computer-based communication among various southern cone intelligence chiefs working together to eliminate dissenters as well as repress left-wing opposition groups in their countries. However, Kissinger's representatives have been able to spare him a formal inquiry, only offering that he would "provide whatever evidence his memory can generate." It is not surprising that Kissinger and his cohorts have gone to great lengths to cover up the role he played in this particularly sinister chapter in U.S.-Latin American history.

# POST-COLD WAR POLITICS

The last 50 years of U.S. regional diplomacy has offered manifold instances of Washington's policy of strong-arming its neighbors in the name of short-term goals, always reflecting a tendency toward intervention and control. The dominant motive behind many of Washington's major initiatives toward Latin America has been a desire to impose its policy goals–whether wanted or not–on the region.

After the collapse of the Soviet Union in 1989, there was considerable scholarly discussion on the direction that U.S. hemispheric policy should take. Washington's stated reason for its major interventions over the last several decades was the threat posed by communism. There was some talk that Washington's hard-line stance against democratically elected, but left-leaning administrations, could now ease up. However, others predicted that the U.S. policy posture toward the rest of the hemisphere would undergo only minimal change because the larger goal-then as before- was the maintenance of U.S. regional preeminence. The U.S. position toward Cuba, the sole force consistently opposed to U.S. influence in the region, has hardened with the strengthening of the U.S. embargo, and much of U.S. diplomacy in the post-Cold War era continues to be predicated upon the political and economic isolation of Cuba.

Aside from Cuba, advancing the spread of neoliberal economics has been a foremost priority for the United States since the end of the Cold War, especially since the middle 1980s. While neoliberalism was treated merely as the preferred alternative to communist economics during the Cold War, now it has become the only option for much of the region, as decreed by the United States and the U.S.-led international financial institutions. These have made "neoliberal market reform" a prerequisite for development assistance and inclusion in the global economy. The goal of a capitalist world market has perhaps eclipsed that of worldwide democracy as the major benchmark for evaluating a society, and in many cases Latin America's states have found themselves on the brink of economic collapse, due mainly to overzealous adherence to Washington's policy prescriptions, recommendations and directives. Instead of alleviating mass poverty and access to shared community power, the spread of neoliberalism has produced many social and economic disconformities.

Evidence that Washington still suffers from Cold War-era insurgency paranoia is bound to affect U.S.-Latin American relations. Where Washington once invoked the threat of a communist spread, then the need to fight drug trafficking and money laundering, it now draws heavily from the George W. Bush administration's anti-terrorist rhetoric. Despite President Bush's early promises to work more attentively with Latin America, a coherent and constructive regional policy has yet to emerge. Instead, heavy-handed diplomacy directed at individuals, movements and leaders who dare to question U.S. policy remains very much the norm.

## *Powell's State Department in El Salvador, Nicaragua and Bolivia*
Under the Bush Administration, Washington increasingly has taken to using the fight against terrorism and drug trafficking to justify its military muscle-flexing. Just as in past decades, U.S. officials openly threaten economic and political retaliation against nations, such as El Salvador, Nicaragua and Bolivia, if leftist candidates who happen to be opposed by Washington succeed in coming to power through free and democratic elections. Under Secretary of State Colin Powell, Washington policy almost certainly reflects an outdated Cold War ideology rather than a more realistic evaluation of contemporary Latin American political realities.

In June 2003, outgoing U.S. Ambassador Rose Likins warned that U.S. private investment would pull out of El Salvador if a candidate from the Farabundo Marti National Liberation Front (FMLN), a former leftist guerrilla group presently holding the largest bloc of delegates in the national legislature, won the presidency in upcoming elections. On June 12, Likins sharply criticized the FMLN, suggesting that the election of its candidate would likely damage relations between the U.S. and El Salvador and justified these statements by pointing to the leftist party's opposition to certain U.S. interests in the region. The FMLN's reservations about the U.S.-backed Central American Free Trade Agreement (CAFTA), the party's rejection of dollarization—which was implemented as a dual currency alongside the *colon* in 2001—and its locally popular stance against the privatization of health care, have won it broad national support for the party as well as its candidate.

Washington's anti-FMLN platform illustrates the potential impact of the State Department's opinion in a country whose economy is heavily dependent upon both direct foreign investment and billions of dollars in remittances from Salvadoran immigrants in the United States. El Salvador's current president, Francisco Flores, who under Salvadoran law is prevented from running for reelection in 2004, quickly seized on Likins' opposition to the FMLN to rally public support for his own party, speaking out on several occasions about the dangers of electing an FMLN president. At a conference in Miami, Flores—taking his cue from Washington—argued that an electoral victory by the FMLN would constitute an "immense risk" for El Salvador because it would jeopardize the fate of the country's immigrants who live in the United States. He speculated that U.S. opposition to an FMLN president would lead to the end of the protected migration enjoyed by Salvadoran immigrants and their possible immediate deportation. Flores also expressed concern for the future of foreign investment in El Salvador, citing meetings with investors who were rethinking their plans for investment in the country in the aftermath of a possible FMLN victory.

Though the FMLN's leftist political positions no doubt provide an impetus for the U.S. campaign against like-minded ideological parties in Central America, the FMLN's past almost certainly has played a large role. From 1980 to 1992, the FMLN fought a bloody civil war against a series of U.S.-backed administrations in the country, and Washington used the group's history of armed conflict, as well as its Marxist political ideology, as justification to consistently oppose its rebirth as a legitimate party. Former ambassador Likins attempted to publicly connect the FMLN to terrorism, criticizing it for supporting other liberation movements and expressing solidarity with communist countries such as Cuba, Vietnam and China. She further questioned the FMLN's positions on democracy and the free market and denounced its general coordinator, Salvador Sanchez Ceron, for sending a letter of support to Cuban President Fidel Castro. Since all of the countries in the hemisphere, excluding the U.S., had diplomatic or consular relations with Cuba at the time, Likins' effort to overplay the implications of the relations between the Marxist FMLN with communist Cuba represented a crafty attempt to connect communism with terrorism. Within the context of Bush's "War on Terror," the attempt to link the two was no idle exercise.

Such use of the terrorist card is reminiscent of U.S. intervention in the Nicaraguan presidential election of November 2001, when U.S. Ambassador Oliver P. Garza targeted the *Frente Sandinista de Liberación Nacional* (FSLN) and its leader Daniel Ortega for having ties to terrorism. In Nicaragua, U.S. embassy officials recalled the harsh and controversial comments made by the Reagan Administration against the FSLN in the 1980s, hoping to lend credibility to their accusations that the party today supports terrorism through its alleged current fraternal links to Iraq, Libya, the FARC in Colombia and ETA, a Basque separatist group. U.S. officials also implied that the election of Ortega would directly undermine the global fight against terrorism, despite his recently transformed public persona of a born-again Christian and middle-of-the-road convert to the free market approach. The State Department's allegations that Ortega would work to provide resources to terrorists in the region in a perceived alliance with Castro and Venezuela's Hugo Chávez further reflected the push by Washington, in particular presidential advisor Otto Reich and recently confirmed Assistant Secretary for Inter-American Affairs, Roger Noriega, to tarnish the public opinion of leftists in Latin America by linking communism and terrorism.

The statements also made by then-U.S. Ambassador to Bolivia Manuel Rocha during the 2002 presidential election in that country, which are strikingly similar to those applied by the State Department in El Salvador and Nicaragua, reflected this pattern of interference in democratic elections since the commencement of Colin Powell's tenure as the head of the agency. On several occasions, Rocha expressed Washington's anxiety over the electoral prospects of Evo Morales, leader of the country's large base of *cocaleros*. The *cocaleros*, who are Bolivian coca farmers opposed to White House-backed policies of forced coca eradication, had become a target of the U.S. "War on Drugs" in Latin America. Morales irritated Washington by threatening to halt payments on Bolivia's foreign debt if elected, and to nationalize foreign-owned industries in the country. In response to Morales' campaign, Rocha warned Bolivians that U.S. aid could be withdrawn if they defied Washington's wishes by electing him as their president. Nevertheless, perhaps as a popular nationalist reaction, Morales received far more votes than he was expected to obtain as a result of Washington's attacks on him.

### *The Fear of Terrorism*

On April 2, 2003, during a trip to Barbados, Otto Reich—who recently had been demoted from his post as acting Assistant Secretary of State for Western Hemispheric Affairs to become Presidential Envoy to the Western Hemisphere—expressed his displeasure with a number of Caribbean leaders who had made statements opposing Washington's decision to attack Iraq without U.N. approval. Reich said he was "very disappointed" with CARICOM, the 15-member Caribbean Community, and suggested that the body "study very carefully not only what it says, but the consequences of what it says." While Reich did not directly accuse CARICOM leaders of supporting terrorism, he equated opposition to U.S. policy with undermining the fight against terror. In the political climate of the time, when an accusation of hindering the "War on Terror" had become sufficient to justify far more than just the public lecturing of dissident regional leaders, Reich's words could rightly have been viewed as an attempt to stifle the free expression of political opinion in the Caribbean.

Washington continues to capitalize on the residues of Cold War simplifications of the fear of communism in the hemisphere in order to justify its controversial activities in the region today. Despite the end of the Cold War, the Bush administration continues its vague and sometimes not so vague attempt to portray leftist groups and governments within the region as a threat to U.S. security interests. This is implicit in Washington's censure of even mildly leftist political parties in El Salvador, Nicaragua and Bolivia. Washington's drive to win the "wars" on terror and drugs, alongside its episodic anti-communist crusades, has become the new justification for U.S. intervention and arm-twisting in Latin America. Washington's attempt to bully the UN Security Council delegations of Mexico and Chile into backing its war plans against Iraq, which eventually led to the sacking of the two countries' highly regarded UN ambassadors, along with its forced recruitment of leaders throughout the region to join the "coalition of the willing" backing the invasion of Iraq, further exemplified this policy of unilateral interference in Latin America.

# NEOLIBERALISM IN THE WESTERN HEMISPHERE

Neoliberal economic reform in Latin America has long been a double-edged sword. On one hand, market liberalization has pushed forward the integration of Latin American countries into the global economy and perhaps will increase economic growth over the long run, which will ostensibly improve living standards in the region. On the other hand, critics argue that Washington-style neoliberalism simultaneously can hinder political growth, economic equality and social advancement in many countries. The dichotomy between the purported effects of neoliberalism in Latin America and the reality of the Washington Consensus has planted seeds of discontent among many citizens of countries that have yet to reap its supposed benefits.

### *The Washington Consensus*
In the mid-1980s, economists both inside and outside of Latin America began to seek solutions to the region's chronic economic ailments, and to strive for an economy that could provide prosperity and growth. In 1990, John Williamson, a senior fellow at the Institute for International Economics in Washington, assembled a list of 10 policy reforms that were among the most commonly suggested for Latin

America, collectively terming them the "Washington Consensus."[31] The logic behind the Washington Consensus was that market intervention by the state should be avoided, because the market was seen as a far better determinant for the allocation of resources than the state.[32] However, since then the tenets of the Washington Consensus have become ever more contentious, as they have not brought the steady growth to Latin America that was promised a decade ago. As a result, many third-world planners began to reassess their faith in the Consensus as an ideal model for international development.

In Argentina, the country's once-booming economy began to decline in the late nineties when dollarization and reliance on foreign borrowing—both neoliberal policy recommendations, at times central to IMF loan requirements—led to grave fiscal difficulties. In 1999, already hard hit by Brazil's financial crisis, Argentina slipped into a steep depression and by October 2000, the country's foreign debt had reached 50 percent of its GDP. Amid widespread protests and an unemployment rate of more than 20 percent, the IMF abruptly cut off aid to Argentina in December 2001, a move which ultimately led to a default on the country's $140 billion foreign debt in January 2002.[33] Despite having once been touted as "South America's most 'European' country"– a reference that recalled its flourishing economy and its advanced social programs – Argentina was left by the international financial community to raise itself out of the economic muck as Washington neoliberals cavalierly ignored their former poster-child of "responsible" development.

The comments of José Maria Figueres, former Costa Rican president and the current Managing Director of the Center for the Global Agenda at the World Economic Forum, demonstrate the growing discontent with the Washington Consensus in Latin America. Figueres has observed that the continent "no longer holds on to the idea that it suffices to liberalize the economy to launch a process of sustainable economic development. Markets don't take care of everything."[34]

### *Honduras and Chiquita Banana*

In the 1990s, Washington's Latin American foreign policy initiatives also reflected the long-standing allegiance of U.S. politicians to major multinational corporations. Perhaps the most egregious example of corporate influence was that of banana giant Chiquita. With its roots in the controversial United Fruit Company, which held immense power over the Honduran government beginning in 1899, Chiquita has continued its progenitor's tradition, extending its corrupting influence to many key institutions and officials in the small and heavily venal country.[35] Despite its often-stifling impact, however, the banana conglomerate has not gone unchallenged. In 1997 and 1998, Chiquita was taken to court by Otto Stalinski, a former official of a rival banana producer, who charged Chiquita with attempted kidnapping, murder, and a multitude of other criminal and civil charges. At the same time, the *Cincinnati Enquirer* published an 18-page exposé on Chiquita's practices, reporting routine unethical behavior by the fruit company.[36]

Chiquita escaped investigation by the U.S. government and managed to buy itself favorable treatment through major donations by its then CEO, Carl Lindner, to the Clinton administration. Usually an important Republican donor, Lindner donated $500,000 to President Clinton's 1996 reelection campaign the day after U.S. Trade Representative Mickey Kantor submitted a complaint to the World Trade Organization (WTO) against the European Union's (EU) "Banana Framework Agreement." Intended to protect the fragile economies of former European colonies in the Caribbean and the Pacific, the EU's formula required that eight to ten percent of banana imports would come from its members' former possessions and placed limits on imports from larger suppliers such as Honduras.[37] Although supported by other affected countries, including Colombia and Costa Rica, the EU's agreement did not please Lindner. In the end, the WTO, under U.S. pressure, ruled that the agreement was in violation of its guidelines.[38] When the EU refused to abide by the ruling, the Clinton administration, in another show of fealty to Chiquita, moved to impose 100 percent tariffs on selected imported goods from the EU, which eventually was forced to back down.

The WTO ruling has had drastic effects on the region's micro-economies.[39] In Dominica, bananas have accounted for 60 percent of its total exports, and many other of the Caribbean islands were in similar straits. With the loss of their banana market to mainland corporations like Chiquita, many residents of the Caribbean were either unable to find work or forced to turn to smuggling and drug trafficking to survive, or plan to begin to illegally migrate to the U.S. Washington, however, appeared to be largely unmoved by their plight. Then-Secretary of State Madeleine Albright neglected to appear at a meeting of Caribbean foreign ministers shortly after the WTO ruling was made, sending a subordinate instead.

### *'Los Chicago Boys'*
Following the violent coup that killed President Salvador Allende, newly-installed General Pinochet placed his confidence in the policies of a group of Latin American economists educated at the University of Chicago and known as *"los Chicago Boys."* These technocrats, who had studied under the legendary Milton Friedman, advocated widespread deregulation and privatization along with a host of other free-market policies.[40] As the first Latin American country to closely adhere to the Chicagoans' prescriptions, Chile rigorously deregulated and quickly privatized its economy, resulting in decreased inflation and new foreign investment. But any economic benefits accrued by the population were far too inadequate to

make up for the political repression of the Pinochet regime. It should be noted that the reforms instituted by Pinochet were mainly at the expense of workers and came in the form of decrees (in the absence of a legislative body and a judicial system) that had a draconian impact upon lower-class Chileans, to the benefit of the nation's middle and upper classes.

However, the application of neoliberalism at the hands of *los Chicago Boys* was not uniformly economically beneficial, as implementing their complicated strategies in the correct sequence was a rarity. Some countries carried out the various stages in different chronological order, which often produced an entirely different outcome, and no country, save Chile, applied the recommendations in their entirety.[41] Some of the countries that experienced the greatest success were the ones that mixed neoliberal policies with elements of state control; one aspect of the process heretofore considered part of the problem rather than the solution.[42] As implementation of neoliberal policies varied among Latin American countries, differing results were also experienced. Pinochet's Chile, which had closely adhered to the tenets of neoliberal reform, experienced some degree of economic upturn, soon to be followed by stark periods of decline. Colombia, which took a much more cautious approach, consequently managed to escape the negative effects of the debt crisis that began in Mexico and later enveloped most of Latin America.

### *The Mexican Peso Crisis*

The event that triggered the region's descent into full-fledged economic crisis was the August 1982 announcement, made by Mexican Finance Minister Jesús Silva-Herzog, that his country would no longer be able to service its foreign debt. Soon after, almost the entire region became embroiled in the crisis, with growth and investment plummeting alongside exploding unemployment levels. Unabated population growth throughout the region also contributed to lowered standards of living and increased poverty. The next ten years would come to be known as Latin America's "lost decade."

A shortage of foreign exchange forced many Latin American governments in the early 1980s to turn to the International Monetary Fund (IMF) for assistance.[43] The Fund used this opportunity to implement its agenda of neoliberal market reform, which consisted of currency stabilization to reduce inflation, structural adjustment to remove price controls and trade tariffs, and allowing the market to determine the most efficient allocation of resources.[44] The state was seen as an albatross, only producing harm when it interfered with the operation of the free market.[45]

At the beginning of 1994, the future appeared bright for the Mexican economy. Investors were confident about its economic prospects after the passage of the North American Free Trade Agreement (NAFTA). However, the political situation in Mexico soon turned sour. A violent uprising in Chiapas, and the assassination of the country's leading presidential candidate, Luis Donaldo Colosio of the *Partido Revolucionario Institucional* (PRI), made investors more cautious.[46] This political pressure negatively affected the value of the peso, causing foreign currency reserves to rapidly fall.[47] The country's foreign reserves were soon insufficient to maintain Mexico's fixed exchange rate, resulting in an unavoidable devaluation of the peso. Investors stopped buying Mexican assets and the prospect of loan default now loomed over the once-resurgent Mexican economy. As much to curb the potential for mass migration of Mexicans into the U.S. as to assist a neighbor in need, the U.S. provided aid and persuaded international lending agencies to do likewise. Additionally, Washington feared that if the Mexican government defaulted on its loans, the anxiety over the stability of Mexico's economy could spread to other countries in the region. Interested in maintaining its leverage in those countries, the U.S. sought to stem such a spread of uncertainty, as economic instability might encourage some Latin Americans to join a potentially more stable market in another arena—the international drug trade.

### *The North American Free Trade Agreement (NAFTA)*

Near the beginning of the 1990s, Washington's economic neoliberals began their quest for free trade arrangements (FTAs) in the Western Hemisphere. As of yet, the only one to be fully implemented is the North American Free Trade Agreement (NAFTA), signed in 1992 by the leaders of Canada, Mexico and the U.S. (Brian Mulroney, Carlos Salinas and George H.W. Bush, respectively), all of whom felt that the agreement would produce millions of jobs and help bring about a more diversified economy in the hemisphere.

Talk of NAFTA was kept more or less out of the public arena in the three countries, as the future signatories were wary of a possible backlash that could follow the public's discovery of the agreement's vulnerabilities. President Bush, and later, President Clinton, secured "Fast-Track" negotiating powers, which allowed them to bypass Congress for much of the negotiation process, and Mulroney and Salinas similarly shielded the NAFTA issue from public debate. This silence was pursued because of the looming realities of the trade agreement: NAFTA could be expected to greatly benefit large multinational corporations who could relocate their installations to Mexico in order to exploit the weak labor and environmental standards there.[48] The Clinton administration was instrumental in finalizing the NAFTA negotiations. Clinton's close friend and then-U.S. Trade Representative, Mickey Kantor, claimed victory in negotiations with Canada and

Mexico, stating that NAFTA's agreements regarding labor and environmental issues had "teeth," but actually he was forced to make significant concessions to both countries in order to gain their assent.[49]

Ultimately, NAFTA survived its gestation period and went into effect January 1, 1994. In the following years, NAFTA took its toll in varying degrees in all three member countries. In the U.S. and Canada, hundreds of thousands of workers were laid off as companies shifted production to Mexico in order to save on labor costs. Claims that Mexico would provide a massive new consumer market for U.S. and Canadian companies also proved largely illusory; most Mexicans could not readily afford domestic manufactured goods, much less imports. Only Mexico received qualified benefits from NAFTA—witnessing an economic boom in the years immediately following the treaty's passage—but even this would prove short-lived and created very few new jobs in the country.

### *The Future of Neoliberalism in Latin America*

Emboldened by the successful implementation of NAFTA, the Clinton administration almost immediately embarked on seeking other free trade agreements across Latin America. Three major regional FTAs were proposed since NAFTA's completion: the U.S.-Chile FTA, the Central American Free Trade Agreement (CAFTA), and the Free Trade Agreement of the Americas (FTAA)—of which only Chile has gone into effect as of this writing. The unfolding FTA arrangements are a point of considerable tension between the United States and a number of Latin American governments, as their leaders attempt to loosen Washington's grip on their economies and institutions. Although once tethered to the United States by compelling economic ties and political naïveté, the burgeoning resistance that some Latin American states have shown toward Washington's much-touted hemispheric economic integration plans may be a signal that U.S. authority is not as overwhelming as it once was for the region.

The Free Trade Agreement with Chile was first conceived in December 2000 when talks began between U.S. Trade Representative, Robert Zoellick, and Chilean Foreign Minister, Soledad Alvear. In order to facilitate negotiations with Chile, newly-elected President George W. Bush pursued Trade Promotion Authority (TPA), which is essentially Fast Track repackaged.[50] After two years of talks, President Bush—now TPA-empowered—informed Congress of his intent to sign an FTA with Chile, pursuant with TPA guidelines. On June 6, 2003, Zoellick and Alvear initiated an agreement to enter into the FTA, although the process was slightly delayed by Washington's desire to reprimand Chile for its opposition to the war in Iraq.[51] The pact was passed by Congress on July 31, 2003, and signed into law by the President.

On a much more expansive scale, the proposed FTAA will encompass all of the states of the Western Hemisphere except Cuba. FTAA talks began in 1998, and are scheduled to conclude in January 2005. This goal is proving unlikely to be achieved, though, as many Latin American countries have become increasingly wary of Washington's economic prescriptions since NAFTA. One saw this in the break-up of the WTO talks at Cancún in October of 2003 and the gutting of the FTAA in Miami in the following November. The Bush administration's latest emissaries to Latin America—Otto Reich and Roger Noriega—have met with significant opposition when attempting to use traditional strong-arm tactics to push through the FTAA. Leading the opposition is Brazilian President Luiz Inácio "Lula" da Silva, who co-chairs the talks with President Bush. Lula, along with Argentine President Néstor Kirchner, Chilean President Ricardo Lagos and now Bolivian President Carlos Mesa, is pushing to move away from the Washington Consensus and toward a higher degree of regional integration and cooperation among Latin American states. As long as these leaders remain in power, the future of the FTAA remains in limbo.[52]

In order to complete the FTAA, Washington also has proposed a Central American Free Trade Agreement (CAFTA). Scheduled to be finalized by December 2003, CAFTA would assist in FTAA talks by focusing Central American trade northward, thus placing extra pressure on free trade holdouts in South America.[53] Opposition to CAFTA has been centralized in El Salvador, where members of the Farabundo Marti National Liberation Front (FMLN) have spoken out against its application. In an unshockingly familiar response, U.S. officials have attempted to undermine this resistance by blatantly interfering in Salvadoran domestic politics, hoping to prevent the victory of the FMLN presidential candidate in the March 2004 election.[54]

Ultimately, each of these trade agreements may share some of the same flaws contained in NAFTA. First, through TPA, the Bush administration will be able to retain the same secretive trade-related negotiation ability that was granted to his father and Clinton.[55] Second, the U.S. seems to be seeking sophisticated economic relationships with the very same dependent Latin American countries that have been specifically criticized by Washington for having weak political infrastructure and an abundance of corruption. One very real consequence of such targeted support could be that strong labor and environmental regulations will not be included in the agreements, as was the case in Mexico, only exacerbating the current underdevelopment of many of these Latin American countries. Finally, as NAFTA already has demonstrated, free trade agreements tend to mainly benefit multinational corporations, causing significant harm to blue-collar workers in all constituent countries.

The states of Latin America have never presented a viable threat to the United States' regional dominance. Instead, the primary threat to Washington has remained the undermining of its dominance over extra-hemispheric hostile forces. Washington's aim, therefore, has always been to maintain enough general stability throughout the hemisphere so that outside incursions might be resisted. This desire, however, has caused U.S. foreign policy toward Latin America since World War II to be dangerously capricious at times, often dictated by misguided obsessions and special interests that, more often than not, have proven to be beneficial only to Washington.

It is important to remember that Latin America is a diverse region, and that the varying circumstances of its constituent countries by necessity preclude a truly homogenous U.S. policy. Nevertheless, save for a few notable departures, Washington historically has dealt with Latin America as a collective, denying each state the benefit of specialized policies and customized development. This attitude toward the region has resulted in policies designed to eradicate some perceived threat against the U.S. or to advance U.S. development, while leaving Latin America palpably behind politically, socially and economically, if need be. During the Cold War, the containment of communism overshadowed the need for democratic political systems that respected human rights. In the 1990s, the Washington Consensus, with its inflexible standards had rolled over what some have considered authentic development goals in many countries. Today, while the war against terror may be rational in theory, it is also true that it has provided the basis for a revitalized pattern of intervention that previously helped to shape Latin America into the distressed region it is today. Whatever the justification, U.S. officials have always been able to overlook the harmful consequences of its baleful actions in Latin America in order to further the cause of the day, as seen from Washington's perspective.

## Washington's Current Relations With Haiti: A Most Peculiar Foreign Policy

After months of seemingly aimless waiting for something to happen in Haiti, Washington is still without what can be called a credible policy toward the island. U.S. policy toward Port-au-Prince seems as unrevisited and unchangeable as Washington's policy toward Havana. The comparison has additional merit because of the Bush administration's personalization of its odium toward Aristide in the same way it has demonized Castro. Washington's Haiti policy is not uniquely a product of Republican Party thinking, because it is almost identical to the Clinton White House's treatment of the Caribbean's other two perceived pariah nations, Cuba, and to a somewhat lesser extent, Venezuela. However, this type of static and ideological-driven policy brings with it very serious dangers.

For the last several years, U.S. policy toward Haiti has been anything but civil. The Bush administration, following the lead of President Clinton before it, has been denying Haiti hundreds of millions of dollars pledged to it by Washington and the rest of the international donors. The State Department insisted that the issue was the flawed senatorial election of 2000, but objective observers would insist that the underlying propellant came from the U.S.'s sulphurous aversion to President Jean-Bertrand Aristide. Washington viewed President Aristide as a potential Castro whose radical personality was capable of triggering unlimited discord on the island.

Haiti's eternal malaise, if anything, continues to worsen as a result of disruptive local politics, shrill rhetoric and the near elimination of overseas assistance. Even though President Jean-Bertrand Aristide (who in November 2000 again won the presidency by a huge margin) agreed to a number of mischievous conditions for U.S. aid to resume, Washington has given no indication that it would be forthcoming, even at this late date. The U.S. campaign of economic asphyxiation and political isolation is not only unseemly, but also gravely damaging to its own best interests.

If this policy continues unaltered, it will, just as it is now doing, bring added turmoil to the island. Inevitably, desperate Haitians will once again be willing to risk the dangerous voyage to Florida over hundreds of miles of open water. Such an exodus could gravely embarrass the Bush White House, just as it did the Clinton administration.

The Democratic Convergence (CD), originally a 15-party coalition of mainly micro-factions, has vehemently rejected Aristide's legitimacy based on charges of electoral fraud in last May's senatorial balloting. The CD even went to the extent of naming Gerard Gourgue as the country's "Provisional President," in the midst of President Aristide's presidential inauguration. Among other preposterous positions, Gourgue called for the return of the commanders of Haiti's repressive armed forces, expelled by the U.S. military in 1994.

Despite its modest popular appeal with the public, the Convergence effectively was awarded a crippling de facto veto by the then-chairman of the Senate Foreign Relations Committee, Sen. Jesse Helms, Aristide's relentless attacker. Having been made a bedrock conviction by Washington's hard right that Aristide must not be allowed to consolidate a functioning administration by any means, Helm's office became the center of legislative maneuvers and propagandistic press releases defaming the Haitian president on a daily basis. The CD leadership knew that in effect, it could use its connection to Helms to veto any move or compromise leading to a resolution of Washington's differences with Aristide. U.S. policy makers also insist that the Democratic Convergence is the country's democratic alternative.

Over the months, the Convergence (and more recently, the kindred body known as the Group of 184) has been the main obstacle to negotiations and resumption of aid to the suffering Haitian public. Aristide first met with its leaders in early 2000 to discuss possible solutions to the stalemate. Regrettably, his offer to include some Convergence leaders in his government and appoint a new impartial electoral body were peremptorily rejected. Aristide's call for initiating a dialogue also was rejected by the Convergence, though he even offered, as a goodwill gesture, to move up the next round of legislative elections.

The State Department and National Security Council have chronically viewed Aristide as a liability rather than as the island's main political asset. Allegations against him routinely have understated his wide support and his unique legitimacy. Aristide has always towered over potential political alternatives and has worked hard to cooperate with Washington's often arrogant demands.

At the end of 2000, the Clinton administration agreed to restore aid once the Haitian leader adopted eight conditions that addressed electoral and economic reforms along with narcotics smuggling, illegal migration and human-rights violations. Later Aristide agreed to additional conditions.

After several requests by Haiti asking for help in addressing the election issue, the Organization of American States belatedly decided to dispatch a delegation to discuss election reforms. Eventually, even high OAS officials began to see the problem as principally due to the opposition's obstructionism rather than Aristide's lack of cooperation.

But as time passed with no softening of Washington's position, the nation began to register extreme privation, as all aspects of its national life began to deteriorate. With this deterioration came the hyper-growth of political polarization, the expansion of lethal political street gangs sponsored by both sides, the soaring of common crime and the entrenchment of both the government and opposition in often extremist positions. Rather than single-mindedly working for reconciliation, Washington played with fire and now all sides are being badly burned.

At this late date, with the U.S. about to hold its own presidential election, failing to display some basic amity to Haiti's population will only add more yellowed pages to Washington's already profoundly jaundiced and mean-spirited treatment of Port-au-Prince, which historically has been frequently characterized by condescension rather than respect, contempt instead of humanity.

[1] "*Constructing a Postwar World: What is the Good Neighbor Policy?*" <http://www.theaha.org/Projects/GIRoundtable/Good_Neighbor/GoodNeighbor1.htm.> Accessed June 2003.

[2] Mace, Gordon and Jean-Philipe Therien, eds. Foreign Policy and Regionalism in the Americas. Boulder, CO: Lynne Rienner Publishers, 1996. 3-4

[3] Bond, Kanisha, et al. "U.S. Policy in Haiti," COHA Occasional Paper, August 2003. U.S. Library of Congress. Submission Pending.

[4] Cohen, Mitchel. "*All the Dictator's Men,* " 1. <www.spunk.org> Accessed May 2003.

[5] http://memory.loc.gov/cgi-bin/query/r?frd/cstdy:@field(DOCID+sv0024) Library of Congress – El Salvador

[6] COHA press release: January 21, 1983 "Human Rights and Certification: El Salvador."

[7] http://www.undp.org/hdr2003/indicator/indic_10_1_1.html

[8] Dinges, John *Our Man in Panama: How General Noriega Used the United States and Made Millions in Drugs and Arms*. New York: Random House, 1990.

[9] "Panama: Land without a compass." COHA Press Release, 12/19/92.

[10] Dinges, *Our Man*

[11] Robert Parry and Douglas Waller. "The Bush-Noriega Relationship," *Newsweek*, Jan. 15, 1990.

[12] Federal Research Division, Library of Congress. http://countrystudies.us/panama/22.htm

[13] COHA, 12/19/92

[14] Dinges, *Our Man*

[15] White House Press Conference, Jan. 5, 1990, http://bushlibrary.tamu.edu/papers/1990/90010500.html

[16] COHA, 12/19/92

[17] Library of Congress Country Studies: Chile. http://memory.loc.gov/frd/cs/cltoc.html

[18] Ibid.

[19] Ibid.

[20] Ibid.

[21] Ibid.

[22] Landau, Saul. "The U.S. overthrow of Chilean democracy 25 years ago." *The Progressive* https://www.theprogressive.org/mplandau998.htm September 1998

[23] Ibid.

[24] Ibid.

[25] *The Progressive.*

[26] BBC News World Edition

[27] Bean, David and Julia Stock. "Social Darwinism to be enshrined in Latin America; U.S. scheduled to be major beneficiary. Press Release: Council on Hemispheric Affairs." June 24, 1992.

[28] *The Progressive*

[29] Ibid.

[30] Vergara, Eva. "Chilean president plans to increase reparations for victims of Pinochet dictatorship." Associated Press. August 13, 2003

[31] IDB America. Magazine of the Inter-American Development Bank. "A new consensus?" Posted June 2002. http://www.iadb.org/idbamerica/index.cfm?&thisid=2229&pagenum=2

[32] Ibid.

[33] Blustein, Paul, "Argentina Didn't Fall on Its Own," *Washington Post*, Aug. 3, 2003

[34] The World Bank Group. Debating the Washington Consensus: World Bank, NGOs suggest new emphasis on social issues. http://web.worldbank.org/WBSITE/EXTERNAL/NEWS/0,,contentMDK:20116211~menuPK:34457~pagePK:34370~piPK:34424~theSitePK:4607,00.html. June 19, 2003

[35] Osweiler, Beth et al, "CEO Lindner and his Chiquita Brand Find it Difficult to Distinguish Right From Wrong," Council on Hemispheric Affairs Press Release, November 11, 1997

[36] *"Cincinnati Enquirer*'s Major Series Breaks Open U.S. Multinational's Wall-to-Wall Skullduggery in the Chiquita Republic of Honduras Banana," Council on Hemispheric Affairs Press Release, May 11, 1998

[37] Osweiler

[38] "The Spotlight Should Also be on Mickey Kantor," Council on Hemispheric Affairs Press Release, January 29, 1998

[39] Assanah, Roy, "The Caribbean's Tangled Way Forward After Banana Defeat," Council on Hemispheric Affairs Press Release

[40] Becker, Gary S. "What Latin America Owes to the 'Chicago Boys'." Hoover Digest 1997 Number 4

[41] Ibid.

[42] Ibid.$\alpha$

[43] Therberge, Alexander. "The Latin American Debt Crisis of the 1980's and its Historical Precursors." April 8, 1999. www.columbia.edu/~ad245/theberge.pdf

[44] Ibid.

[45] Ibid.

[46] Ibid.

[47] Ibid.

[48] "Free Trade Negotiations: The Pace Quickens," Council on Hemispheric Affairs Press Release, Feb. 10, 1992

[49] Hutton, Gregory T. and Hisel, Elza P., "NAFTA Side Agreements: Blind and Toothless," Council on Hemispheric Affairs Press Release. Aug. 17, 1993

[50] Knutson, Ross and Olivia Nelson, "Trade Promotion Authority and the FTAA," Council on Hemispheric Affairs Press Release, November 15, 2001

[51] Perry, Lisa N., "Lagos Humiliates Chile by Not Standing Tall Over Its Iraq Vote," Council on Hemispheric Affairs Press Release, May 16, 2003

[52] Burges, Sean, and Jessica Leight, "Which Way the FTAA? South American regionalism confronts American unilateralism," Council on Hemispheric Affairs Press Release, June 2, 2003

[53] Bailey, Nick, "The Prospects for CAFTA," Washington Report on the Hemisphere issue 23.08, May 30, 2003

[54] Strunk, Chris, "The Bush Administration's Policy of Unilateral Interventions in Latin America," Council on Hemispheric Affairs Press Release, June 25, 2003

[55] "Crisis in FTAA Negotiations Triggers Secret, Invitation-Only FTAA "Mini-Ministerial" Meeting at Exclusive Chesapeake Bay Enclave," Public Citizen Press Release, June 12, 2003

# CHAPTER SEVEN

*Wè jodi, men sonje demen.*

See today, but remember tomorrow is coming.

# Notes on the U.S.-Haiti Solidarity Movement
*Tom Reeves*

This is a reminiscent overview of the U.S.-Haiti Solidarity Movement, from the 1980s, and especially since 1991, to the present. It focuses on the non-Haitian members and groups in that movement in the U.S. It does not cover the solidarity movements in Canada and Europe. It is not meant to be a study of Lavalas or popular organization in Haiti or of what many call the "political crisis" in Haiti today. It depends on testimony from Haitians who helped form and inform the movement. It is partly based on my memories as a participant, partly on records of groups involved, and partly on recollections of about fifty others.

It should always be remembered that the real story of Haiti is that of its people, especially the impoverished peasants who make up more than 85% of the population. From the first successful slave rebellion in 1791 to the armies of Toussaint who defeated the white colonial powers; from the throngs who poured into the streets demanding dechoukaj (a complete uprooting of oppressive institutions) and overthrew Baby Doc to the hopeful majority who chose their first freely elected President in 1991; from the brave underground struggle during the coup to the present confusing time of deprivation - it is the poor of Haiti who have suffered, who have understood the root causes of their suffering, and who have struggled to throw off their bondage. This chapter does not re-tell that story, but is an account by some Americans who understand the role of their government in that oppression and who have stood side by side with the people of Haiti. As U.S. citizens, they know they are ultimately responsible for the bad policies of their government.

These notes are meant to be a contribution toward a history of this important movement, which was perhaps briefly one of the most successful solidarity efforts in U.S. history, and which has become sadly demoralized and disillusioned. Still, the solidarity movement persists, and its impact, though dimmed, is still felt in Washington, and in Port au Prince. Dessima Williams was an official of the revolutionary government of Grenada under Maurice Bishop and a key player during the 1990s with the Haiti solidarity movement. She remains one of the Caribbean's best-known leaders and scholars. Williams told a college class studying Haiti in 1994, "We are part of citizen diplomacy - the only force that can counter the awful effects of many U.S. foreign policies across the world, and in this case Haiti. It is my hope that citizen diplomacy will spread and one day overcome the ill results of ignorance and oppression." [1] These notes are meant to remind us of that task.

# ORIGINS OF THE MOVEMENT

The Haiti solidarity movement in the United States grew out of efforts by Haitian-Americans and Haitians living in exile to gain support from their non-Haitian friends and colleagues. During the Duvalier years, they organized forums and alliances to support refugees and to oppose the brutal dictatorship back home. This was slow work in the 1970s and 80s, when Americans were pre-occupied with other struggles for which they felt responsibility as citizens of the super-power engaged in the Cold War. With Cuba, Vietnam, Cambodia and then Central America, southern Africa, and the Middle East, pulling progressive Americans into action, it was hard to get Haiti on the activist map. Added to that was a preoccupation with the civil rights struggle within U.S. borders, and racism even within the peace and social justice movements. Paul Farmer, in THE USES OF HAITI, points out how effectively U.S. propaganda falsely painted Haiti as the hemisphere's "basket case".[2] This affected how all Americans, including many blacks and progressive whites, viewed the small black nation so close to Florida and so overwhelmed by U.S. military control and economic dominance.

Haitians living in U.S. cities from Boston to Miami and across the country were key in pulling together white and black Americans to support the Haitian struggle. One of those is Philippe Geneus of Boston, who was part of the Committee Against Macoute Propaganda in the early 1980s. "In 1985, I joined the Committee in Solidarity with Haiti (COSAH), and a little later the Committee to Support the Popular Movement in Haiti (KOSMOP). We thought it was important to educate non-Haitians about the political situation in Haiti and to seek their active support. (After Baby Doc fell), we organized a Harvard delegation to Haiti to investigate the jailing and torture of Konpe Plim (Evans Paul), Marino Etienne and others under Prosper Avril - and we alerted Amnesty International, which began to report on Haitian human rights abuses."[3] Geneus says his groups supported Haitian refugees and opposed racist U.S. immigration policies, but they saw support for the political struggle in Haiti as their most important task.

Similar stories are told by Haitians living in Miami and New York where there were already large Haitian populations from the exodus under the Duvaliers. In cities with smaller Haitian populations, direct attempts at building solidarity came more slowly, but were equally important in creating a structure for the Haiti solidarity movement. Max Blanchet of San Francisco remembers being frustrated, after moving from the east coast in the late 1960s, that, "There was not much action out here during the first phase of solidarity work. Most of it centered in New York and later Miami. The newspapers and refugee centers and of course the church were the main focus of action." As the revolutionary struggle in Haiti heated up during 1986, Blanchet says, "Our role as Haitians was to work with the large U.S. progressive community in Berkeley and San Francisco, and to appear on media like KPFA (Pacifica) and KQED (NPR) to tell the public the truth about Haiti." Blanchet says the work first centered on the arrival of small groups of refugees - "it was hard work - we acted as social workers, and the refugees had no families to come to. We were a core group of maybe ten Haitian activists."

Pierre Labossiere was also part of the solidarity work in the Bay area following his work in Central America: "It was 1982. I joined a parade to support the revolution in El Salvador, and I saw a sign demanding freedom for Haitian refugees. I rushed to those holding it and spoke to them in Creole - they didn't understand. 'Oh, you're African-Americans,' I said. 'Oh, you're Haitian!' they exclaimed. That was typical of how we got started working with the solidarity and other progressive groups." Work started with Black organizers in Oakland. Labossiere's membership in the ILWU (Longshoreman's and Warehouse Union) led to union involvement. Blanchet remembers, "There were two wings of American solidarity groups - the church and the political types." Labossiere named the Sanctuary movement as an important religious player in those early days, and the International Action Center as a political center. Blanchet describes the period from 1986 to 1990: "Various Central American solidarity groups joined our activities in what I call the "first phase of solidarity." We consciously sought to join boards of progressive groups, not to use them, but to help them include Haiti on their agenda."

## THE FIRST PHASE OF U.S.-HAITI SOLIDARITY

A central group in this first phase was West-Coast-based Global Exchange, which sent delegations to Cuba, Central America, and soon to Haiti. On the east coast, two important national solidarity groups emerged. The first was the Emergency Coalition for Haitian refugees, led by Haitians to bring together 42 U.S. and Haitian groups in 1982, This was the first full-scale model of Haiti solidarity. The Emergency Coalition later became the National Coalition for Haitian Rights (NCHR). Their initial work focused primarily on rights of refugees and fighting discriminatory U.S. immigration policies. NCHR later led the legal effort to overturn those U.S. policies - from securing the release of many Haitians imprisoned at Krome in Florida to shutting down the U.S. internment camp for people with AIDS (including Haitians) at Guantanamo.

The second national group was the Washington Office on Haiti, formed in 1984 by Christian activists familiar with Latin American and Central American struggles. It included people from the World Council of Churches (Protestant and Orthodox) and from various Roman Catholic peace and justice groups. It called itself an "independent, ecumenical NGO," and worked not only on refugee issues but on support for democracy in Haiti. It became vocal and visible from about 1987. These groups, formed or fostered by activist Haitians, slowly emerged as the U.S. Haiti solidarity movement.

It was during these years that my involvement in solidarity began. Like many other Americans, I came out of a subculture called "The Movement" in the U.S: anti-war, anti-racism and other social justice groups. In particular, most of us had been active in the large U.S. solidarity community engaged in struggles against unjust U.S. policies in Central American and elsewhere. At the time, I was teaching at Roxbury Community College, where more than half the students were of Caribbean descent, and many were Haitians. As early as 1982, the RCC Haitian Club began sponsoring forums to study attempts to oust Duvalier from Haiti.

Just after the overthrow of Baby Doc (February 1986), Philippe Geneus, Frantz Minuty, Freda Laurent and others approached RCC from a new coalition called The Democratic Haitian Resistance (RDA). This included COSAH (Committee in Solidarity with Haiti) and KOSMOP as well as Haitian women's and student organizations. RDA helped organize a conference at RCC The Caribbean Focus, which became a grassroots Caribbean study and action program for the next fifteen years. RDA brought Kompe Plim (Evans Paul) to that conference, directly following his release from prison in March 1986. RDA and other Haitians networked at the conference with American black and white activists, and with Caribbean leaders and scholars like Dessima Williams. Haitians joined Puerto Rican, Jamaicans and Dominican community activists at the conference. Shortly afterward, the celebrated Haitian poet in exile in Boston, Jean Claude Martineau, coordinated a series of courses and pubic events at RCC called "The Haitian Reality." These brought together Haitian-Americans and progressive non-Haitians from all backgrounds. Martineau then traveled throughout the U.S. doing similar work. San Francisco's Laboissiere recalls, "Jean-Claude was crucial to us out here - he came out and his clear yet magical approach galvanized us. Martineau was my mentor in those days."

By the time of the election of Jean-Bertrand Aristide as the first democratically elected president of Haiti in 1990, Haitian-Americans had done their work well across the U.S. A significant beginning had been made toward involving non-Haitian Americans in work to support Haitian refugees, human rights in Haiti, the democratic struggle within Haiti, and especially to fight U.S. policies. Groups like American Friends Service Committee (AFSC) added Haiti to their agenda in Florida, New York and New England. Members of the U.S. Congressional Black Caucus, especially Ron Dellums of California and John Conyers of Michigan, became involved. TransAfrica Forum and several African-American organizations began to target Haiti in their work.

The first local coalitions between Haitian-American and U.S. progressives formed as Haiti solidarity organizations: KONBIT and Haiti Communications Project in Boston; the Bay-Area Haitian-American Council (BAHACO) in San Francisco for example. NCHR expanded into solidarity and human rights work in Haiti itself. The Haiti Action Project formed in New York. There were other groups in Miami, especially the Little Haiti (North Miami) Haitian Community Center, which motivated Catholic church groups in non-Haitian communities to become involved with Haitian refugee organizations, even after Father Gerard Jean-Juste a Haitian priest, played a major role in this work, returning to Haiti at Aristide's request.

# PHASE TWO:
# CITIZEN DIPLOMACY TO RESTORE DEMOCRACY

These groups were small at first and uncertain of their niche in the world of U.S. activism. Then came the shock of the coup that ousted President Aristide in 1991, and the brutal reign of terror and chaos that followed under Raul Cedras and Michel François. As Max Blanchet says, "The second phase of the U.S. Haiti solidarity movement went into high gear."

The meteoric growth and increased militancy of the U.S. solidarity movement was clearly initiated by Haitians and Haitian-Americans from all walks of life who, on hearing of Titid's (popular nickname for Aristide) ouster in late September 1991, poured into the streets of every city and small town in America where Haitians resided.

Such street demonstrations were not new for Haitians in the U.S. - they had been coming out in large numbers to celebrate or protest since the fall of Baby Doc. On January 28, 1986, about 1500 Haitians poured into the streets to celebrate in Miami's Little Haiti - prematurely - an erroneous U.S. State Department announcement of Duvalier's departure. The Miami Herald referred to "looting and rioting" which was violently suppressed by police who arrested about 100 Haitians.

Demonstrations continued until Duvalier did flee in the wake of a massive popular uprising in Haiti. On Feb. 7, 1986, as many as 3,000 were in the streets of Miami, with large groups in smaller cities like Fort Lauderdale, Homestead and Fort Pierce, where large range Haitians took to the streets.[4] Some of the Catholic priests serving Haitians in Florida were key organizers of these demonstrations.

The New York Daily News said nearly 10,000 demonstrated in Manhattan and Brooklyn daily between Feb. 2 and Feb. 10, 1986. [5] In Boston, on Feb. 2, the Globe said 150 gathered at City Hall Plaza where the JFK Federal building is also located - the place where Haitians would demonstrate ever after. Frantz Minuty of COSAH and Myrtha Dupoux used a bullhorn provided by Philippe Geneus, "We must restore all democratic freedoms in Haiti. We too have human rights," said Minuty. Dupoux cried out for the women of Haiti who bore the brunt of Duvalier's reign of rape and violence. The slogans shrewdly aimed at Americans: one banner read, "Massachusetts Taxpayers, Your Money is Enlarging Baby Doc's Bank Account."[6] On Feb. 7, in Boston Haitians marched to the Haitian consulate to confront a cowering "Macoute" consul - with the crowd demanding he be replaced, installing their own candidate, local Haitian activist Jean Geneus. (Geneus was made official Consul by Aristide in 1991, serving until 1998. As of 2003, he was Haiti's ambassador to Argentina.)[7]

In 1990, another round of impressive street rallies by Haitians drew the attention of American activists of many persuasions. This time, the target of protest was the label of being "Haitian" as a "risk factor" for AIDS, and the refusal to allow Haitian blood donors. In April, a Haitian crowd, estimated variously at between 50,000 and 120,000, poured across the Brooklyn bridge to demand an end to such racist practices. Three thousand marched in Boston on April 5, and more than 5,000 in Miami in May.[8] Again, Haitians forged alliances broadly: in San Francisco, New York and Boston, local chapters of the gay militant group, ACT UP, marched side-by-side with Haitian groups.

The coup took place. In 1991 it dashed the first genuine hope for democracy in Haiti, perhaps since independence. To be sure, there were already political splits; even among Haitians in the U.S. There was considerable criticism of Aristide's movement, Lavalas, and of Aristide himself - especially from the far left and in the pages of the ever-radical Haiti Progres (a weekly Haitian newspaper published in Port-au-Prince and Brooklyn, NY). Yet initial policy moves by Aristide - collecting taxes from the rich for the first time, announcing agrarian reform, making headway in trimming bureaucracy, and moving rapidly toward a meaningful minimum daily wage, had increased the hopes of many that this time there could be meaningful change in Haiti.

It should be no surprise that so many Haitians came out and demonstrated - and kept coming out, night after night - to demand the restoration of democracy in Haiti and to blame the U.S. for instigating the coup. But to non-Haitian Americans, even those already engaged in Haitian matters, the passion and clarity of vision, and the incredible unity of those crowds was impressive. In New York, the Times said there were 60,000, the Haitian press cited 120,000; in Miami, between 5000 and 8000 were in the streets almost nightly. In smaller towns with Haitian communities there were impressive numbers, and some arrests and police crack downs, as in Lake Worth and Homestead, Florida. The Herald[9] said that during the first week of the coup d'etat, the crowds moved from looting and burning to singing, dancing, marching for miles on end, and then silent vigils. Even in places like San Francisco and Los Angeles with relatively few Haitians, the solidarity community brought out hundreds.

In Boston, at least 5,000 (the Globe said "more than 2,000" but other estimates were much higher) went to the familiar protest site of City Hall Plaza, and again Philippe Geneus was there with his bullhorn.[10] At Roxbury Community College where I was at the time, Haitian students simply went from classroom to classroom calling for us all to go downtown to Columbus Avenue. I remember the thrill of seeing that throng, sad but determined, peaceful but militant including Haitian matriarchs barely able to get to the plaza with walkers and on grandchildren's arms; business people and nurses; waiters and sanitation workers; Haitians literally just arrived from the island, and teenage Haitian-Americans who could speak little Creole and who had never been to their homeland. An African-American legislator turned to me and said, "Now this is impressive. We could learn from this!"[11]

# AMERICANS FULLY INVOLVED:
# THE SOLIDARITY ARMY GEARS UP

At this point two groups of people joined the ranks and swelled the movement: people, especially from church backgrounds, who had been involved in Haiti but not in politics; and people who had been actively involved in many political struggles in places other than Haiti. This latter group - especially those from earlier solidarity struggles - was a significant force in helping the solidarity movement "take off" in 1991.

As a person with a history of involvement, my feelings at the time may be representative. We fought racial segregation in the U.S. and the laws were overturned. We successfully organized to end the war in Vietnam and we were deeply involved in solidarity work against Apartheid and in Central America.

Along came the masses in Haiti, throwing out the dictators and then electing a liberation theology priest as president. Most of us had never focused on Haiti. We suddenly realized it was the place where slaves first successfully rose up and where blacks defeated the white empires of France, Britain and Spain. Haiti seemed to be one hope of the world in terms of change.

I became involved in solidarity and the struggle for justice in Haiti in 1986 when I joined the campaign to restore Jean Bertrand Aristide to power following the coup d'etat in 1991. Until Aristide's restoration in 1994 and to some extent as late as 1997, there was quite an army of us - black and white U.S. activists from other movements and campaigns, from labor unions to peace groups, from socialist political parties to church social justice committees - who turned our attention and energies to Haiti.

Many members of that solidarity army report similar backgrounds and motivation. They, too, first became involved in Haiti solidarity work in the late 1980s or 1990s after long activism in other areas. Paul Shannon of the American Friends Service Committee (AFSC), who worked with the Haitian-American and U.S. solidarity group, KONBIT, and who joined the New England Observer Delegations to Haiti (NEOD), had been doing grassroots anti-war and social justice work since 1970 - including work for farm workers, the anti-Apartheid struggle, and solidarity work with Central America. Marie Kennedy, Associate Dean and Professor at the College of Public and Community Service, University of Massachusetts, Boston, catalogues a long list of domestic and international social justice struggles in which she was involved from the late 1950s. Sister Lena Deevy, Director of the New England Irish Immigration Center, was a leader in Irish solidarity and refugee struggles. She had been involved in Central America, and anti-Apartheid and anti-racism work, and then Haiti in the 1990s.

Bob Corbett is a philosophy professor from St. Louis who does not consider himself a solidarity activist, but whose "Corbett's Haiti e-mail List" is an important tool for communication among all elements of Haitian and U.S.-Haiti solidarity work. Corbett says that for years before he became involved in Haiti, he was "an activist struggling against much of U.S. foreign policy from Vietnam to the Gulf war." Noam Chomsky is perhaps a special case because of his incredible influence and prominence in every area of progressive politics. Although he says he is "not formally part of anything," he has had a major impact on Haiti solidarity work. Though he was writing about Haiti in the 1980s, he did not visit Haiti until 1993.

Shortly afterward, he began to appear at meetings to support Haitian peasants and others struggling against the military inside Haiti, and he began to include U.S. policy toward Haiti in all of his scathing and insightful indictments of U.S. policy.

A related cadre in the Haiti solidarity army that mobilized after 1991 were those active in other political and liberation struggles, who originally had been involved in Haiti for personal reasons. Chris Tilly, Professor of Economics at the University of Massachusetts at Lowell, and board member of both *Dollars & Sense* magazine and Grassroots International, first became interested in Haiti when, just out of college, he did clerical and manual labor in a hospital with many Haitian co-workers. He had been far more involved in Cuba, where he went specifically for political reasons, and Mexico, where he "found the left stirring in various ways." He also became even involved in South Africa. "When I first worked with Grassroots International in 1991, we had no programs in Latin America. We added our Haitian project that same year."

Scholars, politicians and community leaders from other Caribbean societies who had long stood in support of Haiti became prominent in the new solidarity efforts. In addition to Dessima Williams of Boston, Mel King is the founder of Boston's Rainbow Coalition, former State Representative and mayoral candidate. Representative Byron Rushing; Wellesley Professor Selwyn Cudjoe; and Latina public health activist Milagros Padilla also joined effort.[12]

There is a core of non-Haitians in the Haiti solidarity movement in the U.S. whose first and primary focus has always been Haiti, but who were originally not political. They were first involved in religious work or music, art or other cultural activities, or they had Haitian friends or lovers. Many of them became politicized by the coup.

John Engle facilitates The Experiment in Alternative Leadership, continuing his long-time work with Limye Lavi and Beyond Borders, who work "out of devotion to Christ...for peace and justice." Engle moved to Haiti in 1991 to work for EAPE, an evangelical Christian education group and then helped form Beyond Borders in 1992. Beyond Borders provided housing and other support for many solidarity delegations to Haiti, throughout the coup period and afterward. While in the U.S. doing support work for Beyond Borders, Engle says, "I began to see the need for Americans to do something about bad foreign policy."

Markus Schwartz, a New York musician and Clayton Ross Kilgore, a San Franciso artist, became intrigued by Haitian culture through the arts. "I believe the arts are the single most powerful tool Haitians have to change misconceptions about

Haitian people," Schwartz says. He is part of the Haitian jazz quintet, Mozayik, which has performed in Japan and Cuba with support from the Haitian government. Schwartz still sees his work as non-political, yet his group "occasionally supports solidarity groups by performing." Kilgore joined the Global Exchange and the Quixote Center as part of the international observer team, the International Coalition for Independent Observers (ICIO) for the 2000 elections.

In all quarters of the solidarity movement, a crucial role has been played by women - Haitian women, women from other Caribbean societies, and American women. Haitian-American women's groups have been involved and militant from the start - groups like Asosiyasyon Famn Ayisyen nan Boston (AFAB) in Boston; FANM (Fanm Ayisyen Nan Miyami) in Miami; and Dwa Fanm in New York. Women have provided an anchor for solidarity and the grassroots struggle. Some female activists have been critical of President Aristide for policies adversely affecting women.

Strong women leaders on either, or both, sides of the divide are Bev Bell, who helped Aristide craft his public relations during the exile; Laurie Richardson, a leader in various parts of the movement, including work for the Quixote Center and the Mouvman Paysan Papay (MPP), (and now a critic of both MPP and Aristide) Jane Regan, a sharp critic of Aristide's, but an important link between the solidarity community and the Haitian reality. During the coup she co-directed *Haiti Info*, a biweekly report on the repression there; Michelle Karshan, who worked in the States as a solidarity leader during the coup, and continues as Aristide's foreign press liaison; Laura Flynn, who worked for the Washington Office on Haiti and later for President Aristide; Amy Willentz, author of an excellent book on Haiti under the Duvaliers, (*The Rainy Season)* who translated Aristide's most widely read book, *In the Parish of the Poor,* but who is now a sharp Aristide critic; and Melinda Miles, who became involved as a teenager during the coup period, and now directs Haiti Reborn at the Quixote Center, crafting and coordinating much of the on-going solidarity work to support the democratic process and oppose the U.S./OAS aid embargo.

During the repression under the military junta, Haitian and solidarity women played key roles both in Haiti and in the U.S. Haiti Women was founded in Boston and Haiti in 1993. It sought to solidify the role of women in the Haitian struggle and to expose problems and issues of gender that are key to understanding poverty and oppression in all societies. Dessima Williams, a veteran of similar struggles in her native Grenada, joined Haitian-American and U.S. women in that struggle. A few others involved in this effort were: Myrtha Dupoux of the Democratic Haitian Resistance (RDA) in Boston; Loune Viaud who has recently been honored by the Robert F. Kennedy Memorial Center for Human Rights for her public health work both in Boston and in Haiti; Suzy Castor, an activist, scholar and director of a social research center in Port au Prince; Marie Kennedy, New England Observer Delegation organizer and University of Massachusetts/Boston professor, and Ellen Israel, a teacher's midwives and women's health worker in Boston and Haiti.[13]

## STIMULI IN THE CALL TO ACTION

The use of radio has been widely heralded as a major stimulus for popular action in Haiti. Radio has been equally important for Haitian-American activists, especially in cities like Miami, New York and Boston where there were many Creole radio voices. Film has been another important tool used to focus U.S. opinion on the Haitian reality and to the role played by U.S. Jean-Claude Martineau, the poet, who narrated the classic, *Bitter Cane,* was involved in motivating and narrating another crucial film Hart and Dana Perry's *Haiti: Killing the Dream*, produced by Crowing Rooster films. The movie helped stimulate activism when it was shown nationally on PBS in 1992. Other important films of the media blitz between 1990 and 1995 which informed an American public about Haiti, were Jac Avila and Vanyoka Gee's *Krik, Krak,* Kevin Pina's *Haiti Harvest of Hope,* and Rudi Stern's *Coup de Grace.* Solidarity groups helped involve financiers like Abbie Rockefeller in these media efforts. (These films are described, with contact information, at Windows on Haiti, www.haitiforever.com.)

As in the case of Cuba and Central America, an important tool used to stimulate American political understanding of Haiti have been delegations and study/ work tours, organized by churches, political and community groups, high schools and universities, and individuals. Bob Corbett, a Philosophy Professor at Webster College in St. Louis, is perhaps the person who organized most of these: 30 delegations with 500 participants. These were non-political "work experience" trips; they drew people into the Haitian culture. Many returned home to become involved in solidarity work. A number of universities, from Harvard and Boston College to American University and Stanford, organized trips to Haiti and many students became politicized simply by experiencing the reality of Haitian poverty, and its relationship to unjust U.S. foreign policy.

Melinda Miles, now a full-time Haiti solidarity worker, first went to Haiti in 1993. "I was sixteen, a high school junior. We focused mostly on the sick and dying during that trip, visiting clinics and hospices in Port au Prince and Gros Morne, and visiting peasant families in Brunette... That trip was the first exposure I had to the world and to poverty. I have dedicated to Haiti ever since." Marie Kennedy had no deep involvement with Haiti until she joined a delegation: "going to Haiti, seeing the warmth of ordinary Haitians and the courage of underground activists, seeing and hearing the violence of the military and paramilitary first hand, putting ourselves at risk, and realizing that a few people could make a big difference we came back committed."

After the coup, delegations proliferated and became more overtly political. Among the groups sending groups were Global Exchange, National Lawyers Guild, American Friends Service Committee, Quixote Center, Pax Christi, various Roman Catholic dioceses and individual congregations of many denominations. (These were clearly distinguished by their focus on social justice and political change, from the missionary enterprises in earlier years by all faiths, and more recently by fundamentalist Christians.)

I, myself, was an organizer of a solidarity group organized working with delegations, the New England Observer Delegation to Haiti (NEOD). From 1993 to 1997, NEOD organized eight delegations to Haiti, one to the Boston Haitian-American community to assess their views, and one study and action tour to Haiti and the Dominican Republic, with special focus on Haitians in the Dominican Bateyes (sugar cane plantations).

NEOD was a response to a direct request by the Government of Haiti through Consul General Jean Geneus. Geneus approached Ehrl Dumas of the Haiti Communications Project and me, proposing that we organize a delegation to Haiti. The purpose was to monitor the return of democracy to Haiti as envisaged in the Governors Island accords of September 1993. President Aristide met the delegation in Massachusetts in late October, alerting us to the possibility of the failure of the junta to comply. Aristide asked NEOD to go to Haiti anyway, "to go where I cannot go." NEOD accepted this task, adding to the goal of supporting Aristide's return, two others: to "shine the light" on U.S. and UN activities in Haiti, and especially to meet people from popular organizations and other Haitians to show international solidarity. [14]

Delegations traveling to Haiti the first time, we were amazed to see a highly politically literate peasantry (despite the lowest real literacy rate in the Western Hemisphere), a very mobilized grassroots community, and what appear to be the beginnings of a genuine social and political revolution. Delegates are utterly appalled at both the extraordinary poverty and total breakdown of the country's infrastructure.

This experience is often a pivotal one for our personal and political lives. We came back convinced that positive change must happen in Haiti, that it could happen, that the people of Haiti were determined to make it happen, and that we could play an important role. We truly believed, as our co-chair Dessima Williams told us, that we were a first wave of "citizen diplomats" who would change U.S. policy.

# SOLIDARITY IN FULL SWING

Beginning in 1992, excitement began to build as President Aristide spoke to huge crowds in city after city. In Boston, he received an honorary degree at Roxbury Community College as thousands surrounded the building where he spoke. Haitian activists who had been forced into exile teamed up with Haitian-American groups and the newly organized solidarity coalitions. The Peasant Movement of Papaye (MPP) opened its exile office in Boston and became a center solidarity work.

Haitian consuls and the government of Haiti, in exile, worked with Haitian, Diaspora and solidarity groups to craft very successful public relations and lobby campaign to galvanize people who supported the return of President Aristide.

The U.S. immigration (INS) handling of huge numbers of fleeing Haitians added a sense of urgency to the movement. In September 1992, Bay area Haitian-Americans and solidarity supporters took to sea with the help of the "Peace Navy," to simulate a "refugee landing." The INS took this seriously and became a laughing stock when it incarcerated prominent U.S. citizens as "refugees."

In early 1993, "Camp Clintons" sprang up on college campuses from Dartmouth and Yale to Berkeley, Stanford and the University of California at Davis. These were hastily constructed pens with barbed wire set up on campus malls to mimic the camp at Guantanamo where refugees were housed in blistering heat and primitive conditions. In May, thirty activists were arrested as they blocked the new Federal Building in Oakland, California, which housed local INS offices.[15] During the summer of 1994, Haitians and solidarity activists on both coasts teamed up with Act Up (a gay AIDS activist group) to protest the continuing incarcerations at Guantanamo, discrimination against Haitians, and a special internment camp for those with HIV/AIDS. Members of NEOD and others were arrested in August for blocking access to the Boston U.S. Coast Guard station from which Haitians in INS custody were being sent to Guantanamo.[16]

Between 1992 and 1994, local solidarity coalitions across the country sponsored a stream of public events with exiled Haitian leaders, some of whom came from Haiti at considerable risk. Among these were Father Reynaud Clerisme, Prime Minister Claudette Werleigh, Renée Preval, Haitian-left political leader Ben Dupuy, and MPP leader Chavannes Jean-Baptiste.

The media was clearly courted - local handlers saw to it that President Aristide and many of the speakers not only gave press conferences but also had private meetings with editors at major newspapers and television stations. Special events at city halls and state legislatures resulted in city and state resolutions, as well as heavy lobbying by local and state officials of their U.S. Congressional delegations.[17]

1994 was a peak year for the U.S. Haiti solidarity movement highlighted by the U.S.-imposed return of President Aristide in October. New national and local solidarity groups came into being. Among these were the Haiti Support Coalition (February), Haiti National Network (April), Voices for Haiti (June) and Haiti Women (June). Established efforts like those of the Quixote Center, Washington Office on Haiti, Pax Christi, and TransAfrica Forum, worked around the clock.

Aristide himself crisscrossed the country for a third time, drumming up support, speaking to ever-larger and more enthusiastic audiences. Rep. Joseph Kennedy and the Congressional Black Caucus worked the Congress and lobbied President Clinton. Literally thousands of U.S. citizens became involved from coast to coast.

By late spring, 1994, splits had begun to appear and threatened a unified support for the return of democracy to Haiti. Some groups, notably Kennedy's Haiti Support Coalition and TransAfrica Forum, seemed to support a U.S. intervention implicitly, or - in the case of Kennedy - to demand such intervention outright. [18] Others were clearly very worried about an "invasion" and "occupation" as they called it. Among solidarity coalitions, The Haiti National Network (which spawned Voices For Haiti within months) - which was mobilized especially by NGOs like Oxfam America, and by the Washington Office on Haiti - expressed opposition to direct U.S. intervention, and strongly supported Aristide return.[19]

Other groups, including the Quixote Center and the New England Observer Delegation, were caught in the middle - opposing overt U.S. invasion, but lobbying for U.S. support for Aristide's return, and an end to what many called the "U.S. double game." (Epitomized by an incident in 1993 when a U.S. warship carrying advance advisors to prepare for Governors Island implementation was "turned back" by paramilitary FRAPH members at the Port au Prince harbor.) Even MPP and Haitian government officials claimed to oppose such an invasion - which would clearly violate the Haitian Constitution, and recall the earlier brutal U.S. invasion and long occupation.

Within solidarity and Diaspora groups, a spirited but collegial debate about intervention and/or restoration took place from May until September. NEOD met with TransAfrica for a first discussion in April 1994, moderated by a Haitian government official from Washington, D.C. It seemed to NEOD participants that some others painted the debate sides as either "you are FOR Aristide's return and then you support U.S. intervention, or you do not support such intervention and you are therefore AGAINST Aristide's return." NEOD later told President Aristide, in a letter inviting him to participate in a "Summit" at RCC, "Politically, the solidarity movement, which opposes a U.S. invasion of Haiti, is overshadowed by liberal supporters of Haiti who issue well-meaning calls for U.S. intervention, overlooking the fact that it is ongoing intervention that helps to maintain the putschists in power." The NEOD position, included in the letter to Aristide, called a for a "third way":

> "end all forms of U.S. support for the repression; end U.S. persecution of refugees; stop U.S. violations of the OAS embargo; respect the sovereignty of the Aristide government in negotiations....There is no Knight in Shining Armor...to save Haiti (and to cast the U.S. in that role is preposterous beyond limit). There are no short-cuts to achieving the return of President Aristide in a way that allows the mobilization for basic human needs...in Haiti."[20]

A "Summit" between Aristide and a broad cross-section of Diaspora and solidarity groups took place on May 28. President Aristide debated face-to-face in English and Creole for hours at the RCC student center, at an invitation only meeting of some who were very critical of Aristide, and a majority of whom opposed Aristide's going back as part of a U.S. invasion. A Haitian American present that day, who is now opposed to the Aristide government and who asked not to be named, remembers: "On the one hand, it was impressive, there he was, a head of state, willing to take questions and even attacks from some who opposed him, and others who supported him but had painful misgivings. He spoke in riddles, in parables, and seemed to say both that he would oppose an invasion, might have to do 'things we may not want to do' to restore democracy."

From May until the U.S. invasion began October 2, the split continued, but all groups worked together to support the "restoration of democracy," with Aristide's mysticism providing a cover for the disunity. In Boston, the response to the Summit was the creation of the Haiti Anti-Intervention Network (HAIN). Member groups included Democratic Haitian Resistance (the Haitian resistance group very close to Lavalas). CEDRA (a generally anti-Aristide left-oriented research group) and a variety of other Haitian-American progressive organizations, as well as the New England Observer Delegation (NEOD), Oxfam, Grassroots International, the NLG, AFSC, the Central American solidarity groups and various left political parties.[21]

In some cities, the "split" was simply buried. Pierre Labossiere of BAHACO (Bay Area Haitian Action Council organized 1990) explains, "There was no split in San Francisco - we had lots of discussion and our approach was that we followed the grassroots groups in Haiti - they should be our guide." And we were having great success in building momentum to change U.S. policy. When small towns, churches and others started calling and asking how they could support Haiti, I knew Aristide was going back. Despite our long-time opposition to U.S. interventionism, we just felt he must go back, no matter what or by what method. Even our radical allies deferred to our judgment." Max Blanchet then of BAHACO, now strongly opposed to the Aristide government, partially agrees: "We felt an absolute need to return Aristide to power. We buried our doubts, and perhaps we were right in one sense. We didn't have an alternative solution, and perhaps U.S. intervention would avoid civil war in Haiti."

This confusing state of affairs came to a head when the U.S. troops landed on September 19. Secretary of State Warren Christopher proclaimed to the Security Coalition that the operation was a "coalition" of 33 countries, including Bolivia, Bangladesh and Bulgaria - but of course 90% of the troops and 100% of the command were U.S. (Such a public relations cover is familiar today as "the coalition of the willing.")[22]

HAIN had long planned a TDA (the day after) demonstration for City Hall Plaza in Boston - other coalitions had similar plans in New York and San Francisco. In some cities, these fell apart, and in Miami and New York small crowds of Haitians went to the streets to welcome the U.S. action. In Boston, a handful went to City Hall, including Myrtha Dupoux and Philippe Geneus of Democratic Haitian Resistance with his bullhorn - but the message was muted and divided - no to a U.S. invasion, yes to helping Aristide return. Over the next days, groups met and debated. Many wagged heads and pointed fingers at the U.S. for crashing in with the military as it always does. Yet Aristide had appeared at the U.N. to ask for U.N.

support for "restoration of Democracy," and the U.N. had given its sponsorship, the first time a U.S. led military intervention was approved by the Security Council without veto.[23]

"We were not sufficiently critical of Aristide," says Chris Tilly of NEOD, yet he said he and many others believed "most of the progressives in the Haitian community [were] in favor of the invasion." NEOD had been to Haiti three times, witnessing "repression, violence, empty streets, closed market places, and deathly quiet," yet had also been impressed with courageous popular leaders driven underground, whom they met clandestinely at considerable risk to the Haitians. Now that the "invasion" was a fait accompli, it was not clear to progressives that real democracy would be installed. NEOD, like many others who had been opposed to an invasion - now began to add their voices to that of Aristide himself - "We call on the Americans to complete the task and allow the return of President Aristide and democracy to Haiti," said a flyer at an October 8 demonstration against prolonged U.S. occupation.[24]

When Haitian Consul Jean Geneus approached NEOD with the idea of "going back to Haiti when the President returned," NEOD announced proudly that it would "fulfill [its] original purpose - that of witnessing the restoration of President Jean-Bertrand Aristide to office in Haiti."[25] Many other solidarity organizations made similar decisions.

## GOING BACK WITH TITID

When Aristide was restored to power on October 15, 1994, by a UN sanctioned U.S. force, many progressive Haitian-American and solidarity groups muted their opposition to what they and most grassroots Haitian groups called a "U.S. invasion." Many grumbled about the "Jimmy Carter deal, which gave refuge and payoffs to Cedras, Francois and others considered to be mass murderers guilty of crimes against humanity. Yet the moment was not ripe for quibbling, even over such major compromises.

As Aristide's plane landed, filled with U.S. State Department officials, but also including Rep. Joseph Kennedy and Rep. Maxine Waters of the Congressional Black Caucus, other planes brought solidarity delegations including NEOD, QC, Washington Office on Haiti, Global Exchange and several solidarity activists. Most Haitian-Americans and solidarity activists who witnessed the restoration were swept away, if only momentarily, by the incredible drama of the moment and the obvious joy of the Haitian people who filled the streets and who festooned their neighborhoods with decorations and banners proclaiming their love for Titid and their hope for the future.

At the same time, it was disturbing to see Aristide cut off from his people by a security cordons staffed by U.S. armed forces, isolated behind bullet-proof glass like a bird in a cage....U.S. military control over the ceremony...casts a troubling shadow over Haitian sovereignty." The NEOD report summarized the six-day visit: "(W)e saw the powerful hope of the Haitian people - hope shared by slum dwellers and peasants, merchants and students, young and old. We also felt their fear - fear masked by defiance, but fear nonetheless, since tens of thousands of armed men continue to threaten pro-democracy activists, despite the presence of U.S. troops. And amidst this hope and fear, we repeatedly saw the enormous arrogance of U.S. officials...who think they know what Haiti needs better that the Haitians...do."[26]

The day after dining at the Palace with Aristide, Kennedy and others, we traveled to Haiti's Central Plateau - only "liberated" a few days earlier by U.S. troops, who were already busily at work. The first unit of troops ignored pleas at the prison to free pro-Lavalas prisoners, and staunchly refused to seek out known Macoute and disarm them. "That's not our job," a U.S. officer told us. When we asked too many awkward questions, a helicopter landed with a higher-ranking officer who told Chavannes (who was with us) "don't cause trouble." A "Democracy Enhancement" worker with United State Agency for International Development (USAID) watched MPP leader Jean-Baptiste Chavannes jubilant welcome and said, "This won't last long. He's a demagogue." Chavannes reported to us that USAID was forming bogus community groups and giving them "aid," while trying to woo MPP groups in villages with promises of roads. It would not be long before NEOD and many others in Haiti and outside would see the strains of this bizarre marriage of necessity between the U.S. military and the populist priest in whom the Haitian people placed their trust.

# PHASE THREE (1995-2000): DISILLUSIONMENT AND DIVISION BEGIN

Though divisions in the movement and skepticism about Aristide had been there since before his election, they re-appeared after the Governors Island accord and emerged with increasing force and bitterness. Max Blanchet, of BAHACO in California, remembers before, we had been all for Lavalas and all against the

Haitian military and U.S. policy. We had known better from our own political perspective. We agreed with DeGualle's revealing assessment that the modern state is a cold monster - it has no friends and no enemies, only interests. Yet we had temporarily suspended this judgment. The misgivings flooded the movement immediately on Aristide's return with U.S. troops. A Tet Kole peasant leader told me, while I was in Haiti with Global Exchange in December of 1994, that the viability of Lavalas was dubious. That threw considerable cold water on the enthusiasm of many of us. The real change occurred when the Lavalas movement fell apart openly in 1995. There had been a foretaste with the departure of Konpe Plim (Evans Paul) in 1991. The split between the Aristide faction, Lavalas (FL), and the OPL (the political organization of Lavalas, which had fostered the coalition that won the 1991 election) was disastrous. OPL and FL needed each other equally as partners to bring about change in Haiti.

During the year leading up to the Presidential election in late 1995, Aristide, who had pledged to Clinton that he would not run again, in accordance with Haitian Constitutional term limits, seemed to waver on the issue. When Preval was chosen - some say as the candidate of Aristide, others insist he was tapped by OPL - there was obvious disenchantment by many who favored another candidate - often themselves, as many who knew him claimed was the case for Chavannes.[27] Chavannes stayed with Aristide through the election, in which Aristide referred to himself and Preval as twins.

Chavannes told an NEOD delegation that year, "MPP is one of many rivers that make up Lavalas, but we consider ourselves the biggest one."[28] Chavannes and Gerard Pierre-Charles (an OPL founder and spokesperson) said they wanted to transform a united Lavalas into a table around which all participants were sitting and, indeed, Preval ran on a ticket with the symbol of a table rather than the rooster under which Aristide had run, on the FNCD (Evans Paul's Party) ticket in 1990.

NEOD 5th delegation in March reflected the uncertainty of many solidarity groups: "Re-birth of Democracy or the Coup Continued, Haiti after Five Months of U.S. Occupation." Some grassroots organizers in Haiti denounced Aristide to the NEOD delegation. Rose Anne Auguste at her clinic in the Port-au-Prince neighborhood of Kalfou-Fey was blunt: "Aristide is a puppet in the hands of the U.S....Reconciliation without justice is a policy of treason." NEOD denounced the failure of the U.S. to disarm the former military, and its findings were a harsh criticism of the U.S. presence and strong support for the "Truth Commission" to assure that it would expose those who had committed atrocities.

The election of Preval brought more confusion to the solidarity movement. Aristide now castigated the Preval government. OPL, always a key part of the anti-liberalization coalition in Haiti, now saw its Prime Minister, Rosny Smarth, fall because Aristide and others accused him of a sell out.[29] One leading solidarity activist, who asks not to be identified, said: "By 1996, we were absolutely floored by the charges and counter-charges among Aristide, Preval, OPL, Chavannes and the grassroots groups. Most of us wanted to follow the lead of 'the people,' but it was difficult to know exactly what that meant. On the one hand, many popular organizations that had supported Aristide and Preval now deserted them. On the other hand, as we traveled around, we saw continuing support for Titid among peasants and slum dwellers. Between 1996 and 1999, most of us simply dropped out of Haiti work, or we focused entirely on specific projects like health care or support for peasant groups." Blanchet said the break, in 1996, within the Ti Legliz (little church) movement from which Aristide drew his base, was a final straw for many solidarity activists. By 2000, "the movement had largely disappeared back to a few (Quixote Center, TransAfrica Forum, NCHR, Partners in Health)."

Paul Shannon, the AFSC (American Friends Service Committee) organizer in Cambridge, characterizes this progression as: in 1987, the movement began to grow; from 1991 it was at peak strength until the U.S. invasion in 1994; in 1995 it was trying to find a way to survive; since 2000, it has been gone." Marie Kennedy and Chris Tilly of NEOD would not go that far. "We see the bulk of the remaining solidarity movement focusing on freeing up U.S. and multilateral aid to Haiti, and criticizing U.S. attempts to undermine the Haitian government. This is important work, but we would like to see the solidarity movement broaden its work."

Tilly, other NEOD members, and Haitian activists in Boston tried another tack in 1998-99, organizing a forum to mobilize Haitian-Americans around immigration issues, under the banner of the Haitian Issues Working Group, These activists recognized a strong potential for civic participation by Haitians in the U.S.

Melinda Miles, who worked for the Quixote Center from 1999 until 2003, sees things more positively. "From 1997 to 1999, the Quixote Center's Haiti Reborn program was without full-time staff. This transitional time corresponded to decreasing attention to Haiti in the United States as a whole." Miles remembers that a revival took place in 1999. One part of that was the re-emergence of the Quixote Center as a leader in the solidarity movement," especially with a revitalized Haiti Solidarity Week in 2000, as well as collaboration with the international Jubilee campaign to cancel the debt of Haiti and other developing nations. "The Quixote Center re-established its grassroots donor base," virtually its only funding source, "contrary to the rumor that we receive money from Haiti or foundations supporting

Aristide." "The election of 2000 provided the Quixote Center with an opportunity to validate its belief that the government of Haiti was in power because the Haitian people exercised their sovereign right to put it in power." The Quixote Center joined Global Exchange to set up the International Coalition of Independent Observers (ICIO) to monitor all the elections in Haiti throughout the year 2000. Miles says the Quixote Center's reporting of the ICIO findings "provides the basis for the only complete report on Haiti's elections in 2000."

# PHASE FOURTH (2000 – 2003): DEEP DIVISION, FURTHER DISILLUSIONMENT, AND SIGNS OF REBIRTH

One terrible event in the year 2000 stands out in the minds of many Haitians as well as solidarity people: the murder of Jean Dominique in April of that year. Dominique is widely hailed by those in all parts of the solidarity movement as having been a fearless journalist who exposed and challenged all who he felt had betrayed the Haitian people, violated human rights or yielded to corruption. Through his radio station, Haiti Inter, he pilloried some of Aristide's most violent opponents - like Dr. Rudolph Boulos in the Pharval scandal in which hundreds of Haitian children died from contaminated medications manufactured by Boulos' firm. But Dominique challenged Aristide's close associates as well. Some have felt he might have been the only Haitian capable of challenging Aristide directly for the Haitian people's support. Aristide's ally, Lavalas Senator Dany Toussaint, had threatened Dominique shortly before his murder - the timing is in dispute, like so many other facts. Some say the threat was made six months before the murder, with Dominique's criticism of Boulos coming much closer to the assassination. [30]

Though Aristide personally decried the murder, judicial inquiries seemed stymied at every turn, in coming up with indictments. Over the next three years, three judges involved in the investigations resigned and/or left Haiti. Dominique's widow, Michelle Montas, who took over his work at Haiti Inter, was repeatedly threatened, and on Christmas, 2002, she was attacked and her bodyguard murdered. Montas closed Haiti Inter in early 2003 and chose exile in the United States, claiming the threats were too serious and the government of Haiti provided no protection. She has continued to denounce the investigation as the first indictments were announced in April this year. Even some Aristide supporters acknowledge that those indicted were not the "intellectual authors" of the crime.[31]

Even those who remain active in solidarity with the government of Haiti and its campaign to restore international aid feel the Dominique case is tragic and has not been handled properly. "It was a turning point," says a California supporter "until there is progress there, many folks will believe, with considerable reason, that Lavalas has been involved in serious human rights violations."

The case, as well as strong evidence of other human rights abuses in Haiti has added ammunition to the evidence used by those now opposing Aristide and his government. These include former solidarity activists like Jane Regan, many of the NEOD's delegation members, Laurie Richardson (formerly of the Quixote Center), Max Blanchet, and others who played key roles in the campaign to return Aristide and democracy to Haiti. At ceremonies this April in Montreal, New York and elsewhere to commemorate the life and death of Dominique, opponents and supporters of Aristide stood together in tribute.

## U.S. EMBARGO OF AID TO HAITI PROVIDES A NEW FOCUS FOR SOLIDARITY GROUPS

Meanwhile, the U.S. pursued its course of isolating the Haitian government and depriving it of support. The most overt form of U.S. opposition to Aristide (and Haiti), was its pressure on the Inter-American Development Bank (IDB) to withhold previously approved loans of more than $500 million since 2000. Other loans and investment from the World Bank, the IMF and the E.U., as well as private investments, were either stopped or slowed by what solidarity activists call "the U.S. embargo against Haiti."

The Quixote Center and others in the U.S., working to support what they view as the democratically elected government of Haiti, seized the embargo as a campaign around which to reorganize solidarity. The Quixote Center (QC) launched the "Let Haiti LIVE" campaign to end the embargo. Throughout 2002 and 2003, QC worked with 40 solidarity groups in the U.S., Canada and Haiti, and with the Congressional Black Caucus and other U.S. Congress people. Rep. Barbara Lee of California introduced legislation to force the U.S. to release the aid. Many who had become discouraged with solidarity work began again to be active - including many church people. Miles says frankly, "The reason we began building a coalition was to counteract the polarization in the Haiti solidarity community, which corresponds to the polarization within Haiti. It is our hope that we can unite organizations in the U.S. on the issue of U.S. policy...and its impact on Haiti's progress toward democracy. The Let Haiti LIVE Coalition...advocates for U.S. policies which respect the independence and self-determination of the Haitian people and their Republic.... (O)ur primary goal is to make Let Haiti LIVE a vehicle for dynamic and well-informed grassroots activism to support the Haitian people."

## GROWING UNREST IN HAITI, A NEW KIND OF "SOLIDARITY" IN WASHINGTON

In Haiti, a counter-productive form of activism has been growing - with funding and support from hidden sources. In August and December of 2001, violent attacks took place against government targets, including the National Palace. Armed men carried out the December attack, some in uniform, accompanied by a helicopter later revealed to have been rented in the Dominican Republic. After missing Aristide, who had changed his plan to sleep at the palace only hours before the attack, the group killed one palace guard, suffered its own casualties and sped to the border for refuge. While opponents of Aristide insist the attack was an inside job, meant to garner support for the government, there is considerable independent evidence that this was a genuine coup attempt.

In the wake of the palace attack, pro-Aristide crowds burned Convergence property and struck out at known opposition figures, killing at least one person. The OAS later judged the government guilty of not providing adequate protection and required reparations for those harmed - which the Aristide government in fact paid in order to comply with OAS requirements to restore its aid, though not admitting guilt. Yet the OAS has never placed blame for the attack on the palace or suggested reparations be paid Haiti to atone for it.

Throughout this period, most mainstream media and some progressive media carried reports indicating that Aristide had lost favor with the people, had betrayed his agenda, and that Lavalas was directly responsible for most of the violence. Voices for Haiti was joined by Randall Robinson of TransAfrica Forum, Dr. Paul Farmer of Partners in Health, the film-maker Kevin Pina and others who condemned what they called a systematic campaign of disinformation. The Quixote Center published monthly reviews of articles about the violence and its sources.[32] The independent radical weekly, Haiti Progres, long respected in both solidarity and Diaspora circles, published a series decrying what it called a low-intensity conflict being waged covertly by a Haitian "contra" army, covertly supported from within the Dominican Republic by the Convergence and its U.S. handlers.[33]

The anti-government violence increased in 2003. A heavily armed band wearing t-shirts identifying them as "Armee San Manman" (Motherless Army) carried out organized attacks on a village and police station in the Central Plateau. In these and other incidents, similar attacks killed about 26 people between January and July. Paul Farmer is an internationally recognized public health activist who works in many countries, especially to combat diseases among the poor from Boston's Roxbury to the indigenous communities of Peru. He has long been part of the U.S.-Haiti solidarity movement, with his Partners in Health (Zanmi Lasante) organization, which runs a clinic in Hinche, in Haiti's Central Plateau. One of his clinic medical vans was destroyed in an attack this year on the near-by Peligre electric power station, and his staff and patients have suffered directly from the "Manman" attacks. He says, "When we complained about the former military hassling us (holding guns to our heads, taking our nurses hostage, etc.) NCHR said, initially, 'it didn't happen, pro-government propaganda.'" A journalist visiting the clinic was kidnapped by the armed group and sent an eyewitness account to the U.S. Embassy and to media - yet most media and the Embassy virtually ignored him.[34]

During this period of escalating violence in Haiti, a new self-described Haiti solidarity group appeared in Washington, D.C: the Haiti Democracy Project (HDP), founded in 2000 by James Morrell. Morrell had been a State Department employee working on Haiti's affairs.

Although Morrell calls himself a liberal, the HDP is primarily funded by the Haitian elite right-wing Boulos family, and its board is filled with known rightist Haitian and U.S. political figures. In December 2002, HDP announced the creation of the so-called "Coalition of 184 Civil Institutions" which many considered an attempt to create a more viable opposition than the Convergence, but which overlapped with it. In addition to the Haitian American Chamber of Commerce, the Center for the Development of Free Enterprise and other business interests, the 184 institutions included Chavannes Jean-Baptiste's MPP (Peasant Movement of Papaye). The HDP has directly attacked Haiti Reborn and members of the Congressional Black Caucus, calling them the "highly paid, well-organized pro-Aristide lobby." [35] Melinda Miles counters, "We are not pro-Aristide, we are pro-Haiti. We simply believe the sovereignty of the people of Haiti in selecting their government must be respected. And we are surely not highly paid!"

# SOME SIGNS OF HOPE AND CHANGE IN REGARD TO THE MOVEMENT

Some rays of hope appeared in 2003. The U.S. failed to persuade the OAS General Assembly in Chile in the summer that Haiti had failed to live up to its agreement to resolve the political crisis. The U.S. plan for regime change was taken off the table for the time being. The U.S. had intended he to use the recently adopted OAS charter to support removal of Haiti from membership. U.S. officials made an only somewhat veiled threat that the Charter would allow intervention to replace the government of President Aristide, allegedly for having failed to support "democracy and the free market," in the words of U.S. OAS Representative Roger Noriega.[36] Taking its lead from the Caribbean states of CARICOM, the OAS seems to be moving away from the U.S. position. Already in 2002, the OAS supported the IDB in de-linking international aid release from the political crisis as such. IDB insisted only that Haiti catch up on the arrears to its debt service (the U.S. refuses to consider debt cancellation for Haiti), which Haiti did by July of 2003. As a result, the IDB itself released an amount approximately equivalent to that which Haiti paid on its debt service.

Some human rights organizations, which had previously condemned only violence with suspected Lavalas or Haitian government origins, seemed more willing to take a balanced approach. In its first such condemnation, NCHR made a strong statement in late August against the murder of four Haitian Interior Ministry officials by an armed, uniformed group in the Central Plateau. At the same time, it called for the government of Haiti to condemn violent actions allegedly carried out by police and other officials, and for Lavalas to denounce acts of violence attributed to some of its local leaders.[37]

In Washington in August the first non-public conversations among all factions of the Haiti solidarity movement were initiated. People from within NCHR, QC and even HDP were among those involved. Although the first encounters were unproductive, it was obvious that recent developments in Haiti have made such attempts at a re-united U.S. Haiti solidarity movement not only desirable, but possible. As Merrie Archer of NCHR commented, the most important periods in the Haiti solidarity movement were 1991-1994, and - now. Another alienated solidarity activist from California said, "I have to admit, the embargo - and what seems to be some success in fighting it - have given some new wind to the solidarity movement."

In San Francisco, two long-time activists and friends who now stand on opposite ends of the solidarity spectrum, agreed on some things. Max Blanchet says, "For me the solidarity movement must be critical of U.S. policy - especially if it can be shown to be supporting covert attempts to overthrow the Haitian government. It is absolutely urgent to keep our distance from the Government as it becomes entangled in compromise." Pierre Labossiere says, "The solidarity movement here remains very supportive of the right of the Haitian people to choose its own government. It is our role to expose and fight the CIA, the World Bank and other instruments of U.S. policy that oppress the Haitian people. Let people in Haiti deal with the problems of the Haitian government and the arguments that always flourish in Haitian politics." Marie Kennedy and Chris Tilly in Boston would agree with both: "The government of Haiti should be supported as the sovereign government, and we do not want to help the United States oust that government, but that should not make it immune from criticism."

Melinda Miles of the Quixote Center says that is what her group and others fighting the U.S. aid embargo are doing. "The polarization of the movement is what has to be overcome. Everything today is couched in terms of "pro-Aristide" or "anti-Aristide." The Quixote Center is NOT pro-Aristide, we simply support the sovereignty of the government chosen by the Haitian people. Like the Haitians themselves, we also criticize when it is clear the Haitian government has erred. But as U.S. citizens, our main role is to expose and challenge U.S. policies that erode Haitian sovereignty and harm the Haitian people."

# EPILOGUE:
# COMMENTS FROM SOLDIERS
# IN THE SOLIDARITY ARMY

A questionnaire sent to U.S. solidarity activists received about fifty responses in a month's time. These included eight Haitian Americans active in organizing or coordinating non-Haitian solidarity work, three U.S. expatriates living in Haiti and long part of the solidarity movement, and more than 20 U.S. citizens who were, and most still are, involved in what they would consider "Haiti solidarity work." Several responses came from Americans who do not think they do political work, or even solidarity work as such, but who are connected to the movement in various ways, and who remain involved in Haiti.

# THE RESPONSES

Paul Farmer of Partners in Health, who is widely praised by people on all sides of the controversy about solidarity work for his work at a clinic in rural Haiti, continued to criticize some human rights organizations and media in the United States for "blaming the victim," and for focusing on immediate acts of violence or corruption rather than what he calls the "structure of poverty." He responded briefly to the survey, but noted that his positions have been widely publicized and best represented in his 2002 introduction to the new edition of *The Uses of Haiti*, and in articles written recently in *America Magazine* and *Le Monde Diplomatique.*

"Alas, the 'Haiti solidarity community,' to which I belong, has been almost as fractured as the Haitian political class...Within Haiti and without, the 'Haiti solidarity community' is divided on just about everything. 'The human rights community' is certainly full of strange bedfellows...(it) is riven by deep division (over)...the rights of the poor and their legal rights. The so-called progressive commentary from outside Haiti can also erase history to make a point...Calls to ignore the results of democratic elections are not usually involved in democratic niceties...Most of these complaints come...from the self-appointed leaders of various small movements, each with sponsors in Europe or North America...

"Structural violence (causing misery, hunger and inequality) has been perpetrated from above and without... It will be reflected in local violence...You'd think progressive observers...would make this connection. But many don't....So we hear endless complaints about the corruption of the Haitian government, with no mention of the industrial-strength corruption of the United States...Haiti's 'flawed electoral processes' are dissected while serious allegations of disenfranchisement in Florida are given short shrift"

As for our own international "solidarity community," I sometimes doubt that even we are capable of consensus. My pessimism is based in part on hearing from self-proclaimed Haitian progressives...with some grudge against the elected government. My pessimism is also based on observing a predominantly ahistorical analysis of the current Haitian crisis. The crisis has always been transnational, compounded by the forces of globalization, so comments on "local" problems, whether in Gonaives or a village near the Dominican border, are misleading if they do not bring into relief the connections between the actions of the powerful (few of whom live in Haiti) and the poor.

I would argue that instead of trying to identify 'good' popular organizations in Haiti that people of good will should instead spend some time attempting to identify the powerful, malignant forces and actors that seek to deny sovereignty to the Haitian poor. Most of these actors are not going to be found within Haiti's borders. Are progressive political activists willing to stand up to them and defend Haiti's right to govern its own affairs through a democratically elected government? Are we for or against sovereignty?[38]

A Haitian public health activist, now working among solidarity groups in an east coast city, responded:

"Alas, Paul, he is too dependent on getting handouts and protection from the Haitian government. Aristide IS a monster. We were misled - though some of us had doubts even then. Most solidarity groups know this now, and they spend their resources helping people directly, and don't waste time on a hopeless and corrupted cause. The problem with Aristide is that he has lost all contact with the people - look at whom he entertains at Tabarre. He is going down the same road as Duvalier. There is a strong lobby backed by the interests of some with a stake in the current Haitian economy that supports the government and would distract us by telling us about U.S. evils. We know those evils, but we also know the local evils that are destroying our people. Aristide, if not a murderer himself, is harboring murderers, and those who support him are guilty with him."[39]

Noam Chomsky also responded to the survey. Chomsky, celebrated for his opposition to U.S. empire, came to the Haitian struggle in a major way after a 1993 visit. During that time, he campaigned actively against U.S. policy toward Haiti, speaking for and with solidarity groups and Haitian groups like MPP, as well as the government in exile. About the solidarity movement, he says, "Unfortunately it is now very weak. There was a brief upsurge in the mid-1990s, but I'm afraid it has largely dissipated." Consistent with his well-known thesis, "the manufacture of consent," Chomsky focuses on the role of U.S. media: "The media joined from the start in the campaign to undermine the democratic government of Haiti, openly supporting the Bush-Clinton policies, flatly refused - with extremely rare exceptions - to publish critical facts they knew well about the extent of U.S. support for the military junta...completely falsified the 'liberation,' presenting it as a humanitarian operation when they knew perfectly well that the condition...was that the (Haitian) government adhere to an extremely harsh neoliberal program..." From that point on, Chomsky says, the media "also helps foster divisions (in the solidarity movement) by lining up uncritically with the government efforts to undermine Aristide."

Brian Concannon was active in domestic violence advocacy and Central America solidarity work before going to Haiti as a United Nations volunteer attorney in 1995. He divides his time between the western United States and Haiti, continuing work as an attorney for BAI, the legal advocacy team successful in prosecuting some of those responsible for violence during the coup period. BAI is an independent group, but is funded by the Haitian government. Some of Concannon's thoughts about the solidarity movement - which he continues to work with in the United States - are:

> "Despite many people falling off the bandwagon (for solidarity) and being confused or angry...the movement is growing today, and much better organized and effective than it has been at any time since at least 1995....The Haiti solidarity movement in general seems good at organizing over relatively simple, but severe 'big tent issues': the Duvaliers, the de-facto regime (during the coup)...and immigration issues...The weakness is (on) the deeper issues like the depth of democracy...These...require...more intensive attention."

A key problem now for Concannon is that, "so many overemphasize the role, both good and bad, of one person (Aristide), rather than focusing on the development of institutions and practices." He also points, as do many involved in other solidarity campaigns, to the problem of how to know what is "really going on in Haiti, for people with limited direct knowledge of Haiti. They sometimes hitch on to someone in Haiti they trust, and go wherever that person (or group) goes....The transfer of information across distance, language and cultural barriers is difficult. The solidarity movement needs to find ways of systematically receiving information from a broad spectrum of the grassroots community in Haiti."

Like Chomsky, Concannon blames disinformation: "I think the U.S. government disinformation has been highly successful in dividing or demobilizing the movement.... People who don't believe they are influenced by U.S. policy but find themselves agreeing with it consistently, need to take a hard look at whether this is what the majority of Haiti's people would them to do." The answer, Concannon believes, is to "listen to and take direction from the majority of Haitians, on a daily basis."

Melinda Miles of the Quixote Center strongly agrees: "We truly believe that the hope for the future of Haiti (and the world, really) is to link average Americans with average Haitians. This is where power lies." She feels the polarization in the movement stems from disagreements among "leaders" and groups - including NGOs in Washington - and not from disagreements among average Haitians. "The need to associate everything with either pro-Aristide or anti-Aristide...is deeply poisonous," and she feels the antidote is to maintain close contacts with the Haitian people themselves, "partnerships with grassroots organizations in Haiti." Miles underscores her views by her belief that, "The strength of the Haiti solidarity movement is the power of Haiti itself. Haiti creates life-long activists, and the story of Haiti's struggles creates passion that is unparalleled."

One U.S. political progressive who first went to Haiti from New York with a delegation in 1993 says, "After scarcely a week, I was hooked. This was a culture and a people with a history of struggle for liberation. It is like being a fish on the beach of the U.S. anti-liberation non-culture, being thrown into the water of an honest, popular movement for real change."

Paul Shannon of AFSC, introduced to Haiti by his work with KONBIT who traveled to Haiti in the 1990s, commented, "Haitians and non-Haitians were able to work together, to respect each other and accomplish a tremendous amount of work. It was a great experience working with a movement that was not primarily Anglo; it was a wonderful time!" The impact was incredible - you'd come home almost delirious with an infusion of hope, that change could be possible, that there were genuine radicals working at the local level to create a mass movement in Haiti for change. Yet over the years, I went with delegations sponsored by U.S. NGOs with different ideologies. I watched as local fixers in Haiti steered us toward specific groups who told us more or less what we wanted to hear. I think this is a problem for all sides in the solidarity movement. It becomes very difficult to know who really speaks for the Haitian people, especially when you don't live there and can't speak Creole."

Bob Corbett maintains "Corbett's List" where those of all persuasions can make themselves heard. He spent many years as a political activist "from Vietnam to the Gulf War." For twenty years, he has regularly visited Haiti (50 times) and organized work/experience delegations for Americans to involve them in direct projects of aid and collaboration with grassroots groups in Haiti. Corbett now believes it is impossible, at least for him, to be an honest activist. This seems to apply especially to work in solidarity with Haiti, which he now eschews, providing his e-list instead, which he views as an "important tool for people interested in Haiti for gathering and sharing ideas."

Corbett criticizes not only the solidarity movement but also activism in general. "As an outsider to that work, the greatest weakness seems to me to be a desire not to face up to the level of problems created by Haitian politics and the desire to blame outside sources as the dominant problem in Haiti. Such views seem to me to be dream worlds more influenced by ideology than any open, serious and honest analysis...of the reality of Haiti." Corbett criticizes the use of the term "disinformation" in the questionnaire sent to the respondents: "The question reflects precisely the desire to put such influence into nice good-guy, bad-guy modes, and to ignore the murky, difficult, confused, and contradictory realities..." Corbett goes further: "When I encountered social issues in the world which upset me...I quickly realized actions just on my own... were nearly useless, so I sought out 'solidarity.' But, my intellectual being was torn apart, since every such political group I have EVER encountered played terribly loose with 'truth' in order to move other people to follow their will." After seeing the complexity and contradictions within the groups and movements he'd sought out for solidarity work, Corbett wound up making an either-or choice, which he admits he's uneasy with: "I chose the search for truth...and truth-telling and sharing my views as challenges to others, and to stop participating in political movements...It's a very uneasy compromise and I am in no way deluded that I know 'better' than others."

A woman who was active until recently in the work against the U.S. embargo dropped out of that work and she agrees with the general critique of solidarity work as a whole: "Solidarity movements are inherently unable to deal with the complexity and contradictions of a society like Haiti. I've chosen not to work any more with the local solidarity people who are my friends because I've seen up close in Haiti just how unjust the government is now. The situation with violence and corruption in Lavalas and government circles has deteriorated these last two years. It's terrible. You have to draw the line somewhere and say: this is too much; I can't support these people any longer, even when I know the U.S. policy is also unjust. Because we live here in the belly of the beast, and because we know about the level of atrocities of U.S. policies in the past and we know the current gang in Washington will be doing this again, we just focus on the evil giant. But when I know my friends in Haiti are suffering directly from government injustice, and no-one in the pro-government camp wants to hear about it, I just can't put aside my angers and fears and my loyalty to those who are suffering. Of course, I know the violence and corruption are caused indirectly by U.S. policies, too. Financially, the squeeze the government is under - mostly because of U.S. policies, but also because of greed among the political class - that squeeze creates the situation where extortion and the threats that go with it are the only way to make a living you are accustomed to - whether for the government minister or the local policeman. But understanding that doesn't excuse it. Yet, here in the U.S., those who lead the active solidarity groups say that anything critical of Lavalas or the Haitian government will hurt the movement against U.S. unjust policies. Well, I'm getting out of that bind. I won't play by those rules."

Many Haitian Americans who have struggled for twenty years or more to build support in the U.S. for the Haitian people feel differently. A New York Haitian artist, still involved with the fight against U.S. policies says, "I won't give up despite my misgivings about some of the Haitian government's policies and about the ordinary human condition of self-interest that has caused some men, especially in the political class, to cave in to personal interest and selfishness. No, Aristide was not a saint, a savior. He has feet of clay. Who doesn't? That's not where the focus of the debate should lie. The key question is: what is hurting the Haitian people most in the long-run? What is causing the problem? The answer has not changed: overall, it is the collaboration of the elite in Haiti with their U.S. masters that causes that problem. The middle-classes often can't or won't see it. They are the ones with whom most Americans talk if they know any Haitians. The poor of Haiti: they know! I'll bet on their struggle."

Philippe Geneus in Boston says: "Some so-called radical activists expected radical changes in Haiti, acknowledging that a revolution did not take place in Haiti in 1991. Lavalas remains the only viable progressive movement in Haiti despite the bad apples. The goal of the reactionary forces (national and international) is to make that movement fail, as they did the Sandinistas." Geneus says the government of Haiti frustrates him frequently by not letting people know the facts about the good programs its has been able to accomplish, despite the lack of aid and the impact of neo-liberal IFI policies: among these are literacy campaigns, low-income housing; work to reduce the AIDS infection level, which has gone down; more schools have been built under Lavalas than under all governments before them since independence. Geneus says many accomplishments are almost never mentioned, not even in solidarity publications. "Yes, the government needs to do its homework and report on what it is doing. When progressive non-Haitian people start knowing these facts...more will join the solidarity movement."

Pierre Labossiere of HAC in San Francisco complains, "Those who are hypercritical of Aristide, I don't see them complaining about the Haiti Democracy Project and others who are in league with people like Jesse Helms. Really, we have to keep our eye on the prize, as Martin Luther King used to say. And the prize will be when Haiti is treated as a sovereign nation with its people's choice respected as sovereign."

Another Haitian activist in California asks for his final comment to be in confidence: "But when all is said and done, almost all the political leaders in Haiti these past years have used the 'Marronage' approach - to say one thing to the people, another thing to political allies, and another behind closed doors to those who have the power and the money - and of course to the U.S. in this case. Aristide likes to quote Desssalines that he would surrender ten times to France and betray France ten times. It's not only Aristide who is guilty of that - Chavannes, too, so many others. It's time to be straightforward, to be honest across the board. Until we get some leaders in Haiti who will do that, the solidarity movement in the U.S. will of course not know whom to believe."

Dessima Williams, in Grenada at the time of the survey, responded by asking her friend and co-solidarity activist, Jesi Chancy-Manigat (editor of the CRESFED journal, Rencontre, and board member of the Haitain women's group ENFOFANM) to share their common views. Both women have participated in the growth of the increasingly important women's movement across the whole Caribbean, as well as in specific solidarity struggles for the people of Haiti.

They say, on the one hand, "The contemporary solidarity movement has too much of a humanitarian emphasis and follows a mainstream agenda. It has two extremes - 'Balkinization' at the so-called grassroots level and superficial support of NGO networks. It lacks a genuine understanding of the 'national question,' articulated with a consistent critique of U.S. foreign policy." On the other hand, these women also criticize the other 'solidarity camp.' Those who merely critique U.S. policy in Washington are often lacking in an important ingredient in a solidarity struggle: "Solidarity work in the U.S. should link itself with organizational platforms built up by progressive forces inside the country - university, youth, women, peasants, etc." Generally, U.S. solidarity groups who work with Caribbean societies are apt to be confused by their own perspective as encounters a range of perspectives in the Caribbean: "Because of the influence of so-called anti-imperialist positions, there is no adequate understanding of the unfolding struggles in the Caribbean. Haiti is the best example of that confusion."

Chris Tilly has hope that the confusion can be overcome. Working against the withholding of aid is important, "but I think (more should be done) to spotlight and support progressive grassroots organizing going on in Haiti. The fact that many of these organizations are critical of Aristide is no reason to hold off support from these movements." Tilly also believes the solidarity movement, to be credible, must more publicly criticize the Aristide government. Kennedy and Tilly hope for a fundamental change in the nature of U.S. solidarity work generally. Part of the answer lies in talking about ways that emphasize the people's movements rather than limiting attention to a particular leader or party."

Melinda Miles says, "The Haitian government - some hate it, some love it." That misses the point, she thinks. "The priority of the solidarity movement is to focus on U.S. policies while creating links between Haitians and Americans." She believes those links represent hope for dialogue and "real understanding of the problems of Haiti." Miles continues, "I believe the movement is trying to get back to the same page, but it is so difficult - some of the gaps between us are just too difficult to bridge. But it's worth it - I do believe we can overcome the polarization, if we listen carefully to the people we know, not the organizational leaders. The ordinary folks we know, from our grassroots work in Haiti."

Since 2001 John Engel has worked entirely on improving real communications between people within the movements seeking to bring about change. Engle feels the solidarity movement has been "fragmented and unclear" since about 1995. "There are a lot of good intentioned people, but they often have insufficient habits and practices of dialogue together and with people of opposing views. People are either for Aristide and therefore want to support him...or they believe the Aristide government is so corrupt that supporting it means nurturing a dictatorship." Engle believes there is a way to re-invigorate and possibly re-unite the solidarity movement: "They should be investing more energy in dialogue and rethinking power and leadership. There should be more efforts to make space for a real dialogue, to help build skills in it, to promote it...When this process is good and inclusive, and people are tolerant of others, it is more likely that solutions will come up to overcome differences that will be good and effective."

These views represent an amazing variety of responses to the current crisis in Haiti and the state of the U.S. solidarity movement. They reveal enormous pain, anger, frustration, and gaps between people, disillusion and disappointment, which clearly flawed leaders of the movements in the struggle for justice in Haiti. The comments also show enormous commitment to hearing the voices of the people of Haiti, passionate love of and involvement with the culture and people of Haiti, an ability to entertain and understand the complex social and political environment of Haiti, and a willingness to act carefully based on what they believe the Haitian people have made clear they want.

[1] Transcript, presentation to the "Haitian Reality" course, Caribbean Focus Program, Roxbury Community College, April 1993.

[2] Paul Farmer, *The Uses of Haiti, (4th Edition)*. Common Courage Press, Monroe, ME, 2002.

[3] All quotations without other attribution are taken from responses by email or telephone to the survey of Haiti solidarity activists, both Haitian and non-Haitian.

[4] *Miami Herald*, Jan.29 and Feb. 9, 1986.

[5] *New York Daily News*, Feb. 12, 1986.

[6] Boston Globe, Feb. 2, 1986.

[7] Philippe Geneus (survey response).

[8] *New York Times*, April 28, 1990; *Boston Globe*, April 6, 1990; *Miami Herald*, May 6, 1990.

[9] *New York Times*, Oct. 12, 1991; *Miami Herald*, Nov.24, 1991.

[10] *Boston Globe,* Oct. 5, 1991.

[11] Personal recollection of the writer - whenever "I" or "we" are used, unless within other quotation.

[12] Fourth report of the New England Observers' Delegation to Haiti (NEOD), "At Aristide's Return," November 1994.

[13] Third report of NEOD, "Courage Washing Over Misery," Feb. 1993, and HaitiWomen Announcement (NEOD), July 29, 1994.

[14] First report of NEOD, November, 1993.

[15] Pierre Labossiere (survey response).

[16] NEOD/Haiti Anti-Intervention Network (HAIN) press advisory, Aug. 12, 1994.

[17] NEOD memoranda and Pierre Labossiere (survey response).

[18] Memorandum with press releases and news clippings, office of Rep. Joseph Kennedy, Feb. 8, 1994.

[19] Haiti National Network Agenda and Minutes, NEOD archive, April 9, 1994.

[20] Letter from Chris Tilly to President Aristide, April 17, 1994 (NEOD archive).

[21] HAIN leaflets and press releases, July-October, 1994.

[22] Proceedings of the Security Council, United Nations Documents, Sept. 19, 1994.

[23] Cited in *Ibid.*

[24] NEOD archive.

[25] NEOD 4th report.

[26] *Ibid.*

[27] Personal conversations at the time with MPP leaders and Chavanne's family members.

[28] NEOD, 5th report.

[29] For all references to the "Death Plan," see "Up Against the Death Plan," based on the NEOD 7th report, and published in *Dollars and Sense,* Somerville, MA, March/April, 1996. See also, Lisa McGowan, "Undermining Democracy," Development Gap, Washington, D.C., 1997.

[30] For a thorough summary of the Jean Dominique case through 2002, see the Amnesty International report, "The Jean Dominique Case," April, 2002.

[31] For this and other information about the Jean Dominique and other human rights cases in 2002-2003, see the writer's article, "Still Up Against the Death Plan," *Dollars    and Sense,* Somerville, MA, September 2003.

[32] Haiti Report: U.S. Haiti solidarity group leading the anti-Embargo "Voices for Haiti" campaign: www.quioxte.org/haiti or www.haitireborn.org.

[33] *Haiti Progres:* (French, English summary): www.haiti-progres.com. See especially March 9 and 24 issues, "U.S. Policy in Haiti: A Multi-Front Strategy."

[34] Paul Farmer (email to the writer, August 2003; response survey).

[35] For this and other HDP quotes, see Haiti Democracy Project "Unity Statement," Dec. 26, 2002; and "Broad-based Civil Society Coalition Offers Hope," Dec. 26, 2002; and James Morrell, "Impact of Sept. 11 on U.S. Haiti Policy," paper delivered at conference of the Latin America Studies Association (LASA), Dallas, TX, March 28, 2003.

[36] Roger Noriega, "Reaping the Benefits of Hemispheric Solidarity," speech to the conference of the Council of the Americas, Washington, D.C., April 28, 2003.

# CHAPTER EIGHT

*Men nan la men, annou sove peyi nou-an.*

Hand in hand, let's save our country.

# Charting the Butterfly's Course:
# The Next Generation of Haitian Diaspora in the United States
*Diana Aubourg*

"Because this is the other thing about immigrants ('fugees, émigrés, travelers):
they cannot escape their history any more than you yourself can lose your
shadow."
**White Teeth – Zadie Smith**

## Returning...

In January 2003, Haiti Reborn, a program of the Quixote Center, organized a fact-finding mission to investigate the effects of an unconscionable economic embargo withholding approximately $500 million in humanitarian aid from Haiti.[1] The reader will observe this mission's imprint throughout the book, as four of the contributors explored this complex issue together on the delegation. Of the twenty-one participants, six were of Haitian descent and serendipitously represented the nuances of the Haitian Diaspora in the United States. We were six strands in a rich, multicolored tapestry of an evolving *dyaspora* – young, engaged, and (ostensibly by virtue of our U.S. citizenship) strategically positioned to affect U.S. policy toward Haiti.[2]

We left Haiti at varying ages, under different circumstances (fleeing the Duvalier regime, floating on the Lavalas wave) and returned: one for the first time since age 11; one leading the delegation; one having lived in Haiti previously to work with a grassroots NGO; one who regularly visited Haiti with his U.S. born, biracial daughter; and one having been forcibly deported after incarceration in the U.S now working with Haitian deportees. I was the only one born and raised in the U.S. and thus, perhaps felt the least connected in a cultural sense, though I imagine we all bore our *dyaspora* tags with some conflict – unable to definitively lock ourselves into one national context. Excepting our deported colleague, our most common thread remained that we were transnational, with the U.S. serving as our home base. Indeed, there is an inescapable immigrant shadow which shifts with the sun's position providing shade when we contemplate Haiti's beauty and looming ominously when we weigh our responsibility in shaping Haiti's future. True to the above quote, (and for better or worse) this shadow travels with us.

## The Butterfly's Shadow

In the delegation report, I reflected on my Haitian American identity – or what I deemed a "hyphenated-existence" embedded in black American culture. I touched upon our complicated relationship to black Americans and ruminated over our sense of belonging and displacement, acceptance and rejection:

> Many of us (of Haitian descent and raised in the U.S.) meandered through a profound dissonance between our distinctly Haitian upbringing and our unavoidable existence as the black American under-class. Like many children of immigrants, we struggled with the more superficial things of life: wanting our parents to speak English when our non-Haitian friends were around, begging for McDonalds instead of beans, rice and plantain, debating whether to reveal our Haitian identity less we be ridiculed and wondering why instead of the nuclear-Cosby family we had a steady stream of extended family members staying with us. We didn't understand that the tight rein of discipline exercised by our parents had more to do with their desperate attempts to raise Haitians in America (notice, I've omitted the hyphenation) than healthy notions of child rearing. Before the "Wyclef-phenomenon" we secretly debated amongst ourselves if certain pop cultural icons were Haitian while frantically dissolving ourselves into black American culture in the hopes of "passing". Though the negative experiences were buttressed by such things as endearing relationships with family members and our parents' impartation of their "Haitian pride", our self-concept was marred by the images that defined the Haiti of our generation: Boat people, AIDS, refugees, poverty.[3]

The lamentations of any Diaspora group will include a common stock of words that end in the suffix "tion": persecution, dissolution, assimilation, evolution, confliction. The nouns are endless. With good reason, we Haitian Americans claim these with vigor. Among black immigrant groups in the United States, Haitians have, for the past three decades or so, been dubiously labeled the least socially desirable of the Caribbean transplants. Growing up, we understood that it was often worse to be called a "*Haitian*" than the "n-word."

In my reflections I wrote:

> Ironically, we experienced more racism and discrimination from our Black American brothers and sisters than any other group. As I consider this in retrospect, this was due to at least two kinds of proximity: physical (in the Northeast, we [Black Americans and Haitians] were often clustered together in the same ghettos, housing projects and schools) and existential (we represented the worse of deep, dark, Africa). Undoubtedly, there were the upwardly mobile exceptions that managed to assimilate into white suburban life – they, of course, had their own sets of problems. The vast majority of us living in major cities, however, lived along side our black and brown brethren and negotiated this at least until our parents made the class transition. The strivers who made it to college found solace in the Haitian American associations, in which we discovered the universality of the Haitian American experience – licked our wounds and re-asserted/re-affirmed our history, culture and identity in safer space. Still others, (like my brother) chose paths that lead us to become the "underachieving" black Americans our parents warned us about.

One can find a more layered exploration of these issues in *The Butterfly's Way* edited by Edwidge Danticat whose literary talent has given voice to the experiences of a generation of Diaspora Haitians.[4] The metaphor describes a Diaspora that floats on an undulating, unpredictable course, much like a butterfly. For many Haitian Americans, The *Butterfly's Way* reads like a chorus of "amen's" rising from charismatic churches on any given Sunday – each voice its own sermon preaching to a ready choir about the vices and virtues of *dyaspora* life. By the end, even reluctant readers experience some measure of cultural resonance if not conversion and believers reaffirm their longing for home. Our hearts are touched by the interplay between romance and realism: enslaved *restavèk* children/pastoral landscapes, drowning refugees/Diaspora Haitians protesting discriminatory U.S. policies.[5] With a heavy sigh and *"enfin"*, we accept our issues on display in the public sphere and for the most part, celebrate this mixed bag of shame, celebration and displacement.[6] Pride seeps like mist.

*The Butterfly's Way* is undoubtedly a seminal and defining text of our generation. It issues a formidable challenge to the Haitian Diaspora to probe deeper in our understanding of our identities and experiences; to discern the overarching themes of our generation and move forward with this knowledge. However, there is a next step. And it involves affirming our cultural "shadows" negotiating *dyaspora* status, *as well as* engaging concretely in rebuilding a nation torn by internal strife, crushed by harmful international policy, and plagued by debilitating poverty and underdevelopment.

I write from the perspective of the U.S. born *dyaspora* who, though raised in a Haitian household, spent little time in Haiti growing up up. I struggle with, among other things, speaking *Kréyol* with fluency and understanding the complex machinations of Haitian political life. However, as with many in my generation, I have benefited from some of the best of what the U.S. has to offer by way of institutions, access, and relative privilege. With a Masters degree from a prestigious school, enlightened by extensive travel experiences, and a network of progressive colleagues and friends I successfully made the class transition. My story is far from unique, but rather one of tens of thousands. As such, my cohort and I balance on the precipice of Haiti's transformation from a pitied and marginalized nation-state to a thriving democracy with a place in the world economy. However, with respect to our leadership on the issues explored in this book we are conspicuously "weighed on the scales and found wanting."[7]

This essay by no means speaks authoritatively on the state of the young *dyaspora* community in the U.S., nor will it unfurl a coherent plan of action or framework within which to mobilize disaffected and apathetic young Haitian Americans. I simply offer a snapshot of my generation and provide some context for understanding the barriers in engaging young Haitian Americans in U.S.-based advocacy and direct action to effect change in Haiti.

*"Lè'mal lékol ameriken té kon jouré'm*
(When I went to school Americans used to diss me)
*Yo rélém nèg nwè yo rélém ti réfigié*
(They called me black nigger they called me a little refugee)
*Sang Fezi –Wyclef Jean*

## Who are we? A snapshot...

We are the generation of *dyaspora* in the United States with one foot planted firmly in U.S. soil, and the other extended toward a distant homeland. If we were born or spent most of our lives in the United States, the distance is determined by countless interacting factors: whether we have living memories of Haiti to cradle, whether our parents insisted we speak *Kréyol* at home and eat Haitian food, the extent to which we grafted American culture on to our half/first generation template, and our level of exposure to the political and social problems that persist in our homeland.

We are but one generation removed from *Duvalierism*. Many of us were born into our hyphenated-identities or left Haiti at the heels of Jean Claude (Baby Doc) Duvalier's succession to power in 1971 and came of age in America during his fifteen-year dynastic reign. Born in the 70s, our parents likely hailed from the lower-middle urban class or rural Haiti rather than the elite pedigree of Haitian émigrés who left Haiti in the 50s and 60s. Our parents built their modest nests in the U.S. – clustered on the eastern seaboard - as factory workers, nurses aids and taxi drivers, and we benefited from this country's social welfare and educational systems. Unbeknownst to many of us, we were eating from the same seemingly generous hand of opportunity that supported a brutally repressive regime – sending waves of Haitians to U.S. shores. As our families benefited from lax U.S. immigration policy and refashioned their lives in America during the Duvalier dictatorships, the U.S. dutifully funneled vast sums of foreign aid to Haiti.[8]

In *The Uses of Haiti*, Paul Farmer illuminates the deleterious effects of U.S. policies toward Haiti providing context for the negative images of Haiti that hovered over us as we were growing up. Farmer's main thesis is that Haiti, to its own detriment, has served the purposes of the international community, particularly the United States. Among other things, Farmer discusses the precipitous decline in living standards and per capita income as the U.S. *unconstructively* engaged the Duvalier regimes – particularly with Baby Doc. He points out the steady rise in environmental degradation and external public debt – which increased seven fold from 1973 to 1980. In the first year of Baby Doc's government, Washington provided it with $2.8 million in military aid – a regime that took state-sponsored terrorism to greater levels than the previous dictatorship. [9] Once Baby Doc signed on to a new U.S.-backed economic program, Haiti became the "darling" of the American Business Community.[10] U.S. taxpayer dollars helped to establish assembly plants for U.S. manufactures, which contributed to a 56% decline in Haitian wages.[11]

In 1976, a year after I was born and around the time Haitians were establishing enclaves in New York, Boston and Chicago, 75 percent of Haitians in Haiti fell below the threshold of absolute poverty set by the World Bank.[12] Depending on the level of political engagement of our parents/guardians (and whether we paid any attention to their heated political debates) we had some context for the rivulet of family members from Haiti that poured through our homes and with whom we shared scarce space in our tiny apartments. At the very least, we knew that Haiti was "the poorest country in the Western Hemisphere" and were not permitted to forget it.

In February 1986, we watched Baby Doc's departure on television and the images of ebullient throngs on Haiti's streets celebrating what we then understood to be a new beginning. *Dechoukaj* became a household term.[13] Like babies, we were unwittingly christened in the *Lavalas* waters that rose miles away and gushed forth. We witnessed a savior-like figure emerge out of the chaos that followed the end of Duvalierism. As the flow of refugees persisted unfettered, we met first, second, and third cousins our age who were active in the *Lavalas* movement – but ignorance/indifference left us far removed from their lived experiences. In 1990, fully entrenched in our Diaspora lives, we saw Haiti briefly recast in a prism of hope rather than despair as two-thirds of the populace voiced their preference. The following year, when a *coup d'état* deposed Haiti's first democratically elected government, we were somewhere between our last years in high school and first years in college. By then, we may have formulated an independent assessment of Haiti's political situation, but more than likely our views were an extension of the animated debates we heard at home, family gatherings, and on Haitian radio and television programs.

***

We are largely a generation of "firsts" in the dynamic unfolding of our immigration story in America: the first to absorb, en masse, black American culture and translate it to our baffled and indignant parents; the first to transform traditionally white Catholic inner-city schools into little Haitian havens; the first to befriend black Americans and Latinos in our neighborhoods and defy our parents admonishments to "don't be like them;" among the first to create Haitian student associations at high schools and institutions of higher learning; and among the first to meet and exceed our parents expectations and enter prestigious institutions and professions. Those of us raised in the inner city lived through the crack epidemic and surge in black-on-black violence and as such, were among the first to disgrace our parents with our participation in illicit behavior and involvement in U.S. courts and prison systems.

For many of us, *Haitian* was a dirty word for as long as we can remember. But in the late 80s and early 90s, we discovered that even our blood was "dirty" and would be discriminated against. According to the U.S. Centers for Disease Control, we were one of four high risk groups for HIV, along with other "Hs:" Homosexuals, Hemophiliacs, and Heroin users. In 1990, in a powerful expression of U.S. Diaspora solidarity, we marched across the Brooklyn Bridge in protest. In 2003, we wage a different war, as Haiti ranks the highest HIV rate (5.6%) in the Caribbean and blacks in the U.S. account for half of all new reported HIV infections.[14]

As young blacks in the U.S. we matured in and were shaped by the Hip-Hop Generation. We negotiated its defining force in our lives with our *dyaspora* identities. Our numbers swelled in New York's ghettos, Hip Hop's organic incubator, and we took part in creating the most influential musical genre of the 21st century. In desperate attempts to shield us from the corrupting influence of our non-Haitian peers, our parents barred the music and its cultural markers (high-top fades, bulk jewelry, dreadlocks and dreams of rap stardom) from crossing the threshold of their homes. But we triumphed and fell in love with the first medium that spoke, in lucid detail, to our experiences as black youth. We were, after all, in the same "boat" as our black and brown brethren (we discovered) and Hip Hop proved the balm that nursed our wounds and the bridge that permitted us to cross-over to black urban subculture. We pledged our loyalties and were tacitly accepted - though we didn't wave our Haitian flags at rap concerts until the Fugees and Wyclef emerged.

Along this journey, we were politicized. We absorbed Public Enemy, KRS-1, Tribe Called Quest, De La Soul and others who deconstructed our lives as blacks in America. As a result, we embraced expressions of black pride, though most of us failed to link this to Haiti's unique history as the world's first black republic. Through what is known as "conscious rap" we began to contemplate our role in the black struggle and the universality of our experiences as blacks in the U.S. and globally. Ironically, as we fought against self-hatred, police brutality and apartheid through Hip Hop, we still feared rejection from our peers for being Haitian.

Now, we stand as test cases in this rather unscientific immigrant experiment. Our parents wonder about our commitment to the homeland, *Haiti Cherie*, and we doubt that we will be able to effectively transfer to our children the language, food, and customs of our parents. We look back and now appreciate our parent's stubborn insistence that we retain a Haitian identity distinct from the dominant culture – for now our biculturalism is an asset. We welcome our immigrant shadow but cherish our blue passports. Some of us believe our relative success is testimony enough to our industry in the U.S., others, however, have begun to ask if we could and should be doing more for Haiti.

*Piti, piti, wazo fe nich li*
**(Little by little the bird builds its nest)**
*Haitian Proverb*

## Guiding the Butterfly...

In June 2002, the Trinity College Haiti Program held a symposium entitled: *"The Emerging Presence in the U.S. of the Haitian Diaspora and its Impacts on Haiti"*. In this daylong forum, Haitian Americans involved in policy, program, and research related to Haiti and Diaspora issues delved into four themes: Leadership, Advocacy, Interfacing, and Innovation. The stated goal was to increase "understanding of the Diaspora's capacity to shape – or indeed to lead – the debate around [Haiti] issues".[15] The symposium offered a glimpse into U.S. Diaspora views on a wide array of practical concerns such as civic participation and our role in influencing U.S. policy toward Haiti, polarization/fragmentation within our community, the resulting crisis in leadership and mobilization of resources for investment in Haiti. Further, the symposium was a gathering of "who's who" in the U.S. Diaspora community including Marie St. Fleur, the first Haitian American to hold an elected seat in Massachusetts; Phillip Brutus, the first Haitian American elected to the Florida legislature; Dr. Joseph Baptiste, the founder of the National Organization for the Advancement of Haitians (NOAH); Joseph Bernadel, co-founder and director of the Toussaint L'Ouverture High School for Arts and Social Justice, the first public school in the U.S. founded by a Haitian Americans and other respected community leaders.

A reading of the Symposium report reveals that it captured some of the leading voices in the U.S. Diaspora community. As with most forums, the issues addressed were too vast and complex to be dealt with concretely in the time allotted. However, the discussants and participants made comments in reference to young Haitian Americans that are important to highlight in this essay. Joseph Baptiste, President of NOAH, expressed a common assessment of my generation:

> "The second generation does not have the same level of commitment toward Haiti as the first. For those in the third generation, most don't even speak Creole. Sometimes I jokingly refer to them as fake Haitians. As a testimony to the disconnect many young Haitians have with regard to Haiti, it's insightful to note that when NOAH organizes a delegation to Haiti, many of the delegates are going to Haiti for the very first time."[16]

Indeed, Baptiste's observation would apply to me. Though I was taken to Haiti as a toddler, I had no recollection of this visit and returned, in a way, some 25 years later to experience Haiti for the first time with a delegation. The conference participants discussed the need for young Haitian Americans to "bridge the cultural gap" by visiting Haiti. Dimy Doresca, representing the Haitian American Students Association at Georgetown, added to this by urging for a "Haitian Peace Corps" of sorts:

> "Among the various ideas floated, the following stood out as most significant: the need to give young Haitians a real picture of Haiti: the need for young Haitians to volunteer their time to go to Haiti and see how things are for themselves."[17]

The need to reconnect young Haitian Americans with Haiti was an overarching theme. The Symposium report closes with the following:

> "Among the topics discussed widely...were such themes ...as the importance of providing opportunities for members of the Haitian American Diaspora not born in Haiti, i.e. its one and a half, second and third generation members, to become more knowledgeable about Haiti and to find realistic channels for making positive contributions to its growth and development."[18]

In writing this essay, I sought to get a sense of what my Haitian American peers were thinking: if they thought about issues affecting Haiti and their Diaspora identity and whether they in fact had an interest in "getting a real picture of Haiti" as the experts prescribed. I talked with my relatives and friends, randomly distributed an informal survey over the Internet and conducted a handful of interviews with Haitian Americans active in Haiti-related work. The survey yielded nothing close to a representative sample, due largely to the fact that it was sent out under time constraints during the summer months. Nonetheless the responses were interesting and worthy of note.

When asked to describe the most pressing challenges facing Haiti, Haitian Americans and the Haitian Diaspora, a 31-year old urban planner born in Boston responded: "A lack of organized stewardship between Haitian and Haitian Americans [on] the present condition of Haiti. The gap between the two is flooded with pride and an unwillingness to compromise on many levels. There also seems to be overwhelming denial, with regard to the mounting failures of the family unit and its far-reaching impacts." On family, a 33-year old respondent also from Boston offered, "I believe second generation Haitians in this country should focus more on the immediate family first. Ask themselves questions such as: What are you doing personally to promote Haitian consciousness, awareness and culture in your community? Can your child speak and converse in Creole? How much do they know about Haitian culture and history? How often have they visited the country, if ever?"

A 32-year old research assistant born in New York felt that Haitians lacked a collective voice: "I believe we as people contribute to identity crises among second and third generation members." A 30-year old doctoral student in speech pathology focused on the need to both assist Haiti and retain our identities. She states, "the most pressing challenges facing Haitian Americans and the Diaspora is what we can do to aid the country and to make our voices heard. Other challenges include maintaining our ethnic identification and culture as we assimilate and intertwine with U.S. and other cultures." Some respondents simply listed the challenges: Corrupt government, embargoed relief funds, creating roads, creating a sustainable health care system, and the HIV/AIDS epidemic. One respondent, a 30-year old occupational therapist, focused on how the current conditions in Haiti have thwarted our parents dreams of returning home: "Our parents, who are retiring, want to go back home to Haiti. We the children who are left behind, are fearing for their safety and well being because of the troubled state of Haiti."

There was consensus, both in the survey responses and in discussions, that young Haitian Americans have an important role to play in affecting U.S. policy towards Haiti. One respondent stated emphatically, "Yes – education/privilege has afforded many of us the opportunity for a real dialogue about the ongoing conditions of Haiti. We have the [right] of the vote to affect policy change." Another wrote, "I believe that the Haitian Diaspora has an obligation to get involved in U.S. policies towards Haiti. I believe that Haiti needs us now and that things will get worse if we turn our backs on her." A respondent shared the following, " We invest in 401K's, mutual funds, stocks, etc. because we expect some type of dividend, a return on our investments. Is it too much to ask this group to invest THEIR TIME to the present and future of Haiti? The return on this type of investment, in the long-term, will be far greater than any of us can imagine." One respondent stated simply, "If Haitian Americans aren't willing to play a role, who will?"

There was also an emphasis on electoral politics as an effective mechanism to exert influence on U.S policies: "our biggest role is [to] vote and make our voices heard." Joe Thelusca, National Coordinator of the Haitian League, an organization that works to involve Haitian Americans in U.S. politics, reasoned that we need to establish political credibility: "We have not demonstrated to either [political] parties

[that] we can make an impact in the political arena...it boils down to our fundraising capacity and voting power [to influence elections]." Civic engagement, according to Thelusca, will increase the level of aid to Haiti and change harmful trade policies.

Of course leadership is an ever-contentious issue - and in this respect, the Haitian American community is no different from other minority groups struggling to define themselves in the mainstream. Ronald Aubourg, who has been active in the Haitian American community in New York, discussed the failure of our parent's generation, the "old guard," to "relinquish their stakes" and step aside for new, vibrant, and more effective leadership. While political leadership is key, many with whom I spoke discussed the critical role of *cultural* leadership – and with this, the conversation invariably shifted to discussing the influence of Wyclef Jean and Edwidge Danticat on our generation. To many, Wyclef Jean (and his former rap group the Fugees) revolutionized Haitian American identity and propelled Haitian pride among *dyaspora* youth to unfathomable levels. Wyclef epitomized fusion – blending hip hop, rock, Haitian *kompa*, reggae, R&B, and other forms with biting social commentary and rallying cries for Haitian solidarity and pride. We listened to his songs and for the first time heard Haitian *Krèyol* on mainstream radio and in concerts. We had been "fusing" our whole lives but Wyclef proved a convincing spokesperson who, along with Danticat, legitimized our identities to the world.

Ginau Mathurin, 33, founder of EchodHaiti.com (www.echodhaiti.com), a website designed to draw young Haitian Americans back to Haitian culture, believes that culture will be the single mobilizing force for Haitian Americans. He states, "I don't think that it's going to be politics – it will be that [cultural] bridge. Once you cross that bridge, you feel that you can travel to the other side [Haiti]." For Mathurin, Wyclef and Danticat served as these essential bridges that not only translated our experiences to the dominant culture but also connected us to our Haitian roots in ways a political forum or dense historical analysis of Haiti could not. He reiterated, "people like Danticat and Wyclef have been a big help because they created a bridge. Wyclef was a breakthrough – we could be affirmed." Others maintain that these cultural phenomena are only skin-deep, superficial, and lacking the substance needed to produce tangible outcomes. There is no utility in promulgating a false dichotomy between culture and politics. For some (perhaps a majority) culture, in the form of music, literature and websites, will be a more effective draw, while for others, a delegation trip to Haiti or a fundraising effort could strengthen the bonds that many critics of this *dyaspora* generation say are weak.

Finally, I would be remiss not to mention existing efforts by young Haitian Americans to engage their peers in shaping Haiti's future. In addition to the plethora of websites, chat rooms and informal salon discussion groups that create fora for dialogue and debate, there are efforts underway to facilitate the building of bridges discussed earlier. I will highlight two such efforts with which I am most familiar.

The 10th Department Organization for Haitian Empowerment (10th DOHE) was founded in 2002 by a small group of Haitian and second generation Haitian Americans with the goal of "spreading a message of hope and empowerment to the 10th Department."[19] 10th DOHE also seeks to strengthen transnational ties between the Haitian Diaspora, Haiti, and international communities to dispel negative stereotypes against Haitians and people of Haitian descent. 10th DOHE provides networking opportunities to facilitate positive social change through education, cultural awareness, grassroots mobilization, advocacy initiatives, and information exchange. The Republic of Haiti has nine geographical regions or departments and the Haitian Diaspora symbolically represents the 10th.

10th DOHE is organizing a national march to be held in Washington D.C. in March 2004. The 2004 march will commemorate Haiti's bicentennial and demand an end to, among other things, unfair immigration policies, racial discrimination against Asylum seekers, unfair economic and trade polices, and the withholding of international aid to Haiti. Such grassroots mobilization efforts in the nation's capital will empower the Haitian diaspora to collectively address issues that impact Haitians abroad and in Haiti, while promoting Haitian pride, culture, and Haiti's sovereignty. A practical goal of the march is to link Haitian Americans to the initial efforts of rebuilding their family's geographical area or department. The idea is to provide Haitian Americans with a deeper connection to their roots in Haiti. According to Eugenia Charles-Mathurin, one of its founders, the 10th DOHE will also create a program to involve second and third generation Haitian American youth in fundraising for grassroots educational projects in Haiti and exchange programs to reconnect them with Haiti.

Another effort is more narrowly concerned with "reversing the brain drain" by creating an extensive database of Haitian American professionals interested in sharing their skills with public and private institutions in Haiti. The Haitian American Skills Share Foundation, founded in 2002 by Marx Vilaire Aristide, seeks to "reverse Haiti's brain drain by providing Haitian Americans opportunities to return to Haiti and share their skills. In so doing, the Foundation seeks to systematically contribute to Haiti's long-term development." This effort involves encouraging Haitian American professionals to lend their skills and experience to Haiti as volunteers; maintaining a database of Haitian American professionals volunteers and Haitian institutions that want to receive volunteers; and placing Haitian Americans with organizations and institutions in Haiti on the basis of needs, skills and interests.

There is clearly overlap in these initiatives and according to Charles-Mathurin, the organizations will seek to collaborate. These initiatives will also face considerable challenges – from garnering financial support at home to ensuring a safe environment for those Haitian Americans who travel to Haiti. When asked if s/he was interested in lending skills to improve Haiti, one respondent to the informal survey, a 28-year-old public health professional, wrote:

> "I would definitely be interested in lending my skills to improve the health conditions in Haiti through creating a sustainable infrastructure for public health and research. My concerns at this time are: lack of support from the government, my level of involvement would be useless and my safety would be jeopardized once involved."

The central focus, however, for both of them is to draw on the resources of the 1.5 million Haitians that reside in the United States - over 70% of whom are under age 40 – to both improve the polticical, social and economic conditions in Haiti as well as build bridges between Haiti and the next generation in the U.S.[20]

***

*Piti, piti, wazo fe nich li.* Little, by little, our families built nests in the U.S. designed to nurture and protect us from a culture that threatened to swallow us whole. As life would have it, these nests bore holes and loose twigs - often teetering on unsteady branches. We are now, little by little, building our own nests in this country with remnants of our parents toil. This nest-building is a slow process and our collective Diaspora experience in the U.S. is but a blink to students of history. We are young, both in age and Diaspora identity. Though we may exude confidence in certain settings, by and large, there is still an uncertainty in our gait and tentativeness in our step. Why is this? We remember the teasing and taunting endured while growing up, the searing labels branded on our person and the unrelenting dissonance between our lives at home and interactions with the outside world. As a friend reflected, "We grew up on the dark side of the Haitian American experience." We are working to forgive and move on. Having survived, we are in collective therapy – breaking the silence to share our experiences with each other, reclaiming our parent love of konpa music, returning to or visiting Haiti for the first time, forging our natural affinity to the Haitian struggle, and perhaps discovering a sense of responsibility to assist in rebuilding our country.

The butterfly, delicate and resilient, will continue along its eclectic path. Indeed, its patterns are beautiful. But as I write, a humanitarian emergency unfolds in Haiti in which the majority of the population cannot live (as the title of this book implores) because they lack adequate health care, education, clean water, and security. Consequently, we cannot afford to sit idly and watch the butterfly float aimlessly. Herein lies the challenge for my generation of *dyaspora* in America.

*Bibliography*

Danticat, Edwidge
        2001 The Butterfly's Way. Soho Press.
Farmer, Paul
        2003 The Uses of Haiti. Monroe, Main: Common Courage Press.
Smith, Zadie
        2000    White Teeth. Vintage International: Vintage Books.
"The Emerging Presence in the U.S. of the Haitian Diaspora, and its Impact on Haiti": A
        Symposium Report. The Trinity College Haiti Program. Trinity College,
        Washington, DC. October 2002

---

[1] For the full report, "Investigating the Human Effects of Withheld Humanitarian Aid", go to the Haiti Reborn website at: www.haitireborn.org

[2] *Dyaspora*, in addition to describing Haitians living abroad, is used in a number of contexts. Its negative connotation refers to, among other things, Haitians who abandoned Haiti in times of political/economic turmoil or who express political views that are unsympathetic or critical of the Haitian government and people.

[3] "Investigating the Human Effects of Withheld Humanitarian Aid", A report of the Haiti Reborn/Quixote Center Delegation, January 11-19, 2003.

[4] Danticat, 2001

[5] Unpaid child servants that are often treated as enslaved persons.

[6] In French "enfin" means "at last, finally, or after all" but in Haitian *Kreyol* it is used with a tone of resignation or "oh, well".

[7] Biblical reference: Daniel 5:26

[8] The U.S. government issued over one million entry visas to Haitians between 1956 and 1985. From Libete: A Haitian Anthology, Charles Arthur and Michael Dash (Markus Wiener: Princeton, 1999).

[9] Farmer, 2003, *Introduction*

[10] Farmer, 2003, pg. 97

[11] According to Farmer, Haiti grew to be the world's ninth largest assembler of goods for U.S. consumption under Jean Claude's regime. This was a direct result of U.S.-backed offshore assembly, which exploited cheap Haitian labor, poor labor standards, and the worst living conditions in Latin America.

[12] Farmer, 2003, pg 100

[13] The "uprooting" or outing of Duvalier supporters and public killings of ton ton macoutes – the regime's paramilitary force.

[14] United States Centers for Disease Control: www.cdc.gov

[15] "The Emerging Presence in the U.S. of the Haitian Diaspora, and its impact on Haiti: A Symposium Report. The Trinity College Haiti Program, Trinity College, Washington D.C. October 2002.

[16] Pg. 6

[17] Pg. 9

[18] Pg 23

[19] website: www.10thdepartment.org

[20] 1990 Census data

# Epilogue
### *March 17, 2004*

On February 29, 2004, in the earliest and darkest hours of the day, Haiti experienced its thirty-third coup d'etat. Within hours, anticipation turned to terror as a pseudo-reconstituted Haitian Army advanced on the capital, Port-au-Prince. The data indicates that the United States implemented a regime change in Haiti with operators from within. It is an indignation that Haiti's spirit of freedom has been dishonored and insulted during the 200th anniversary of Haiti's declaration of independence.

For weeks before the coup, Haitians erected barricades throughout the country to support Aristide on one side and to protest him on the other side. The US administration put high pressure on Aristide and none on his opponents... empowering the opposition to refuse all negotiated solution.

Most Haitians will tell you that the situation today is a repetition of history.
- The Army has reemerged to assist the traditional Haitian elite in taking power once again.
- The United States helped out with the removal of the democratically elected government.
- A government has been constituted in Haiti without the participation of even one single poor person. Not one peasant, not one fisherman, not one market woman, not one brave student.

There is an established pattern in U.S. policies to undermine Haitian efforts for democracy, pro-poor economic policies and national sovereignty in Haiti.

We were reminded of the role the United States plays in Haiti, as well as the role played by tradition. It's a tradition in Haiti for the tiny elite to suck every bit of profit out of the country, all of it made on the backs of the Haitian poor. It's a tradition for those elite to use soldiers to terrorize, exploit, mutilate, and murder the population. It's a tradition in Haiti that the rich get richer and the poor get poorer, and the gap between the classes is filled with the broken dreams – and, more often than not, the broken bodies – of the Haitian poor.

Unfortunately there are some U.S. traditions at play in Haiti, too. There is our imperialistic tradition to control this hemisphere and much of the world beyond. There is our tradition of supporting Haiti's elite, our tradition of training Haiti's soldiers. Most disturbing perhaps is our time-honored tradition of racism – most starkly revealed in our treatment of the poor Haitians who flee to our shores seeking refuge.

The book *Let Haiti live* is part of a discussion by organizations and individuals to reflect on U.S. policies in Haiti. It is also a document to inform those who want to see changes in these policies. As Americans we must not be silent or indifferent, but rather should extend our solidarity to the most mistreated people in our hemisphere.

The Let Haiti Live Coalition has shown that we can make a difference on U.S. policy. We can make our government treat Haiti more justly. Join us today – visit www.lethaitilive.com and be part of a mission to demand a better life for the Haitian people.

Melinda Miles and Eugenia Charles

# ACRONYMS

| | |
|---|---|
| **ACLU** | America Civil Liberties Union |
| **AFSC** | American Friends Service Committee |
| **AJH** | Association of Haitian Journalists |
| **AP** | Associated Press |
| **APA** | Administrative Procedure Act |
| **BAHACO** | Bay Area Haitian American Council |
| **BAI** | *Bureau des Avocats Internationaux,* Bureau of International Lawyers |
| **BIA** | Board of Appeals |
| **BTC** | Broward Transitional Center |
| **CAA** | Cuban Adjustment Act of 1966 |
| **CAFTA** | Central American Free Trade Agreement |
| **CAMEP** | Metropolitan Central Autonomy for Potable Water |
| **CARICOM** | Caribbean Community and Commonwealth |
| **CD** | *Convergence Democratique,* Democratic Convergence |
| **CEP** | Provisional Electoral Council |
| **CHPP** | Haitian Conference of Political Parties |
| **CIA** | Central Intelligence Agency |
| **CNG** | *Conseil National du Gouvernement,* National Council of Government |
| **CNOE** | National Council of Electoral Observation |
| ***Coordinadora*** | Nicaragua Democratic Coordinating Committee |
| **COSAH** | Committee in Solidarity with Haiti |
| **CPJ** | Committee to Protect Journalists |
| **DHS** | Department of Homeland Security |
| **ESAF** | Enhanced Structural Adjustment Facility |
| **EU** | European Union |
| **FANM** | *Fanm Ayisyen Nan Myami,* Haitian Women of Miami |
| **FBI** | Federal Bureau of Investigation |
| **FIAC** | Florida Immigrant Advocacy Center |
| **FL** | *Fanmi Lavalas,* the Lavalas Family political party |
| **FRAPH** | Revolutionary Front for the Advancement and Progress of Haiti |
| **FSLN** | *Frente Sandinista de Liberacion Nacional* |
| **FTAA** | Free Trade Area of the Americas |
| **G184** | Group of 184 |
| **G8** | Group of Eight |

| | |
|---|---|
| **GDP** | gross domestic product |
| **HAC** | Haiti Action Committee (Bay Area, CA) |
| **HAIN** | Haiti Anti-Intervention Network |
| **HASCO** | Haitian American Sugar Company |
| **HDP** | Haiti Democracy Project |
| **HERO Act** | Haitian Economic Recovery and Opportunity Act |
| **HIPC** | Heavily Indebted Poor Countries Initiative |
| **ICCPR** | International Covenant on Civil and Political Rights |
| **ICESCR** | International Covenant on Economic and Social Rights |
| **ICIO** | International Coalition of Independent Observers, co-coordinated by the Quixote Center and Global Exchange |
| **IDB** | Inter-American Development Bank |
| **IHRED** | Haitian International Institute for Research and Development |
| **IFES** | International Foundation for Election Systems |
| **IFIs** | International Financial Institutions |
| **IMF** | International Monetary Fund |
| **INS** | formerly the Immigration and Naturalization Service, now the Department of Homeland Security's Bureau of Immigration and Customs Enforcement |
| **IRI** | International Republican Institute |
| **KONAKOM** | Congress of National Democratic Movements |
| **KOSMOP** | Committee to Support the Popular Movement in Haiti |
| **LCHR** | Lawyers Committee for Human Rights |
| **LHL** | Let Haiti LIVE: Coalition for a More Just U.S. Policy |
| **MOCHRENA** | *Mouvement Chretien pour une Nouvelle Haiti,* Christian Movement for a New Haiti, political party |
| **MPP** | *Mouvman Peyizan Papaye,* Peasant Movement of Papaye |
| **MSF** | *Medecins Sans Frontiers,* Doctors Without Borders |
| **NAFTA** | North American Free Trade Agreement |
| **NCHR** | National Coalition for Haitian Rights (formerly Haitian Refugees) |
| **NDI** | National Democratic Institute |
| **NED** | National Endowment for Democracy |
| **NEOD** | New England Observers Delegation |
| **NGOs** | non-governmental organizations |
| **NPR** | National Public Radio |
| **OAS** | Organization of American States |
| **OIG** | Office of Inspector General |

| | |
|---|---|
| **OPL** | *Organisation du Peuple en Lutte,* Organization of People in Struggle; formerly the *Organisation Politique Lavalas,* Lavalas Political Organization |
| **ORR** | Office of Refugee Resettlement |
| **PAHO** | Pan-American Health Organization |
| **PAPDA** | *Platfom Ayisyen pou Pledwaye pou yon Devlopman Alternatif,* the Haitian Platform to Advocate for an Alternative Development |
| **PIH** | Partners In Health |
| **PNH** | Haitian National Police |
| **PPN** | National Popular Party |
| **QC** | The Quixote Center |
| **RCC** | Roxbury Community College |
| **RDA** | Democratic Haitian Resistance |
| **RSF** | *Reporters Sans Frontiers,* Reporters Without Borders |
| **SAC** | Structural adjustment credit |
| **SAP** | Structural adjustment program |
| **SMP** | Staff-monitored program |
| **TB** | tuberculosis |
| **TGK** | Turner Guilford Knight Correctional Center |
| **TNH** | *Tele Nasyonal d'Haiti,* Haitian National Television |
| **UDHR** | Universal Declaration of Human Rights |
| **UNDP** | United Nations Development Programme |
| **UNESCO** | United Nations Educational, Scientific and Cultural Organization |
| **UNHCR** | United Nations High Commissioner for Refugees |
| **UNO** | National United Opposition (Nicaragua) |
| **USAID** | United States Agency for International Development |
| **WB** | World Bank |
| **WHO** | World Health Organization |
| **WOH** | Washington Office on Haiti |
| **ZL** | *Zanmi Lasante,* Partners In Health |

# TIMELINE

**1492**
Christopher Columbus lands on the island called Hayti/Quisqueya/Bohio and changes its name to "Hispaniola." The native Taíno Arawak population is virtually destroyed within 50 years.

**1697**
The Treaty of Ryswick grants French sovereignty over Saint Domingue, the area known today as Haiti.

**1779**
Haitians send troops to Battle of Savannah

**1791**
A slave revolt against French colonialism begins under the leadership of Boukman and Toussaint-Louverture. Over the next ten years, Toussaint manages to defeat the island's French settlers, Spanish colonists, a British expeditionary force, and a mulatto *coup* and win control of the colony.

**1801**
Toussaint is proclaimed Governor-General of Saint Domingue. Napoleon Bonaparte dispatches an expeditionary force of 22,000 troops – the largest force ever to cross the Atlantic – to recover the colony from black control. Toussaint is quickly captured through French trickery and dies in exile. The first Haitian Constitution outlaws foreign ownership of land.

**1804**
Napoleon's forces are defeated under the leadership of Jean-Jacques Dessalines. Independence is declared and the name "Haiti" is reclaimed. Haiti becomes the world's first independent black republic and the second independent state in the Americas.

**1825**
Haitian President Boyer signs an agreement with the government of France. In return for 150 million francs and 50% tariff breaks, France officially recognizes the independence of Haiti.

**1915**

Following the assassination of the Haitian president, 2,000 U.S. Marines invade Haiti, invoking the Monroe Doctrine. U.S. investment in Haiti triples between 1915 and 1930.

**1917**

U.S. State Department drafts a new Constitution for Haiti, repealing the prohibition against foreign land ownership.

**1922**

The U.S. consolidates Haiti's external debt.

**1934**

U.S. Marines leave Haiti after 19 years, leaving behind a U.S. trained army to maintain control.

**1953**

Haiti is the first Caribbean republic to sign a treaty with Washington encouraging private U.S. investment on very favorable terms.

## The Duvalier Dictatorships: 1957-1986

**1957**

François "Papa Doc" Duvalier is installed as President through Army-controlled elections. The army is reorganized and elite units are placed under his direct command. Duvalier creates a private presidential militia -- the Volontaires de la Sécurité Nationale, better known as the *Tontons Macoutes* -- which grows to outnumber the army. Duvalier crushes political opposition, arresting or forcing into exile political rivals, dissolving trade unions, repressing student political activities and banning or attacking opposition newspapers.

**1963**

The first boatland of Haitian refugees arrives in the United States.

**1964**

Duvalier suspends elections and declares himself "President for Life."

**1971**
François Duvalier, having amended the constitution to lower the age requirement, dies and names his 19 year-old son, Jean Claude "Baby Doc" Duvalier, as his successor.

**1981**
The U.S. makes an agreement with Haiti to interdict boats and return refugees.

**1985**
The killing of four students in Gonaives sparks a national protest movement against Jean-Claude Duvalier.

**Feb 7, 1986**
Sustained popular mobilization forces Jean-Claude Duvalier to flee into exile in France on a U.S. jet.

## Post-Duvalier Period
A provisional government, the National Council of Government (CNG), assumed control after Duvalier fled. Every CNG member save one had served as high-ranking officer in Duvalier's military or as a senior minister in Duvalier's government. General Henri Namphy, who governed the CNG, was among the most senior officers in the Haitian Armed Forces. While political unrest continued, public discourse, stifled for 30 years under the Duvaliers, burst out into the open.

**March 29, 1987**
A new constitution is adopted in a national referendum.

**November 29, 1987**
Elections are aborted after the military execute a campaign of violence. At a polling place in Port-au-Prince, armed men attack citizens waiting in line to vote and kill approximately 30. A new Provisional Electoral Council is hand-picked by the National Council of Government to set new elections.

**January 17, 1988**
Leslie Manigat is declared the winner of a presidential election marked by massive abstention and fraud. The government was civilian in name only. The military's involvement in drug trafficking and contraband grow unabated during Manigat's tenure.

**June 20, 1988**
After 135 days in power, Manigat is forced from office after attempting to assert civilian control over the military. General Henri Namphy, the original leader of the National Council of Government, declares himself leader of a second Provisional Governing Council (CNG II), places Haiti under strict military control and suspends the 1987 Constitution.

**September 11, 1988**
As Father Jean-Bertrand Aristide, a harsh critic of Namphy, is leading Sunday mass at the Church of St. Jean Bosco in Port-au-Prince, a group of armed men bursts into the packed church. Armed with military weapons and machetes, the attackers shoot and slash worshipers. Twelve people are killed and dozens are wounded in the attack.

**September 17, 1988**
Namphy is overthrown in a coup d'état. Lt. General Prosper Avril, a former Duvalier advisor, declares himself President.

**January 1990**
General Avril's government declares a state of emergency and suspends key provisions of the Constitution. Numerous human rights workers and political opponents of the military government are seized, beaten, tortured and deported.

**March 5, 1990**
Soldiers fire on demonstrators and kill an 11 year-old girl, Rosaline Vaval, in the southern city of Petit-Goâve. This death galvanizes the political opposition. Schools and shops close as demonstrators fill the streets despite the army's violent attempts to repress them.

**March 10, 1990**
General Avril resigns after the popular movement takes to the streets in nation-wide protest. Supreme Court Justice Ertha Pascal-Trouillot is installed as interim President.

**October 18, 1990**
Father Jean-Bertrand Aristide announces his candidacy for president under the auspices of the National Front for Change and Democracy (FNCD).

## The Aristide Presidency & the Coup d'État

**December 16, 1990**
Haiti successfully holds its first democratic election. Father Jean-Bertrand Aristide wins 67% of the popular vote.

**January 6, 1991**
Roger Lafontant stages an unsuccessful attempted coup d'etat.

**February 7, 1991**
Aristide is inaugurated as President of the Republic of Haiti.

**September 30, 1991**
General Raoul Cédras orchestrates a coup d'état against President Aristide. Hundreds are killed in the first week of the coup. Aristide resides in Washington DC during most of his exile.

**October 2, 1991**
OAS condemns the coup and calls for a trade embargo. U.S. Sec. of State James Baker states, "It is imperative that we agree, for the sake of Haitian democracy and the cause of democracy throughout the hemisphere, to act collectively to defend the legitimate government of President Aristide."

**October 7, 1991**
In a rapid change of course, White House Spokesman Marlin Fitzwater states, "We don't know [if Aristide will return to power] in the sense that the government in his country is changing and considering any number of different possibilities."

**February 1992**
Bush administration unilaterally relaxes embargo to allow U.S. assembly plants to operate in Haiti.

**February 24, 1992**
Washington Protocols are signed between President Aristide and the Haitian Parliament in which Aristide agrees to replace his Prime Minister with a compromise candidate.

**May 24, 1992**
President Bush orders the U.S. Coast Guard to intercept all Haitians leaving the island in boats and return them to Haiti without hearing their claims for political asylum.

**June 10, 1992**
Marc Bazin is ratified by *coup* leaders as the *de facto* prime minister. Bazin had been the U.S.-favored presidential candidate in the 1990 elections.

**January 1993**
President Clinton imposes a naval blockade to prevent Haitian refugees from fleeing to the U.S.

**January 18, 1993**
The Haitian population unanimously boycotts illegal elections.

**February 1993**
US/OAS mission is deployed throughout Haiti to monitor human rights violations.

**July 3, 1993**
The Governors Island Accord is signed by President Aristide and *coup* leader Gen. Raoul Cédras. Cédras agrees to step down by Oct. 15, and President Aristide is scheduled to return on October 30. The agreement was made under UN/OAS auspices with intense international pressure on President Aristide. It provides that the military hold power through a period of transition.

**August 1993**
As called for in the Governor's Island Accord, a new "government of consensus" is installed with business leader Robert Malval as Prime Minister.

**October 11, 1993**
U.S. troop carrier, the USS Harlan County, carrying 200 U.S. and Canadian soldiers, turns back from landing when about 100 *attachés* demonstrate at the port.

**December 15, 1993**
Prime Minister Malval resigns. Before his resignation, Malval proposed expanding the government to include well known Duvalierists and Tontons Macoutes.

**December 26, 1993**
Neo-Duvalierist group, FRAPH, sets more than 1,000 homes on fire in the urban slum Cite Soleil, killing at least 70 people.

**April 1994**
Aristide supporters are massacred in Raboteau, a shantytown in Gonaives.

## Aristide's Return to January 1, 2004

**October 15, 1994**
Accompanied by 6,000 U.S. troops, later to be replaced by 6,000 UN troops, Aristide returns to power to serve what remains of his term. General Cédras and General Philippe Biamby (chief-of-staff) go into exile in Panama. Michel François (police chief) retreated to the Dominican Republic.

**April 1995**
Constant disruptions of law and order result from Haiti's ineffective justice system and lack of sufficiently trained police force.

**June & July 1995**
Local and legislative elections take place. Lavalas wins a landslide victory in the Senate and Lower House. Voter turnout is scarce, however, and election results are contested. Of the 27 participating parties, 23 refuse to recognize the results.

**November 1995**
Prime Minister Smarck Michel resigns and is replaced by the Foreign Minister Claudette Werleigh.

**December 17, 1995**
Presidential elections take place, but only 25% of the voters participate. The race is won by former Prime Minister René Préval, and for the first time in Haitian history, power is yielded from one elected leader to another.

**February 7, 1996**
Préval is inaugurated and Rosny Smarth later becomes Prime Minister.

**October 18, 1996**
Structural adjustment plan framework accepted.

**December 1996**
Divisions within the Lavalas Political Organization are manifested by Aristide's formation of the Fanmi Lavalas (Lavalas Family).

**April 1997**
Elections take place for 9 senators, two deputies, members of 564 local assemblies and 133 municipal representatives. Popularly considered fraudulent elections, voter turnout is extremely low, with less than a 10% presence at the polls.

**June 1997**
Prime Minister Rosny Smarth resigns.

**November 1997**
1,200 UN troops withdraw. 300 police instructors and 400 U.S. troops remain.

**February 1998**
The Organization du People en Lutte, formerly known as the Organization Politique Lavalas, no longer demands that the results of the April 1997 elections be repealed.

**January 1999**
President Préval appoints Education Minister Jaques Edouard Alexis as Prime Minister. As a result of its expired term, President Preval refuses to recognize parliament.

**March 1999**
A new government and provisional electoral council (CEP) are sworn in.

**July 16, 99**
President Preval signs the Provisional Electoral Law, nullifying the 1997 elections and preparing for the fall elections.

**March 27, 2000**
After numerous election delays, the U.S. calls the date of June 12 the "line in the sand" for the new Haitian parliament to be seated. According to Article 152 of the Haitian Constitution, the parliament is seated for its second session after a recess on the second Sunday in June. Sanctions against Haiti are threatened, including economic and diplomatic isolation and the denial of U.S. visas to those seen obstructing the democratic process.

**April 3, 2000**
Radio journalist Jean Leopold Dominique is assassinated in the parking lot of his radio station, Radio Haiti International, on Delmas. (NYT)

**May 21, 2000**
Local and legislative elections are held. International observers praised Haiti's elections as largely peaceful, free and fair. The CEP announced that more than 60% of the registered voters participated, the largest turn out since Dec 1990.

**May 22, 2000**

A group of political parties calling themselves the Group de Convergence claim electoral irregularities. Their principle claim is that one million ballots were stolen, unobserved by national and international observers. This was denied by the CEP.

**June 1, 2000**

The CEP releases election results stating that of the eight departments that had held the vote FL won 16 out of 17 seats in the senate in the first round. Of the 83 seats in the House of Deputies, FL won 28 outright.

**June 2, 2000**

The OAS observation mission notes that according to the provisions of the Electoral Law the methodology used to calculate the vote percentages for Senate candidates is not correct.

**June 16, 2000**

President of the CEP, Manus, seeks asylum in a foreign mission crosses the border to the Dominican Republic en route to the U.S.

**August 22, 2000**

Haiti's newly elected parliament convenes. FL spokesman Yvon Neptune was appointed president of the Senate.

**November 26, 2000**

Elections are held for president and eight senate seats. The CEP reports 60% voter turn out with Aristide winning 92% of the votes cast.

**February 7, 2001**

Jean-Bertrand Aristide, 47, is inaugurated without disturbance, although 10 people were arrested due to a plot to use bomb to disturb the ceremonies. The Democratic Convergence inaugurates its own president, Gerard Gourge.

**April 6, 2001**

The United States Executive Director at the Inter-American Development Bank uses his influence to stop disbursement of four pending humanitarian loans.

**November 8, 2001**

The U.S. Congressional Black Caucus takes up the issue of de facto economic sanctions, which have been in place in Haiti since 1997 (when efforts to privatize state-owned enterprises failed). They send a letter to President George Bush.

**December 17, 2001**

A coup attempt is unsuccessful in the early hours of the morning. Two police officers are killed. Thousands pour into the streets to defend democracy. Some protesters destroy offices and homes belonging to the Convergence.

**December 2001**

The U.S. government secretly changes its policy towards Haitian refugees, requiring indefinite detention.

**January 2002**

High-level OAS/CARICOM delegation investigates the political impasse in Haiti.

**February 22, 2002**

U.S. Congressional Black Caucus unanimously agreed that the U.S. should lift its veto on disbursing millions of dollars in aid to impoverished Haiti. "The failure to find a solution to the political impasse between Aristide's government and the opposition party coalition could lead to anarchy in the near future," warned Conyers in a written statement.

**March 4, 2002**

Senator Yvon Neptune is appointed Prime Minister. Neptune was a senator for the Western province of Haiti, and former spokesman for the Lavalas Family party. Senior Lavalas officials agreed Senator Neptune was a good choice.

**July 2, 2002**

The OAS releases its report on the coup attempt of December 17, 2001. Their findings do not include conclusive evidence that the attack was intended to be a coup. They call on the Haitian Government to investigate and prosecute all offenders in reprisal attacks.

**August 2, 2002**

During a prison break in Gonaives, popular leader Amiot Metayer is freed from jail. Along with him several criminals convicted for their participation in the Raboteau massacre are freed as well, most notably Jean Tatoune.

**September 4, 2002**

The OAS unanimously agrees to Resolution 822 calling for new elections, disarmament, increased security and normalization of economic relations between Haiti and the international financial institutions, among other things.

**October 29, 2002**
Over 200 Haitians arrive in Miami seeking asylum. Their dramatic arrival is covered by the U.S. press.

**January 2003**
Government of Haiti cuts petrol subsidy to encourage the re-engagement of the IMF.

**March 19, 2003**
High-level OAS/CARICOM delegation arrives in Haiti.

**April 23, 2003**
Attorney General John Ashcroft issues a decision to detain all Haitians, even those granted bonds, on the basis of Homeland Security. He cited an increase in third world nations using Haiti as a staging point as the reason.

**May 8, 2003**
Haitian authorities reach an agreement with the IMF on its Staff-Monitored Program (SMP).

**June 20, 2003**
The Ministry of Commerce and Industry approves two projects to create Free Trade Zones, including on on the Maribahoux Plain at the border with the Dominican Republic.

**September 22, 2003**
Longtime community leader from Raboteau, Gonaives, Amiot "Kiben" Metayer, is found murdered near Saint Marc.

**September 2003**
The 47th Haitian legislature closes it session after proposing three amendments to the 1987 Constitution: 1. To formally abolish the Haitian Army, 2. To remove life restrictions on dual citizenship, and 3. To replace three-member mayoral cartels with a single mayor.

**October 9, 2003**
The Group of 184, led by factory owner Andre Apaid, Jr. joins the political opposition, the Democratic Convergence.
The World Bank's private sector financing arm approves its first loan to Haiti since 1998, for the free trade zone project at the border of the Dominican Republic on the Maribahoux Plain.

## November-December 2003

Anti-government protesters clash with pro-government supporters several times. The Group of 184 and Democratic Coverngence begin to advocate a violent overthrow of the Haitian government. Most violence occurs when opposition marchers deviate from the agreed-upon routes for their protests and intentionally confront pro-government protesters. Some 100 people are injured, and approximately 45 are killed. The Haitian National Police use tear gas and fire shots in the air but do not use unnecessary force to break up protests.

## December 19, 2003

President Aristide revives a compromise proposal from the Haitian Conference of Catholic Bishops. He encourages the opposition to accept their proposal, which would create a nine-member council to oversee the next elections. The Democratic Convergence rejects President Aristide's invitation for compromise, and declares it will only participate if President Aristide steps down or is removed from power.

## December 26, 2003

The Inter-American Development Bank begins disbursement on loans held up since 2000.

## January 1, 2004

The Haitian people celebrate the 200th Anniversary of their victory over slavery. Opposition members, including the Group of 184 and the Democratic Convergence, protest the bicentennial.

# CO-SPONSORS

Our deepest gratitude to all those individuals and families who supported the preparation of this book:

Ann & Doug Christensen
Barbara Parsons
Brian Lochen M.D.
Bill Larsen
Carol A. Binstock
Clyde A. Woods
Connie Barna
Cynthia Tshcampl
Erika Bourguignon
Eveline Hodges
Evans Dure
Gordon & Elizabeth Stevenson
Handmaids of the Sacred Heart of Jesus
I.C.M. Sisters U.S. District
In Memory of Rodrigue & Paula Macajoux
Jane Wentworth
Jim Carlson
Joan M. Maruskin
Joe DuRocher
John & Patricia Ginda
John Murnin
Karel R. & Hermine Dahmen
Linden P. Martineau
Lois Van Tol
Lorraine Oatman Patterson
Maria Concetta Grifoni
Mary & Anthony Lopresti

Mary Ann & James Hubert
Max S. Bell Jr.
May & Serge Parisien
Micheal Barfield
Milton Carpentier
Nadege Volcy
Omnes Barthelemy
Our Lady of Victory Missionary Sisters
Pastors John G. Lemnitzer & Kim M. Sternes
Pat & Maureen Coffey
Patrick Francis
Paul Miller
Mark Peters
R A Desutter
R M Olson
Rev William C. Konicki
Richard G. Morris
Richard Vanden Heuvel
Rob Hardley
Ruth E H Beeton
Sally Sommers
Sarah Brownell
Sharel & Joe Zelenka
Shelley A. Sandow
Sisters of the Holy Names NY Province
Therese Marie Rittenbach

# RESOURCES

If you would like to get active on behalf of the Haitian people, we suggest these organizations:

Haiti Reborn, a program of the Quixote Center, works in the United States on behalf of the Haitian people to build an active grassroots solidarity mvoement and to advocate for a more just U.S. foreign policy. Haiti Reborn acts as a center of information to combat negative stereotypes, and provides in-depth political, economic and social analysis. To complement this work at a structural level, Haiti Reborn funds community-based initiatives which empower Haitians at the grassroots.

Contact: Haiti Reborn/Quixote Center
P.O. Box 5206, Hyattsville, MD 20782
(301)699-3443 x195, fax: (301)864-2182
Website: www.quixote.org/haiti, email: haiti@quixote.org

The Quixote Center is a multi-issue justice and peace center founded in 1976. It is a non-profit organization whose mission is to work with people who have few resources for their struggles. We strive to make our world, our nation, and our church more just, peaceful and equitable in their policies and practices.. The Quixote Center includes a wide range of social justice programs. In addition to Haiti Reborn, these are:

- *Catholics Speak Out* encourages reform in the Roman Catholic Church and adult responsibility for faith. In particular, the project works towards equality and justice within the Church and dialogue between the laity and hierarchy on issues of sexuality, sexual orientation and reproduction. Contact: cso@quixote.org.

- *Equal Justice USA* is a grassroots program of the Quixote Center that mobilizes and educates ordinary citizens around issues of crime and punishment in the U.S. Our work brings into public focus the racial, economic and political biases that permeate our legal system. By transforming our culture of vengeance and violence, we build support for an alternative public policy that is both effective and humane. Contact: ejusa@quixote.org

- *Interfaith Voices* is a public radio program promoting religious tolerance and interfaith respect and understanding across the United States. Contact: Maureen Fiedler at: faithmatters@quixote.org. Listen on the Web: www.interfaithradio.org.

- The *Nicaraguan Cultural Alliance* proudly present fine art materials from Nicaragua. The proceeds support the Nicaraguan artists and artisans who created the original works. Contact: nca@quixote.org.

- *Priests for Equality* works on issues of gender equality in the Catholic Church and in society as large. They are currently translating the Bible into gender inclusive language. Contact: pfe@quixote.org.

- *The Quest for Peace* is a peace and justice organization providing developmental aid to the rural poor in Nicaragua through our partner John XXIII in Managua since 1985. Contact: quest@quixote.org.

**Partners In Health:** The mission of Partners In Health is to provide a preferential option for the poor in health care. By establishing long-term relationships with sister organizations based in settings of poverty, Partners In Health strives to achieve two overarching goals: to bring the benefits of modern medical science to those most in need of them and to serve as an antidote to despair. We draw on the resources of the world's elite medical and academic institutions and on the lived experience of the world's poorest and sickest communities. At its root, our mission is both medical and moral. It is based on solidarity, rather than charity alone.

When our patients are ill and have no access to care, our team of health professionals, scholars, and activists will do whatever it takes to make them well – just as we would do if a member of our own families – or we ourselves – were ill.

Contact: Parnters In Health
641 Huntington Ave, 1st Floor, Boston, MA 02115
(617)432-5256, Fax: (617)432-5300
Website: www.pih.org, Email: info@pih.org

**The Haiti Solidarity Network of the Northeast** is a non-profit organization whose goals include:

- Show solidarity with our Haitian brothers and sisters, through prayers and meetings
- Inform ourselves and others regarding Haiti
- Visit our brothers in various parts of Haiti through personal delegations
- Support financially and manually self-help projects in Haiti
- Publicize true information about Haiti
- Strengthen Haiti's independence through whatever non-violent means necessary

HSNNE holds a monthly meeting on the second Tuesday every month at 7:30pm (September to June) at St. Joseph's Social Service Center, 118 Division Street, Elizabeth, NJ. All are welcome.

Contact: Haiti Solidarity Network of the Northeast
437 Glenwood Avenue, Teaneck, NJ 07666
(201)836-4738
Email: delinois@earthlink.net, Georgette Delinois, President of the Board

**Oblates of Mary Immaculate Office of Justice, Peace and the Integrity of Creation** have a presence in more than 70 countries worldwide and have maintained an active presence in Haiti for more than fifty years. Members of the congregation have supported the foundation of schools, and clinics, and have actively promoted different development initiatives though the many parishes where they have served over the years. The congregation's international community has supported many development projects and has been active in supporting efforts to establish a just, democratic political system, which respects human rights, safeguards human dignity and responds to the many challenges of poverty and development.
Contact: Seamus Finn, OMI
391 Michigan Ave., NE, Washington DC 20017
(202) 483-0444, Fax: (202) 483-0708
Website: www.omiusa.org, Email: seamus@omiusa.org

# Pax Christi USA Haiti Task Force: The Haiti Task Force represents a
deep commitment of Pax Christi USA to the people of Haiti since 1985. The HTF educates and advocates for just U.S. policies toward Haiti and networks with grassroots organizations throughout the U.S. and in Haiti that are dedicated to work for justice and improvement of the quality of life for the people.

Contact: Pax Christi USA Haiti Task Force
110 Lee Drive
Huddleston, VA 24104
(540) 297-6493
Email: delrauth@aol.com, Adele and Bob DellaValle-Rauth, Chairs

**The Office of the Americas,** founded by Theresa and Blase Bonpane in 1983, is a non-profit educational corporation dedicated to furthering the cause of justice and peace through broad based programs including:

- Delegations to areas of conflict.
- The International March for Peace in Central America.
- Fact finding missions to Iraq, Peru, Colombia, Chiapas, Ecuador, Guatemala, Honduras, El Salvador, Nicaragua, Costa Rica and Panama.
- Private diplomacy in areas of conflict.
- Formation of the Coalition for World Peace immediately after 9/11/01.
- Regularly scheduled programs on radio and TV under the title, WORLD FOCUS.
- News Commentary for Pacifica Radio.
- Background briefings for journalists.
- Expert Witness testimony in Federal Immigration Courts.
- Coalition Building with military families, immigrant workers, other justice, peace and solidarity organizations.
- Speakers Bureau for universities, high schools and monthly educational salons.
- The files of the Office of the Americas are preserved at the Department of Special Collections of the U.C.L.A. Research Library (collection 1590).

Contact: Office of the Americas
8124 West Third Street Suite 202
Los Angeles, CA 90048
(323)852-9808
Website: www.officeoftheamericas.org, Email: ooa@igc.org

**St. John the Baptist Church,** El Cerrito, CA
Contact: Father John Maxwell
Email: jmaxwell@pacbell.net

**Haitian Ministry Commission of the Diocese of Richmond**
The Haitian Ministry Commission of the Diocese of Richmond oversees the twinning relationship between the Dioceses of Richmond and Hinche, Haiti. The Haitian Ministry Commission has the following responsibilities: First, it is the

primary advisory body to the Bishop in the area of ministry with Haiti and with the Haitian people of our diocese. Second, it is charged with the implementation of the pastoral plan on Haitian ministry and with making recommendations to the Bishop. Third, it is charged with the promotion of understanding of Haitian ministry and the fostering of effective communication regarding it throughout the Diocese.

Contact: Cosmas Rubencamp, CFX, Executive Secretary
811 Cathedral Place
Richmond VA 23220-4801
804-359-5661, ext. 221
Website: www.richmonddiocese.org/haiti, Email:
crubencamp@richmonddiocese.org

**Jubilee USA Network** is an alliance of churches, diverse faith communities, labor, environmental, solidarity, and community organizations building a grassroots movement to achieve the complete cancellation of unjust and illegitimate debt owed by countries with high levels of human need, and an end to unjust economic policies imposed on those nations. Working in solidarity with partners around the world, Jubilee USA promotes its mission through public education, grassroots organizing, media outreach, policy analysis and advocacy.

Contact: Jubilee USA Network
222 East Capitol Street, NE, Washington DC 20003
(202) 783-3566, Fax: (202) 546-4468
Website: www.jubileeusa.org, Email: coord@j2000usa.org

**Fondasyon Trant Septanm** Created in 1996, the Foundation is a national umbrella group for the victims' associations resulting from the September 30, 1991 coup d'etat. It responds to the needs of its member groups with a unified organization and legal structure, aiding in the processes of psychological rehabilitation and socioeconomic reintegration, and supporting the coup victims in their struggle for justice and reparation. The foundation has sought to create public space for victims' expression, organizing a weekly march to 'Martyrs Square' where victims speak out about the political, economic and social violence perpetrated against them. Its struggles against substandard law enforcement, military and judicial corruption and impunity have resulted in, most notably, the fall 2000 Raboteau trial -- the first case ever against police and military personnel involved in a coup-era massacre.

Contact: Lovinsky Pierre-Antoine
c/o Bureau Avocats Internationaux, 45, Avenue John Brown, B.P. 19048, Port-au-Prince, Haiti
Email: lovinskypa@yahoo.fr

**The Marin Interfaith Task Force on the Americas** (MITF) is a grassroots organization founded in 1985 in response to the U. S. role in El Salvador. MITF has since expanded its focus to include all of the Americas. Our Mission Statement: Proceeding from our hope for and commitment for world peace, our mission is to educate North American citizens about realities in the Americas, and the role the U.S. plays there and provide humanitarian aid and support for projects in the region.

Contact: Marin Interfaith Task Force
PO Box 2481, Mill Valley CA 94942,
Phone: 415-924-3227
Website: www.mitfcentralamerica.org, Email: mitf@igc.org

**10th Department Organization for Haitian Empowerment (10th DOHE)**, a nonprofit organization that seeks to strengthen transnational ties between the Haitian Diaspora, Haiti and the international communities to dispel negative stereotypes against Haitian people. 10th DOHE provides networking opportunities to facilitate positive social change through education, cultural awareness, grassroots mobilization, advocacy initiatives, and information exchange.

Contact: 10th DOHE
P.O. Box 2322, Washington, DC, 20013-2322
Phone: 202-508-3891, Fax: 202-452-5512
Website: www.10thdepartment.org, E-mail: 10thdohe@10thdepartment.org

**Rochester Committee on Latin America**, a task force of Rochester NY's Metro Justice for education and political action.

Contact: Rochester Committee on Latin America
Phone: 585-381-5606, Fax: 585-381-3134
E-mail: interconnect-mott@juno.com,

# ACKNOWLEDGEMENTS

*The editors would like to thank:*

Each of the contributors to this book, for taking time out of your lives to share your perspective on a country we all hold dear;
Marianne Miles and David Packard, for your unparalleled and invaluable assistance in the editing of this book;
Christopher Miles, for creating the Let Haiti LIVE website (www.lethaitilive.org) and designing the cover of this book;
The staff of the Quixote Center – Carol Binstock, Mark Buckley, Bill Callahan, John Clark, Jan DeWright, Maureen Fiedler, SL, Jane Henderson, Rea Howarth, John Judge, Trisha Kendall, Dolly Pomerleau, Tom Ricker, Alexandra West, and Saul Wolf – for their support in this project; and
The board of the Quixote Center – Nancy Allen, Bill D'Antonio, Jack Bresette, Frank Debernardo, Jeff Garis, Njoki Njehu, Natacha Thys, and Lisa Zimmerman – for your guidance to the Quixote Center.
Haiti Reborn Interns/volunteers – Jennifer N. Costanza, Micheline Fleurant, Myles Duffy, D'Wanna Lee, and Dawan Jones.

*Eugenia Charles thanks:*
My husband Ginau Mathurin for his generous support and patience throughout this process and his mother Degrace Nestor-Mathurin for helping us look after our daughter Mika along with my brothers-in-law Jeph, Jean-Michel and Yves Mathurin. Special thanks to my courageous mother Emilia Louis and the rest of the family and friends for their moral support: Momprene, (wife) Jasmide and (daughter) Charline Charles, Lionel and (daughter) Djenny Charles, Louiskel and (son) Christope Charles, Horiol and (son) Isaac Charles, Myllion and his new wife, Eric Charles, Jean-Claude Charles, Avelita Charles, Irmathe Previlon and husband Patrice, my nieces and nephews Michelle, Gabrielle, Patrick and Joshua Previlon; Ymose Vincent and Herold Champagne, Jean-Denis, Verdieu, Edwidge, Gladys, and Denise Pierre-Louis; My grandmother Elinette Ferdinand and her children, Canord Louis, the Britt's family particularly Richard D. Britt and wife Jackie, Marlin and Clinton Alton Britt. Carole B. and Simon Seaforth and family, Marie-Ange Jean-Claude and family, Anne V. Russell and Freya Bernado, Mildred Charles and Chyna Dorcean, Marcia Francis, Nadine Rose Antoine, Martine Dorvilus and family, Ivon Alcime and family, and members of Theatre Mapou, Myrnette Joachim and Arnold Joseph, Clairemicia Abbichet and family (Loseline). My Haitian brothers and sisters in Haiti particularly Lovinsky Pierre-Antione for his

undying passion and devotion to see a better Haiti and family, Jean Gabriel Fils and family, Guylene Viaud (Loune) for her candid spirit dedication to Haiti, Mary Kay Smith and Rosie Fawzi.

*Melinda Miles thanks:*
My partner, Joe Duplan, for sharing the beauty and complexity of your homeland with me, each and every day, and for being a supporter of all my work. My Haitian sister, Eugenia Charles, for teaching me so many things about your culture and your country, and for collaborating on so many grand adventures. Deepest thanks to Chris, Mom and David for putting their time and energy into my project. To Anne Marie and Memere, for your love and support. This book is also dedicated to the members of my extended Haiti family, including Anous Anold, Guypson Catalis, the Duplan sisters – Surzi, India and Regine – and their children, Michelle Karshan, Riva Precil, Rafael, Marc and Lodz Duplan, Pat Dillon, rjm, Ron Voss, Domond Bertony, Moira Feeney, Pierre Labossiere, Cousin Dody, Gerard Nelson, Timothee Samuel, Daniel Tillias, Jean Desnor, Father Ronel Charelus, Sister Jackie Picard, Sister Vivian Patenaude, Sister Nazareth, Father Jomanas Eustache, Prince Luc, and Didier Civil.

*Our deepest appreciation to:*
**Our Haitian partners, for their undying dedication to building an independent democracy in Haiti.**

# Author Biographies

**Adam Taylor:** Currently serves as Executive Director of Global Justice, an organization that he co-founded in 2001 to educate, train, and mobilize students around issues of human rights, development, and social justice. Taylor also serves on the Boards of Jubilee U.S.A. Network and Sojourners magazine. Taylor worked in AIDS prevention in Zambia with Africare in 2000. Taylor worked as a Fellow at the Carr Center for Human Rights Policy in 2001. Taylor serves as an Associate Minister at Shiloh Baptist Church. He received his Masters in Public Policy from the JFK School of Government, Harvard University (2001) and a BA from Emory University with a major in International Studies (1998).

**Paul Farmer, M.D., Ph.D.,** is the Maude and Lillian Presley Professor of Medical Anthropology at Harvard Medical School and Medical Director of the Clinique Bon Sauveur, a charity hospital in rural Haiti. An infectious disease physician as well as anthropologist, Dr. Farmer has worked in communicable-disease control in the Americas for over a decade. Along with his colleagues in the Program in Infectious Disease and Social Change in the Department of Social Medicine at Harvard Medical School, Dr. Farmer has pioneered novel, community-based treatment strategies for tuberculosis— and also sexually transmitted infections (including HIV) and drug-resistant typhoid— in resource-poor settings. Along with his clinical work in Haiti, Dr. Farmer is an attending physician in infectious disease at Brigham and Women's Hospital in Boston and Chief of the hospital's newly formed Division of Social Medicine and Health Inequalities. Dr. Farmer has written extensively about health and human rights, and about the role of social inequalities in the distribution and outcomes of readily treatable diseases.

**Congresswoman Barbara Lee:** Barbara Lee was first elected to the House of Representatives for the Ninth District of California in a 1998 special election to fill the seat of retiring Congressman Ron Dellums. She is currently the Co-Chair of the Progressive Caucus, Chair of the Congressional Black Caucus (CBC) Task Force on Global HIV/AIDS, Whip for the CBC, member of the CBC Haiti Task Force, and a member of the CBC Minority Business Task Force.

Throughout her political career, Barbara Lee has sought to bring her training as a social worker to bear on the problems and challenges that confront the East Bay of California, the nation, and the world. She has worked to provide for the basic needs of Americans: health care, housing, education, jobs, and the creation of livable communities in a peaceful world. These objectives underlie Lee's work on the International Relations Committee and the Financial Services Committee, where she has been one of the leading voices for Haiti. As part of her international focus, Lee has also strengthened the international response to HIV/AIDS by creating the framework for the Global Fund to Fight AIDS, TB, and Malaria as a new mechanism to raise and disburse funds to help impoverished countries like Haiti fight the Global AIDS pandemic. During the past year, she has successfully pushed the Bush Administration to release its hold on $146.9 million in Inter-American Development Bank loans to improve Haiti's roads and medical care. Lee has also recently introduced The New Partnership for Haiti Act of 2003. This legislation partners Haitians and Americans together to execute an environmentally-sound approach to rebuilding Haiti. It proposes to develop basic sanitation, water, and other health infrastructures in Haiti, as well as beginning a Peace Corps-like program for health professionals and engineers interested in going to Haiti to help with the development process.

**Randall Robinson:** is an internationally respected foreign policy advocate and author. He established TransAfrica in 1977 and was its president until 2001. The mandate of TransAfrica was to promote enlightened, progressive U.S. policies towards Africa and the Caribbean. While president of that organization, he spearheaded the U. S. campaign to end apartheid in South Africa. His leadership in support of the pro-democracy movement in Haiti – which included a 27-day hunger strike - also caused the United States Government to lead the 1994 multinational effort to return to power Haiti's first democratically elected – but violently overthrown – government.

Randall Robinson is an author whose works include national best sellers (i) *Defending the Spirit*, (ii) *The Debt – What America Owes to Blacks*, and (iii) *The Reckoning – What Blacks Owe to Each Other*. He is a graduate of Harvard Law School. Twenty-one universities have bestowed upon him honorary Ph.D's in recognition of the impact he has had on U.S. foreign policy. He is the recipient of numerous awards for his global humanitarian work, and among the organization that have honored him thusly are The United Nations, the Congressional Black Caucus, Harvard University, Essence Magazine Awards Show, ABC-News Person of the Week, The Martin Luther King Center for Non-Violent Change, the NAACP, and Ebony Magazine Awards Show, to mention a few.

**Kim Ives** is a writer and editor with Haiti Progres newspaper and a documentary filmmaker who has directed and worked on many films about Haiti (Bitter Cane, The Coup Continues, Rezistans). He also works with the Haiti Support Network (HSN) and was a co-editor of the new book Haiti: A Slave Revolution, published with the International Action Center (IAC). He has led numerous delegations to Haiti and frequently speaks about Haiti before church, student, and community audiences and on Haitian and U.S. radio programs, most frequently Pacifica's WBAI-FM in New York.

**Tom F. Driver:** author, photographer, lecturer, and peace activist is the Paul J. Tillich Professor of Theology and Culture Emeritus at Union Theological Seminary in New York. Through most of the 1990s he was Chairperson of the Haiti Task Force of Witness for Peace. His earlier research on Haitian popular religion is reflected in his book, *Liberating Rites: Understanding the Transformative Power of Rituals* (Westview Press, 1997). Since retirement from teaching he has worked with Witness for Peace and the Presbyterian Peace Fellowship on the critique of U.S. policy in Latin America and the Caribbean. He and his wife, Anne L. Barstow, have created two videos: *Colombia: The Next Vietnam?* (2001) and *Colombians Speak Out about Violence and U.S. Policy* (2003). Contact: tfd3@columbia.edu.

**Brian Concannon, Jr:** Human rights lawyer and activist Brian Concannon Jr. has worked for the Bureau des Avocats Internationaux (BAI) in Port-au-Prince, Haiti since 1996. The BAI was established by the Haitian government to help victims and the justice system prosecute human rights cases, mostly from Haiti's 1991-1994 de facto military dictatorship. The office represents human rights victims in court, and helps them advocate inside and outside of the courtroom. It works closely with judges, prosecutors, police and government officials, providing legal, technical and material assistance, as well as policy advice. The BAI trains Haitian law school graduates, hosts U.S. law student interns and works with U.S. law school clinics through its clinical program. The BAI's most prominent case to date is the prosecution of the 1994 Raboteau Massacre, considered the best complex prosecution in Haiti's history. After six weeks of trial ending in November 2000, the jury convicted 53 defendants for an attack on a pro-democracy neighborhood, including the de facto dictatorship's top military and paramilitary leaders.

Before joining the BAI, Mr. Concannon was a human rights observer for MICIVIH, the U.N./O.A.S. human rights mission in Haiti. He is a graduate of Georgetown University Law Center (J.D.) and Middlebury College (B.A.), and held a Brandeis International Fellowship in Human Rights, Intervention and International Law from 2001-2003. Mr. Concannon writes and speaks often about justice, human rights and the democratic transition in Haiti.

**Mario Joseph, Esq.:** Haiti's most prominent human rights lawyer, has led the Bureau des Avocats Internationaux (BAI) in Port-au-Prince, Haiti since 1996. The BAI was established by the Haitian government to help victims and the justice system prosecute human rights cases, mostly from Haiti's 1991-1994 de facto military dictatorship. The office represents human rights victims in court, and helps them advocate inside and outside of the courtroom. It works closely with judges, prosecutors, police and government officials, providing legal, technical and material assistance, as well as policy advice. The BAI is training the next generation of Haitian Human Rights lawyers through its apprenticeship program. Mr. Joseph was the lead attorney for the victims in the BAI's most prominent case, the 2000 Raboteau Massacre trial. The Raboteau case is considered the best complex prosecution in Haiti's history.

Before joining the BAI, Mr. Joseph worked on human rights cases for the Catholic Church's Justice and Peace Commission. Also an educator, Mr. Joseph has held a variety of teaching and administrative posts. He is a graduate of the Ecole Normale Superieure, Haiti's leading teaching college, and the Gonaives Law School. He speaks frequently on human rights in Haiti on Haitian radio and television, and is a member of the Law Reform Commission.

**Melinda Miles:** Co-Director, Haiti Reborn/Quixote Center. Miles has been working on Haiti issues since 1993. She has coordinated the Haiti Reborn program at the Quixote Center for five years. Miles has coordinated over a dozen delegations to Haiti, ranging in size from four to 26 participants, and has acted as a press spokesperson for the International Coalition of Independent Observers (for Haiti's 2000 elections). She has authored the reports, *"Elections 2000: Monitoring Participatory Democracy in Haiti,"* and *"Investigating the Human Effects of Withheld Humanitarian Aid."*

**Marie Clarke:** is the National Coordinator of Jubilee USA Network, the U.S. arm of the international Jubilee movement for debt cancellation for impoverished countries. Jubilee has almost 70 member church denominations, labor, environmental and citizen groups, 12 regional groups and about 9000 individual members. Marie was previously a director of Quest for Peace at the Quixote Center and a member of the Jubilee USA Coordinating Committee. She has extensive experience in grassroots development work in Nicaragua and domestic and international advocacy work. In Nicaragua, Marie participated in sustainable development work through Nicaraguan partners in thirty of the most impoverished municipalities. Prior to directing Quest for Peace, Marie worked as an associate at NETWORK: A National Catholic Social Justice Lobby. Marie lived in developing countries for 12 years.

**Cheryl Little:** Cheryl's extensive involvement in the community dates back to 1985 when, upon her graduation from law school with honors, she began working at the Haitian Refugee Center and distinguished herself as one of the nation's leading advocates for Haitians. Since 1996, she has served as the Executive Director of the Florida Immigrant Advocacy Center, Inc., (FIAC) an agency she co-founded, which provides free legal help to immigrants of all nationalities and which strives to protect the basic rights of immigrants. FIAC serves the most vulnerable immigrants including asylum seekers, the homeless, victims of domestic violence, those with AIDS or in detention, and migrant farm workers. FIAC was the recipient of American Immigration Lawyers Association's (AILA) 2001 Pro Bono Award and The Florida Bar Foundation's Steven M. Goldstein Award for Excellence for FIAC's collaborative effort to successfully enforce legal rights of immigrants applying for citizenship.

Cheryl is the author of "Intergroup Coalitions and Immigration Politics: The Haitian Experience in Florida," published in the University of Miami Law Review and "INS Detention in Florida," published in the University of Miami Inter-American Law Review. Additionally, she has co-authored a number of reports regarding the plight of immigrants at Krome's Detention Center and in Florida's County Jails.

**Marleine Bastien, LCSW:** see Ms. Bastien's contribution for her biography.

**Tom Ricker** is the policy coordinator for the Quest for Peace, a program of the Quixote Center that funds community development initiatives in Nicaragua, and has been active in the Central America solidarity community since 1995. He received a Ph.D. in Political Science from the University of Maryland in 2001 and has written on labor rights in Nicaragua, the Sandinista revolution and U.S. foreign policy in Central America. Tom has also taught international relations and political economy at the University of South Florida, University of Maryland, and the George Washington University.

**Larry Birns:** Founded the Council on Hemispheric Affairs in 1975 and has since served as the director of COHA. He has written widely on U.S.-Haitian affairs among many other Latin American themes.

**Curtis Morales:** Author and editor, Curtis Morales serves as a COHA Research Associate and is a member of its editorial board.

**Kanisha Bond:** COHA Research Associate and a second-year M.P.P. candidate at Georgetown Public Policy Institute in Washington, DC, where she studies international development and crime policy. A longtime resident of Scranton, PA, Kanisha graduated from Bucknell University in Lewishburg, PA in 2002 with a B.A. in international relations and Spanish, and has studied both in the U.S. and Spain. Currently, Kanisha is working to complete a research practicum that employs econometric methods to explain the cross-country industrial organization of organized crime; her primary research interests are the intergovernmental response to global criminal activity and the historical social policymaking and implementation patterns in Latin America and the Caribbean Basin. Upon graduation in May 2004, she plans to continue such research somewhere in the Western Hemisphere.

**George Dorko III:** COHA Research Associate, graduated from Washington and Jefferson College with a BS in Political Science and Spanish. He is currently second year graduate student at the University of Pittsburgh pursuing his master's in Public and International Affairs (MPIA), majoring in Global Political Economy. George's research interests include the economic development of Latin America.

**Charles Willson** is a native of Atlanta, Georgia, who currently attends the University of Georgia. Willson has had other work published with the Council on Hemispheric Affairs and in various publications including the Miami Herald. A tireless traveler, history buff, and thorough editor, his research interests outside of Haiti include ethnic politics in Israel and the history of Pan-Africanism.

**Tom Reeves:** was Professor of History (1972) and Director of the Caribbean Focus Program (1983) at Roxbury Community College until his retirement in 2001. Caribbean Focus was a grassroots study and action program with field study and work projects in Haiti, the Dominican Republic, Jamaica, Puerto Rico and Cuba. He was a founder of the New England Observer Delegations to Haiti which sponsored delegations of community activists and academic and political leaders to Haiti during the coup period and afterward. He was at various times a civil rights, peace and AIDS activist, serving as director of the National Council to Repeal the Draft in the early 1970s, and as organizer of Act Up Boston in the 1990s. He was jailed for his civil rights work in Alabama, for his draft resistance in Washington, D.C., and for civil disobedience in support of people with AIDS in Boston, and (also in Boston) against incarceration of Haitians by the U.S. at Guantanamo. He was a speech writer for George McGovern, Mark Hatfield and other Senators during the Vietnam War. He is author of numerous articles in periodicals ranging from the NACLA Report and Dollars & Sense to Gay Community News, and of the book, The End of the Draft, published by Random House. He is a writer for and distribution director of The Guide to Gay Travel, Politics and Culture.

**Diana Aubourg** was born and raised in Cambridge, Massachusetts. Her parents emigrated from Haiti to the United States in 1972. Ms. Aubourg currently directs Africa policy and programs for the Pan African Children's Fund (PACF), a U.S. black church initiative that supports orphan care projects throughout Sub Saharan Africa and the Caribbean.

Ms. Aubourg has been active in the fight against global AIDS for over five years and works with a growing network of black clergy, activists and intellectuals to raise awareness about the African AIDS crisis. She is a founding member of the Pan African Charismatic Evangelical Congress (PACEC) – which mobilizes U.S. black churches around foreign and development policy affecting people of African descent and serves on the board of the Jubilee USA Network, an international campaign to cancel the debt of impoverished nations. Prior to her position with PACF, Ms. Aubourg worked as a research associate with the Right to Development Project at the François-Xavier Bagnoud Center for Health and Human Rights at Harvard University.

Ms. Aubourg graduated with a B.A. in Policy Studies from Syracuse University and a Master in City Planning from the Massachusetts Institute of Technology (MIT) with a focus on international development planning. She currently resides in

Dorchester, MA, where she is an active member of the Azusa Christian Community – an inner-city ministry that supports direct service to thousands of high-risk youth and their families.

# INDEX